BUILDING STUDENTS' HISTORI LITERACIES

How can teachers incorporate the richness of historical resources into classrooms in ways that are true to the discipline of history and are pedagogically sound? Now in its second edition, this book explores the notion of historical literacy, adopts a research-supported stance on literacy processes, and promotes the integration of content-area literacy instruction into history content teaching. Providing an original focus on the discipline-specific literacies of historical inquiry, the new edition presents a deeper examination of difficult histories and offers new strategies that can be applied to all genres of historical inquiry. Nokes surveys a broad range of texts, including those that historians and nonhistorians both use and produce in understanding history, and provides a wide variety of practical instructional strategies immediately available to teachers. Featuring new examples and practical resources, the new edition highlights the connection between historical literacies and the critical reading and communication skills that are necessary for informed civic engagement.

Equipped with study guides, graphic organizers, and scoring guides for classroom use, this text is an essential resource for preservice and practicing teachers in literacy and social studies education.

Jeffery D. Nokes is a professor in the History Department at Brigham Young University, where he helps direct the history teaching and social science teaching programs.

BUILDING STUDENTS' HISTORICAL LITERACIES

Learning to Read and Reason
With Historical Texts and Evidence

Second Edition

Jeffery D. Nokes

Routledge
Taylor & Francis Group

NEW YORK AND LONDON

Cover image: © Getty Images

Second edition published 2022
by Routledge
605 Third Avenue, New York, NY 10158

and by Routledge
2 Park Square, Milton Park, Abingdon, Oxon, OX14 4RN

Routledge is an imprint of the Taylor & Francis Group, an informa business

© 2022 Jeffery D. Nokes

First edition published by Routledge 2012

Library of Congress Cataloging-in-Publication Data
A catalog record has been requested for this book

ISBN: 978-1-032-02472-1 (hbk)
ISBN: 978-1-032-01405-0 (pbk)
ISBN: 978-1-003-18349-5 (ebk)

DOI: 10.4324/9781003183495

Typeset in Bembo
by SPi Technologies India Pvt Ltd (Straive)

To Isaac, Raelynn, Grace, Emery, and Truman

CONTENTS

FIGURES

FOREWORD

Early in my professional career, I published an article on promoting reading comprehension in social studies. The article was a response to comments I frequently encountered when working with preservice and in-service teachers whose students were either struggling with comprehension of dense social studies texts or were reluctant readers: "I'm not a reading teacher; students should already know how to read when they get to middle school. My job is to teach them social studies content." Over the course of my career, I have sought to understand the reading and literacy challenges students encounter in social studies as well as empirically document why it is crucial for all middle and high school teachers to be teachers of reading and content.

This inquiry path for me began when I was a high school history, civics, and economics teacher. I remember facilitating lessons in which students analyzed primary and secondary sources to answer overarching questions, such as What inequalities can (or will) democracy tolerate? and How can democracies find compromise? While the content had the potential to be very engaging, many students experienced difficulty with comprehending informational texts and struggled with independently developing a critical understanding of multigenre sources. More recently, I conducted a study in a middle school to explore how students engaged in general and disciplinary literacy practices when reading visual and text primary sources. While students were able to answer questions, their responses reflected a surface-level reading. Few used sourcing unless cued to do so, and the ability to successfully contextualize the sources was a rare observation. In general, most students failed to reason, to question, or to think critically about the content. Dr. Jeffery Nokes has observed similar struggles in his research on student reading and writing in history. The wealth of his knowledge in this area is well cited within this text.

It also affirms the extensive expertise and awareness of the fields of history education and disciplinary literacy.

Like Dr. Nokes, I have grappled with the challenges of helping students develop literacy skills to read and write critically in social studies. Students consistently exhibit difficulties with academic language gaps (a lack of content knowledge to contextualize or interpret texts), comprehension gaps (an inability to accurately derive meaning from text), inaccurate use of evidence (a failure to inference or overreliance on literal meaning), little motivation for reading (reluctant and uninterested readers), and writing gaps (a lack of skills in the use of argumentation and evidence-informed claims). Overcoming these barriers is of utmost importance given the literacy aims of social studies to teach critical inquiry. Critical inquiry empowers students to be informed and engaged citizens who are capable of using their reading, writing and speaking skills to practice empathy and to pursue civically minded, justice-oriented solutions in a pluralistic democracy. The fundamental import of literacy in inquiry is well known. The College, Career, and Civic Life (C3) Framework centers literacy as a core inquiry skill in the education of informed and action-oriented children and youth. A recent volume released by the National Academy of Education (NAEd) compiled scholarship articulating the need for civic reasoning and discourse as well as how these could be enacted to improve the overall state of civics education in K–12 schools. The NAEd contends disciplinary and general literacy skills are essential in cultivating these citizenship skills. Scholars also argue reading and writing in social studies are not so much about literacy skills as they are about how to use reading, writing, and speaking as tools of critical thinking, historical reasoning, civic discourse, and informed action. These aims are thoughtfully expressed in Dr. Jeffery Nokes's new edition of *Building Students' Historical Literacies: Learning to Read and Reason with Historical Texts and Evidence*. Moreover, this book presents authentic, classroom-tested approaches capable of overcoming the literacy challenges so deeply entrenched in traditional social studies classrooms. It is a model of the literacy and inquiry purposes promoted in the NCSS *College, Career, and Civic Life (C3) Framework* as well as the *Common Core State Standards for History and the Social Sciences*.

Building Students' Historical Literacies: Learning to Read and Reason with Historical Texts and Evidence offers practical, research-informed strategies for helping students become more critical readers and skillful writers and speakers. Not only is it an essential resource for social studies and history teachers, but it is also a well-written, easy-to-follow guide for improving student literacy and civic preparation skills. Dr. Jeffery Nokes outlines the inquiry-oriented habits of mind historians use when working with sources and argues how these reading, thinking, and writing tools are essential for negotiating the complexities of contested issues and (mis)information in contemporary society. For Dr. Nokes, historical literacy is civic preparation and critical literacy is vital for informed civic engagement. The skills historians exercise when working with sources are the same practices students and adults should employ to become skeptical researchers when using the internet, socially responsible media users, and bias and perspective detectors when reading. Dr. Nokes challenges educators to teach students to source texts for perspective recognition, approach texts with historical skepticism, corroborate information across multiple sources offering diverse and divergent perspectives, situate sources in the contexts of time and place, question trustworthiness and relative value of different accounts, and use and vet evidence wisely in support of claims, interpretations, and argumentation. Beyond these well-known historical thinking practices, Dr. Nokes introduces skills of substantiation and rebuttal, academic humility, historical empathy, and open-minded deliberation. These affective and cognitive skills offer a needed extension and timely response to the growing challenges associated with online reading and social media use.

The value of this book resides in its convincing ability to rethink folkways of teaching. It is well known that teachers, influenced by the *apprenticeship of observation*, tend to rely upon instructional practices they learned from their own experiences as students. These default options provide a set of predictable strategies (or conventional practices often including a steady diet of lecture, textbook, film, and worksheets) that teachers can fall back on when they are uncertain about how to proceed pedagogically. Dr. Jeffery Nokes contends that this persistent instruction not only fails to make content palatable for students but also consistently ignores the perspectives of traditionally marginalized students and yields minimal long-term learning or historical literacy development. The dismal performance on the NAEP Grades 4, 8, and 12 U.S. history exam, whereby fewer than a fifth of students met knowledge and skill proficiency over the last 25 years, offers evidence that conventional history instruction needs revision. Even more pressing is the growing complexity of dis- and misinformation permeating the sources of information students and adults turn to. *Building Students' Historical Literacies: Learning to Read and Reason with Historical Texts and Evidence* offers a refreshing and well-supported discussion of ways to help students to do more than simply comprehend a wide array of historical sources but to also develop the disposition and ability to think critically about multigenre sources as well as leverage evidence from these in pursuit of critical inquiry. Recognizing that these practices are not inherently flawed, Dr. Nokes contends that the intentional, purposeful use of instructional methods (e.g., information transmission, knowledge construction, or problem-solving) matters greatly in their effectiveness. Hence, this book presents an extensive review of relevant research to guide teachers in questioning and rethinking their literacy and history instruction. The expansive discussion of research also makes a sound case for why historical inquiry is critical for K–12 learning. Dr. Nokes, rightfully, argues that teachers have a responsibility to build students' historical literacies and effectively offers a real-world model for centering historical inquiry and disciplinary literacies in history teaching.

What is most notable in *Building Students' Historical Literacies: Learning to Read and Reason with Historical Texts and Evidence* is the extension of well-known reading and writing approaches. According to Dr. Jeffery Nokes, historical literacy is the ability to negotiate a wide array of sources and create texts and resources valued within the discipline of history using agreed-on inquiry methods. His discussion of literacy formation begins with the ability to locate and identify relevant sources. This step is often overlooked in other methods for teaching historical thinking. Similarly, the usefulness of a source and its accuracy depends on the question(s) a historian (or student) uses to guide an inquiry. Knowing the purpose for reading is a foundational step in learning how to evaluate the evidence within sources. As with other approaches, credibility and accuracy are often not contextualized in this manner, leaving students to misapply or misunderstand this step when attempting to think like a historian. Yet another distinction of Dr. Nokes's approach to disciplinary literacy is the role of historical empathy. Garnering much more scholarly attention in the research within the last few years, empathy counters deficit notions of inferiority frequently imposed upon the past by apprentice historians. A dimension of empathy noted within this text is care which inspires actions to rectify injustices. The added discussion of affective domains of literacy enhances the usefulness and merit of this outstanding instructional resource. Open-mindedness, healthy skepticism, and academic humility further students' interpretative skills while also helping students recognize the limits of their own knowledge and inferences. Within the pages, teachers will find strategies for guiding students in understanding how historical knowledge is constructed, why not all interpretations are equally valid or reliable, and the role of judgment in determining the strength of arguments and evidence use.

Building Students' Historical Literacies: Learning to Read and Reason with Historical Texts and Evidence is a comprehensive and pioneering resource for teaching inquiry as active and iterative literacy processes necessary for meaning construction. Moreover, it empowers educators to attend to gaps in history teaching that rarely practice authentic disciplinary skills associated with the professional activities of historians. Grounded in experiential descriptions, Dr. Nokes offers an approachable process for rethinking historical literacy and well-documented method for integrating these practices in social studies classrooms. When historical literacy is an explicit objective of instruction, students can safely and with success delve deeply into sources and use a host of strategies (prediction, connecting prior knowledge, codebreaking, investigative thinking, confirmation bias checks, etc.) to infer meaning and engage purposefully with the texts. Dr. Nokes's vision of inquiry prepares students to skeptically consider the relevance and value of sources in light of their questions. Applications of this text in teaching history and social studies will likely yield students who can read and think critically, are informed and engaged participants in democracy, and are capable of using their understanding for the benefit of society. Drawing on the most recent research in the field, Dr. Jeffery Nokes's historical literacy processes will attend to many of the struggles and challenges students encounter in working with a wide array of texts and sources in history and social studies. I am glad that I had an opportunity to read *Building Students' Historical Literacies: Learning to Read and Reason with Historical Texts and Evidence*. It is a resource I will continue to reference and recommend to teachers and colleagues.

Tina L. Heafner, PhD
Professor of Social Studies Education
University of North Carolina at Charlotte

AUTHOR

Jeffery D. Nokes is a professor in the History Department at Brigham Young University, where he helps direct the history teaching and social science teaching programs. He earned a PhD in teaching and learning from the University of Utah, with an emphasis on literacy in secondary history classrooms. A former middle school and high school teacher, he has focused his research on history teaching and learning, historical literacy, and preparing young people for civic engagement. He is the author of *Building Students' Historical Literacies: Learning to Read and Reason with Historical Texts and Evidence* and coauthor of *Explorers of the American West: Mapping the World through Primary Documents*. His newest book is *Teaching History, Learning Citizenship: Tools for Civic Engagement*. Jeff has published many journal articles and book chapters on the topics of historical literacy, literacy instruction, and teacher preparation. He has received middle school, high school, and university teaching awards, including the Karl G. Maeser Excellence in Teaching Award from Brigham Young University in 2019. He currently teaches courses on the historian's craft, teaching historical literacies to young people, teaching methods for prospective social studies and history teachers, and Utah history. Jeff lives in Riverton, Utah, with his wife, Gina, where he enjoys backpacking, camping, and spending time with his children and grandchildren.

ACKNOWLEDGMENTS

I acknowledge, with gratitude, the help that I have received throughout my career and on this project, including both the first and second editions of this book. I appreciate the professors during my undergraduate career who helped me develop some fundamental historical literacies, particularly Robert Kenzer. I appreciate the many mentors I have had throughout my teaching career, especially Scott Crump and Barry Lehto. Professors Jan Dole, Doug Hacker, Suzanne Wade, Kay Camperell, and Emily Swan patiently supported me throughout my graduate education, as my notions of teaching historical literacies took shape. Many others have been helpful in the completion of this project. I gratefully acknowledge the advice of Professors Sam Wineburg, Roni Jo Draper, and Brian Cannon, and prospective history teachers, Lauren Angarola, Jenna Hatch, and Emily Shaw, who provided helpful feedback on early drafts of chapters from a preservice teacher's perspective. I appreciated my interaction with the Content Area Literacy Study Group at BYU, which opened my eyes to new literacies and gave me critical feedback on my ideas about historical literacies. I acknowledge the energy and foresight of Karen Adler, the Senior Editor for Literacy Education at Routledge who proposed creating a second edition and to Emily Dombrovskaya and others at Routledge for their assistance on the project. I express thanks to the anonymous reviewers who provided great insights for making substantial changes for this edition. I am particularly thankful for my wife, Gina, who has supported me throughout my career and the completion of this second edition. And I'm thankful for my good children who have been understanding of my investment in this project. While the ideas of many others have inspired my writing, I take sole responsibility for the contents of this book.

PART I

Exploring the Critical Literacies used in Historical Inquiry

Literacy is central to the work of historians. They ask questions about the past, read about how others have answered those questions, seek evidence of many genres, apply thinking strategies and habits of mind, read and analyze evidence, construct interpretations, make claims about historical events and conditions, substantiate their claims using evidence, and communicate their interpretations through argumentative writing and speaking. This book explores the critical reading, thinking, and writing strategies used by historians as they engage in historical inquiry. Its purpose is the help history teachers introduce these literacies to young people in order to help them become more critical readers and more skillful writers and speakers. An argument that I make throughout this book is that the skills and habits of mind that historians use during inquiry have applications for the reading and writing required for civic engagement in the 21st century. Students who possess these critical reading skills and who exhibit these habits of mind engage in historical inquiries with greater zeal and learn history better. But more important, they are equipped with tools necessary to negotiate the internet, social media, and polarized news outlets—the sites where individuals research the controversial issues of today.

Part I of this book explores the concept of historical literacies. In Chapter 1, I describe my experiences as a middle school and high school history teacher, testing out historical inquiry lessons in my classroom and discovering through trial-and-error practical and engaging instructional methods. I also describe my transition into life as an educational researcher where I have continued to learn how to help students use critical reading strategies during historical inquiry. In Chapter 2, I contrast traditional history instruction with history instruction that engages students in historical inquiries. I propose that teaching young people the critical reading strategies associated with historical literacies prepares them for civic engagement. In Chapter 3, historians become models of reading, thinking, and writing. I describe the texts they read and create and the skills and habits of mind they use as they engage in inquiry. Chapter 4 explores ideas for teaching

DOI: 10.4324/9781003183495-1

historical literacies to young people. General research on literacy is used to identify tools for building students' historical literacies. In Chapter 5, I continue to explore the question, what is history? I contend that until students understand how historical knowledge is constructed, they will be unable to participate effectively in historical inquiry. Finally, in Chapter 6 I discuss critical intertextual analysis. Using a model lesson that includes a variety of genres of historical evidence and a range of strategies and habits of mind, I provide a vision of critical reading that could be the long-range outcome of programs that build historical literacies.

By the time you have finished reading the chapters of Part I you should be able to do the following:

- Contrast the methods and impact of conventional history instruction with those of historical inquiry and historical literacy instruction and summarize the research-based support for the latter.
- Compare and contrast the roles of evidence, secondary sources, tertiary sources, and public histories and describe methods of promoting historical literacy with each category of resource.
- Analyze the concept of historical literacy, considering Freebody and Luke's four roles of the reader (code breaker, meaning maker, text user, and text critic), and describe how and why barriers to students' historical thinking can be minimized when a teacher supports students in each of their four roles.
- Describe and demonstrate historians' strategies and habits of mind for working with evidence, accounts, and traces.
- Explain the steps of explicit strategy instruction and tell how it is different from implicit strategy instruction.
- Define the notion of epistemic stance and contrast the typical epistemic stances of students with the epistemic stance required for sophisticated historical thinking. Describe instructional methods that help students assume a more sophisticated epistemic stance.
- Make connections between the strategies essential in historical literacies and the strategies needed for informed civic engagement and explain how teachers can help students transfer historical literacies to informed civic engagement.

These objectives should result in teachers who are better prepared to build students' historical literacies and engage them in historical inquiries.

1

WHY TEACH HISTORICAL LITERACIES

Evaluating the Source and Context of This Book

Will reading this book be worth your time? The purpose of this chapter is to convince you that it will. You should begin to see how the historical literacies presented throughout the book serve a vital role in preserving democracy by informing civic engagement.

> As you read this vignette, consider the similarities between the way historians investigate evidence and the way individuals should conduct online research and use social media responsibly.

Several years ago, as my family sat around the dinner table, two of my sons who competed on the high school cross-country team had a conversation about sugar. One had recently tried to eliminate sugar from his diet. He thought that doing so would improve his performance as a runner. However, after cutting sweets, his times did not improve. The younger brother had a sweet tooth and would never sacrifice sugar. In recent weeks, his times had improved, and he had started to outpace his older brother. Did the consumption or nonconsumption of sugar have anything to do with their performance on the track? During the dinnertime discussion, the younger brother tried to convince the elder that sugar was good for a runner. He made a compelling case, comparing his sugar-enhanced times to his brother's stalling performance. Going for the knockout punch, he pulled his cell phone out of his pocket. Within a few minutes, he found a website that stated unequivocally that sugar was an important part of a young runner's diet.

Up to that point in the conversation, I had remained a silent listener. I was nearly convinced that runners needed sugar. Then I asked to see my son's phone. The site he had found had a professional appearance, with images that gave the impression that it had been created by a nutritionist or someone in the

DOI: 10.4324/9781003183495-2

medical field. Taking his phone, I searched for information about the creator of the website. Eventually I found the name of the organization responsible for the webpage. Searching for more information about that organization, I eventually found that it was affiliated with one of the major producers of soft drinks in the United States. Both boys could understand the problems associated with making decisions about sugar consumption based on evidence provided by one of America's largest purveyors of sugar. Undaunted, my sugar-consuming son went back to his phone to search for a more authoritative source that would support his argument.

This book is about historical literacy. But the applications of its content extend beyond the reading, thinking, and writing that occur in history classrooms. It is intended for history teachers, but the impact has the potential to reach beyond schools. The literacies described in its pages can enhance young people's ability to engage in historical inquiry. These same literacies, with minor adjustments, can also advance their capacity to wisely research current issues using the Internet, use social media responsibly, and distinguish bias in the telling or retelling of a news report. For young people (and old people) who turn to their cell phones to answer all types of questions, the ideas of this book might save them from minor or major mistakes. In a democratic society in which individuals increasingly research political issues online, the critical reading and argumentative writing strategies described in this book are of existential importance. History classrooms that teach students to approach texts with mild resistance, cross-check information found in one source with other sources, provide evidence-based substantiation for claims, and seek alternative perspectives when researching, prepare young people for informed civic engagement in the 21st century's polarized environment. These critical reading strategies that are exhibited by historians, if taught in history classes, have the potential to solidify history's indispensable place in the curriculum, a position debated in the 21st century (Alterman, 2019).

Two of the most basic historical thinking skills are *sourcing*, considering the source of the information one receives, and *contextualization*, thinking about what was happening when a document was created. So it is important to introduce myself to the reader, sharing something about the context that motivated me to write this book. In this chapter, I describe my growing interest in the critical thinking associated with historical literacies and historical inquiry throughout my 30-year teaching career. I describe some of the experiences I had as a middle school and high school history teacher, experiences that ground my understanding of history teaching in the practical realities of the classroom. I also describe some of my experiences as a researcher as my understanding of historical literacy and historical inquiry have evolved. I introduce the major themes of the remaining chapters of this book to help the reader follow my logic in putting this book together in the sequence that I have.

historical literacies: the ability to negotiate/read and create/write the kinds of texts that are valued in history, including the ability to gather and weigh evidence from multiple sources, make informed decisions, solve problems using historical accounts, and persuasively defend interpretations of the past

Historical Literacies in My Classroom

What insights for teaching historical literacies can you gain from my teaching experiences?

My interest in the critical reading strategies that I now call historical literacies began early in my teaching career when a colleague of mine gave me a collection of documents related to the Boston Massacre to use with an eighth-grade U.S. history class. Being a young teacher, I was happy to try just about anything that I was given. I gave students the documents as I received them and assigned students to try to figure out what really happened at the Boston Massacre. Then I stepped back and watched students work. The documents presented conflicting evidence that at first perplexed these 13- and 14-year-olds. I was not much more familiar with historical reading than the youngsters were. But I instinctively knew that the perspective of the eyewitnesses, American or British, loyalist or patriot, made a difference in their account of the event. I tossed that concept to the students to consider, and their debate gained energy and sensibility. Even an inexperienced teacher like me could see that something special was taking place that day. The level of engagement was high as students argued about the trustworthiness and relative value of the different accounts. Many students became passionate about their interpretations. Some contested the minute details of the event. The students' excitement in learning during a challenging reading task was something I had not witnessed before in my classroom, which typically involved textbook reading, lectures, and documentary videos. The students learned a great deal through the activity, but I learned even more—I caught a glimpse of what a history classroom might be like if I engaged students in historical inquiry.

historical inquiry: opportunities for students to explore authentic questions about the past, with space to construct their own interpretations, support in their use of evidence, and a chance to share their ideas and receive feedback.

Over the next several years, I began to collect activities like this Boston Massacre analysis—activities during which students would sort through primary source documents and attempt to answer a historical question. My teacher instincts told me that this was good teaching. I soon discovered that when I planned and structured the activity correctly, with an interesting question and the right documents, graphic organizers, and student groupings, engagement was high. And students learned the historical content better. I gained a clearer understanding of what inquiry looked like—something I had rarely experienced personally as a student. However, in the days before the internet, it was extremely time-consuming to find primary sources, and I, as a typical teacher, was expected to serve as a student government advisor, assistant basketball coach, mock trial team coordinator, and on multiple committees. Regrettably, most of my lessons followed a more traditional format with students listening to me lecture. But in my heart, I understood that there was a better way to help students learn historical content. Over the years, I shortened lectures and increased the frequency of activities during which students would construct their own interpretations based on documents and other historical evidence.

I was on a constant lookout for new texts that I could incorporate in my classroom, and the harder I looked, the more I discovered. For instance, one afternoon while reading the newspaper, I found an obituary of a gentleman with a Japanese surname. Reading closer I found that he had been forced to relocate from California during the early years of World War II—sent to the internment camp at Topaz in central Utah. I cut out the obituary and took it to class the next day because it fit in with the lesson I was teaching. As students analyzed the obituary, they made discoveries that went beyond what I had noticed. One student pointed out that the man's parents had traditional Japanese names, he had a traditional Japanese given name but an Americanized nickname, and his children had traditional American names. She had identified evidence of the process of assimilation in this family. Another student noticed that the obituary used active voice except for the line about him being sent to an internment camp. She suggested that the obituary made it sound like the forced removal happened but it was not anyone's fault. The way it was written eliminated blame from anyone. She thought that it showed a spirit of forgiveness by the gentleman's family. Other students disagreed. The students' analysis of the obituary solidified a thought that had been growing in my mind for some time—my students had the ability to be not only consumers of historical knowledge, remembering things that others had figured out, but also they had the potential to be producers of original understandings, developing independent interpretations of historical events—interpretations that had significant value and that could be evaluated by peers in rigorous collaborative and deliberative discussions.

For the next few years, I continued to add to my collection of document-based inquiry activities and found better ways to nurture students' historical thinking. And as I did, I gained increasing appreciation from students and growing attention from colleagues, parents, and community organizations. The students at Elk Ridge Middle School chose me as the "teacher of the year" the same year that the regional chapter of the Daughters of the American Revolution selected me as their outstanding history teacher. Then, after 12 years in middle schools, I moved to Bingham High School, where, in my second year, I was named "most inspirational teacher" by the students. That same year I was honored as the Utah High School history teacher of the year by Utah's chapter of the National Council for the Social Studies. I joked with my teaching colleagues that the awards were a result of my being the only teacher in the building who wore a tie to school every day. But in the back of my mind, I knew that a great deal of my success was a result of my efforts to engage students in historical inquiry.

Then in 2006, after 15 years of teaching middle school and high school history, I became a teacher educator and researcher at Brigham Young University. Since then, I have continued to study history teaching, with a specific focus on building secondary students' historical literacies. The most important insight I have gained is that research on literacy applies not only to written historical evidence but to all types of historical resources, such as artifacts, photographs, architecture, and music. And looking back on my 15-year career, I always seemed to understand the value of helping students learn with multiple genres of evidence—I just never considered my efforts as building historical literacies, which I do now. Whether I was helping students use raw data from census records to discover trends in immigration or helping students understand the symbols in a political cartoon or helping them create a museum exhibit displaying their interpretation of a historical event of their own choosing, I was building students' historical literacies.

Historical Literacies in the Research

> How has research on teaching shaped your ideas about teaching practices? What more could be done to connect teachers with research that has classroom applications?

In the mid-1990s, after a few years of teaching, while working on a master's degree, I stumbled, quite by accident, onto an article that changed the way I viewed history teaching. Dr. Camperell, my content-area literacy professor, assigned me to find a research article related to reading within my discipline. "You might look at the *Journal of Educational Psychology*," she suggested. I went to the library and found the floor with bound periodicals. Discovering the journal Dr. Camperell had suggested, I pulled one off the shelf and opened it to the table of contents. I do not know whether it was luck or fate, but in that volume was one of the most influential and oft-cited articles related to historical literacy. It's title immediately caught my attention—it had the words *reading* and *historical text* in it—just what I needed. What was even more appealing to me was that in the appendix, there were eight documents related to the Battle of Lexington. Thrilled, I made a copy of the article and put the eight documents in my Revolutionary War file so that I could teach with them the following year.

When I began to read the article, I discovered two ideas that were worth much more than the eight documents. First, there is a purpose in teaching history even more important than building students' historical content knowledge, namely nurturing their historical thinking skills. By helping students read and reason like historians, history teachers could prepare them to survive and thrive as adults in an Information Age. The enhanced content knowledge that resulted from engagement in multiple text activities, which I had observed in my classroom, was an important by-product of this type of teaching. However, the real value of students' engagement in multiple text analyses was in their development of historical thinking skills. Second, individuals were systematically studying history teaching. These researchers, like Wineburg (1991), the author of the article in the *Journal of Educational Psychology*, were defining "historical literacies" and were experimenting with instructional strategies that helped students analyze texts with greater sophistication.

Later, I entered a PhD program in "teaching and learning" with a focus on literacy. I continued teaching high school history. I discovered that research on building students' literacies had numerous classroom applications for helping students think historically. In my practice, research-based approaches to literacy instruction, such as explicit strategy instruction, helped me improve students' ability to engage in historical thinking. For my dissertation, I systematically studied what I had observed repeatedly in my classroom. Eight colleagues agreed to teach lessons that I developed, including 10 reading lessons focused on either building content knowledge or building historical literacies using either textbooks or collections of primary sources. My research demonstrated that students learned better—both content knowledge and historical reasoning skills—with primary sources than they did with the textbook. Additionally, students showed significant improvement in their ability to use some of the historians' critical reading strategies when they were given explicit strategy instruction (Nokes et al., 2007). I completed my degree and continued teaching the high school students I adored until moving to Brigham Young University in 2006.

The Importance of Critical Reading in the 21st Century

Why does the lack of critical reading skills, particularly skills for reading online texts and social media, threaten democracy? How can historical literacy instruction help?

My views on the process and importance of nurturing the critical literacies asso-ciated with historical thinking continued to evolve over the years. Having grown up before the internet or social media were available, watching the way these technologies change the way people communicate and interact is fascinating. I have been amazed by the power of these media to reform the world. In 2010, I watched with interest and hope as individuals facing oppression and poverty used social media to coordinate antigovernment protests and uprisings across much of the Arab world. Arab Spring, as these rebellions were called, resulted in civil wars and regime change in a few nations. In other locations, the insurgen-cies were contained, as government officials shut down the internet or blocked social media sites that were being used to foment revolt. Government forces and counterinsurgent groups met protesters with violence, the effects of which continue to be seen in many nations more than a decade later. In most of north-ern Africa and across the Middle East, Arab spring faded without the needed democratic or economic reforms that had inspired its rise. The events of the 2010 Arab Spring demonstrated the powerful political role that the internet and social media could play.

On the home front I have been dismayed to watch the increasing polarization of America's democratic institutions and news media. Daily newspapers that used to present accurate though biased reports have been replaced by social media and politicized news outlets that care less about accuracy than on instigating emo-tion-driven action. Americans' changing sources of information have opened the door for fake news and foreign meddling in U.S. politics. Social media creates echo chambers in which Americans hear and repeat the same bogus stories and opinions, reposting with increased ire and decreased critical thought. Politicians and special interest groups tap into anger to solidify support, adding fuel to the fire with their hostile and deceptive rhetoric. Russian trolls use social media to exaggerate extremism and raise doubts about democratic institutions among Americans (Bodine-Baron et al., 2018). Research backs up what seems obvi-ous—Americans are unprepared for the new demands for critical reading that current trends related to social media and online reading create (Breakstone et al., in press).

An insurrection at the U.S. Capitol building on January 6, 2021, removed any doubt about the urgency with which teachers must improve their teach-ing of critical literacies. On that day, a mob of supporters of President Donald Trump attacked the Capitol during a joint session of Congress that had con-vened to count the electoral votes that would transfer the presidency to Joe Biden, the legitimate winner of the November 2020 presidential election. Like most Americans, I watched in disbelief as rioters desecrated some of the most beloved icons of American democracy. Behind the attacks were President Trump's unfounded claims of a stolen election based upon allegations of widespread elec-tion fraud, claims for which no trustworthy evidence exists. Among the accusa-tions were unfounded news reports that voting machines in some states had been programmed to change Trump votes to votes for Biden. Weeks after the election, claims of a stolen victory through widespread voter fraud continued to be circulated by politicized news agencies and by some politicians, including Donald Trump. Yet election officials in each state—both Republican and Democratic officers—reported that the handful of incidents of voter fraud that had occurred did not impact the outcome of the election. The January 6 Capitol insurrection has convinced me of the existential importance of teaching the critical literacies associated with historical reading, thinking, and writing.

The skeptical reader might ask, How can teaching young people the literacies necessary to engage in historical inquiry protect fragile democracy? This book answers that question. To summarize here, important similarities exist between the literacies needed to read, think, and write historically and to research, communicate, and take action in democratic societies with polarized and unscrutinized outlets of information. Among other concepts, this book addresses the following:

- *healthy skepticism*—historians are mildly resistant to the evidence they receive. They will not accept information without running it through a screening process first. The best historians are even skeptical of evidence that they want to believe. Internet researchers and social media users, likewise, should be mildly resistant to the ideas they find—even those ideas they want to believe—and critically evaluate them before acting on them or sharing them.
- *perspective recognition*—historians think carefully about the perspective of the person from whom information is coming. They seek information from alternative perspectives. They give historical characters the benefit of the doubt, understanding that their perspective in the past differed from that of modern individuals. Likewise, those researching political issues should seek out diverse perspectives and gather evidence about the issues from multiple points of view. In working with political opponents, activists must understand that differences of opinion generally grow from differences in perspective, not from evil intent.
- *sourcing*—historians carefully consider the source of the evidence they find, keeping in mind the perspective, biases, and insights of the person behind the evidence. Effective online research and responsible social media use require sourcing, a careful vetting of the person or organization behind information.
- *corroboration*—historians cross-check the information found in one source with information found in other sources. When historians encounter plausible but conflicting information, they do not simply believe one source and discount the other, but they construct a synthesized interpretation. Individuals researching political issues should cross-check information found on one website with information on others, gleaning the best information from each source.

- *argumentation*—historians construct and defend evidence-based interpretations through argumentation. They substantiate claims with carefully vetted evidence. They expect their colleagues to do the same. Likewise, in discussions of controversial political issues, individuals should use evidence to back up their claims. The public should demand strong evidence to substantiate claims. Evidence should be scrutinized, even when an individual wants to believe what is being argued.
- *substantiation* and *rebuttal*—historians construct interpretations from evidence. They recognize the need to substantiate their claims with evidence and to acknowledge evidence that seems to contradict their claims, offering an explanation. In contrast many political activists develop their opinion first, then cherry-pick evidence to support their opinion, suppressing contradictory evidence. Such actions run counter to informed civic engagement and damage democracy.
- *academic humility*—historians are willing to change their minds in the face of better evidence. Of all the traits that are essential in a democracy, the willingness to rethink one's position is perhaps the most vital. Like historians, activists must go where the best evidence takes them, remembering others' perspectives.
- *historical empathy*—historians imagine the perspective of people in the past and care about historical characters. Many of them take action in the present based on the wrongs they have identified in the past. Likewise, those who study current issues do so cognitively and emotionally, ready to take action when they recognize inequity or other problems.
- *collaborative deliberation*—historical inquiry involves social interaction, as historians build on the work of their peers and as their work undergoes peer review. Informed civic engagement is also social in nature as diverse people work together to solve problems and address issues in a manner that achieves the common good.

Students who have developed these attributes and skills in history classrooms, and who have been taught to apply these strategies in civic engagement are better prepared to face the unprecedented challenges of negotiating social media and using online sources of information as they take informed action.

An Overview of the Book

How is this book organized? How can understanding its organization help you study more efficiently and effectively and apply ideas more appropriately?

This book, written for prospective, new, and practicing history teachers, is a synthesis of my teaching experiences and the research conducted by me and many others on building historical literacies. It emerges from the 15 years of failures and successes in the classroom that have been followed by 15 years of studying what the best teachers do. I write it as a teacher turned teacher-educator and as a tinkerer turned researcher. The uniqueness of this book lies in its practical classroom application of research. Its importance rests in the need to prepare young people for the challenges associated with online reading and social media use in the polarized political climate of the 21st century.

Each chapter in the book opens with a vignette. These vignettes, with few exceptions, are quasi-autobiographical—I once taught a lesson that resembles each narrative. In the vignettes, I try to capture the thinking of teachers as they establish objectives, gather resources, plan instruction, and carry out their lessons. The vignettes are intended to introduce the major themes of that chapter. Each is framed by questions before and after the story to help the reader focus on the concepts that will be unpacked on the pages that follow. Two chapters, the first and last, serve as framing chapters for the book. Chapter 1, which you are reading now, discusses the origins and importance of the ideas discussed in subsequent chapters and previews some of those concepts.

The next section, Part I, includes Chapters 2 through 6. In these chapters, I define *historical literacies* and discuss critical literacy instruction. Chapter 2 contrasts instruction that builds historical literacies with traditional history instruction, promoting a paradigm shift and new vision of teaching history. Chapter 3 further defines *historical literacies*, contrasting the reading of historians in their scholarly work with the reading of history students in schools. This chapter previews the texts, reading strategies, and habits of mind that constitute historical literacies. In Chapter 4, I consider historical literacies within a context of general literacy and outline a theoretical framework for understanding literacy. This chapter establishes a pedagogical model for teaching and assessing historical literacies that I refer to throughout the book. In Chapter 5, I describe history as a discipline, suggesting that students must understand the nature of historical inquiry and historical knowledge before they can develop historical literacies. Chapter 6 describes a historical inquiry lesson that requires students to use a range of critical historical literacy strategies as they evaluate a variety of genres of historical evidence. I include this lesson to demonstrate how skillful readers apply strategies flexibly as they gather evidence from many genres of text and formulate an argument.

In Part II of this book I include chapters that break down the teaching of individual skills or habits of mind using a specific genre of historical text, each chapter focusing on one skill and one genre. The correlation between the skills and genres, while not arbitrarily chosen, is not meant to indicate that certain aspects of historical thinking are used exclusively with certain genres. Instead, the skills and habits of mind associated with historical inquiry extend across all genres of evidence. Specifically, Chapter 7 discusses the use of historians' strategies of sourcing, corroboration, and contextualization in working with primary sources. Chapter 8 focuses on the process of making observations and inferences with prehistoric and historic artifacts. Chapter 9 explores second-order concepts, ideas related to historical procedures and organizational structures in history. This chapter gives suggestions for helping students analyze visual texts. In Chapter 10, I consider historical empathy and perspective taking using various types of historical fiction. Chapter 11 promotes healthy skepticism using textbooks, a genre usually written in a style that discourages critical reading. In Chapter 12, I consider reductionist traps that can cause confusion about the need for historical interpretation. In this chapter, I discuss historical inquiries that use audio and video texts. Chapter 13 addresses the important skill of argumentative historical writing, using quantitative historical data.

I conclude the book with another framing chapter. Chapter 14 draws on the vignettes used throughout the book to present a template for creating powerful historical literacy lessons. In addition I provide suggestions for overcoming the barriers that might prevent a teacher from using inquiry in their history classroom.

The first edition of this book was published in 2013. In 2020, I was approached by Karen Adler at Routledge and asked whether I would be interested in updating this book in a revised second edition. The reviewers who helped us consider the idea agreed that the concepts of this book continue to be of importance but that changing conditions required major revisions. So the current edition is substantially different from the first edition. After the first edition was published, a great deal of research has been conducted that provides additional insights into the most effective methods of teaching and assessing historical literacies. Educational researchers know more about teaching argumentative writing and working with students who have learning disabilities, for instance. I have tried to incorporate this new research into the ideas included in this edition. I have shortened vignettes in this edition to make room to include more practical resources for teachers—study guides and rubrics. I restructured the book to make certain that readers understood that isolated strategies do not correspond to certain genres of evidence, but that all the strategies must be applied in concert with all types of texts. I gave argumentative writing and assessment a more prominent place in the current edition. I added examples associated with inquiries related to difficult histories and included more research related to the response of youth of color to historical inquiry instruction. I updated the examples to reflect teaching resources of the 21st century—gone are the overhead projectors and trips to the school computer lab that represent my classroom experience but do not reflect the realities of today's schools. The most substantial change in the current edition is the explicit connection between historical literacies and the critical reading and communication skills that are necessary for informed civic engagement. The current political climate has demonstrated the need for readers and speakers to have the tendency and ability to think critically about the information they receive and share on social media and in internet research. Building students' historical literacies can help.

Questions for Consideration

1. Review the bullet list on pages 10–11 of historical literacy strategies and habits of mind that have applications in civic engagement. Can you think of additional ways to apply historical thinking skills or habits of mind to civic engagement? What can a teacher do to help students transfer these strategies from the history classroom to the civic arena?
2. How do current political conditions create a need for individuals to use social media responsibly, research the internet with care, and evaluate their news sources? To what degree do these changing conditions elevate the importance of history instruction?
3. Why is instruction on historical literacies essential in classrooms that use inquiry? What are the dangers in engaging students in historical inquiries without building their historical literacies?

Additional Reading and Viewing

- The website https://cor.stanford.edu/videos/ includes a series of videos introducing the Stanford History Education Group's research on civic online reasoning, which transfers the historical literacies of sourcing and corroboration to internet reading with some specialized adaptations.
- The article Breakstone, J., Smith, M., Wineburg, S., Raparort, A., Carle, J., Garland, M., Saavedra, A. (in press). Students' civic online reasoning: A national portrait. *Educational Researcher,* accessible at https://stacks.stanford.edu/file/druid:cz440cm8408/Students%27%20Civic%20Online%20Reasoning_2021.pdf provides an excellent description of the struggles of so-called digital natives to critically evaluate online texts.
- The article, Nokes, J. D., Dole, J. A., & Hacker, D. J. (2007). Teaching high school students to use heuristics while reading historical texts. *Journal of Educational Psychology, 99*(3), 492–504, describes my dissertation research.
- The book Swan, K., Lee, J., & Grant S. G. (2018). *Inquiry Design Model: Building inquiries in social studies.* National Council for the Social Studies and C3 Teachers, provides a practical guide for creating inquiries in history and social studies classrooms using the Inquiry Design Model.

References

Alterman, E. (2019, Feb. 4). The decline of historical thinking. *The New Yorker.* https://www.newyorker.com/news/news-desk/the-decline-of-historical-thinking

Bodine-Baron, E., Helmus, T. C., Radin, A., & Treyger, E. (2018). *Countering Russian social media influence*. RAND Corporation. https://www.rand.org/content/dam/rand/pubs/research_reports/RR2700/RR2740/RAND_RR2740.pdf

Breakstone, J., Smith, M., Wineburg, S., Raparort, A., Carle, J., Garland, M., Saavedra, A. (in press). Students' civic online reasoning: A national portrait. *Educational Researcher*

Nokes, J. D., Dole, J. A., & Hacker, D. J. (2007). Teaching high school students to use heuristics while reading historical texts. *Journal of Educational Psychology, 99*(3), 492–504

Swan, K., Lee, J., & Grant S. G. (2018). *Inquiry design model: Building inquiries in social studies*. National Council for the Social Studies

Wineburg, S. S. (1991). On the reading of historical texts: Notes on the breach between school and academy. *American Educational Research Journal, 28*(3), 495–519. doi:10.3102/00028312028003495

2
BUILDING HISTORICAL LITERACIES
A New Purpose for History Teaching

Most teachers teach the way they were taught. The purpose of this chapter is to make you question—even doubt—the time-honored history teaching methods of lecture and textbook reading, replacing them with a new vision of history teaching that includes historical inquiry and the building of historical literacies.

As you read the following vignette, compare the learning activities described with your experiences studying history in middle school and high school.

Ms. Cordova, the principal at McArthur Middle School, walks down the hall of the social studies department during third period. She notices the lights are off in Mr. Hanks's classroom and, glancing in, observes that he is showing students a video. Most students are filling out a worksheet. Ms. Cordova is distracted by loud voices coming from the next classroom down the hall and continues walking. As she approaches, she hears students reciting in unison the names of the presidents of the United States in chronological order. Continuing down the hall, she hears the hum of voices coming from another classroom and peeks in to see students sitting in small groups studying passages on Greek city-states in their world history textbook. In the next classroom, she hears Mr. Adams, one of the most popular teachers, involved in an animated lecture on the causes of World War I. Students laugh at his exaggerated German accent. As she passes his door, she sees that he is dressed in the uniform of a German soldier. From the silence in the hall ahead, she wonders whether the next classroom is empty. But, looking in, she sees that it is full of students who sit quietly at their desks either reading their textbook and taking notes or snoozing.

Finally, Ms. Cordova sees Mr. Rich's classroom, the class she has come to observe. As she enters, students' behavior appears somewhat chaotic. Some

DOI: 10.4324/9781003183495-3

FIGURE 2.1 Photograph of child laborers used in Mr. Richis's inquiry lesson (Hine 1908).

students sit at desks arranged in small groups. Other students huddle around Mr. Rich's computer browsing the internet. A few students stand at the whiteboard flipping through papers on a table and drawing some type of chart on the board. Mr. Rich is engaged with three students in one of the groups. As Ms. Cordova approaches, Mr. Rich nervously welcomes her, inviting her to join the students' discussion. Students pay little attention to her. They are looking at a black-and-white photograph of children working in a textile mill (see Figure 2.1).

Ms. Cordova listens as students debate whether the photograph is staged or spontaneous. When they turn to Mr. Rich for an answer, he points them toward his computer where another group of students is looking for information about the photographer. Two students get up and walk toward that group while the others continue to flip through the documents on their table, finally focusing on an excerpt from a historical novel, *Lyddie*, describing working conditions in textile mills (Paterson, 1991).

Ms. Cordova moves through other groups where students are engaged in similar conversations using the same collection of documents. A student explains to her that they are debating the question written on the whiteboard: "To what degree was child labor in 19th-century factories worse than child labor on family-owned farms of earlier generations?" Ms. Cordova watches students rummage through graphs, political cartoons, a map, an excerpt from a historical novel, photographs, diary entries, letters, and song lyrics. She hears students using terms like *account, unreliable, accurate, evidence,* and *corroborate.* She sees them adding annotations to the margins of the texts they read and taking notes on a Venn diagram (see Figure 2.2). More interesting to her, she senses in these young people an ability to not simply comprehend a wide variety of historical texts, but the disposition and ability to think critically about them.

Ms. Cordova likes the level of engagement in Mr. Rich's classroom. But she does not fully appreciate the fundamental difference between the instructional methods used in the other history classrooms and the way Mr. Rich teaches. Videos; memorization drills; lectures, no matter how entertaining; and textbook

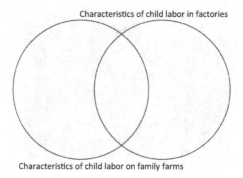

Characteristics of child labor in factories

Characteristics of child labor on family farms

FIGURE 2.2 Venn diagram used to organize notes on child labor.

reading assignments, whether done individually or in groups, represent efforts to transmit to students a historical narrative that has been produced by others. Students' role in these activities is to receive, manage, remember, and repeat information. Lectures, videos, and textbooks simply represent different media through which information is conveyed. In contrast, in Mr. Rich's classroom, students construct their own understandings and interpretations of history using many of the same types of texts that historians use. Students' role in his class is to semi-independently solve historical problems, building their own understanding of the past in the process. Students in Mr. Rich's class are immersed in inquiries that require historical literacies.

> How would Mr. Rich's lesson require a completely different way of thinking about history teaching than a traditional lesson? How would he plan and assess differently? How would classroom management be different? How are teachers' and students' roles different?

Research on Traditional History Instruction

Much of my career has been spent working with colleagues like the hypothetical teachers in McArthur Middle School's Social Studies Department. Many have taught with impressive energy, passion, and humor. But most have used traditional instructional methods. Early in my career, I taught in much the same way. Research suggests that we were typical of history teachers across America, lecturing, showing documentaries, and assigning textbook reading (Lee & Weiss, 2007; Nokes, 2010; Ravitch & Finn, 1987). However, an ever-increasing number of innovative teachers regularly engage students in inquiry methods that nurture historical reading, reasoning, and writing skills (Grant, 2018). In this chapter I consider the methods and materials of traditional classrooms and the results of traditional instruction. I establish a definition of historical literacies that I use throughout this book. I reimagine history teaching, making a case for historical literacy instruction that involves historical inquiry—authentic and semi-independent investigations of historical questions—like the learning activity designed by Mr. Rich.

Traditional Methods

In spite of a substantial body of research that shows the ineffectiveness of traditional history teaching approaches like lecture, why do you think that these methods continue to be so common?

In popular culture, the image of the history classroom includes a monotone teacher at the front of the room, lecturing to dozing teenagers about topics like the Hawley Smoot Tariff that everyone but the teacher perceives to be irrelevant (see https://www.youtube.com/watch?v=dxPVyieptwA; Chinich & Hughs, 1986). Many adults experienced history classrooms where days were spent reading a textbook chapter and answering the questions at the end. They remember history classrooms that were teacher-centered—the teacher doing most of the talking, with the students being assessed on their ability to remember what the teacher or textbook told them. Students' involvement was limited to listening to the teacher, reading the textbook, taking notes, and, in the best cases, working together with peers to prepare for dreaded exams that would assess their ability to remember a wide range of historical facts—tidbits of information that would quickly be forgotten after the exam. These adults, looking back on their high school days, often summarize their experience thus: "I hated history in high school, but I really like it now." Does this image, presented in popular culture and in the collective memory of adults, reflect the reality of today's history classrooms?

traditional history instruction: instruction designed to transmit historical information to students, usually through lecture, textbook reading, or documentary videos, with students repeating the historical information back on exams

The National Assessment of Educational Progress (NAEP) provides some of the best data on the teaching that has taken place in history classrooms of 30 years ago and today (Lee & Weiss, 2007; Ravitch & Finn, 1987). As part of the 1987 assessment, nearly 8,000 seventeen-year-old students were asked how often they engaged in different activities in their history class. Seventy-three percent of students reported that they "listen to the teacher explain a history lesson" daily, and almost 60% reported reading from their history textbook daily. In contrast, only 12% of students reported "analyzing historical events in small groups" daily. About twice as many claimed to "memorize information" every day. The report concludes that

> in the eyes of the students, the typical history classroom is one in which [students] listen to the teacher explain the day's lesson, use the textbook, and take tests. Occasionally they watch a movie. . . . They seldom work with other students, use original documents, write term papers, or discuss the significance of what they are studying.
>
> (Ravitch & Finn, 1987, p. 194)

Jumping ahead two decades, the 2006 NAEP survey of 4th, 8th, and 12th graders showed few changes in instructional methods. The survey asked students how they studied history or social studies. It did not offer the response of "listening to the teacher," like the earlier survey did, but the most frequently selected option, reported to have been done daily by more than half of the secondary students, was the option most like it: "discussing the material studied." Additionally, 32% of 4th graders, 42% of 8th graders, and 34% of 12th graders reported to have read daily from a textbook. Although the percentage of students experiencing daily textbook reading had declined, many history teachers continued to use traditional activities (Lee & Weiss, 2007).

As part of my dissertation, a research assistant and I spent 72 hours observing eight high school history teachers for six consecutive class sessions over a 3-week period. We found that these teachers lectured over 56% of the time, with more than half of the lectures involving little interaction with the students. In addition, students in these classrooms spent 23% of class time engaged in reading assignments that, in most cases, involved their textbook. The remaining time was divided relatively evenly between assessments and cooperative learning. Several teachers provided brief mini-lessons on skills such as how to make a poster, write a paper, or engage in a debate. However, lessons on skills occupied just a few minutes over the 72 hours of observations. In contrast, traditional methods of history instruction, lectures and textbook reading, occupied almost 80% of class time (Nokes, 2010).

More recently, a collaborative of 34 researchers across six states spent 3 years investigating the presence of *authentic pedagogy* in 52 social studies classrooms. They defined authentic pedagogy as instruction that "challenged students to construct knowledge through disciplined inquiry in order to produce work that has value beyond success in school" (Saye et al., 2013, p. 90). Authentic pedagogy is the antithesis of traditional instruction where information is transmitted then regurgitated back on exams. Results of these observations showed that almost 80% of teachers provided a minimal or limited level of authentic pedagogy, instead relying on more traditional methods of instruction. Skipping ahead

5 years, in Grant's (2018) review of history teaching practices, he contends that the promotion of inquiry by the National Council for the Social Studies (NCSS, 2013) has led to an increase in inquiry methods in history classrooms. However, he concludes that history teachers' inexperience with nontraditional teaching methods ensures the continued use of conventional lecture-and-textbook instruction in many history classrooms.

To say that lecture and textbooks have no usefulness in history classrooms would be wrong. To the contrary, you will see examples of historical inquiry lessons that include the reading of textbook passages described later in this book. And lecture serves an important role in many inquiry lessons, as teachers provide students with basic background information needed to engage in inquiry. However, my contention throughout this book is that lecture and textbook reading designed solely to transmit information, in the absence of opportunities for students to construct their own interpretations from historical evidence, do little to promote historical literacy and may even discourage it.

In summary, students' surveys, my observations, and recent research all suggest that traditional activities continue to have a prominent place in history classrooms in spite of their proven ineffectiveness and dullness. Certainly, the image of the droning history teacher is exaggerated in the movies, although the instructional methods depicted seem accurate. Through both lectures and textbook reading, teachers maintain control of the historical accounts that students hear. Students' role in traditional history classrooms is primarily to listen, manage information, record it in their notes, memorize it in preparation for exams, and report it back to the teacher during assessments. Evidence exists that suggests that the quintessential image of a history class continues to be accurate.

Traditional Materials

Why do expensive and boring textbooks continue to be so commonly used in history classrooms as "informational" texts?

The classroom observations that I conducted as part of my dissertation research revealed patterns in the resources that history teachers used with their students. The eight teachers I observed employed textbooks about five times as often as they used primary sources. Textbooks were used as expository or *informational texts*, intended to transmit information. Students were not encouraged to critically evaluate or question the validity of textbook passages but to remember the information in the textbooks without question. They summarized textbook passages and used textbooks to find answers to factual questions. Students watched documentary videos and listened to lectures for the same reason they read textbooks: to receive information. During my observations, some teachers never exposed students to primary source documents, artifacts, photographs, music, or other historical sources that a historian might use as evidence (Nokes, 2010).

Both the 1987 and 2006 NAEP surveys corroborate the findings of my observations of the materials used in history classrooms. In 1987, almost 60% of the students reported that they were exposed daily to textbooks. One third of students reported watching movies weekly. In contrast, only 12% reported using documents or other original sources at least once a week and 45% said that they never used primary source documents (Ravitch & Finn, 1987). Changes between the 1987 NAEP survey and the one conducted in 2006 cause some optimism. The 2006 survey showed a significant drop in the percentage of students who reported using the textbook daily—from almost 60% in 1987 to 32% in 2006. The 2006 survey also showed an increase in the frequency of primary source use, particularly in middle and high schools. Still, 39% of 4th graders, 28% of 8th graders, and 20% of 12th graders claimed to have never used primary sources in their history classes (Lee & Weiss, 2007). And although primary sources may be increasingly common in history classrooms, my observational study found that when primary sources were used, the teacher typically read and explained the document to the students. Students listened and took notes on the information contained in the primary source, as they would have done during a lecture or when reading a textbook. Reisman (2012) observed primary sources being used in a similar manner—to reinforce information found in a textbook. During the 3 weeks of my observations, I saw only one extended lesson and two brief activities that engaged students in inquiry with primary sources (Nokes, 2010).

Results of Traditional Instruction

> Why do you think that traditional instruction causes confusion in students about the nature of history as a discipline?

Traditional history instruction, in spite of its dullness, would be celebrated if it properly prepared students for college, career, and a lifetime of informed civic engagement. However, this is not the case. One of America's favorite pastimes is to mock fellow Americans' ignorance of historical facts. For example, in 2019, the Woodrow Wilson Foundation (now called the Institute for Citizens and Scholars) sponsored a survey that found that only 27% of Americans younger than the age of 45 were able to demonstrate a basic understanding of U.S. history (Riccards, 2019). These results echoed a 2011 issue of *Newsweek* that asked in the headline "How Dumb Are We?" (Romano, 2011). The *Newsweek* article reported that 38% of the 1,000 Americans given a U.S. citizenship test failed. The good news, if there is any to be found, is that Americans are not becoming much dumber: Romano (2011) cites studies that show that shifts in Americans' civic knowledge since the 1940s have averaged out to less than 1%. In other words, today's Americans have a similar grasp of history as that of their parents and grandparents—and, on average, their grasp of history and civics is poor.

Even older research suggests that Americans' struggles with remembering historical facts go back many generations. For example, over a century ago, Bell and McCollum (1917) tested elementary students, high school students, normal school students, and university students on their knowledge of basic historical facts. Average scores for the different groups ranged from 16% to 49%. They concluded that "this does not show a very thorough mastery of basic historical facts" (Bell & McCollum, 1917, p. 274). Many history teachers, even those without an inclination to rethink their methods, are aware of the ineffectiveness of traditional instruction in promoting long-term learning. I have heard on many occasions comments similar to the following, made by a student teacher I worked with: "I need to give the test tomorrow [Friday] because the students will forget over the weekend everything we have been studying."

Struggles with learning history are not confined to remembering historical facts but include difficulties in processing historical information. For example, the 2010 NAEP assessment found that only 20% of fourth graders demonstrated proficiency in historical thinking and writing. Even more alarming, only 17% of 8th graders and 12% of 12th graders showed proficiency (National Center for Educational Statistics, 2011). Students' lack of skill in using historical evidence to solve simple historical problems mirrors their lack of content knowledge. Put bluntly, most students find history classes boring and are not very good at remembering history or using historical evidence.

Researchers raise other concerns about the teaching of a single historical narrative. Stahl and Shanahan (2004) suggest that traditional instruction causes students to view texts as bearers of information. Objective-sounding history textbooks stand above criticism, unquestioned by student-readers (Paxton, 1999). How different this is from historians' view of texts as "'speech acts' produced for particular purposes by particular persons, at particular times and places" (Stahl & Shanahan, 2004, p. 96).

In addition to questioning the value of traditional instruction, some researchers contend that what occurs in most history classrooms is not history teaching at all. VanSledright (2002), for example, makes a distinction between heritage teaching and history teaching. He claims that heritage teaching exposes students to a single historical narrative, carefully tailored to "create a sense of pleasure and joy in being who we are" (Vansledright, 2002, p. 11). However, the traditional narrative rarely celebrates accomplishments outside of the white, male, American or European realm. Students in heritage classrooms rehearse this "official history," as policymakers hope to build patriotism. VanSledright (2002) contrasts heritage instruction with history teaching, which opens the past to evidence-driven inspection and revision. He encourages teachers to engage students in historical inquiry using rigorous methods of questioning, weighing evidence, and understanding contexts before passing judgment. He concludes, ironically, that history teaching is rare in America's history classrooms, adding that much of society is satisfied with heritage teaching rather than history teaching.

---

heritage teaching—presenting history as a single narrative that celebrates culture in a way intended to build pride in certain people's identity

---

But not everyone is satisfied. Heritage instruction is particularly unappealing to students of color. The traditional textbook narrative largely ignores minority perspectives and experiences, often presenting history as a whitewashed narrative of freedom and progress (Bostick, 2021; Loewen, 2008). The failure of textbooks to adequately address problems of racism, slavery, ethnic cleansing, and other difficult histories has led Loewen (2008) to call traditional instruction "lies" that teachers tell students. Research shows that students from different backgrounds experience the same history instruction differently and even learn content differently. Students of color, whose heritage is ignored or marginalized in the traditional historical narrative presented in most textbooks, naturally react with indifference or contempt for history classes (Epstein, 2000; Peck, 2018). The failure of students of color to remember the history they are taught is driven by their distrust of it. Understandably in these circumstances, the history children of color learn from their families holds much greater personal significance than the history they read in textbooks and hear in schools (Epstein, 1998).

In 2019, recognizing the problems associated with the traditional historical narrative, particularly the impact of such instruction on children and youth of color, the *New York Times* created the 1619 Project (1619 Project, 2021). This project marks 1619, the year that enslaved Africans were first brought to Virginia, rather than 1776, as the founding date of America. The 1619 Project condemns the racist, slave-holding Founders and America's racist history and celebrates, instead, the resilience and contributions of people of color. Creators of the 1619 Project intended to correct serious flaws in traditional heritage instruction. But they did so by replacing the heritage curriculum with a counter-heritage curriculum rather than with history instruction. In 2020, in response to the 1619 Project, the Trump administration sponsored a commission that produced the *1776 Report* (1776 Report, 2021). This report, prepared by politically conservative scholars, doubled down on America's traditional heritage curriculum, downplaying the role of slavery and race in the nation's history in favor of themes of liberty and capitalism. The political struggle between the 1619 Project and the *1776 Report* represents only the most recent battle in the ongoing history wars (Barton, 2012), which would be more accurately called the heritage wars.

In what ways are *the* 1619 Project and *the 1776 Report* similar in their promotion of something other than history teaching?

Both the *1776 Report* and the 1619 Project have been criticized by academic historians for distorting history in order to promote a political agenda. Both publications suggest that *a* story of American history is *the* story, a concern previously raised about textbooks (VanSledright, 2008). By focusing on heritage and counter-heritage rather than historical inquiry, both approaches leave students without the skills needed to acknowledge alternative perspectives when studying the past. Students may leave class proud of the Founders or angry at the Founders but with few skills to help them think deeply about the Founders' contexts or to wrestle with the inconsistencies between the Founders' words and actions. Ironically, students in history classes that focus on heritage or counter-heritage rarely learn about the nature of history as a discipline. They cannot comprehend why the same historical event might be reported and remembered in different ways by different people, instead just choosing one side and condemning the other. They rarely gain the skills needed to sort through contemporary debates over history with sophistication.

To summarize, in spite of the efforts of history teachers, traditional instruction that consists of lectures, textbook reading, and videos, does not yield significant long-term learning for most students. Historical content knowledge that students passively receive and rarely use is quickly forgotten. Within weeks of when facts are taught, students retain little beyond the simplistic and erroneous notions of pop history that everyone learns just by living in a society inundated with historical allusions (Wineburg, 2007). Furthermore, students leave traditional history classrooms with little ability to engage in historical reading, reasoning, or writing because their time has been spent managing information rather than engaging in historical thinking. What does not work for white students is even less effective with students of color who often respond to traditional instruction with indifference or contempt. The antidote for the traditional heritage narrative cannot be found in a counter-heritage narrative, but instead can be administered through instruction on historical literacies. An honest appraisal of ongoing studies of general historical knowledge creates doubts about the value of traditional history instruction today, 50 years ago, or 100 years ago. Traditional instruction has never worked well for the majority of students.

Redefining History Instruction

What do you see as the primary advantages of the presence of historical inquiry and historical literacy instruction in classrooms?

Increasingly, history educators are redefining the purpose of teaching history. Many question the value of traditional instruction that focuses exclusively on distributing historical information, much of it mere trivia. Of what value, for example, are history lessons that require a future welder, surgeon, or waitress to memorize information about the structure of Viking ships or the names of obscure vice presidents of the United States, particularly when such unused factual knowledge is not retained. History educators suggest—and this is the theme of this book—that instead, history teachers should build students' historical literacies: students' ability to gather and weigh evidence from multiple sources, make informed decisions, solve problems using historical accounts, and defend their interpretations of the past in writing and speaking. Instead of focusing solely on historical information, teachers have the potential to prepare students to survive and thrive for a lifetime in a world in which digital texts must be evaluated, conflicting news accounts must be compared, and information accessed through social media must be questioned (McGrew et al., 2018). Historical literacy is crucial for participation in a democratic and increasingly globalized world where both accurate and inaccurate information is equally available and nearly indistinguishable on people's cell phones (Wineburg, 2018).

Historical inquiry promotes a more sophisticated view of the world than heritage or counter-heritage instruction. By acknowledging multiple perspectives, historical inquiry nurtures *informed patriotism*, an appreciation of remarkable Americans and unique American institutions while acknowledging the flaws and inequities that have tormented and continue to plague American society. A more accurate understanding of history, including the ability to recognize diverse perspectives, allows a young person to see patriotism both in an aged woman who stands and places her hand over her heart and a young man who kneels and bows his head as the American flag is unfurled. History teaching, with the express purpose of building historical literacy, is crucial in the development of informed patriotism.

---

informed patriotism—an appreciation of unique and commendable American institutions and individuals, tempered by an understanding of America's flaws and inequities, with a commitment to make America better

---

The call for reform is becoming more common in mainstream discussions about history teaching. For instance, the Common Core State Standards for History and Social Studies, adopted by most of the states in the United States, call for history teachers to expose students to multiple accounts, help students consider the sources of documents, introduce students to the distinction between primary and secondary sources, teach students to use evidence to argue a claim, require students to synthesize information from different texts, and expect students to be fluent with various types of texts (Common Core State Standards, 2010). In response to the Common Core, the National Council for the Social

Studies created the C3 Framework (adding the third "c" of civic preparation to the college and career preparation highlighted in the Common Core.) The C3 Framework promotes inquiry pedagogy, suggesting that all students should be taught and encouraged to ask authentic questions, think critically about evidence, read like disciplinary experts to the degree possible, and apply concepts and strategies in their own lives and in civic engagement (NCSS, 2013; Swan & Lee, 2014). The National Council for History Education (NCHE, n.d.) promotes *habits of mind* that reflect historians' unique ways of seeing the world, including the tendency to "interrogate texts and artifacts, posing questions about the past that foster informed discussion, [and] reasoned debate and evidence-based interpretation" ("History's Habits of Mind"). Increasingly, educational leaders envision teachers promoting historical inquiry in every history classroom.

Making the Case for Historical Literacy Instruction

What are some of the similarities between historical reading and online reading? Which skills are valuable in both processes?

Mr. Rich is a composite character. He represents a growing number of history teachers who make historical inquiry and historical literacy instruction an integral and daily part of their classrooms. Researchers are investigating the results of innovative historical literacy instruction like Mr. Rich's lesson on child labor.

For example, VanSledright (2002), a teacher education professor, was convinced that elementary students would benefit by investigating evidence and independently constructing historical understandings. He spent much of a school year helping 23 fifth-graders study historical controversies, explore teacher-prepared "archives," produce document-based group presentations, and debate conflicting interpretations of historical events. He helped students "learn history by doing it" (VanSledright, 2002, p. 196). His ambitions were confronted by three formidable challenges as students (a) struggled to understand the difference between historical interpretation and the reality of the past, (b) continued to search for the single "correct" historical narrative, and (c) imposed present conditions, values, and standards on people and events of the past. In spite of these challenges, he saw students "deeply drawn into the process of investigating the past" (VanSledright, 2002, p. 150) and taking "to the task of reading texts with considerable zeal" (p. 152). His teaching methods were highly engaging.

VanSledright's lessons were not only engaging but they advanced students' critical reading skills. The eight students with whom VanSledright did follow-up interviews had developed a more sophisticated understanding of the nature of historical inquiry. They interpreted evidence, recognized bias, distinguished between primary and secondary sources, and corroborated across texts. These

10- and 11-year-olds became more willing to insert themselves into the historical discussion, one suggesting that he would rather rely on his interpretation of primary sources than on either of two contrasting interpretations made by other investigators. VanSledright (2002) tentatively celebrated the "conditional successes" of his work with the youngsters (p. 134).

In 2005, I studied the impact of historical literacy instruction on high school students (Nokes, et al., 2007). Eight teachers taught a 4-week unit on the 1920s and 1930s that I had planned. During the unit, all of the activities that students did in all the classes were the same except for 10 one-hour literacy lessons. Teachers were assigned to different treatment conditions during these lessons. In two of the classes, teachers conducted traditional reading activities—"read the textbook and answer these questions" about the historical content. In two other classes, teachers continued to use the textbook, but they discussed and practiced historians' strategies with students. Students were taught to read the textbook with a more critical eye. In two of the classes, teachers used documents and other authentic historical texts and students answered questions about the historical content. In the last two classes, students read the same collection of documents and received instruction on historians' reading and reasoning strategies. In this fourth treatment condition, students were taught to pay attention to perspective, synthesize across texts, and use other critical reading strategies. Students in the two treatment conditions that studied documents scored significantly higher than the students who studied textbooks on tests of their content knowledge, regardless of whether their lessons had focused on content or historians' strategies. However, only the students that were taught historians' strategies while working with primary sources showed significant growth in their ability to read and reason like historians. On posttests, these students paid greater attention to the source of the document, they more skillfully compared and contrasted conflicting accounts, and in the end, they wrote about historical controversy with greater sophistication. One important conclusion of my study, and others like it (Reisman, 2012), is that if a teacher focuses exclusively on content instruction, students are not likely to develop critical reading strategies. If, on the other hand, a teacher spends a significant amount of time teaching historical literacies, students will start to use the strategies, will interact more deeply with texts, and, as a result, will learn the content better. Traditional teachers would be surprised to learn that under the proper conditions, when some content instruction is replaced by literacy instruction, greater content knowledge is developed.

Other researchers have fostered historical disciplinary knowledge with middle school (Ashby, Lee, & Shemilt, 2005; Levstik & Barton, 2015), high school (Bain, 2005; Britt & Aglinskas, 2002; De La Paz et al., 2014, 2017; Lesh, 2011; Nokes et al., 2007; Reisman, 2012; Young & Leinhardt, 1998), and undergraduate students (Hynd et al., 2004; Perfetti et al., 1995) with positive results. They have documented success in teaching historical reading strategies to students with learning disabilities (De La Paz, 2005) and to students in international settings (van Boxtel & van Drie, 2012, for example). They have discovered strategies for teaching students to discuss controversies (Wissinger & De La Paz, 2016) and to write with greater sophistication (Monte-Sano, 2008; Wissinger et al., 2021). Student-participants in these studies developed a more sophisticated view of historical interpretation, improved in their historical reading and writing skills, used historians' strategies for working with texts, became more sensitive to perspective, and, as a by-product, increased in historical content knowledge.

Unsurprisingly, contrasting views exist on the importance or usefulness of teaching historical reading with primary sources. Some have identified a teaching practice they have labeled "death by sources," as students become tired of engaging in source analysis without a vision of why they are reading historical documents (Barton, 2018, p. 9). Without an inquiry-driven purpose, students read historical documents like they do the textbook, trying to memorize information rather than evaluate and use evidence to answer an authentic question. Students become frustrated trying to remember information that comes in disconnected and fragmentary documents that lack a logical flow or narrative. The experience of reading primary source documents can be frustrating to students who are just looking for an answer (Lesh, 2011).

Others contend that devoting too much time to help students read like a historian, an admittedly futile goal, distracts teachers from other noble goals of history teaching, such as helping students construct a civic identity and preparing them to participate in a democracy (Barton & Levstik, 2004). Others argue that students cannot be taught to read like university-trained historians. Although this argument is accurate, this same challenge does not guide instruction in other fields. For instance, few students can slam dunk a basketball, but that does not prevent physical education teachers from teaching them basketball skills and letting them play. And the studies cited previously show that with the proper support students are able to read in more sophisticated ways when they are given opportunities to engage in historical inquiry.

Others argue that because few students will become academic historians, they do not need to learn to read like historians. However, advocates of historical literacy instruction acknowledge that producing little historians is not their ultimate objective. Instead, they contend that the literacy strategies developed in inquiry-focused history classrooms have applications for everyone in democratic societies. They argue that historical reading skills can be applied in online reading, when evaluating social media, when constructing evidence-based arguments, and are vital for civic engagement (e.g., see the Stanford History Education Group's lessons related to civic online reasoning at https://cor.stanford.edu). Recent research shows that the application of these skills in online reading is not instinctive but requires instructional support, a point discussed later in this book. Even skeptics of historical literacy instruction admit that 21st-century readers need the skepticism and skills that are central to historical literacies.

To summarize, three research-based reasons suggest that history teachers should build students' historical literacies. First, when framed appropriately, working with documents can be highly engaging for students—much more so than traditional instruction consisting of lectures and textbook reading. Second, students who engage in inquiry by actively piecing together historical events from documents interact with content more deeply and learn historical content better. This should not be surprising given current research on learning, which shows that individuals learn best when they are active, that is, solving a historical mystery using documents, rather than passive, that is, watching a documentary video (Bransford et al., 2000). Third, students who are taught historical reading strategies exhibit more sophisticated critical reading and thinking skills, are more skilled in constructing historical understandings, and are better prepared to be lifelong learners of history. They are more likely to be able to know where to find reliable sources when they have questions about historical events and are more likely to seek corroborating evidence rather than rely on a single source. Furthermore, students who are historically literate are better prepared to thrive in a democratic society during this Information Age. They are better prepared for online reading, to participate responsibly in social media, and to be informed patriots, serving as knowledgeable voters, conscientious jurors, wise consumers, and sensible users of social media, roles that require an individual to sort through conflicting messages, pay attention to sources, and interpret evidence.

Defining *Historical Literacies*

What are some of the advantages of thinking about historical literacies rather than merely historical reading?

The concept of literacy means different things in different settings and is currently being defined and redefined in the research. There is a movement in education to make a distinction between *reading* and *literacy*. *Reading* involves constructing meaning with traditional texts that include words, sentences, and paragraphs. *Literacy*, on the other hand, involves constructing meaning with a wider variety of sources including traditional texts but, in addition, images, sounds, or other resources (Cope & Kalantzis, 2000). For instance, most propaganda posters from World War I combine words and images. The designers of posters use not only loaded language but also emotive colors and art to achieve a particular purpose. To effectively comprehend a poster and use it as evidence, a viewer must attend to not only the words but the images as well. Thus, literacy includes the ability to read in the traditional sense (i.e., words, sentences, paragraphs) and the ability to construct meaning with nontraditional texts (i.e., colors, images, sounds). In the vignette that opened this chapter, some of Mr. Rich's students debated the authenticity of a photograph of child factory workers. Their analysis incorporated both traditional texts (i.e., a historical novel excerpt) and nontraditional resources (i.e., exploring the Internet to investigate the source of the photograph). Because the study of history involves both traditional texts and nontraditional texts, this book focuses on building a wide range of literacies including, but not limited to, students' reading abilities.

Furthermore, the term *literacy* denotes an individual's ability to construct meaning with some sort of resource—a text. Remaining true to the term's original denotation, then, literacy within a field (i.e., scientific literacy, historical literacy) is defined as an individual's ability to interact appropriately with the texts that are valued within that discipline (Draper et al., 2010; Moje, 2008). In contrast, some current uses of the term *literacy* have drifted from its original meaning, suggesting that rich content knowledge within a field qualifies an individual as literate in that field. It should be noted that rich background knowledge often facilitates the comprehension of texts, but content knowledge may not be necessary, on one hand, or sufficient for comprehension, on the other. For example, research has shown that historians with expertise in one field (i.e., medieval China) are able to analyze historical texts from a different, unfamiliar field (i.e., the antebellum United States; Wineburg, 1998). In contrast, some individuals may know much historical information but be unfamiliar with historical thinking processes (Wineburg, 1991). In spite of a wealth of historical knowledge, an individual remains historically illiterate when he/she does not know how to construct historical interpretations using evidence.

So historical literacy, as defined in this book, is the ability to appropriately negotiate (read) and create (write) the texts and resources that are valued within the discipline of history using methods approved by the community of historians. Historical literacies require a mature understanding of the nature of the discipline of history and the ability to approach a historical problem from an appropriate frame of mind. Historical literacies include the use of historians' strategies for comprehending and evaluating the vast array of artifacts and records that are useful in making inferences about the past.

Chapter Summary

This book calls for a revolution in the way history is taught. History teachers must face the harsh reality that traditional methods and materials do little to build students' long-term content knowledge or to promote critical thinking skills. I make the case for redefining history teaching by placing historical inquiry and historical literacies at the center of instruction. When students use historians' methods to study primary source materials, they become more active and engaged, learn historical content and critical thinking skills, and are better prepared to thrive in a democratic society in which easily available information must be vetted. This chapter defines historical literacy as the ability to negotiate and create texts that are authentic in historical inquiry and sets the stage for the further exploration of historical literacies in the chapters that follow.

Questions for Consideration

1. What are the main problems of heritage teaching? How might a shift from heritage teaching to history teaching lead to a resolution of the constant "history wars" over the content that should be taught?
2. What is the difference between patriotism and informed patriotism? How does the notion of informed patriotism allow a person to see protests for justice as a form of patriotism? How can historical inquiry promote informed patriotism?
3. How can historical inquiry invite the perspectives of diverse groups into the study of history? Why might young women, members of the LGBTQ community, and youth of color feel more included in history classes that promote inquiry?
4. Imagine that you are a new teacher hired into a department with colleagues who primarily use traditional methods. How might you convince them to devote time to historical inquiry? What resources could you use to strengthen your argument and to substantiate your claims about the benefits of historical literacy instruction?

Additional Reading and Viewing

- For a comprehensive review of research on teaching historical reading see Reisman, A. & McGrew, S. (2018). Reading in history education: Texts, sources, and evidence. In S. Metzger & L. Harris (Eds.), *International handbook of history teaching and learning* (pp. 529–550). Wiley Blackwell.
- For an article that offers an alternative critical perspective on teaching historical literacies see Barton, K. C. (2018). Historical sources in the classroom: Purpose and use. *HSSE Online, 7*(2), 1–11.
- A free PDF version of the National Council for the Social Studies C3 Framework can be accessed at https://www.socialstudies.org/sites/default/files/c3/c3-framework-for-social-studies-rev0617.pdf.
- A 2½-minute video highlighting "a better way to learn history" produced by the Stanford History Education Group can be found at https://www.youtube.com/watch?v=zSey4WALf8I.

References

1619 Project. (2021). The 1619 Project. *The New York Times Magazine.* https://www.nytimes.com/interactive/2019/08/14/magazine/1619-america-slavery.html
1776 Report. (2021). https://trumpwhitehouse.archives.gov/wp-content/uploads/2021/01/The-Presidents-Advisory-1776-Commission-Final-Report.pdf

Ashby, R. A., Lee, P. J., & Shemilt, D. (2005). Putting principles into practice: Teaching and planning. In M. S. Donovan & J. D. Bransford (Eds.), *How students learn: History, mathematics, and science in the classroom* (pp. 79–178). National Academies Press.

Bain, R. B. (2005). "They thought the world was flat?" Applying the principles of *How people learn* in teaching high school history. In M. S. Donovan & J. D. Bransford (Eds.), *How students learn: History, mathematics, and science in the classroom* (pp. 179–213). National Academies Press.

Barton, K. (2012). Wars and rumors of war: The rhetoric and reality of history education in the United States. In T. Taylor & R. Guyver, (Eds.), *History wars in the classroom: Global perspectives* (pp. 187–202). Information Age Publishing.

Barton, K. C. (2018). Historical sources in the classroom: Purpose and use. *HSSE Online*, 7(2), 1–11. https://hsseonline.nie.edu.sg/journal/volume-7-issue-2-2018/historical-sources-classroom-purpose-and-use

Barton, K. C., & Levstik, L. S. (2004). *Teaching history for the common good.* Mahwah, NJ: Lawrence Erlbaum.

Bell, J. C., & McCollum, D. F. (1917). A study of the attainments of pupils in United States History. *Journal of Educational Psychology, 8*(5), 257–274. doi:10.1037/h0074477

Bostick, D. (2021). The classical roots of White supremacy. *Learning for Justice, 66.* https://www.learningforjustice.org/magazine/spring-2021/the-classical-roots-of-white-supremacy

Bransford, J. D., Brown, A. L., & Cocking, R. R. (2000). *How people learn: Brain, mind, experience, and school.* National Academy Press.

Britt, M. A., & Aglinskas, C. (2002). Improving students' ability to identify and use source information. *Cognition and Instruction, 20,* 485–522. daoi:10.1207/S1532690XCI2004_2

Chinich, M. (Producer), & Hughs, J. (Director). (1986). *Ferris Bueller's day off. [Motion picture].* Los Angeles, CA: Paramount Pictures.

Common Core State Standards. (2010). *Common core state standards.* http://www.corestandards.org/

Cope, B., & Kalantzis, M. (Eds.). (2000). *Multiliteracies: Literacy learning and the design of social futures.* Routledge.

De La Paz, S. (2005). Effects of historical reasoning instruction and writing strategy mastery in culturally and academically diverse middle school classrooms. *Journal of Educational Psychology, 97*(2), 139–156. doi:10.1037/0022-0663.97.2.139

De La Paz, S., Felton, M., Monte-Sano, C., Croninger, R., Jackson, C., Deogracias, J. S., & Hoffman, B. P. (2014). Developing historical reading and writing with adolescent readers: Effects on student learning. *Theory & Research in Social Education, 42*(2), 228–274. doi:10.1080/00933104.2014.908754

De La Paz, S., Monte-Sano, C., Felton, M., Croninger, R., Jackson, C., & Piantedosi, K. W. (2017). A historical writing apprenticeship for adolescents: Integrating disciplinary learning with cognitive strategies. *Reading Research Quarterly, 52*(1), 31–52. doi:10.1002/rrq.147

Draper, R. J., Broomhead, P., Jensen, A. P., Nokes, J. D., & Siebert, D. (Eds.). (2010). *(Re)imagining content-area literacy instruction.* Teachers College Press.

Epstein, T. (1998). Deconstructing differences in African-American and European-American adolescents' perspectives on U.S. history. *Curriculum Inquiry, 28,* 397–423. doi:10.1111/0362-6784.00100

Epstein, T. (2000). Adolescents' perspectives on racial diversity in U. S. history: Case studies from an urban classroom. *American Educational Research Journal, 37*(1), 185–214. doi:10.2307/1163476

Grant, S. G. (2018). Teaching practices in history education. In S. Metzger & L. Harris (Eds.), *International handbook of history teaching and learning* (pp. 419–448). Wiley Blackwell.

Hine, L. (1908). *Doffers in Cherryville Mfg. Co., N.C. Plenty of others [black and white photo-graph]*.Washington, DC: Library of Congress Prints and Photographs Division. https://www.loc.gov/pictures/resource/nclc.01358/?co=nclc

Hynd, C., Holschuh, J., & Hubbard, B. (2004).Thinking like a historian: College students' reading of multiple historical documents. *Journal of Literacy Research, 36*(2), 141–176. doi:10.1207/s15548430jlr3602_2

Lee, P. J., & Weiss, A. (2007). *The nation's report card: U.S. History 2006 (NCES 2007–474)*. Retrieved from U.S. Department of Education, National Center for Education Statistics website: http://nces.ed.gOv/nationsreportcard/pubs/main2006/2007474.asp#pdflist

Lesh, B.A. (2011). *Why won't you just tell us the answer? Teaching historical thinking in grades 1–12*. Stenhouse.

Levstik, L. S., & Barton, K. C. (2015). *Doing history: Investigating with children in elementary and middle schools* (5th Ed.). Routledge.

Loewen, J. W. (2008). *Lies my teacher told me: Everything your American history textbook got wrong*.The New Press.

McGrew, S., Breakstone, J., Ortega, T., Smith, M., & Wineburg, S. (2018). Can students evaluate online sources? Learning from assessments of civic online reasoning. *Theory & Research in Social Education, 46*, 165–193. doi:10.1080/00933104.2017.1416320

Moje, E. B. (2008). Foregrounding the disciplines in secondary literacy teaching and learning: A call for change. *Journal of Adolescent and Adult Literacy, 52*(2), 96–107. doi:10.1598/JAAL.52.2.1

Monte-Sano, C. (2008). Qualities of historical writing instruction: A comparative case study of two teachers' practice. *American Educational Research Journal, 45*(4), 1045–1079. doi:10.3102/0002831208319733

National Center for Education Statistics (2011). *The Nation's Report Card: U.S. History 2010 (NCES 2011–468)*.Washington, DC: Institute of Education Sciences, U.S. Department of Education. https://nces.ed.gov/nationsreportcard/pubs/main2010/2011468.aspx

National Council for the Social Studies (2013). *The college, career, and civic life (C3) frame-work for social studies state standards: Guidance for enhancing the rigor of K-12 civics, economics, geography, and history*. Silver Spring, MD: NCSS. https://www.socialstudies.org/sites/default/files/c3/c3-framework-for-social-studies-rev0617.pdf

NCHE. (n.d.). *History's habits of mind*. https://ncheteach.org/Historys-Habits-of-Mind.

Nokes, J. D. (2010). Observing literacy practices in history classrooms. *Theory and Research in Social Education, 38*(4), 298–316. doi:10.1080/00933104.2010.10473438

Nokes, J. D., Dole, J. A., & Hacker, D. J. (2007).Teaching high school students to use heu-ristics while reading historical texts. *Journal of Educational Psychology, 99*(3), 492–504. doi:10.1037/0022-0663.99.3.492

Paterson, K. (1991). *Lyddie*. Lodestar Books.

Paxton, R.J. (1999). A deafening silence: History textbooks and the students who read them. *Review of Educational Research, 69*(3), 315–337. doi:10.3102/00346543069003315

Peck, C. (2018). National, ethnic, and indigenous identities and perspectives in history education. In S. Metzger & L. Harris (Eds.), *International handbook of history teaching and learning* (pp. 311–333).Wiley Blackwell.

Perfetti, C.A., Britt, M.A., & Georgi, M. C. (1995). *Text-based learning and reasoning: Studies in history*. Lawrence Erlbaum Associates.

Ravitch, D., & Finn, C. E. (1987). *What do our 17-year-olds know: A report on the first national assessment of history and literature*. Harper & Row.

Reisman, A. (2012). Reading like a historian: A document-based history curriculum intervention in urban high schools. *Cognition and Instruction, 30*(1), 86–112. doi:10.10 80/07370008.2011.634081

Reisman, A. & McGrew, S. (2018). Reading in history education: Texts, sources, and evidence. In S. Metzger & L. Harris (Eds.), *International handbook of history teaching and learning* (pp. 529–550). Wiley Blackwell.

Riccards, P. (2019). When it comes to American history knowledge, Woodrow Wilson Foundation finds that only one state can pass U.S. citizenship exam. https://woodrow. org/wp-content/uploads/2019/02/WW-AHI-50-State-Release-02.14.19-fnl.pdf

Romano, A. (2011). How dumb are we? *Newsweek, 151*, 13/14, 56–60.

Saye, J. & Social Studies Inquiry Research Collaborative. (2013). Authentic pedagogy: Its presence in social studies classrooms and relationship to student performance on state-mandated tests. *Theory and Research in Social Education, 41*(1), 89–132. doi:10.1080/00 933104.2013.756785

Stahl, S. A., & Shanahan, C. H. (2004). Learning to think like a historian: Disciplinary knowledge through critical analysis of multiple documents. In T. L. Jetton & J. A. Dole (Eds.), *Adolescent literacy research and practice* (pp. 94–115). Guilford.

Swan, K. & Lee, J. (2014). *Teaching the college, career, and civic life (C3) framework: Exploring inquiry-based instruction in social studies.* National Council for the Social Studies.

van Boxtel, C., & van Drie, J. (2012). "That's in the time of the Romans!" Knowledge and strategies students use to contextualize historical images and documents. *Cognition and Instruction, 30*(2), 113–145. doi:10.1080/07370008.2012.661813

VanSledright, B. (2002). *In search of America's past: Learning to read history in elementary school.* Teachers College Press.

VanSledright, B. (2008). Narratives of nation-state, historical knowledge, and school history education. *Review of Research in Education, 32*(1), 109–146. doi:10.3102/009 1732X07311065

Wineburg, S. (2018). *Why learn history (when it's already on your phone).* University of Chicago Press.

Wineburg, S. S. (1991). On the reading of historical texts: Notes on the breach between school and academy. *American Educational Research Journal, 28*(3), 495–519. doi:10.3102/00028312028003495

Wineburg, S. S. (1998). Reading Abraham Lincoln: An expert/expert study in the interpretation of historical texts. *Cognitive Science, 22*(3), 319–346. doi:10.1207/ s15516709cog2203_3

Wineburg, S. S. (2007). Forrest Gump and the future of teaching the past. *Phi Delta Kappan, 89*(3), 168–177. doi:10.1177/003172170708900305

Wissinger, D. R., & De La Paz, S. (2016). Effects of critical discussions on middle school students' written historical arguments. *Journal of Educational Psychology, 108(1)* 43–59. doi:10.1037/edu0000043

Wissinger, D. R., De La Paz, S., & Jackson, C. (2021). The effects of historical reading and writing strategy instruction with fourth-through sixth-grade students. *Journal of Educational Psychology, 113*(1), 49. doi:10.1037/edu0000463

Young, K. M., & Leinhardt, G. (1998). Writing from primary documents. *Written Communication, 15*(1), 25–68. doi:10.1177/0741088398015001002

3

DEFINING HISTORICAL LITERACIES
What and How Do Historians Read and Write?

When someone says "history text," what do you think of? By the time you finish reading this chapter, you should think not only of a textbook but of the wide variety of documents, artifacts, images, and objects that historians use as evidence. You should also be able to describe historians' strategies and habits of mind for working with evidence and for writing.

As you read this vignette, think about all the different types of resources available today that provide evidence of how people in the past have lived. Think about how a teacher might enrich history lessons by engaging young people with this evidence.

Mrs. Francis reads an article about how archaeologists use a research method called dendrochronology to determine when ancient cliff dwellings at Mesa Verde, Colorado, now abandoned and in ruins, were originally built. She discovers that the process involves taking a cross-section sample from timbers used in construction. Using the distance between tree rings, archaeologists identify the climatic pattern in the years leading up to the time the tree was cut down, presumably for the construction of the home. Comparing these tree ring patterns to core samples taken from living ancient trees located nearby, they search for a similar series of wet and dry years. Once they find a match they can state, with some authority, what year the tree that was used in the construction of the home was harvested and, by implication, the year the cliff dwelling was built.

While reading the article, Mrs. Francis has an epiphany. Her eyes are opened to the vast number of resources, like a log used in the construction of the cliff dwelling, that archaeologists, historians, scientists, anthropologists, and others use to construct an understanding of the past. She also begins to consider the number of different skills required to become historically literate. She contemplates

DOI: 10.4324/9781003183495-4

how she could introduce her eighth-grade American history students to the process of dendrochronology. She thinks that it might be worth exposing students to tree ring dating in order to show them how scientists, archaeologists, and historians work together to construct an understanding of the distant past. Dendrochronology is a simple enough process that most students would be able to understand it. She recognizes that the logs are only one of many pieces of evidence used to track the evolving culture of the Ancestral Pueblo people, and she determines to develop a lesson during which students evaluate evidence of the Ancestral Pueblo culture as part of a unit on the pre-Columbian Indigenous cultures of America.

On the day of the lesson, Mrs. Francis briefly lectures, giving students background information on the Ancestral Pueblo who lived in the Four Corners region of the United States until about 800 years ago. After lecturing for a few minutes, she asks students how historians might know when the Ancestral Pueblo moved out of the Four Corners region. After all, they left no written records about when or why they abandoned their homes. The question catches students off guard—many of them have not considered how historians know what they claim to know. She tells the students that archaeologists have used many clues to speculate about important turning points in the ancient history of the Ancestral Puebloan people.

Mrs. Francis models for students the processes involved in dating the movement of the Ancestral Pueblo. She shows them how archaeologists use dendrochronology to date the construction of the Ancestral Puebloan homes and to identify when that construction ended, roughly 750 years ago. She highlights the role of *observing*—noticing the tree ring patterns—and *inferring*—making reasoned conjectures based on observations. She explains that dendrochronology has led archaeologists to infer that the Ancestral Pueblo built homes on the plateau tops of Mesa Verde centuries before building homes in the cliffs. Archaeologists have also used dendrochronology to infer that about the same time construction ended on the mesa tops, construction began in the cliffs. They can also make inferences about when construction in the cliffs ended. She concludes her lecture by asking the questions, *Why* did the Ancestral Pueblo move from the mesa tops to the cliffs after living there for centuries, and *why* did they move from their cliff dwellings? What else can we infer about the culture of these ancient people based on observations of their homes and other artifacts that they left behind.

Mrs. Francis has gathered photographs of dwellings and artifacts that archaeologists have used to make inferences about the Ancestral Pueblo culture. She has placed the photographs in digital file folders labeled *cliff dwellings, petroglyphs, cordage artifacts*, and *stone artifacts*. She prepares a graphic organizer designed to help students record observations they make—what they see; inferences they make—what they think; and questions they have—what they wonder (see Figure 3.1; Richards & Anderson, 2003). She places students in groups with the assignment

Name _____

Analysis of Ancestral Pueblo Artifacts

Instructions: As you analyze each artifact give it a name in the first column, draw a sketch of it or paste an image of it in the second column, then describe what you see, what you think, and what you wonder in the remaining three columns.

Artifact	Sketch	What do you SEE? (Observations)	What do you THINK? (Inferences)	What do you WONDER? (Questions)

FIGURE 3.1 "See, Think, Wonder" graphic organizer.

Artifact	Sketch	What do you SEE? (Observations)	What do you THINK? (Inferences)	What do you WONDER? (Questions)

In the space below, choose one of the following questions or make up one of your own and describe how observations and inferences based upon the artifacts help you answer the question. Be sure to talk about the evidence in the artifacts that led you to your conclusions.

a. Why did the Ancestral Puebloan people abandon their cliff dwellings?
b. What was daily life like for someone who lived among the Ancestral Pueblo in 1200 AD?
c. How did technology change among the Ancestral Pueblo while they lived in the Mesa Verde area?
d. What natural resources were especially valuable to the Ancestral Pueblo?
e. What can we learn about the Ancestral Pueblo from their artistic creations?
f. Your question:

FIGURE 3.1 (Continued)

to think about how the artifacts can help modern researchers understand the Ancestral Puebloan culture. She shows students a list of questions they can think about at the bottom of the graphic organizer. Although each student has their own computer with the images, she encourages students to collaborate, sharing their observations and comparing their inferences.

As Mrs. Francis moves from group to group, she listens to students discuss inferences they make from the artifacts. One group debates why the Ancestral Pueblo moved from the mesa tops to the cliffs. Some students argue that climate change drove them to the cooler locations, pointing out the cliff-shaded homes. Others suggest that the move had to do with protection from enemies, showing the defensive positions of the dwellings. She watches as students carefully analyze the photographs she has purposefully selected to promote careful observations and nuanced inferences. For example, she intentionally chose two photographs of the same cliff dwelling taken from the same position at different times of the year so that observant students might make inferences about the Ancestral Pueblo people's seasonal use of solar heating in south-facing dwellings (see Figures 3.2 and 3.3).

FIGURE 3.2 Photograph of cliff dwelling taken on a winter day. (Photograph printed with permission of Bruce Schundler.)

FIGURE 3.3 Photograph of cliff dwelling taken on a summer day. (Photograph printed with permission of Bruce Schundler.)

> Long ago in the north
> Lies the road of emergence!
> Yonder our ancestors live,
> Yonder we take our being.
>
> Yet now we come southwards
> For cloud flowers blossom here
> Here the lightning flashes,
> Rain water here is falling!

FIGURE 3.4 The song lyrics for the Hopi Turtle Dance (Ortman, 2012).

Mrs. Francis finds that different groups have focused on many features of the Ancestral Puebloan culture. For instance, some students have inferred that the Ancestral Pueblo were farmers who also hunted. Others suggest that they had religious beliefs related to nature. One points out that they did not seem to have anything made of metal. She works to make sure that students can justify each inference using the evidence found in artifacts. For instance, when she presses one student to account for why he inferred that they hunted and ate mountain sheep, he explains that he saw many mountain sheep etched in petroglyphs.

At the end of the lesson Mrs. Francis debriefs with students. During part of the debriefing after a short debate, the class collaboratively concludes that several interrelated causes probably led the Ancestral Pueblo to move into the cliffs. Based in part on their background knowledge, they infer that climate change may have created drought and food shortages that may have increased raiding and warfare over the limited supplies of water and food. During the debriefing students also discuss other inferences they made based on the artifacts they reviewed. As the discussion continues, Mrs. Francis emphasizes that the Ancestral Pueblo people experienced cultural change over decades and centuries and that a changing climate appears to have played a major role in that transition. To conclude the lesson, Mrs. Francis gives students the song lyrics used in the Turtle Dance at the Santa Clara Pueblo (see Figure 3.4), an Indigenous village thought to have descended from the Ancestral Pueblo (Ortman, 2012, p. 188). She asks students to compare the song to the archaeological evidence they have investigated to see which inferences it corroborates. Before leaving class, as an exit slip, students write a brief introduction to the Ancestral Pueblo culture that could be placed on a virtual museum website that shows photographs of the artifacts they analyzed. Their description provides museumgoers with a basic understanding of who the Ancestral Pueblo were, prior to looking at their artifacts.

> How do the "texts" and the writing assignment used in this lesson differ from the conventional assignment to read the textbook and answer factual questions? How do the texts and activity in this vignette give students a more accurate sense of the nature of history as a discipline?

Historical Literacies

What are the advantages and disadvantages of defining "texts" broadly?

Some of the most engaging historical inquiry lessons, like Mrs. Francis's, involve students in an analysis of artifacts rather than written forms of historical evidence. You might react, "This is not literacy! They are not reading anything!" However, students engage in many of the same processes used in traditional reading when they attempt to construct meaning with artifacts and other types of evidence. For instance, Mrs. Francis's students engage in historical literacies by using evidence to support claims. Working with artifacts, students find that current understandings of the past are influenced significantly not only by historians but by a host of other researchers as well.

The work of archaeologists, historians, scientists, anthropologists, and others, whose intent is to describe and interpret the past, involves the construction of meaning with a wide variety of resources. Mrs. Francis realized that what looks like an old log becomes a *text* to be read by someone who knows how to make sense of its markings and skillfully interpret them. Architecture styles, trends in music, prehistoric garbage dumps, census numbers, family patterns in modern nomadic societies, ancient artifacts, modern artifacts, and written records—especially written records—are the building blocks with which history, the interpretation of the past, is constructed. The world abounds in print and digital, visual and aural, natural and man-made texts, useful in the study of history. But the usefulness of texts comes only when an individual knows how to read them. Historical literacy involves a search for data—evidence with which to build defensible interpretations of past events—from this vast array of texts. Using Mrs. Francis's classroom as an example, in this chapter, I (a) define the concept of historical literacy, (b) consider historians as models of historical literacy, and (c) establish the need for secondary students to receive historical literacy instruction.

historical text: any object of any genre that is used to (a) construct an understanding of the past, (b) show the way people think about and study the past, and (c) communicate the understanding of the past to others

Defining the Concept of Historical Literacy

How would you explain what historical literacy is to elementary, middle school, or high school students?

Historical literacy is the ability to construct meaning with multiple genres of print, nonprint, visual, digital, video, audio, and multimodal historical texts; critically evaluate texts within the context of the work historians have previously done; use texts as evidence to develop original interpretations of past events and conditions; and create multiple types of texts that meet discipline standards. As mentioned in Chapter 2, historical literacy is different than general historical knowledge. Historical literacy is not the possession of an encyclopedic knowledge of historical facts but the ability to glean appropriate information about the past from resources of many genres. It is the ability to engage in historical processes—to not simply possess knowledge but to know how to build it. Historical literacy connotes the ability to not only learn from the historical accounts that others have written but also to independently develop new interpretations of the past and to communicate them to others, in speech, writing, or visual displays. Although historians are expected to construct interpretations that are new to the world, students' independently constructed interpretations might be new only to them or their classmates.

Mrs. Francis's lesson serves as a good model of historical literacy. She introduced and supported students' work with familiar and unfamiliar genres of texts, such as the cliff-dwelling ruins, artifacts, and song lyrics. She provided students with some background knowledge prior to exposing them to the texts. In doing so, she helped students understand what archaeologists and historians have hypothesized about the Ancestral Pueblo. The majority of time in her lesson was spent with students exploring evidence, developing hypotheses, and defending their ideas before their peers. In her interaction with students, she repeatedly pulled them back to the texts, asking them to justify their interpretations using evidence. In the end, students produced an authentic text, the type of public history that a museum curator might write for a virtual exhibit.

Historians as Models of Historical Literacies

A description of historical literacy must begin with a consideration of the literacies of historians. Specifically, I explore the following questions: Which texts are essential to historians' inquiries? Which literacy skills do historians employ? and Which habits of mind characterize historians' work?

Which Texts Are Essential to Historiansis' Inquiries?

If a historian researched and wrote a biography of you, what documents, artifacts, photographs, and evidence would be useful to them?

The work of historians primarily involves the study of written records, with artifacts, such as those in Mrs. Francis's lesson, supplementing the written record.

Historians spend much of their research time in archives, searching through collections of documents, such as old newspaper articles, trial transcripts, church records, journal entries, and letters, for sources of information related to their topic of interest. Historical literacy involves searching for materials, skimming, distinguishing relevant from irrelevant information, and evaluating the accuracy and usefulness of sources. As a general rule, when working with written texts, historians value primary sources, firsthand accounts related to their inquiry, over other types of evidence. They do so for much the same reason that those investigating a crime scene would value eyewitness testimony over hearsay accounts. Primary sources, although influenced by the writer's involvement in an event and their limited point of view, are not distorted by any other individual's interpretations. In spite of their admitted imperfections, primary sources provide the purest evidence about the past. Historians seek all possible primary sources related to their inquiry and construct an interpretation through a critical analysis and synthesis of primary source evidence. Historical literacy includes the ability to gather sources, recognize and account for point of view, identify corroborating and conflicting evidence, and build logical and defensible interpretations.

---

primary source: a firsthand account of an event or conditions, produced by an eyewitness and recorded in a journal, a letter, an oral history, an interview, a memoir, a sketch, or in some other genre

---

Along with written records, historians draw on a number of scientific, oral, visual, numeric, and anthropologic sources and artifacts to construct interpretations of the past. For example, historians use the findings of anthropologists who study modern nomadic societies to make inferences about prehistoric nomadic groups who left behind no written records and few artifacts. Ice core samples give clues about climatic fluctuations—something absent in written records and a new lens through which to view historical events. Scientific fields of study, such as paleobotany, explore the prehistoric record found in evolving plant life, helping historians trace the origins and spread of agriculture. Census records capture patterns in immigration, providing data to supplement the more personal records kept by some immigrant families. And historical archaeology, the study of artifacts at historical sites (such as the quarters of those enslaved at Mount Vernon), corroborates or raises questions about interpretations that would otherwise be based solely on written records. From tree rings that give hints about home construction to magazine ads that show the fashionable length of women's hair, historians draw from a wide range of resources to supplement written records. Thus, Mrs. Francis's lessons, although nearly devoid of written texts, included numerous sources that historians and archaeologists would use as evidence to interpret the past.

Rarely do historians pioneer an entirely new topic of study; instead, their work is generally grounded within a field of research on similar topics. Thus, historians must be aware of secondary sources and skillful in working with these secondhand accounts produced from primary sources. Historians pay attention to other historians' interpretations of their topic. They ask how other historians have dealt with evidence and whether flaws exist in the their work. They explore what others have omitted that is worthy of consideration and whether new evidence has been uncovered. They consider and often write about how the study of a historical topic has evolved over time, a process labeled historiography. Within the context of prior work, they consider how their fresh perspective leads to new and better interpretations of the past. Historians understand that secondary sources, like primary sources, reflect the values, interests, and interpretations of the individuals who produce them. Historical literacy involves the ability to distinguish primary from secondary sources and to work with both in appropriate ways. It includes the ability to use source information, including the context of the document's creation, whether a primary or secondary source, to build meaning with it.

> secondary source: (a) a historical account, such as a monograph or journal article, produced by a historian using primary source evidence or (b) a contemporary hearsay account

Historians produce a variety of texts, including monographs, journal articles, maps, cartograms, population pyramids, charts, graphs, and diagrams, intended to help others understand the past and to persuade others to accept their interpretations. These texts are used to convey historical ideas to fellow historians as well as to individuals who lack disciplinary expertise—students of history or newspaper readers, for example. Historians' writing often integrates narration, description, and argumentation. Thus, historians' literacies include not only the ability to read and critically analyze multiple genres but to produce multiple types of text— each a secondary source if related to the topic of their research.

In addition, the historical record includes public or popular histories produced as museum exhibits, historical novels, feature films, and popular books. Although of less importance to many historians, some historians focus their academic careers on creating public histories that have popular appeal. Teachers must not underestimate the influence of students' experiences with popular culture on their understandings of the past. For instance, not long after the release of the movie *Forrest Gump*, researchers found that young people's conception of the Vietnam War era had been shaped significantly by its plot (Wineburg, 2007). Ironically, the media that are the least helpful to most historians (i.e., public and popular histories) are often the most influential in the lives of nonhistorians.

Because of the profound influence of public and popular histories such as feature films, it makes sense that history teachers spend time helping students think critically about public histories, weighing them against historical evidence and secondary sources.

public history: a historical account published primarily for a lay audience rather than for historians including feature films, museum exhibits, historical fiction, webpages, and historic sites

Expository texts, most notably history textbooks, complete the list of the types of texts that individuals might encounter when learning about history. Textbooks, encyclopedia articles, Wikipedia, a teacher's lecture, and other expository texts represent, for the most part, tertiary sources—thirdhand accounts of historical events, far removed from the primary sources that serve as evidence. Expository sources generally follow a traditional historical narrative, providing few explanations of how evidence was used or how interpretations were made. Textbooks contain few explicit attempts to persuade the reader that their account of historical events is accurate. Instead, expository texts, by their very nature, give the impression that they are above question or critique, simply providing facts (Paxton, 2002). Expository texts generally inspire less interest than other types of historical texts (Logtenberg et al., 2011), although they are ubiquitous in history instruction and are often even referred to as *the* text.

expository texts: thirdhand or tertiary historical accounts, such as textbooks, Wikipedia, and traditional history lectures that present historical events and conditions in a manner that appears to be free from interpretations, simply the facts, and above question.

To simplify things for students, I categorize texts as either evidence, secondary sources, tertiary sources, or public/popular histories as shown in Figure 3.5. This figure illustrates for students that all historical interpretations should be based directly or indirectly on some form of historical evidence, although some public and popular histories, produced to entertain, have little or no evidence base. It should be noted that a text's placement in this categorization system is based on the way a historian uses it. For instance, textbooks are normally tertiary sources, but to a historian who investigates the evolving portrayal of African Americans in the public school curriculum, textbooks published in different eras would become primary sources. The movie *Birth of a Nation* (Griffith et al., 1915) would serve as a tertiary source for a historian investigating the origins of the Ku Klux Klan, but as a primary source for a historian studying White southerners'

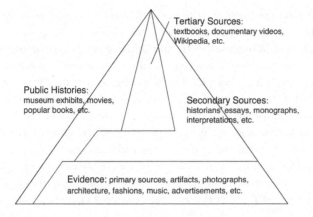

FIGURE 3.5 A visual categorization of historical texts and evidence.

perceptions of race in 1915, the time the movie was produced. With this understanding, the categorization system shown on this chart can help teachers and students remember the purposes for using different types of texts and to identify the approaches most helpful in working with them.

Which Literacy Skills Do Historians Employ?

What specific and specialized reading strategies do historians use that make them unusually active, careful, and critical readers?

Perhaps more than any discipline area, researchers have explored the literacies used by historians as they construct meaning with historical texts. Researchers suggest that historians are extraordinarily active readers, comparing them to attorneys who interrogate evidence (Wineburg, 1991, 2001). Historians are both analytical and imaginative as they read, carefully examining evidence while trying to conceptualize what things were like in the past. Historians do not view texts as conveyers of information, as students often do, but as the product of individuals with emotion, limited perception, a particular point of view, conflicts of interest, and personal insights. Furthermore, historians acknowledge that texts and contexts can be interpreted in multiple ways, opening the door for historical debates, continued investigation of old questions, regular revisions of history, and a need for argumentative writing. Reading a historical text requires more than the comprehension of the meaning of words and sentences; it requires an understanding of the subtext—the context, audience, purposes, biases, and insights of the author (Lesh, 2011; Perfetti, et al., 1999; Wineburg, 1994).

Historians use a number of strategies as they critically analyze evidence. For example, they pay attention to a document's source and keep that source in mind as they read. Wineburg (1991) and other researchers identify this technique as *sourcing*. Sourcing is used universally by historians regardless of their field of expertise. When they pick up an unfamiliar text they look first at the author, consider the context of the document's creation, identify the author's audience and purpose, and begin to build expectations about the document's content even before reading (Wineburg, 1991). When source information is missing they use the content of the text to make inferences about the source (Nokes & Kesler-Lund, 2019). Texts are viewed as extensions of individuals. Historians' reading, then, is an exchange with people, separated by time and place but connected through the writing/creation and reading/interpretation of texts.

> *sourcing: paying attention to the author or creator of a piece of evidence, along with the creator's audience, purpose, and involvement in the event described, and using this information to comprehend and evaluate the evidence*

Additionally, historians compare and contrast evidence from multiple sources, a strategy labeled *corroboration* (Wineburg, 1991). Corroboration involves checking and cross-checking one piece of evidence against others (VanSledright, 2002). As historians encounter new information in a primary source, they search for verification in other sources, holding new interpretations as tentative until substantiating evidence can be found. Historians also pay attention to and account for conflicting evidence. Corroboration helps historians evaluate the accuracy and reliability of various sources. Additionally, corroboration, when coupled with sourcing, allows historians to gain the advantage of having multiple perspectives of an event. For instance, if studying the Battle of Little Bighorn, historians would corroborate across oral histories from the Sioux and Cheyenne, written records from the U.S. Army, artifacts from the battle site, personal writings that provide insight on Native American and U.S. military leaders, and other sources (Lesh, 2011). Their interpretations are bolstered when multiple sources substantiate their conclusions.

> *corroboration: cross-checking evidence found in one text with evidence found in other texts, paying particular attention to similarities and differences*

One of the challenges of studying the past is that it is always done through the lens of the present. Today's values, attitudes, and environment differ from those of past generations. This explains why the actions of historical characters often seem odd to people today. It is difficult, particularly for young people, to consider the past without making judgments based on modern standards. In contrast historians attempt to understand the past on its own terms as they investigate historical texts. Researchers have labeled historians' efforts to understand the physical and cultural context of a text's creation as *contextualization* (Wineburg, 1991). Historians use their rich background knowledge and clues in texts to imagine the context of the document's creation (Wineburg, 1998). They attempt to construct meaning with the document with that context in mind, putting out of mind, as much as possible, the present.

> *contextualization: imagining the setting of an event and of a document's creation, including the physical and social setting, and understanding the event and the content of the document with that setting in mind*

Different aspects of the context can take on importance. The linguistic context is important in comprehending written texts because the meaning and use of words can change over time. For instance, during Shay's Rebellion, when George Washington wrote to General Benjamin Lincoln asking if the farmers of Massachusetts were "mad," he was not asking whether they were angry but if they were crazy (Washington, 1786). The physical context gains significance in working with artifacts. For instance, archaeologists painstakingly document the precise location of artifacts in relation to other artifacts in an archaeological dig. The physical context carries implications about the way an artifact may have been used. Many aspects of the physical context may be important, such as the topography of a battlefield, the distance between two cities, prevailing wind directions, or the proximity of a body of water.

Contextualization includes more than the physical context of an event. The timing of a document's creation can influence its usefulness as a source. Individuals who write immediately after an event often remember details, but they lack the perspective that time can give. In Wineburg's (1991) research, when analyzing documents related to the battle of Lexington, one historian pointed out that one account had been written by an eyewitness at the end of the Revolutionary War, several years after the battle. When that account did not match other eyewitness accounts, the historian concluded that the author might have confused events from later battles with his memory of Lexington (Wineburg, 1991).

Furthermore, contextualization involves a consideration of the broad context of an event—the macro-context, as well as the immediate context—micro-context. The macro-context includes societal norms, the language of the time period, etiquette, common values, generally accepted theories, and significant national and international events. The micro-context includes immediate factors that influence an event such as the weather, the day of the week of the event, and whether the people involved in the event had had a good night's sleep. Students can sometimes infer some elements of the micro-context from documents, but they have a more difficult time imagining the macro-context. Research shows that contextualization is particularly difficult for students, more difficult than sourcing or corroboration (Nokes et al., 2007; Reisman, 2012). Most students lack the rich background knowledge that is helpful in contextualization.

Historians employ a number of other interrelated strategies when analyzing evidence and constructing interpretations. For example, *historical empathy* is a lens through which historians frame historical evidence (Endacott & Brooks, 2018). Historical empathy is the process of imagining an individuals' context and perspective to understand their actions. Perspective recognition is the understanding that others, including people in the past, see the world differently. Historical characters often take actions that might surprise a modern researcher, given modern values, priorities, and perspectives. They may condemn historical characters as being unintelligent or immoral when their behavior differs from modern norms. Historical empathy replaces this deficit view of people in the past—the notion that people in the past were intellectually and culturally inferior to people today—with the understanding that both today and in the past, people's decisions generally make sense to them given their knowledge, technologies, and values (Foster, 2001; Lee, 2005; Lesh, 2011).

> *perspective recognition: the ability to use the context that historical characters lived in to understand their actions, knowing that those actions, though strange to people today, probably made sense to people at the time*

> *deficit view of the past: the erroneous notion that people of the past were unintelligent or immoral, an idea that emerges when modern values and current worldviews are used to judge their actions*

In addition to perspective recognition, Barton and Levstik (2004), suggest that historical empathy has a second element: *care*. Historical empathy involves caring about the people and events of the past enough to take action in the present. For example, historians who study the enslavement of African Americans in the United States have created an organization called Historians Against Slavery (see https://www.historiansagainstslavery.org/main/). This organization applies the nearly universal disgust of the history of slavery to motivate individuals to take action to combat the current slave trade. The feelings associated with a study of slavery are a significant element of historical empathy.

historical empathy: using evidence, imagination, and reasoning to imagine the factors that made historical actors' actions seem rational to them (perspective recognition), and feeling an emotional attachment to historical characters that inspires caring action today (care)

In addition to sourcing, corroboration, contextualization, and historical empathy, historians make inferences, reading between the lines as they construct interpretations. Historians make inferences about historical motives, purposes, causes, or trends. VanSledright (2002) points out that often the greatest challenge historians face is not synthesizing information from conflicting sources but filling in gaps when no evidence exists, employing what is referred to as *historical imagination*. Collingwood (1993) shows that what is inferred, is imagined. Unlike pure imagination, historical imagination is constrained by evidence, reason, and earthly realities like gravity and time (Collingwood, 1993; Levesque, 2008). The development of historical inferences and interpretations involves skillfully using evidence when it is available; employing sourcing, corroboration, and contextualization; and blending logic and imagination to fill in the gaps when the historical record is fragmentary, contradictory, or silent. As Collingwood (1993) described, history is "a web of imaginative construction stretched between certain fixed points provided by [critically analyzed evidence]" (p. 242).

historical imagination: creatively filling in gaps in the historical evidence with logical inferences constrained by evidence and earthly realities and inserting one's understandings when facing conflicting evidence

Which Habits of Mind Characterize Historians' Work?

What is the difference between a historical reading strategy and a habit of mind displayed by historians?

In addition to the strategies described above, there are several habits of mind that historians demonstrate—ways of thinking about historical evidence and acceptable methods of constructing historical interpretations. For example, historians approach a historical question with a mature *epistemic stance*—a sophisticated understanding of the way historical knowledge is constructed (Reddy & VanSledright 2010). They understand that history is not the past but, instead, is a study of the past based on the incomplete and imperfect record that has been left behind. They acknowledge that there is not a single historical narrative but that multiple interpretations are possible. Furthermore, they understand that not all interpretations are equally valid, making judgments based on the way evidence was used. The ways of thinking about the nature of historical knowledge and how it is constructed are addressed more fully in Chapter 5, where epistemology is considered.

> *epistemic stance: approaching historical inquiry with a sophisticated under-standing that historical interpretations are constructed through an analysis of evidence and that alternative interpretations are possible based on the research-er's priorities and perspectives.*

Additionally, historians maintain a *healthy skepticism* as they approach texts. They do not accept information in any text at face value but critically evaluate text content with the source in mind. Texts do not convey information but, instead, represent an individual's limited viewpoint, parts of which the historian may or may not accept as reliable based on a great number of factors. Historians maintain the power of the "line item veto" to discount any part of a text that they judge to be inaccurate (Wineburg, 1994, p. 121).

> *healthy skepticism: a mild resistance to information that a person receives until it has been scrutinized*

Historians' healthy skepticism does not prevent them from giving each piece of evidence a fair review. To the contrary, historians maintain an *open mind*, with the ability to simultaneously consider several contradictory, tentative interpre-tations. They understand that new evidence, which regularly surfaces, or new ways of thinking about the past lead to a constantly evolving understanding of history. Perfetti and his colleagues (1999) hypothesized that as historians engage in inquiry, they not only construct an understanding of an event (labeled a "situ-ation model" in literacy research), but they also construct alternative explana-tions (labeled "hypothetical situation models" by Perfetti). As more evidence is encountered, historians lean more strongly toward certain interpretations, but alternative interpretations are not completely dismissed. A colleague of mine and I watched this process as historians collaboratively analyzed evidence. We found that they frequently acknowledged the plausibility of their peers' ideas even when they doubted the accuracy (Nokes & Kesler-Lund, 2019). By doing so they demonstrated *academic humility* by considering and exhausting many plausible alternative interpretations before reaching a conclusion. Thus, historians, though skeptical about all interpretations, remain open to new, evidence-based theories. Ironically, Wineburg (1991) found that students were much more confident in their naïve understanding of the past than were historians of their sophisticated interpretations.

---

academic humility: the willingness to remain open-minded about one's under-standings, willing to change one's mind in the face of better evidence

---

Historians' habits of mind are based on their understanding of important concepts related to historical methodology and general historical thinking. Such concepts include *evidence, accounts, traces, change, continuity, time,* and *cause.* A correct understanding of these concepts, sometimes labeled second-order concepts or metaconcepts, is a key to historians' work (Lee, 2005). More is said about metaconcepts in Chapter 9.

Historians' unique literacy strategies are not limited to reading but also include writing strategies. For example, historians recognize the relationship between reading and writing, establish a clear purpose for reading, and read with their writing task in mind (Monte-Sano et al., 2014; Nokes & Kesler-Lund, 2019). They write for particular audiences and tailor their writing to the needs of that audience (Nokes & Kesler-Lund, 2019). In high-quality historical writing, the author takes a stand and substantiates their claims using evidence (Goldberg et al., 2011; Monte-Sano et al., 2014). Historians are not only excellent readers but are skilled writers as well. Chapter 13 focuses on argumentative historical writing.

The Need for Secondary Students to Receive Historical Literacy Instruction

---

Why do you think young people struggle with historical reading and writing?

Historians' professional activities contrast sharply with traditional history teaching methods. There exists, perhaps, no other discipline where the work of students differs more drastically from the work of professionals. In science, students do labs. In gym class, they play sports. In English class, they write poetry. In music class, they perform in ensembles. And in industrial arts, they work with the same tools carpenters use. However, in history, students typically listen to lectures and memorize information, activities that do not reflect historical thinking. Students are so distanced from historical processes that they typically have no inkling of how historians go about their work. Several years ago I interviewed 30 fifth graders, asking, among other things how they thought historians spent their time. Students confused the work of historians with paleontologists, history makers (such as explorers or pilgrims), or simply admitted they did not know what historians did. They imagined historians surfing Wikipedia, watching the History Channel, or listening to lectures, all processes more closely associated with the way students learn history than with historical inquiry. Most students cannot imagine the work of historians because they have never experienced anything like it.

Unfortunately, many people are satisfied with traditional history teaching. In fact, the teaching of historical literacies has been controversial in the past. For example, the U.S. educator and eventual president Woodrow Wilson was afraid that the complex cognitive processes of historical thinking exceeded students' abilities. He contended that "we must avoid introducing what is called scientific history in the schools for it is [a] history of doubt, criticism, examination of evidence. It tends to confuse young people" (VanSledright, 2002, p. vii). Even as late as the 1960s, some psychologists discouraged teaching history through inquiry to young people (Hallam, 1970), favoring instead the sharing of concrete events. They presumed that even high school students were cognitively unprepared for historical thinking, a notion subsequently dispelled by scores of studies mentioned throughout this book.

Yet the confusion of young people in working with historical texts has also been well documented. Without support, they struggle when exposed to historical documents and asked to engage in historians' literacies. For example, Wineburg (1991) compared think-aloud protocols of historians with the protocols of advanced high school students as they negotiated meaning with multiple texts related to the Battle of Lexington. He found that the students, unlike the historians, struggled with contradictions in the accounts, focused on remembering facts, and appreciated the straightforward, and what they perceived as objective, account in a textbook passage. The students misunderstood the nature of historical thinking, assuming that their purpose in reading was to remember information rather than to construct and interpret meaning. Other researchers have discovered similar types of challenges when students read multiple historical texts. Stahl et al. (1996) found that high school students focused on information that was repeated in multiple texts but failed to notice, or chose to ignore, contradictions. VanSledright (2002) suspected that fifth-grade students inappropriately applied background knowledge from Disney's movie *Pocahontas* in interpreting the causes of the "Starving Time" in the Jamestown colony. In my research, I found that after several lessons on the use of contextualization, students did not employ this strategy on a posttest writing task (Nokes, et al., 2007). More recently I found that even when eighth graders noticed the source of a document, they did not use that knowledge to construct a stronger argument (Nokes,

2017). And other studies further document students' struggles to engaging in historical reading and reasoning (Britt & Aglinskas, 2002; Seixas, 1993). How can teachers involve students in historical inquiries without causing the confusion that Woodrow Wilson and others feared?

The success of Mrs. Francis's lesson used to introduce this chapter is not imaginary. I watched both middle school and high school students engage in historical reading on many occasions when I, as their teacher, created the proper conditions and gave them the support they needed to do so. Mrs. Francis's lesson represents the growing movement among history teachers and researchers to engage students, as young as early elementary grades, in historical reading and thinking (Bain, 2005; Lee & Ashby, 2000; Levstik & Barton, 2015; Nokes, 2014; Stahl & Shanahan, 2004; VanSledright, 2002). As described in Chapter 2, the National Council for the Social Studies' C3 Framework encourages teachers to help students identify the source of documents, differentiate between facts and interpretations, consider multiple perspectives, hold interpretations as tentative, interrogate historical data, and marshal evidence to support interpretations (NCSS, 2013). In other words, history teachers are encouraged to immerse students in the texts, literacies, and habits of mind of historical inquiry—this is the new standard of history teaching. But in the face of the research that shows that it is difficult for students to process historical documents does this kind of teaching produce results?

A recent review of literature by Scandinavian researchers found that in the past 20 years, 1,300 research articles had been published on history teaching (Anonymous, in press). One of the two major themes that these researchers found was the effectiveness of teaching historical thinking. Scores of studies have shown that (a) students are able to engage in more sophisticated historical reading and writing when they are given instruction, support, and opportunities to practice; (b) students can engage in historical empathy when given appropriate texts, topics, and instruction; (c) students of different ages, ability levels, racial backgrounds, and nationalities improve when instruction and texts are tailored to their backgrounds and ability levels; (d) effective inquiry lessons can be designed around many local, national, and world history topics; and (e) resources for teaching inquiry-driven history lessons that revolve around historical literacies are available across numerous webpages (see the list of online resources in Chapter 14).

To summarize, students rarely spontaneously engage in historical reasoning even when given primary source documents—the processes are extremely challenging for them. But with instruction, students develop historians' literacies and habits of mind. They can overcome many of the challenges of historical thinking if teachers make historical literacy an explicit objective of their instruction.

Chapter Summary

Historical literacies include the ability to construct historical interpretations with primary and secondary sources, artifacts, scientific evidence, and other sources as historians do—both consuming and producing texts of multiple genres. The texts important in history include evidence, secondary sources, tertiary sources, and public histories. Historically literate individuals are strategic in working with texts, using sourcing, corroboration, contextualization, and other strategies. They make evidence-based inferences. Historically literate individuals exhibit certain habits of mind such as skepticism, open-mindedness, and academic humility. Yet students rarely demonstrate historical literacies unless they are taught to do so. But with such instruction, they begin to use historians' texts, literacies, and habits of mind with increasing sophistication.

Questions for Consideration

1. How do you think historians' reading strategies and habits of mind, as explained in this chapter, compare to the reading of other disciplinary experts such as biologists, mathematicians, and engineers? What implications do these differences carry for instruction for students?
2. How do historians' reading and writing strategies compare to the critical reading strategies needed for online reading and civic engagement? What are the instructional implications of these similarities?
3. How have you learned strategies like sourcing, corroboration, and historical empathy for working with documents? Have you received instruction on these strategies, figured them out in dependently, or are they new to you?

Additional Reading and Resources

- "History's Habits of Mind," produced by the National Council for History Education can be found at https://ncheteach.org/Historys-Habits-of-Mind.
- Sam Wineburg's pioneering research on historians' reading is reported in the article Wineburg, S. S. (1991). On the reading of historical texts: Notes on the breach between school and academy. *American Educational Research Journal, 28*(3), 495–519. doi.org/10.3102/00028312028003495.
- Additional research on historians' reading and writing processes that I conducted with a colleague is reported in the article Nokes, J. D. & Kesler-Lund, A. (2019). Historians' social literacies: How historians collaborate and write during a document-based activity. *The History Teacher, 52*(3), 369–410.
- Bruce VanSledright reports on his yearlong work with fifth graders in the book VanSledright, B. (2002). *In search of America's past: Learning to read history in elementary school.* Teachers College Press.

References

Anonymous (in press). History education under construction: Conceptual, intellectual and social structure within a knowledge domain (2000–2019). *European Journal of Education.*

Bain, R. B. (2005). "They thought the world was flat?" Applying the principles of *How people learn* in teaching high school history. In M. S. Donovan & J. D. Bransford (Eds.), *How students learn: History, mathematics, and science in the classroom* (pp. 179–213). National Academies Press.

Barton, K. C., & Levstik, L. S. (2004). *Teaching history for the common good.* Lawrence Erlbaum.

Britt, M. A., & Aglinskas, C. (2002). Improving students' ability to identify and use source information. *Cognition and Instruction, 20*, 485–522. doi:10.1207/S1532690XCI2004_2

Collingwood, R. G. (1993). *The idea of history.* Oxford University Press.

Endacott, J. L., & Brooks, S. (2018). Historical empathy: Perspectives and responding to the past. In S. Metzger & L. Harris (Eds.), *International handbook of history teaching and learning* (pp. 203–225). Wiley Blackwell.

Foster, S.J. (2001). Historical empathy in theory and practice: Some final thoughts. In O. L. Davis, E. A. Yeager, & S.J. Foster (Eds.), *Historical empathy and perspective taking in the social studies* (pp. 167–181). Rowman & Littlefield.

Goldberg, T., Schwarz, B. B., & Porat, D. (2011). "Could they do it differently?": Narrative and argumentative changes in students' writing following discussion of "hot" historical issues. *Cognition and Instruction, 29*(2), 185–217. doi:10.1080/07370008.2011.556 832

Griffith, D. W., & Aitken, H. (Co-producers), & Griffith, D. I. (Director). (1915). *The birth of a nation [Motion picture].* Epoch Producing Corporation.

Hallam, R. N. (1970). Piaget and thinking in history. In M. Ballard (Ed.), *New movements in the study and teaching of history* (pp. 162–178). Indiana University Press.

Lee, P.J. (2005). Putting principles into practice: Understanding history. In M. S. Donovan & J. D. Bransford (Eds.), *How students learn: History, mathematics, and science in the classroom* (pp. 31–77). National Academies Press.

Lee, P. J., & Ashby, R. A. (2000). Progression in historical understanding among students age 7–14. In P. N. Stearns, P. Seixas, & S. Wineburg (Eds.), *Knowing, teaching, and learning history. National and international perspectives* (pp. 199–222). New York University Press.

Lesh, B.A. (2011). *Why won't you just tell us the answer? Teaching historical thinking in grades 1–12.* Stenhouse.

Levesque, S. (2008). *Thinking historically: Educating students for the twenty-first century.* University of Toronto Press.

Levstik, L. S., & Barton, K. C. (2015). *Doing history: Investigating with children in elementary and middle schools* (5th Ed.). Routledge.

Logtenberg, A., Van Boxtel, C., & van Hout-Wolters, B. (2011). Stimulating situational interest and student questioning through three types of historical introductory texts. *European Journal of Psychology of Education, 26*(2), 179–198. doi:10.1007/ s10212-010-0041-6

Monte-Sano, C., De La Paz, S., & Felton, M. (2014). *Reading, thinking, and writing about history: Teaching argumentative writing to diverse learners in the Common Core classroom, grades 6–12.* Teachers College Press.

National Council for the Social Studies (2013). *The college, career, and civic life (C3) framework for social studies state standards: Guidance for enhancing the rigor of K-12 civics, economics, geography, and history.* NCSS. https://www.socialstudies.org/sites/default/files/c3/ c3-framework-for-social-studies-rev0617.pdf

Nokes, J. D. (2014). Elementary students' roles and epistemic stances during document-based history lessons. *Theory and Research in Social Education, 42*(3) 375–413. doi:10. 1080/00933104.2014.937546

Nokes, J. D. (2017). Exploring patterns of historical thinking through eighth-grade students' argumentative writing. *Journal of Writing Research, 8*(3), 437–467. doi:10.17239/jowr-2017.08.03.02

Nokes, J. D., Dole, J. A., & Hacker, D. J. (2007). Teaching high school students to use heuristics while reading historical texts. *Journal of Educational Psychology, 99*(3), 492–504. doi:10.1037/0022-0663.99.3.492

Nokes, J. D. & Kesler-Lund, A. (2019). Historians' social literacies: How historians collaborate and write during a document-based activity. *The History Teacher, 52*(3), 369–410.

Ortman, S. G. (2012). *Winds from the North: Tewa origins and historical anthropology.* University of Utah Press.

Paxton, R. J. (2002). The influence of author visibility on high school students solving a historical problem. *Cognition and Instruction, 20*(2), 197–248. doi:10.1207/S1532690XCI2002_3

Perfetti, C. A., Rouet, J.-E., & Britt, M. A. (1999). Toward a theory of documents representation. In H. van Oostendorp & S. R. Goldman (Eds.), *The construction of mental representations during reading* (pp. 99–122). Erlbaum.

Reddy, K., & VanSledright, B. (2010). *Epistemic change in history education.* Paper presented at the annual conference of the College and University Faculty Assembly, Denver, CO.

Reisman, A. (2012). Reading like a historian: A document-based history curriculum intervention in urban high schools. *Cognition and Instruction, 30*(1), 86–112. doi:10.1080/07370008.2011.634081

Richards, J. C., & Anderson, N. A. (2003). What do I see? What do I think? What do I wonder? (STW): A visual literacy strategy to help emergent readers focus on storybook illustrations. *The Reading Teacher, 56*(5), 442–444.

Seixas, P. (1993). Popular film and young people's understanding of the history of Native American-White relations. *The History Teacher, 26*(3), 351–370. doi:10.2307/494666

Stahl, S. A., Hynd, C. R., Britton, B. K., McNish, M. M., & Bosquet, D. (1996). What happens when students read multiple source documents in history? *Reading Research Quarterly, 3* i, 430–456. doi:10.1598/RRQ.31.4.5

Stahl, S. A., & Shanahan, C. H. (2004). Learning to think like a historian: Disciplinary knowledge through critical analysis of multiple documents. In T. L. Jetton & J. A. Dole (Eds.), *Adolescent literacy research and practice* (pp. 94–115). Guilford.

VanSledright, B. (2002). *In search of America's past: Learning to read history in elementary school.* Teachers College Press.

Washington, G. (1786, December 4). *[Letter to Benjamin Lincoln].* Founders Online, National Archives. https://founders.archives.gov/documents/Washington/04-04-02-0374-0002

Wineburg, S. S. (1991). On the reading of historical texts: Notes on the breach between school and academy. *American Educational Research Journal, 28*(3), 495–519. doi:10.3102/00028312028003495

Wineburg, S. S. (1994). The cognitive representation of historical texts. In G. Leinhardt, I. Beck, & C Stainton (Eds.), *Teaching and learning in history* (pp. 85–135). Erlbaum.

Wineburg, S. S. (1998). Reading Abraham Lincoln: An expert/expert study in the interpretation of historical texts. *Cognitive Science, 22*(3), 319–346. doi:10.1207/s15516709cog2203_3

Wineburg, S. S. (2001). *Historical thinking and other unnatural acts: Charting the future of teaching the past.* Temple University Press.

Wineburg, S. S. (2007). Forrest Gump and the future of teaching the past. *Phi Delta Kappan, 89*(3), 168–177. doi:10.1177/003172170708900305

4

TEACHING HISTORICAL LITERACIES

Supporting Students as Active Readers and Writers

The last chapter discussed how historians read. This chapter breaks down the reading process into four subprocesses that strong readers engage in. These four subprocesses are referred to throughout this book. They serve as diagnostic tools for identifying students' struggles and can guide teachers as they plan inquiries, prepare texts, and teach historical literacy lessons. This chapter also addresses writing processes.

As you read the following vignette, think about how Mr. Nguyen might have taught the lesson differently. Was it a mistake for him to use the political cartoon? What more could he do to help students work with it?

Mr. Nguyen remembers a history lesson on progressivism he taught in an eighth-grade U.S. history class early in his career when he primarily used traditional methods. Before he lectured on Theodore Roosevelt's trustbusting policies he started class by having students spend a few minutes analyzing a political cartoon from that era. In preparation for the lesson, he had found the perfect political cartoon: an image painted in 1904 of an octopus-like monster, labeled "Standard Oil," with tentacles wrapped around a statehouse, other government buildings, and business executives (see Figure 4.1). The monster's eyes are fixed on the White House and a tentacle is reaching that direction (Keppler, 1904). Mr. Nguyen was excited by his discovery of this cartoon because it is a wonderful primary source that shows the fears of proponents of Theodore Roosevelt's trustbusting. He hoped that during the analysis of the cartoon students would become curious about the conditions that existed at the time.

When class started, Mr. Nguyen displayed the cartoon using a projector and asked students to analyze it. There was a long silence, but because he knew the value of "wait time," he waited. After a minute of quiet, he called on several

DOI: 10.4324/9781003183495-5

FIGURE 4.1 A political cartoon (Keppler, 1904).

students to explain the cartoon. One student after another awkwardly struggled through their flawed explanations. Their answers showed a range of challenges. Most lacked the historical background knowledge needed to understand the symbols on the cartoon. Some did not understand the nature of political cartoons. They lacked specific strategies for making sense of what they were looking at. Others thought the cartoon had to do with current events involving the oil industry. After listening to students struggle, Mr. Nguyen explained the political cartoon to the class and jumped into his lecture. Later he wondered why the activity had flopped. He had found what he thought was a great text, provided time for students to reflect, and asked open-ended questions. Why did the students struggle like they did? When he talked about his frustration with another history teacher later that day, his colleague replied, "That's why I don't use primary sources. The kids just cannot read them."

Since that lesson, Mr. Nguyen has had a lot of time to think about how poorly the activity with the political cartoon went. Fortunately, through the years he has experimented with different teaching methods, has become more familiar with research on teaching, and is now convinced that his colleague was wrong—students could work with political cartoons and other primary source evidence if teachers structured lessons in the right ways. He realized that his first mistake was that he wanted students to read the cartoon merely because it was part of the narrative of the lecture. There was no intent on his part to encourage students to question or critique the political cartoon as part of a historical inquiry. He later realized that with support and opportunities for independent inquiry, students could not only make sense of the political cartoon, but they could engage in even more sophisticated historical literacies. For example, with practice conducting historical inquiries, students might even ask who had produced the cartoon. They might ask questions about the context of its creation, its intended audience, and its historical impact. They might seek other documents or artifacts to cross-check its message or to investigate contrasting opinions. Rather than viewing the cartoon as a way to transmit or receive information, they might use it as evidence in historical inquiry.

This botched activity also showed him that simply providing students with the right text is not enough to build historical literacies. Students must be taught strategies for working with texts. And, more important, students need opportunities for inquiry. They need to use historical texts and artifacts, like the political cartoon, not simply to gain information but also as one of multiple pieces of evidence to interpret historical controversies. Furthermore, students must comprehend a text before they can analyze it. He thought about how teachers can help students by breaking down the process of analysis into simpler steps, each of which students could accomplish with the proper support. Instead, many teachers find it easier to read documents to students, telling them how the documents illustrate a historical theme rather than helping students read them for themselves or use them to build their own interpretations. Such instruction does little to foster students' historical literacies.

Have you had teachers who were especially good at helping you work with challenging resources? What did they do that helped you?

In this chapter, I explore how research on reading and literacy, and on teaching reading in the traditional sense (i.e., instruction on reading words, sentences, paragraphs, and books), can inform instruction on building students' historical literacies with both language-based (letters or speeches) and non-language-based (art or music) texts. I consider (a) general literacy strategies and historical literacies, (b) a framework for understanding reading processes and historical literacies, (c) a framework for understanding writing processes, (d) two models of literacy instruction, and (e) warnings about the potential misapplication of general reading research to building students' historical literacies.

General Literacy Strategies and Historical Literacies

As you read this section try to identify the difference between a metacognitive strategy and a cognitive strategy?

Students have a difficult time working with texts as diverse as political cartoons, diary entries, textbooks, artifacts, or televised debates, unless they possess general comprehension skills in addition to historical literacies. History teachers can cooperate with language arts and other content-area teachers to build these general abilities. Often literacy strategies are useful in the reading of both traditional print texts and nontraditional texts, such as the political cartoon described in the introduction of this chapter. There are several general skills and elements of general reading instruction that apply to building historical literacies. For instance, concepts such as close reading; metacognition, particularly the monitoring of one's comprehension; vocabulary instruction; and the categorization system of before-, during-, and after-reading strategies apply to building historical literacies. I introduce each of these four concepts.

Close Reading

Research on reading has shown that proficient readers purposefully vary their reading speed. When searching through large bodies of text, looking for relevant passages, they may simply skim. However, when encountering dense or complex texts, good readers slow down, pause and reflect while reading, annotate the text, think about the author, pay attention to details, reread passages, ask questions, and seek clarification from other sources—practices that have been labeled *close reading*. The ability to select an appropriate reading speed is important for historians, who are able to quickly sift through volumes of material in an archive, searching for documents relevant to their research project. Upon making a discovery, they might spend hours, days, or even a career carefully analyzing a single text. History teachers should encourage students to be purposeful in choosing their reading speed, pointing out the appropriate conditions for skimming, close reading, or moderate reading speeds. Students are more likely to engage in close reading when teachers give them a manageable reading load—a few short passages to be considered carefully rather than long reading selections.

---

close reading: the purposefully slow and careful reading of a document, often accompanied by highlighting or annotating the document, discussing the content with peers, or taking notes on important content.

Unlike some other general literacy strategies, experts on historical thinking value the strategy of close reading. For instance, Reisman (2012) included close reading as one of four historical reading strategies that she fostered. Using historians as models, advocates of close reading encourage students to slow their pace, consider the source, ask questions about the text, and reflect deeply about the context surrounding its production. During close reading, readers are encouraged to consider the specific words an author uses, and the specific claims and evidence that an author employs. Students can be taught to adapt these questions when working with artifacts or visual evidence such as photographs. For instance, during close reading students might think about why a photographer took a picture from a certain angle. Embedded within the teacher resources of the Stanford History Education Group website are lessons on close reading through which teachers provide reminders and support to help students think deeply about the short passages they meticulously analyze (Stanford History Education Group, 2012).

Metacognition

Research on reading shows that good readers tend to be metacognitive, or reflective on their reading and thinking processes (Baker, 1994; McKeown & Beck, 2009). One of the key metacognitive practices is monitoring one's comprehension—paying attention to whether one understands what is read and noticing when comprehension breaks down (Theide et al., 2009). Surprisingly, early research on reading suggests that many young readers do not pay attention to whether they understand what they are reading (Baker, 1984; Markham 1979). Once, when I asked a student to summarize what he had just read out loud to the class, he responded, "How am I supposed to know? I just read it." In some students' way of thinking, reading consists of the correct pronunciation of words; they are unaware that reading really only occurs when one comprehends what is read. In historical literacy, as in general reading, students must be taught the importance of monitoring their comprehension and being aware when they do not understand, recognizing that this is a problem.

Additionally, metacognition includes an awareness of strategies that can be used when comprehension breaks down. Generally speaking, students can reread, ask questions, look for additional sources, or, when appropriate, skip a passage when they do not understand what they are reading. When working with artifacts or photographs, students might discuss observations with peers, focus on parts rather than the whole, or consider the context of the artifacts' discovery or the photographs' creation. Research on reading suggests that good readers are aware of a repertoire of strategies that they can employ to improve their comprehension and use of texts (McKeown & Beck, 2009). Thus, metacognition requires knowledge of oneself, including one's strengths and weaknesses as a reader or historian; a knowledge of the reading and writing task at hand, including the texts, strategies, and processes involved in completing the task; and an awareness of how successfully the activity is proceeding (Baker, 2002). Students engaged in historical thinking should be aware of the task at hand, know the cognitive tools available to them, and should have a sense, throughout the process, of how they are doing.

Skillful writing involves a great deal of metacognition (Hacker et al., 2009). Writers think about their purpose and set goals for their writing that evolve as the process moves forward. They imagine an audience, anticipate the audience's reaction, and adjust their writing accordingly. They read what they have written, reflect on their language, diagnose potential problems, and make revisions, all under the control of their own metacognitive monitoring. Writing is so interrelated with metacognitive activity that Hacker et al. (2009) argue that "writing is applied metacognition" (p. 161).

> *metacognition: thinking about thought processes, including monitoring one's success in comprehension, considering strategies that might improve success, setting goals, and planning for writing, in order to take charge of one's own learning process*

Vocabulary and Literacy

The development of a rich vocabulary is a basic element of general literacy instruction. Students need knowledge of word meanings in order to read and write. Such is also the case when working with written historical texts—students must know the meaning of the words that they encounter. There is history-related vocabulary that history teachers might need to define for students. Reading research supports the notion that there is no better way for students to learn history-related vocabulary than to be immersed in discussions that allow them to hear and use unfamiliar words in context (Baumann, 2009). History teachers should consider students' vocabulary needs when selecting texts, and should provide vocabulary support when needed for students to comprehend and critique the texts they are using.

Before-, During-, and After-Reading Strategies

Expert readers use cognitive strategies, thinking strategies like visualizing a setting or predicting an outcome, to improve their comprehension. Research on the practices used by effective readers often categorizes strategies as those used before reading, during reading, and after reading (Pearson & Dole, 1987). For instance, before good readers start to read an unfamiliar text they might preview the text to get a feel for what it is about, activating their background knowledge (Langer, 1984). They establish a purpose for reading and may make predictions about what they will read. Thus, even before reading, they take an active role in learning with the text (Ogle, 1986). During reading, good readers vary their reading speed, monitor their comprehension, summarize, make inferences, seek clarification when needed, ask questions, and continue to make and verify predictions (Paris et al., 1991). They may visualize in their mind's eye the things they are reading. They make connections to other things that they have read, world events, or their personal experiences (Tovani, 2000). After reading, good readers summarize, continue to ask questions, and find others who have read the same text or who have not read the text with whom they can discuss it (Paris, et al., 1991).

> *cognitive reading strategy: a way of thinking or mental tactic, employed before, during, or after reading that improves the reader's comprehension or use of a text*

Although some of these strategies might not apply directly to historical literacies, some certainly do, and the notion of before-, during-, and after-reading strategies might be an effective way for a history teacher to discuss strategic reading with students (e.g., see Hairrell et al., 2011). For instance, *before* a historian reads a text or analyzes an artifact, they look at the source (Wineburg, 1991). In addition, they approach texts with the appropriate epistemic stance (VanSledright, 2002) and with healthy skepticism. *During* reading, a historian often goes back and forth between different texts making direct comparisons using the strategy referred to as corroboration (Wineburg, 1991). *After* reading, a historian uses the text as evidence, citing or paraphrasing it in their writing. History teachers might find it convenient to teach students using the before-, during-, and after-reading framework to help students remember what they should be doing at each stage of working with historical evidence. To summarize, reading researchers have explored constructs such as close reading, metacognition, vocabulary instruction, and before-, during-, and after-reading strategies that are directly applicable in building historical literacies.

> How might Mr. Nguyen in the vignette at the start of this chapter have used the concepts of close reading; metacognition; vocabulary; and before-, during-, and after-reading strategies to improve the students' analysis of the political cartoon?

A Framework for Understanding Literate Processes and Historical Literacies

> As you read about the four roles of the reader, think of examples from your own reading experiences where you have struggled in each of these roles. What might a teacher have done to have supported you in each role?

Research on literacy can provide a helpful framework for understanding the roles of students as readers of historical texts. One such framework, which I use throughout this book, is the four resources model, developed by literacy researchers Freebody and Luke (1990). This model presents the reader as active throughout their interaction with a text, engaging in the four roles of *code breaker, meaning maker, text user,* and *text critic.* This book addresses students' historical literacy needs in terms of these four roles. I provide a general description of each followed by a synthesis of the four resources model of literacy as applied in developing students' historical literacies.

Code Breaker

The code breaker is able to effectively decipher a symbol system. In Freebody and Luke's (1990) model, the code breaker is able to interpret the meaning of letters in traditional print texts, recognize the sounds associated with letters, and use letters and the sounds they represent to form words and sentences both in reading and in writing. Acknowledging a literate individual as a code breaker is important for history teachers for three reasons. First, history teachers must develop instructional accommodations for students who struggle with breaking the code in traditional reading—students who lack basic reading proficiency. History teachers can accommodate struggling readers by providing audio recordings of text, encouraging parents to read with students on homework assignments, finding simple texts, or modifying complex texts into simpler language. Additionally, teachers must become involved in helping students resolve this serious threat to their academic and social well-being. Although it is not the primary responsibility of a history teacher to build students ability to decode in the traditional sense, when a teacher identifies a student who cannot read, the history teacher should seek the resources provided by the school, such as reading teachers, counselors, and special education departments, in order to help that student. The focus of this book is not on building students' ability to decode written text.

Second, traditional print texts sometimes contain unfamiliar conventions or symbols—codes to which history students have had no exposure. For example, the symbols BCE and CE are commonly used in place of the more familiar symbols BC and AD in working with dates. Students might need to be taught the meaning of these symbols. Similarly, students might be unfamiliar with other symbols in historical print texts, such as the "long *s*" symbol, commonly used in the 18th century, which looked like the letter *f* but represents the sound of the letter *s*. Furthermore, old handwritten documents in cursive script can be difficult for students to decode. When students cannot decode, the teacher can either change the text, by transcribing or translating it, or change the students by teaching them new decoding strategies.

Third, when building historical literacies, the concept of code breaking must be projected onto the variety of sources used in historical inquiry, such as the ability to decode the symbolic images in a political cartoon. Much of Mr. Nguyen's frustration with students in the introduction of this chapter stemmed from students' inability to decode the political cartoon and Mr. Nguyen's failure to recognize their struggles as a decoding issue. Different formats of text, such as political cartoons, propaganda posters, artifacts, music, photographs, artwork, radio broadcasts, and debates, use different symbolic codes. When a history teacher provides students with historical evidence, it is the teacher's responsibility to teach students to decode any unique symbols, such as a long *s*, an unfamiliar abbreviation, or an oil tank with tentacles. This process is part of building students' historical literacies.

A wide range of valuable resources for historical inquiries may present decoding issues for students. For example, a cartogram is a map with the relative size of states or nations distorted to represent a statistic other than land shape and size. A cartogram that represents world population expands China and India and shrinks Canada and Australia (for examples of cartograms, see http://archive. worldmapper.org/about.html). Someone unfamiliar with the purpose or structure of a cartogram might have difficulty decoding what the shapes and sizes mean. However, with brief decoding instruction, a cartogram becomes a valuable resource for historical inquiry. Musicians, artists, political cartoonists, and others have unique symbol systems that require some decoding, and history teachers cannot assume that students have the skills needed to decode the multiple genres useful in studying history. Instead, a teacher should be sensitive to students' decoding needs and adjust instruction appropriately. Before students can use historical texts as evidence, they must be able to decode the symbolic system associated with constructing meaning with that text.

Meaning Maker

The meaning maker constructs meaning with the code that has been broken. In traditional reading, the meaning maker can summarize a passage, demonstrating basic comprehension. Similarly, in working with nontraditional texts, such as a data table or painting, the meaning maker can summarize the factual information contained in the table or describe the subject of a painting. It should be noted that code breaking and meaning making go hand in hand. For example, as an individual attempts to break the code and find meaning in a table from an early 20th-century census, they would have to identify the meaning of numbers located in columns and rows (see Figure 4.2). Doing so would involve some traditional decoding—reading the name of the country at the top of each column and the state listed to the left of each row, some numerical decoding—reading the numbers located in each cell, and some structural decoding—understanding the meaning of columns and rows. The ability to break this code allows individuals to then begin to construct meaning, discovering, for example, that almost one half of a million German immigrants resided in New York in 1890 (Durand & Harris, 1913).

It should be noted that sometimes the meaning that readers construct is highly subjective, such as in listening to a piece of music or viewing abstract art. In all cases, the making of meaning integrates both the readers' background knowledge and the content of the text being read. In some cases, two people with different backgrounds will comprehend the same text differently, a notion understood very well by historians. Even in cases where the construction of meaning is highly subjective, the teacher can discern comprehension problems. For example, struggling readers often rely heavily on background knowledge rather than the text during the meaning-making process, reaching conclusions that are unwarranted given the evidence in the text. Teachers can assess students' capabilities as code

DIVISION OR STATE AND CENSUS YEAR	Total foreign born.	Northwestern Europe.							
		Eng-land.	Scot-land.	Wales.	Ireland.	Ger-many.	Nor-way.	Swe-den.	Den-mar
MIDDLE ATLANTIC.									
New York:									
1 1910	2,748,011	146,870	39,437	7,464	367,889	436,911	25,013	53,705	12,
2 1900	1,900,425	135,685	33,802	7,304	425,553	499,820	12,601	42,708	8,
3 1890	1,571,050	144,422	35,332	8,108	483,375	498,602	8,602	28,430	6,
New Jersey:									
4 1910	660,788	50,375	17,512	1,202	82,758	122,880	5,351	10,547	5,
5 1900	431,884	45,428	14,211	1,195	94,844	121,414	2,296	7,337	3,
6 1890	329,975	43,785	13,163	1,069	101,059	106,181	1,317	4,159	2,
Pennsylvania:									
7 1910	1,442,374	109,115	32,046	29,255	165,109	195,202	2,320	23,467	3,
8 1900	985,250	114,831	30,386	35,453	205,909	226,796	1,393	24,130	2,
9 1890	845,720	125,145	32,081	38,301	243,836	230,516	2,238	19,346	2,
EAST NORTH CENTRAL.									
Ohio:									
10 1910	598,374	43,347	10,705	9,377	40,062	175,095	1,110	5,522	1,
11 1900	458,734	41,745	9,327	11,481	55,018	212,829	639	3,951	1,
12 1890	459,293	51,027	10,275	12,905	70,127	235,668	511	2,742	
Indiana:									
13 1910	159,663	9,783	3,419	1,498	11,266	62,179	531	5,081	
14 1900	142,121	10,874	2,805	2,083	16,306	77,811	384	4,673	
15 1890	146,205	11,200	2,948	888	20,819	84,900	285	4,512	
Illinois:									
16 1910	1,205,314	60,363	20,755	4,091	93,455	319,199	32,913	115,424	17,
17 1900	966,747	64,390	20,021	4,364	114,563	369,660	29,979	109,147	15,
18 1890	842,347	70,510	20,465	4,138	124,498	338,382	30,339	86,514	12,
Michigan:									
19 1910	597,550	42,737	9,952	786	20,434	131,586	7,638	26,374	6,
20 1900	541,653	43,839	10,343	838	29,182	145,292	7,582	26,956	6,
21 1890	543,880	55,388	12,068	789	39,065	135,509	7,795	27,366	6,
Wisconsin:									
22 1910	512,865	13,959	3,885	2,507	14,049	233,384	57,000	25,739	16,
23 1900	515,971	17,995	4,569	3,356	23,544	268,384	61,575	26,196	16,
24 1890	519,199	23,633	5,494	4,297	33,306	259,819	65,696	20,157	13,
WEST NORTH CENTRAL.									
Minnesota:									
25 1910	543,595	12,139	4,373	1,023	15,859	109,628	105,303	122,428	16,
26 1900	505,318	12,022	4,810	1,288	22,428	125,191	104,895	115,476	16,
27 1890	467,356	14,745	5,315	1,470	28,011	110,955	101,169	99,913	14,
Iowa:									
28 1910	273,765	16,788	5,162	2,434	17,756	98,759	21,924	26,763	17,
29 1900	305,920	21,027	6,425	3,061	28,321	123,277	25,634	29,875	17,

FIGURE 4.2 A portion of a table from the 1910 census (Durand & Harris, 1913).

breakers and meaning makers by asking comprehension questions such as "What is the main idea of this paragraph?" "What event does this painting depict?" and "How many tons of steel were produced in Pittsburg in 1910?" When a teacher anticipates or identifies comprehension problems, they should provide instruction to address students' needs as code breakers and meaning makers.

Because historians, as seasoned readers, often engage in code breaking and meaning making without conscious effort, these two elements of literacy are often left out of the discussion of historical reasoning. However, code breaking and meaning making are not automatic with many students. Thus, it falls on the shoulders of history teachers to help students with these two important elements of historical literacy, prerequisites for more sophisticated analyses. As is the case with code breaking, if students struggle with meaning making, the teacher can either alter the text, by providing a modified, simplified translation (Wineburg & Martin, 2009), or alter the reader, by fostering in them an improved ability to comprehend, perhaps by introducing unfamiliar vocabulary to them. The approach the teacher chooses should be based on their instructional objectives. As a student grows in historical literacy, they become increasingly capable of constructing meaning (code breaking and meaning making) with an increasing number of text genres and increasingly complex texts.

It should be noted that historical meaning-making can be tricky for students because historical questions require historians to seek for meaning that is often very different from the meaning intended by the writer. The historian's interest may not be in the message of the text but in its subtext and the message it sends about the historical period in question. For example, the writer of a letter from colonial Massachusetts might have intended to give a description of the local Indigenous cultures to a friend in England. However, a historian might use such a document to construct meaning about the effects of Puritan religious doctrines on colonists' beliefs about American Indians. As Lee (2005) states "historians can ask questions about historical sources that those sources were not designed to answer" (p. 37). Thus students need to seek for the meaning in texts that answers historical questions rather than simply the literal meaning intended by the author. Students and historians, and not the text, are the meaning makers.

Text User

Freebody and Luke (1990) label the third role of the reader as that of a text user. Young people are adept text users. They sift through social media to learn about the status of friends and celebrities. They post images and write entries to share their lives with others. They review memes and forward them to friends. After reading a novel, a text user wants to talk about it. Text users conduct internet searches on their phones with a practical purpose in mind. They read about their hobbies and their friends and current events. Most young people spend a great deal of time as text users engaging in literate practices independent of any school assignment. Good readers find ways to conduct research and to apply the understandings that they construct with texts, and quite often those applications involve authentic and self-initiated reading and writing.

In comparison, historians provide an excellent model of professionals who use text in their work. Historians gather and use evidence of a variety of genres to develop and substantiate interpretations of the past. Historians' reading and writing is always purposeful. Early in their research, during archival work, historians search for texts that are relevant and useful. They evaluate evidence in terms of their purposes—does it provide insights into their questions? If so, does it support or conflict with their emerging interpretations? As historians gain confidence in their understandings, they reflect on how they will use the evidence to substantiate their interpretations. As they write, they quote or paraphrase texts as evidence. Thus, historians spend the bulk of their research time acknowledging a need for text, searching for appropriate text, determining how they will use various texts, and producing texts that communicate their findings. The work of historians revolves around the use of texts for discipline-driven purposes.

Often, in history classrooms, students are asked to use texts in a manner that is irrelevant to them, uninteresting from their perspective, and only indirectly related to historical literacies. Answering the questions at the end of a chapter in a history textbook is certainly a way to use text. Such an assignment might build students' general literacies, particularly the skills of skimming and summarizing. However, such an assignment does not require students to use texts as a historian would and so does not build students' historical literacies. In contrast, the vignettes that open each chapter of this book describe students using texts while engaging in authentic historical inquiries. Students use historical texts in discipline-driven rather than school-driven learning activities.

Text Critic

Freebody and Luke (1990) further describe proficient readers as text critics, critically evaluating texts. Information Age technologies give individuals unprecedented access to ideas, information, and opinions (Wineburg, 2018). Good readers are able to screen incoming information in order to ascertain its relevance, accuracy, and usefulness. Researchers have found, however, that many students struggle to critically evaluate information, particularly when it is found online. For example, Leu and his colleagues (2007) discovered that seventh-grade students accepted information on a bogus website about the Northwest Tree Octopus, a fictional species, because it was rich in details, interesting, and had colorful images (which had been digitally falsified). Even when directly confronted by a researcher and told that the site was inaccurate, some of the students continued to argue that it was reliable (Leu, et al., 2007). One by-product of building students' historical literacies is increasing their ability to think critically about all the texts to which they are exposed, although the transfer of historical reading skills to online reading is not guaranteed (McGrew et al., 2018), a point discussed in Chapter 5.

As described in Chapter 3, historians are, above all else, critical readers. They do not accept information found in texts at face value, but they interpret it based on its source and how it relates to other texts. Because history requires this type of critical analysis of texts, history classrooms are ideal locations to nurture students' critical thinking. History teachers must encourage students to question every author (Beck et al., 2020), including the textbook author; recognize that history is always interpretive in nature, and thus open to revision; and search for the voices of those silenced in the traditional historical narrative. Lee (2005) suggests that

> once students begin to operate with a concept of evidence as something inferential and see eyewitnesses not as handing down history but as providing evidence, history can resume once again; it becomes an intelligible, even powerful, way of thinking about the past.
>
> (p. 37)

Much of the basis for the difference between historians' reading and history students' reading is the lack of experience for most students in engaging as a text critic.

The Four Resources Model in Developing Students' Historical Literacies

The four resources model provides a suitable framework for considering historical literacy for several reasons. First, the four resources framework suggests that readers are active in the construction of meaning. Meaning does not reside on the page or in the picture but is built in the mind of the reader or viewer as their background knowledge interacts with their experience with the text. History classrooms that promote historical literacy acknowledge students' active role in constructing understandings. They encourage students to develop independent and original historical interpretations rather than merely learn the history written by others. There is no expectation that every student in the class will develop the same interpretations. Nor are students evaluated by how closely their construction of an event matches that of the textbook narrative. Of course, giving students room for individual thinking does not mean that incorrect interpretations do not exist. It simply means that teachers are as interested in the inquiry process as in answers. When students' thinking is derailed, leading them to gross errors that are unlikely to be corrected by continued study, teachers need to provide correction. For instance, some students reached the conclusion that the Holocaust was a fabrication during one poorly conceived and executed history lesson (Taff, 2014). Students should not have been given the leeway to reach such an unfounded and dangerous conclusion. In the absence of gross misunderstandings, however, teachers who promote historical inquiry invite students to discuss, disagree, and debate historical ideas, always demanding that students support their interpretations with evidence.

Second, in classrooms that are committed to building students' historical literacies, teachers nurture students' ability to decode and construct meaning with a great variety of texts. Implied in this assumption is the notion that teachers expose students to a variety of genres, and devote class time to helping students learn various symbol systems. History teachers who are devoted to building students' historical literacies take the time to explicitly discuss with students the skills used in reading various texts. They do not simply read and explain texts to students, as the frustrated Mr. Nguyen eventually did. Instead, they discuss openly with the students how meaning is constructed, then allow students to construct meaning for themselves. Historically literate students are skillful in finding meaning in political cartoons, music, art, architecture, artifacts, documents, and other genres because their teachers help them learn how to do so. Part II of this book gives specific ways of supporting students' work with different types of texts.

Third, historically literate students are able to critically evaluate texts using the unique literacies of historians. They engage in sourcing, corroboration, and contextualization. They exhibit historians' habits of mind in withholding judgment, recognizing interpretations as tentative, and approaching all texts with a healthy skepticism and academic humility. They use their imagination, fueled by text-based evidence, to produce reasoned speculation when the historical record is silent. They view texts not as conveyors of truth but as evidence and accounts. And they take an active role in sifting through the evidence, independently building historical interpretations, and communicating them through argumentative speaking and writing,

A Framework for Understanding the Writing Processes

In historical inquiry, a strong relationship exists between reading and writing processes, with the materials historians have read integrated into written arguments, descriptions, and narrations. Strategies, too, are used across reading and writing. Sourcing is not just a reading strategy but is used in writing to bolster an argument. For instance, when a historian introduces evidence in a monograph or a thesis-driven lecture, they frequently begin by writing or talking about its source. Researchers on writing generally break the writing process down into three main subprocesses: planning, composing, and revising (Hayes, 2006). In addition, researchers acknowledge the role of metacognition, as writers coordinate these three processes.

Planning

> As you read this section consider how it might help teachers provide better writing instruction if they present the writing process as three subprocesses: planning, composing, and revising.

Planning involves establishing a purpose for writing, setting goals, considering content, and exploring ways of organizing ideas. Expert writers anticipate the background and needs of their audience as they plan. Research has found that experts not only spend more time planning than novices, but the quality of their planning is superior (Nokes & De La Paz, 2018). In contrast to young people, whose planning is generally content-focused, expert writers spend time thinking conceptually about their work, what they want to accomplish with their writing, and about the best approach to accomplish their goals. Research has found that teachers can help students plan conceptually for writing by reminding them about their audience and their rhetorical goals as they write (Wollman-Bonilla, 2001).

How does planning for historical writing specifically compare with general ideas about planning? In a recent study, a colleague of mine and I observed historians engaged in historical inquiry analyzing a series of documents, then designing a memorial. We found that historians began to plan for writing as soon as they started to read. The planning stage of writing was integrated into their analysis of the documents. Their discussions while exploring evidence were framed by their subsequent writing task—designing a monument. For example, one group of historians discussed how different individuals who produced the accounts of the event they studied would have created different types of memorials. Several groups discussed the audience that would view their roadside memorial as they planned for writing. The way they read was influenced by their planning (Nokes & Kesler-Lund, 2019). One of the best ways that teachers can help students in their role as planners is to support them during their analysis of evidence, a process described throughout this book.

Composing

The act of forming letters and words on paper or a computer screen is referred to as composing or translation (Hayes & Flower, 1980). This process has two elements: *text generation* (thinking of what to write) and *transcription* (writing it). For young students this dual process can be challenging, particularly because transcription sometimes distracts from text generation. For example, a writer who has to look around to find a particular letter on a keyboard or who has to think about how to spell a word is less able to focus on the ideas they want to write about. For this and other reasons, research has found that young people are able to construct an oral argument easier than they are able to construct a written argument (Salahu-Din et al., 2008).

A challenge students face while composing historical arguments is that they are generally unaccustomed to producing unique insights in their writing. Students tend to engage in what has been referred to as *knowledge telling* rather than *knowledge transforming* writing (Scardamalia & Bereiter, 1987). To explain, knowledge telling is the process of reporting back what a person knows about a topic, merely retrieving information from memory. Traditional history instruction and conventional assessments reward and reinforce this type of writing. However, such knowledge telling is inferior to the reading, thinking, and writing that can occur in the reimagined classrooms promoted in this book. As students develop independent interpretations based on evidence, they instead engage in knowledge transforming writing, evaluating and reworking ideas in order to defend independently developed claims. Ideas for supporting students as knowledge transforming text composers are shared throughout this book.

Revising

Revising writing is a complex process that involves critical reading, evaluation, and rewriting. The writer critically reads what they have written, comparing it to an imagined ideal text; identifies weaknesses and errors; makes substantial revisions in terms of content and organizational structure; and edits the text to remove grammatical errors or to improve clarity (Hayes, 2006). Unsurprisingly, revising is an extremely difficult process for students for a number of reasons. For example, students may not know what an ideal text looks like, so they have no way of measuring up their writing against a model text (Limpo et al., 2013). Specifically, students might not know what argumentative historical writing looks like—they do not see it in history textbooks. In addition, young people have a difficult time thinking about and revising large sections of text, instead focusing on sentence-by-sentence editing (Piolat et al., 2004). Rather than evaluating and refining their ideas during the process of revising, they merely edit their words. Ideas for supporting students in their role as revisers are described throughout this book.

Two Models of Literacy Instruction

> As you read this next section consider the differences between explicit strategy instruction and implicit strategy instruction and when it might be best to use one or the other.

General research on literacy provides not only a model for understanding the roles of readers but provides models of instruction designed to help teachers build students' literacies. The two models that are featured most prominently in this book are *explicit strategy instruction* and *implicit strategy instruction*. Both types of teaching are based on Vygotsky's theory of sociocultural learning (1986). Vygotsky suggested that all learning is social in nature and that learning is facilitated when a more knowledgeable individual, such as a mother, a baseball coach, or a history teacher, designs appropriately challenging activities for the learner and provides temporary support, referred to as *scaffolding*, for the learner as they engage in the activity. As the learner becomes more able to engage in the activity independently, the teacher gradually removes the scaffolding. A key to Vygotsky's model is that activities must be designed at an appropriate level of difficulty, referred to as a Zone of Proximal Development (ZPD). The ZPD includes tasks that an individual cannot do independently but can do with assistance. As the learner's skills grow, scaffolding is removed, and the learner engages in the activity independently. Learning has occurred. A new task can then be assigned at a slightly higher level of difficulty (within a new ZPD) with the required scaffolding.

> *scaffolding: the temporary support that teachers give students to help them learn during tasks that would be too difficult for them to do independently*

> *Zone of Proximal Development (ZPD): region where learning occurs according to sociocultural theories of learning, represented by appropriately challenging tasks that students can perform with scaffolding that they would be unable to perform on their own.*

Explicit Strategy Instruction

Explicit strategy instruction is designed to provide training, practice, and support in doing activities that students could not do independently—activities within their ZPD. Explicit strategy instruction includes four stages: *direct instruction* of the strategy, *modeling*, *guided practice*, and *independent practice* (Nokes & Dole, 2005). During the first stage, *direct instruction*, the teacher openly discusses the strategy with students, naming it, describing the process, discussing the appropriate conditions for its use, and selling its effectiveness. For instance, instead of having students flounder in their attempts to make sense of the political cartoon, Mr. Nguyen might have introduced students to the strategy of "identifying the symbols" as a first step in reading a political cartoon. Furthermore, during direct instruction, he could have described the process of "identifying the symbols" such as looking for labels on images, like "Standard Oil" written on the monster; identifying unlabeled symbols, such as the White House; interpreting symbolic actions, such as reaching a tentacle for the White House; and attending to subtle symbols, such as the focus of the eyes of the monster on the White House. Thus, Mr. Nguyen would have named the strategy "identifying the symbols" and described the steps involved in engaging in the strategy.

Following direct instruction on the strategy, the teacher *models* the strategy for students. The key element in modeling is thinking aloud as students listen. For instance, Mr. Nguyen might start by identifying the symbols that are labeled. He might say,

> When I read a political cartoon, I start by identifying the symbols. It is easiest to identify the symbols that are labeled. I can see that "Standard Oil" is written across the monster's body so that helps me identify the monster as a symbol representing Standard Oil, which was an oil company founded in 1870. Next, I look for unlabeled symbols that I recognize. This building looks like the White House, and I think the White House would represent the president of the United States. This other building might represent a state government but I am not really sure. I do not know whether that is really important at this point. But I will keep that in the back of my mind. Next, I want to look for symbolic actions. Do any of you see anything that the monster is doing that might be symbolic?

His question shifts the modeling from himself to the students. When a student offers a response, Mr. Nguyen might ask the student to explain their thinking to the class in order to have them model thought processes for peers.

It is important that during the modeling stage that the teacher model processes rather than outcomes, a subtle but important distinction. In the vignette at the start of the chapter, Mr. Nguyen's interpretation of the political cartoon did not reflect the modeling of a strategy but rather demonstrated the outcome of his strategy use. He explained his interpretation of the cartoon rather than explaining the processes he used to figure out what the cartoon meant. In order for modeling to be effective the teacher must not simply give the answer, but reveal the normally hidden thought processes of those who engage with a strategy. Doing so models for students a strategic way to solve a problem.

Next comes a period of *guided practice*, during which students have an opportunity to engage in the strategy with scaffolding in place. Scaffolding might include such things as peer support, posted reminders about strategic processes, graphic organizers, the teacher or class completing some of the process together, working with simplified texts, or individualized help from the teacher. For example, after this lesson on reading political cartoons, Mr. Nguyen might have displayed a poster in his classroom listing the steps involved in reading a political cartoon (see Figure 4.3). After working together to make sense of the Standard Oil cartoon, he might have chosen a different political cartoon from the same era, perhaps showing a different perspective, giving the students the assignment to analyze it

---

How to Analyze a Political Cartoon as a Historical Source

Step 1: Identify the symbols
- Look for labels
- Identify recognizable symbols
- Attend to subtle symbols
- Consider symbolic speech/captions
- Interpret symbolic actions

Step 2: Identify the relationship between symbols
- Attend to physical location of important symbols
- Interpret actions connecting symbols

Step 3: Interpret the author's methods and message
- Identify exaggerations
- Gather information about the artist
- Consider the artist as a source
- Summarize the artist's stance

Step 4: Critique the cartoon
- Identify your initial reaction
- Consider flaws in the artist's logic
- Consider information the artist has omitted
- Find contrasting opinions
- Offer your critique of the cartoon

FIGURE 4.3 A poster listing steps in analyzing a political cartoon.

in small groups. He could display a poster with the steps used in analyzing political cartoons and provide one-on-one help as needed. This kind of scaffolding is what makes guided practice *guided*.

The final stage of explicit strategy instruction is *independent practice*, during which the teacher assigns students to engage in the target activity without support. Independent practice allows the students and the teacher to assess their ability to engage in literate activities, providing important information about whether students are prepared to move on to more challenging tasks. In the case of Mr. Nguyen's class, he might assign students to find a current political cartoon online and prepare a written analysis.

Providing explicit strategy instruction requires a paradigm shift by history teachers. In contrast to exclusively content-focused lessons, explicit strategy instruction focuses on students' development of skills and literacies. Content knowledge becomes a by-product of students' work with texts like political cartoons. Admittedly, explicit strategy instruction takes time. Certainly, teachers can cover more historical information when they do not take the time to teach skills. However, the trade-off between the coverage of more information, information that 100 years of research shows is not likely to be retained, and the development of historical literacy skills that allow students to actively engage with content is worthwhile.

---

explicit strategy instruction: a method of teaching students to use cognitive strategies that includes (a) direct talk about the strategy, (b) modeling of the strategy, (c) opportunities for students to practice the strategy with scaffolding in guided practice, and (d) opportunities for students to engage in independent practice of the strategy without support

---

Some researchers have developed a systematic method of providing explicit strategy instruction and metacognitive instruction over the course of a school year. They call it the *cognitive apprenticeship*, based on the traditional apprentice relationship between a master craftsman and a novice. In a cognitive apprenticeship, the teacher serves as an expert who gradually turns responsibility for inquiry over to novice students as they gain skills. Early in the year, the teacher does a great deal of direct instruction and modeling, making students aware of both cognitive and metacognitive processes that lead to successful inquiry. Over time, the teacher takes a less active role and provides more *coaching* as students engage in the activity with the teacher giving advice as they work. The objective of cognitive apprenticeships is for students to become independent in the inquiry process, having developed a repertoire of historical thinking strategies and the metacognitive know-how to appropriately use them (De La Paz et al., 2014, 2017).

> *cognitive apprenticeship: the systematic use of strategy instruction, modeling, coaching, and scaffolding by an expert (the teacher) to induct novices (students) into a new discipline, with the expert gradually granting greater autonomy and responsibility to the novice as they become more skillful*

Implicit Strategy Instruction

Another way that teachers can provide literacy instruction is through implicit strategy instruction (Dole, 2000). As mentioned, one of the drawbacks of explicit strategy instruction is the amount of time required to do it well. Another disadvantage is that some of the students may already possess the literacies that the teacher is targeting. For them, explicit instruction is frustratingly slow and tedious. Implicit strategy instruction, on the other hand, is a research-proven teaching alternative based on many of the same Vygotskian notions. It engages students in a target literacy or strategy, but instead of speaking openly about the strategy with students and modeling the strategy, the teacher simply creates an assignment that requires students to engage in the strategy and then explains the assignment to the students. For instance, Mr. Nguyen might create a study guide for students to complete as they analyze the political cartoon. The study guide might give a brief description of the nature of political cartoons and ask students to list the symbolic images that are labeled, list the unlabeled images that they recognize, list subtle symbols, and identify symbolism in speech, captions, or actions. The study guide could walk students through each of the steps of analyzing the cartoon without explicitly discussing strategies.

Alternatively, Mr. Nguyen might design an activity where students are placed in a group where they follow written instructions that guide them through the process of identifying the symbols in the political cartoon. Students then switch to a new group where a new set of instructions walks them through the process of identifying the relationship between the symbols. Students would continue to regroup and move through the steps of analyzing a political cartoon. Regardless of the structure of the activity, the main idea of implicit strategy instruction is that the teacher designs activities that walk students through literate processes without taking a significant amount of class time to talk openly about these processes. Students use the strategies without conscious awareness. The intent is that with repeated exposure to implicit strategy instruction students will discover and begin to internalize literate processes.

> *implicit strategy instruction: an instructional method that involves students in the use of a strategy usually through a structured assignment, without explicit*

discussion of the strategy, with the intent that students will discover the strategy and start to use it on their own

Advantages and disadvantages of implicit strategy instruction exist. On one hand, implicit strategy instruction takes considerably less class time, is often a more familiar teaching approach than explicit strategy instruction, and is faster paced and less tedious than explicit strategy instruction. On the other hand, it takes repeated exposures to target strategies before many students discover and internalize them. Some students might never develop the target skills. And implicit strategy instruction can be more work for the teacher, who must break down literate processes into tasks that students can manage and then design activities that provide scaffolding. Implicit strategy instruction, unlike explicit strategy instruction, is difficult to provide "on the fly" as needs spontaneously arise. Most researchers suggest that a combination of explicit and implicit strategy instruction is the best approach to building students' literacies (Dole, 2000).

Why do you think that the history classrooms that are most successful in developing students' historical literacies include a mix of explicit and implicit strategy instruction?

Potential Misapplication of General Literacy Research

Although general research on literacy provides helpful suggestions for building historical literacies, care must be taken to not overgeneralize the applications. In particular, there are issues with the notion of text in general reading research, strategies in general reading research, metacognition and strategy selection, and a focus on strategy use. I describe each of these four concerns in the following subsections.

What are some of the conditions during which general research on reading and writing might not apply directly to historical literacies?

Texts in General Reading Research

Although there is a growing acceptance of alternative formats of text (Cope & Kalantzis, 2000; Draper et al., 2010), much of the research on reading focuses on traditional print text, that is, words, sentences, and paragraphs. This narrow focus of reading research ignores the vast array of sources that historians use. Furthermore, this research ignores the unique literacies needed to work with these diverse texts. Reading a propaganda poster is a different process than reading a textbook excerpt. History teachers should not feel limited to language-based texts in their search for appropriate resources for teaching historical literacies. Instead, they should consider the wealth of evidence available and carefully choose texts that will meet their objectives.

Additionally, history teachers need to be wary of the classifications of text in general literacy research. In some cases, such classifications may impede historical literacies. For instance, one of the troubling trends in current literacy research, from a historical literacy perspective, is the classification of certain types of texts as *informational texts*. The implication of this classification is that there are texts, such as textbooks, that are intended to transmit information directly to students. Well-intended literacy advocates might suggest reading strategies for working with informational texts that discourage critical thinking, such as *finding the main idea* or *summarizing*. Using these strategies leads students to accept information found in informational texts at face value—an approach that hinders, rather than promotes, historical thinking. Instead, students might read two textbooks and contrast their accounts, considering why the authors chose to present events differently. Such an activity reinforces the idea that historians do not recognize any texts as informational, which is one of the traits that make them gifted readers. Instead, historians view texts as *accounts* or *evidence*, concepts discussed more thoroughly in Chapter 9. Students tend to consider texts as conveyors of information, and the classification of some texts as "informational" might reinforce this view, discouraging healthy skepticism and impeding historical literacies.

Strategies in General Reading Research

In some cases, strategies suggested in general reading research, such as inference making, carry over into work with historical evidence. However, in some cases general reading strategies conflict with historical thinking. For example, text-to-self connections, the personal connections that an individual makes with a text, conflict with the strategy of contextualization that historians use. When text-to-self connections are made in the reading of historical texts, students impose their personal experiences, including modern perspectives and values, on historical people and events. The personal connections might interfere with students' ability to engage in perspective recognition or historical empathy. Thus, what might be considered good reading is bad history. Historical literacies represent a unique skill set that includes some general literacy skills, excludes other general literacy skills, and includes some skills unique to historical inquiry. Because of its uniqueness, the responsibility for building students' historical literacies cannot be passed off to language arts teachers. As stewards of the discipline, history teachers must make sure that schoolwide literacy programs, such as the expectation to read and summarize textbook passages as *informational texts*, do not interfere with historical literacies.

Metacognition and Strategy Selection

General literacy research suggests that reading often proceeds without problems that would require conscious strategy use. Often, comprehension occurs nearly automatically. Good readers constantly monitor their reading and when they experience a comprehension problem they employ a strategy, such as visualization, looking up challenging vocabulary, asking a question, or rereading, in order to restore it. The strategies used to restore comprehension are sometimes referred to as *fix-up strategies*. Historical reading strategies such as sourcing and corroboration should not be considered fix-up strategies. They are not employed only when naturally proceeding comprehension breaks down. But they must be employed constantly and consistently throughout every historical reading task. For instance, a student should not be taught to attempt to read a diary entry and if it does not make sense then look at the source. Instead, students need to understand that the source always matters and that the comprehension, critique, and use of historical texts is impossible without sourcing. Thus, the strategies used in historical inquiry are not selectively chosen fix-up strategies, but they must be constantly used when working with historical evidence.

The Focus on Strategy Use

Some advocates of reading strategy instruction have been criticized because in their efforts to promote literacy strategies they lose focus on what really matters: building students' ability to comprehend and use texts in inquiry and, by extension, apply these same tools when working with social media and online texts. The historical literacy strategies featured in this book must be considered tools to achieve the end of fostering in students the ability to read and reason with historical texts and in the reading they do outside of school. Certainly, creative teachers can find other ways to achieve these same ends. However, how sad it would be for history teachers to focus on building students' ability to use a handful of strategies, such as *sourcing*, without promoting historical thinking, historical problem solving, or argumentative historical writing.

> How does knowing that the literacies associated with historical reading and writing differ from literacies in other disciplines change your view of your role as a history teacher?

Chapter Summary

General research on both literacy and teaching literacy has numerous implications for history teachers who desire to build students' historical literacies. There are some direct applications of literacy research such as with close reading, metacognition—particularly monitoring one's comprehension, vocabulary instruction, and the categorization system of before-, during-, and after-reading strategies. Readers of all texts, including historical texts, should take active roles as code breakers, meaning makers, text users, and text critics. As writers, students take on the roles of planners, composers, and revisers. Teachers can improve students' ability to engage in historical reading, reasoning, and writing through explicit and implicit strategy instruction. Despite the numerous applications of general literacy research to historical literacy, there are enough differences in texts and literacies that history teachers are cautioned to avoid inappropriately apply teaching practices associated with general literacy instruction when engaging students in historical inquiry.

Questions for Consideration

1. · How could teachers improve lesson plans by anticipating the struggles students might have as code breakers, meaning makers, text critics, text users, planners, composers, and revisers? How can a teacher support students in each of these roles?
2. When students struggle during an activity, how might it help teachers if they can diagnose students' difficulties as related to one or more of the roles of readers and writers? What symptoms might a teacher expect to see if a student is struggling as a code breaker, text critic, planner, or in one of their other roles?
3. How might a history teacher respond to schoolwide literacy programs that discourage historical thinking by promoting the use of informational text or highlighting knowledge telling rather than knowledge transforming writing?

Additional Reading and Viewing

- A collection of posters and charts that could be displayed in a classroom as scaffolding to support students' use of historical thinking strategies can be found at the Stanford History Education Group's website at https://sheg.stanford.edu/history-lessons?f%5B0%5D=topic%3A7#main-content#main-content.
- A good review of current research on writing, including the processes of planning, composing (translating), and revising can be found at Hayes, J. R. (2006). New directions in writing theory. In C. A. MacArthur, S. Graham, & J. Fitzgerald (Eds.), *Handbook of writing research* (pp. 28–40). Guilford Press.
- A description of Freebody and Luke's idea of the four roles of the reader is found in this article: Freebody P., & Luke, A. (1990). Literacies programs. Debates and demands in cultural context. *Prospect: Australian Journal of TESOL, 5*(3), 7–16.

• A good overview of the Cognitive Apprenticeship model of instruction can be found in Dennen's work at Dennen, V. P. (2004). Cognitive apprenticeship in educational practice: Research on scaffolding, modeling, mentoring, and coaching as instructional strategies. In D. H. Jonassen (Ed.), *Handbook of research on educational communications and technology* (pp. 813–828). Lawrence Erlbaum.

References

Baker, L. (1984). Spontaneous versus instructed use of multiple standards for evaluating comprehension: Effects of age, reading proficiency, and type of standard. *Journal of Experimental Child Psychology*, *38*(2), 289–311. doi:10.1016/0022-0965(84)90127-9

Baker, L. (1994). Fostering metacognitive development. In H. Reese (Ed.), *Advances in child development and behavior* (Vol. 25, pp. 201–239). Academic Press.

Baker, L. (2002). Metacognition in comprehension instruction. In C. C. Block & M. Pressley (Eds.), *Comprehension instruction: Research-based best practices* (pp. 77–95). Guilford.

Baumann, J. F. (2009). Vocabulary and reading comprehension: The nexus of meaning. In S. E. Israel & G. G. Duffy (Eds.), *Handbook of research on reading comprehension* (pp. 323–346). Routledge.

Beck, I. L., McKeown, M. G., & Sandora, C. A. (2020). *Robust comprehension instruction with Questioning the Author: 15 years smarter.* Guilford.

Cope, B., & Kalantzis, M. (Eds.). (2000). *Multiliteracies: Literacy learning and the design of social futures.* Routledge.

De La Paz, S., Felton, M., Monte-Sano, C., Croninger, R., Jackson, C., Deogracias, J. S., & Hoffman, B. P. (2014). Developing historical reading and writing with adolescent readers: Effects on student learning. *Theory & Research in Social Education*, *42*(2), 228–274. doi:10.1080/00933104.2014.908754

De La Paz, S., Monte-Sano, C., Felton, M., Croninger, R., Jackson, C., & Piantedosi, K. W. (2017). A historical writing apprenticeship for adolescents: Integrating disciplinary learning with cognitive strategies. *Reading Research Quarterly*, *52*(1), 31–52. doi:10.1002/rrq.147

Dennen, V. P. (2004). Cognitive apprenticeship in educational practice: Research on scaffolding, modeling, mentoring, and coaching as instructional strategies. In D. H. Jonassen (Ed.), *Handbook of research on educational communications and technology* (pp. 813–828). Lawrence Erlbaum.

Dole, J. A. (2000). Explicit and implicit instruction in comprehension. In B. M. Taylor, M. E. Graves, & P. vanden Broek (Eds.), *Reading for meaning: Fostering comprehension in the middle grades* (pp. 52–69). Teachers College Press.

Draper, R. J., Broomhead, P., Jensen, A. P., Nokes, J. D., & Siebert, D. (Eds.). (2010). *(Re)imagining content-area literacy instruction.* Teachers College Press.

Durand, E. D., & Harris, W. J. (Directors). (1913). *Thirteenth census of the United States taken in the year 1910, volume 1, population 1910, general report and analysis.* Government Printing Office.

Freebody P., & Luke, A. (1990). Literacies programs. Debates and demands in cultural context. *Prospect: Australian Journal of TESOL*, *5* (*3*), 7–16.

Hacker, D. J., Keener, M. C., & Kircher, J. C. (2009). Writing is applied metacognition. In D. Hacker, J. Dunlosky, & A. C. Graesser (Eds.), *Handbook of metacognition in education* (pp. 154–172). Routledge.

Hairrell, A., Simmons, D., Swanson, E., Edmonds, M., Vaughn, S., & Rupley, W. H. (2011). Translating vocabulary research to social studies instruction: Before, during, and after text-reading strategies. *Intervention in School and Clinic, 46*(4), 204–210. doi:10.1177/1053451210389606

Hayes, J. R. (2006). New directions in writing theory. In C. A. MacArthur, S. Graham, & J. Fitzgerald (Eds.), *Handbook of writing research* (pp. 28–40). Guilford Press.

Hayes, J. R., & Flower, L. S. (1980). Identifying the organization of writing processes. In L. W. Gregg & E. R. Steinberg (Eds.), *Cognitive processes in writing* (pp. 3–30). Erlbaum.

Keppler, U. J. (1904). Next. *Puck, 56,* 1436. http://www.loc.gov/pictures/item/20016 95241/

Langer, J. (1984). Examining background knowledge and text comprehension. *Reading Research Quarterly, 19*(4), 468–481. doi:10.2307/747918

Lee, P. J. (2005). Putting principles into practice: Understanding history. In M. S. Donovan & J. D. Bransford (Eds.), *How students learn: History, mathematics, and science in the classroom* (pp. 31–77). National Academies Press.

Leu, D. J., Zawilinski, L., Castek, J., Banerjee, M., Housand, B. C., Liu. Y,. & O'Neil, M. (2007). What is new about the new literacies of online reading comprehension? In L. S. Rush, A. J. Beagle, & A. Berger (Eds.), *Secondary school literacy: What research reveals for classroom practice* (pp. 37–68). National Council of Teachers of English.

Limpo, T., Alves, R. A., & fidalgo, R. (2013). Children's high-level writing skills: Development of planning and revising and their contributions to writing quality. *British Journal of Educational Psychology, 84*(2), 177–193. doi:10.1111/bjep.12020

Markham, E. M. (1979). Realizing that you don't understand: Elementary school children's awareness of inconsistencies. *Child Development, 50,* 643–655.

McGrew, S., Breakstone, J., Ortega, T., Smith, M., & Wineburg, S. (2018). Can students evaluate online sources? Learning from assessments of civic online reasoning. *Theory & Research in Social Education, 46*(2), 165–193. doi:10.1080/00933104.2017.1416320

McKeown, M. G., & Beck, I. L. (2009). The role of metacognition in supporting reading comprehension. In D. Hacker, J. Dunlosky, & A. C. Graesser (Eds.), *Handbook of meta-cognition in education* (pp. 7–25). Routledge.

Nokes, J. D., & De La Paz, S. (2018). Writing and argumentation in history education. In S. Metzger & L. Harris (Eds.), *Internationalf handbook of history teaching and learning* (pp. 551–578). Wiley Blackwell.

Nokes, J. D., & Dole, J. A. (2005). Helping adolescent readers through explicit strategy instruction. In T. L. Jetton & J. A. Dole (Eds.), *Adolescent literacy research and practice,* (pp. 162–182). Guilford.

Nokes, J. D., & Kesler-Lund, A. (2019). Historians' social literacies: How historians collaborate and write during a document-based activity. *The History Teacher, 52*(3), 369–410.

Ogle, D. M. (1986). K-W-L: A teaching model that develops active reading of expository text. *Reading Teacher, 39*(6), 564–570. doi:10.1598/RT.39.6.11

Paris, S. G., Wasik, B. A., & Turner, J. C. (1991). The development of strategic readers. In R. Barr, M. L. Kamil, P. Mosenthal, & P. D. Pearson (Eds.), *Handbook of reading research,* Vol 2 (pp. 609–640). Longman.

Pearson, P. D., & Dole, J. A. (1987). Explicit comprehension instruction: A review of research and a new conceptualization of instruction. *Elementary School Journal, 88*(2), 151–165. doi:10.1086/461530

Piolat, A., Roussey, J. Y., Olive, T., & Amada, M. (2004). Processing time and cognitive effort in revision: Effects of error type and of working memory capacity. In L. Allal, L. Chanquoy, & P. Largy (Eds.), *Studies in writing, Vol. 13, Revision: Cognitive and instructional processes* (pp. 21–38). Kluwer Academic Press.

Reisman, A. (2012). Reading like a historian: A document-based history curriculum intervention in urban high schools. *Cognition and Instruction, 30*(1), 86–112. doi:10. 1080/07370008.2011.634081

Salahu-Din, D., Persky, H., & Miller, J. (2008). *The nation's report card: Writing 2007 (NCES Document No. 2008–468)*. National Center for Education Statistics. https://nces. ed.gov/nationsreportcard/pdf/main2007/2008468.pdf

Scardamalia, M., & Bereiter, C. (1987). Knowledge telling and knowledge transforming in written composition. In S. Rosenberg (Ed.), *Cambridge monographs and texts in applied psycholinguistics. Advances in applied psycholinguistics, Vol. 1. Disorders of first-language development; Vol. 2. Reading, writing, and language learning* (pp. 142–175). Cambridge University Press.

Stanford History Education Group (2012). *Charting the future of teaching the past.* http:// sheg.stanford.edu/

Taff, R. H. (2014, May 26). Turning Holocaust denial into homework. *Wall Street Journal,* https://www.wsj.com/articles/SB10001424052702303701304579550262302288806

Theide, K. W., Griffin, T. D., Wiley, J., & Redford, J. S. (2009). Metacognitive monitoring during and after reading. In D. Hacker, J. Dunlosky, & A. C. Graesser (Eds.), *Handbook of metacognition in education* (pp. 85–106). Routledge.

Tovani, C. (2000). *I read it but I don't get it: Comprehension strategies for adolescent readers.* Stenhouse.

VanSledright, B. (2002). *In search of America's past: Learning to read history in elementary school.* Teachers College Press.

Vygotsky, L. (1986). *Thought and language.* MIT Press.

Wineburg, S. (2018). *Why learn history (when it's already on your phone).* University of Chicago Press.

Wineburg, S., & Martin, D. (2009). Tampering with history: Adapting primary sources for struggling readers. *Social Education, 73*(5), 212–216.

Wineburg, S. S. (1991). On the reading of historical texts: Notes on the breach between school and academy. *American Educational Research Journal, 28*(3), 495–519. doi:10.3102/00028312028003495

Wollman-Bonilla, J. E. (2001). Can first-grade writers demonstrate audience awareness? *Reading Research Quarterly, 36*(2), 184–201. doi:10.1598/RRQ.36.2.4

5

WHAT IS HISTORY?

Establishing the Need for Historical Literacies in Historical Inquiry

Some children have no idea where milk, eggs, peanuts, or hamburger comes from when they see it in a grocery store. Similarly, most young people have never considered where history comes from. They erroneously believe that history is simply the past—what happened. History just exists. This chapter addresses the need to help students understand history as a human construction, opening the door for them to apply historical literacies as they engage in historical inquiry.

> As you read the following vignette consider how Mrs. Hansen helps students understand the constructed and interpretive nature of history.

During a unit on the Middle Ages in her 10th-grade world history class, Mrs. Hansen decides to conduct a historical inquiry activity during students' study of the Crusades. She determines to give them excerpts from multiple primary and secondary sources showing medieval Muslim, Christian, Jewish, and modern historians' perspectives. She selects a historical question that she feels is simple enough for her students to understand, but complex enough to allow for different interpretations: To what degree were the Crusades motivated by religious or worldly factors? (Mitchell & Mitchell, 2002). She hopes that her class will be unable to reach a consensus on this question and that a discussion, properly structured, will help them become more skillful at using historical evidence. She wants students to develop a more mature understanding of the nature of history, recognizing that historical events are open to multiple interpretations but that through the skillful use of evidence, learners of history can make defensible claims.

Mrs. Hansen searches online and through several anthologies of world history primary sources and finds a number of texts that she decides to use. She discovers several versions of Pope Urban II's speech at the Council of Clermont

DOI: 10.4324/9781003183495-6

in 1095 (Halsall, 2021). She chooses one recorded by Fulcher of Chartres, which she anticipates will sway students toward the notion that the Crusades were religiously motivated. Continuing her search, she finds an account produced by a Jewish witness, Ibn al Athir, describing the Christian conquest of Jerusalem and the subsequent looting (Reilly, 2007). She is confident that this will sway students toward the notion that the Crusades were motivated by greed. She finds a letter written by Stephen of Blois that includes mixed evidence including quotes that suggest a materialistic purpose—"You may know for certain, my beloved, that of gold, silver, and many other kinds of riches, I now have twice as much as you, my love, supposed me to have when I left you"—juxtaposed with claims that he was "prepared to die for Christ" (Perry & Xue, 2001). She finds online a passage written by Beha ed-Din, a Muslim witness of a massacre during the Third Crusade (Richard The Lionheart Massacres The Saracens 1191, 2001). Turning to secondary sources she finds two conflicting historians' perspectives in an anthology on opposing viewpoints in world history (Mitchell & Mitchell, 2002). She continues to search for texts that will allow the class to develop mixed interpretations and to have a healthy discussion on the topic. By the day of the Crusades activity, she has gathered eight sources, which she edits to manageable lengths, copies, and places in folders for 10 groups of students.

Mrs. Hansen has had to lay the groundwork for this lesson since the first day of the school year. Her lesson on the Crusades is just one of many lessons designed to help students develop a more mature understanding of the way historians construct historical knowledge. She believes, for several reasons, that the Crusades activity will allow students to practice constructing and defending evidence-based interpretations. First, she has chosen a question and texts that are likely to foster alternative interpretations among her students—revealing to them that multiple perspectives are possible. Second, she has chosen texts that are packed with quotes and explicit references that support alternative interpretations, allowing students to cite concrete evidence in defense of their claims. She has made certain that the evidence is fairly simple to find within these texts. Third, she has previously taught students strategies for working with historical evidence, such as perspective recognition, corroboration, and contextualization. Fourth, she has created a safe classroom environment where students have been encouraged to test historical ideas with their peers—a classroom where all plausible ideas are subject to an even-handed, peer-led critique.

The 90-minute class period at Mrs. Hansen's school requires some creative lesson planning on her part. She determines to follow the format of the "Document-Based Lesson" (Reisman, 2012). She intends to start class with a mini-lecture to build background knowledge, followed by explicit strategy instruction on the use of evidence to support an interpretation. When students are adequately prepared, she will have them work with the eight documents in small groups for most of the rest of the class period. During this inquiry, students will explore in small groups the packets of documents she has collected. She intends to end the period with a debriefing on the activity, during which students will share their interpretations and evaluate their peers' ideas and she can talk about the way historians construct historical knowledge.

On the day of the lesson, Mrs. Hansen begins class by asking the central question: To what degree were the Crusades motivated by religious or worldly factors? She points out that this is a question that is still debated by historians. She suggests to students that before they start to explore this question on their own, she should give the class some settled facts about the Crusades and the Crusaders—general information that historians agree on. She transitions into a short lecture during which she introduces students to concepts, background information, and vocabulary that will help them understand the documents they read. This lecture is not simply intended to give students information that they will be tested on but to also give them information that will help them comprehend the documents. She ends the lecture by paraphrasing two historians. The first, Mayer (2002), contends that European Crusaders were drawn to Jerusalem because it was the place where Jesus had lived, "the center of a spiritual world," and the thought of it being under the "yoke of heathen domination" was unbearable (p. 156). The second historian, Finucane (2002), argues that "the crusaders, then, were aided not only by their own religious zeal, cupidity, curiosity, and many other motives that pushed them eastward, but also by the turmoil and rivalries among the Moslems themselves" (p. 165). For the first historian, the simple answer to the central question is that the Crusaders were primarily motivated by religious factors. For the second historian, the answer is more complicated.

Next, Mrs. Hansen previews for the class the documents that students will explore. She reminds them about the distinction between primary and secondary sources and encourages them to pay attention to whether each document comes from a medieval Christian, Muslim, Jewish, or a modern point of view. She also points out that these sources come from a variety of time periods, reminding them about the strategies of sourcing and contextualization, both strategies that she has taught students before. She models the use of evidence by thinking aloud, anticipating what a person might say if motivated by religion or by worldly factors. She explains how the documents allow a historian to enter the minds of the Crusaders so they can figure out what the Crusaders were thinking. Because a person's motivation is hidden, historians have to try to figure out why people did what they did using the things they wrote and the traces they left behind as evidence.

Mrs. Hansen explains that in a few minutes, students are going to get into groups of three or four and receive a text set that includes excerpts from eight primary and secondary sources. Along with the texts, she will give each student a graphic organizer that provides a place for them to record information about the source and context, a place to cite evidence that Crusaders were religiously motivated, a place to include evidence that Crusaders were motivated by other factors, and a place to corroborate across sources (see Figure 5.1). "Let me use one of the texts that will be in your text set to show you how

Crusades Documents Analysis Guide

Document	Source and Context	Evidence of religious motivation	Evidence of worldly motivation	Similarities and differences from other texts
Document 1				
Document 2				
Document 3				
Document 4				
Document 5				
Document 6				
Document 7				
Document 8				

FIGURE 5.1 A graphic organizer designed to support students' work with Crusades documents.

I would analyze it. You can follow along with me on your graphic organizer," she adds as she starts passing them out.

Continuing her modeling, she projects on the screen Fulcher of Chartres' record of the speech made by Pope Urban II, saying:

The introduction to this document helps me understand the source. This is a speech the pope made in 1095 that marks the start of the Crusades. However, I know that at that time they did not have audio or video recorders, so I wonder how someone remembered the words of this speech. The pope might have read a written speech, and we might get the record from his written text, but it looks like in this case we find out about the speech from one of the listeners—this is Fulcher of Chartres' record. I wonder how soon after the speech was made that he wrote this down, because I know that over time, he might have forgotten exactly what was said. If I had more time to study this, I would probably look to see whether there were other records made of this speech, or even if the pope's record exists somewhere, but for now I will trust that this is a decent summary of the speech but might not be word for word the way it was given.

Mrs. Hansen continues: "Now I can see on my graphic organizer that there is a place to record source information so I would write . . ." She models how to use the graphic organizer as she fills out the source information. Then she begins to read the text, which is full of religious references. She writes on the whiteboard several specific quotes that she recommends that students write on their graphic organizer under the heading "evidence of religious motivation." She also includes a few quotes that she suggests the students write in the column for "evidence of worldly motivation." As she finishes reading the first document, she points out that within this one text, there appears to be more evidence on the side of the argument that they were fighting for religious reasons. But she reminds students that these ideas came from the pope and that they have other documents to consider.

When Mrs. Hansen is certain that students understand how to complete the assignment, they form groups, and she distributes the text sets. She circulates during the activity providing suggestions, prompting strategy use, modeling historical thinking, and complimenting students on their use of documents. When 15 minutes remain in the class, she asks students to turn their attention to her so that they can talk as a class about what they discovered in their groups. She starts the debriefing by asking students their answers to the central question. She finds that most students think that religious motives were the primary cause but that other factors played a role. Mrs. Hansen draws on the board a continuum with "religious factors" written on one side and "other factors" written on the other side (see Figure 5.2). Students are then encouraged to quickly approach the board and use a marker to plot their position along the spectrum. After they finish, she starts the discussion again. She asks students to consider why there is such a broad range of interpretations when they all used the same evidence. In the discussion that follows she helps students see the constructed nature of their historical interpretations. However, she also helps them see that although multiple interpretations are possible, criteria exist for evaluating interpretations. The most noteworthy criterion is the evidence they used to back up their claims. She helps students see that they must carefully consider the accounts and evidence in order to arrive at a defensible interpretation.

Crusades motivated
by religious factors

Crusades motivated
by worldly factors

| 1 | 2 | 3 | 4 | 5 | 6 |

FIGURE 5.2 An instrument for recording students' interpretations about the causes of the Crusades.

The discussion continues until the bell rings signaling the end of class. Students leave the classroom continuing to argue their interpretation, talking about the evidence that they found that was most compelling.

How can Mrs. Hansen present the graphic organizer in a manner that makes it feel less like a worksheet and more like a resource for collecting evidence and organizing students' thoughts to help them use evidence to make a stronger case for their interpretation?

Developing an Appropriate Epistemic Stance for Working With Multiple Texts

Mrs. Hansen did not use the technical terminology with her students, but one of her primary objectives with this, and several other similarly structured lessons across the school year, is to help students develop a more sophisticated epistemic stance in order to improve their ability to work with historical texts. *Epistemic stance*, as it applies to history, is defined as an individual's understanding of the nature of historical knowledge, where historical knowledge comes from, and how it is constructed. I begin this chapter by considering the nature of historical knowledge, what history is, and how historians construct history. I next explain and explore the concept of epistemic stance, with a focus on two immature stances common among students: objectivism and subjectivism, followed by the sophisticated stance typically taken by historians: criterialism (VanSledright & Maggioni, 2016). Next, I consider instructional methods, like Mrs. Hansen's, using multiple historical texts, intended to help students develop a more mature epistemic position. I conclude with a consideration of methods for assessing students' epistemic stance.

epistemic stance: the mindset that a person approaches history with, based on their understanding of the nature of historical knowledge, where it comes from, how it is constructed, and their role in constructing historical understanding

Historical Knowledge

As you read this section consider the difference between history and the past. Why is it important to understand the distinction when engaged in inquiry?

The past, as it was, is lost to us. We do not know what Stephen of Blois or other Crusaders were thinking or feeling as they gathered their gear and began their trek to Jerusalem. And we cannot ask them. Without the means to travel back in time, we are left with only the remnants of the past—artifacts and writings—to try to make sense of it. The Crusaders left a scattered trail of evidence about their experiences, some of which has survived until today and been discovered by individuals interested in trying to comprehend their actions. Historians' work involves sifting through spotty evidence, searching for clues, interpreting the meaning of those clues, and reconstructing stories about the past. They attempt to write not only interesting stories but also stories that can be justified, given the existing evidence, and are fair to the characters of their stories—individuals who lived under circumstances often very different from our own. History, then, is not "what happened" but is a study of the past, filled with inferences, decisions about significance, interpretations, inclusions and omissions, generally accepted facts, and sometimes even speculations.

history: an evidence-driven study of the past

In spite of historians' efforts to avoid imposing themselves on their understanding of the past, they cannot evade doing so. VanSledright (2002) admits that "[w]e imbue scattered artifacts and historical residue with meaning, and in the process—despite heroic efforts to do otherwise — we concoct more or less evidence-based fictions" (p. 144). Collingwood (1993) argues that "the past is . . . in every detail an imaginary picture" (p. 245). Levesque (2008) agrees that some element of "historical imagination" is necessary as historians reconstruct, reenact, and rethink the states of minds of historical actors. However, VanSledright, Collingwood, and Levesque all acknowledge the role of evidence in constraining and guiding historians' imaginations. For instance, Levesque makes a distinction between historical imagination and pure imagination, arguing that historical imagination is exercised within the parameters of evidence and reality. Historians understand that historical knowledge is influenced by available evidence; by their colleagues' attachments and interests; by limited human perception, both the producers and the analyzers of evidence; and by disciplinary norms. It is impossible to reconstruct things as they really were or to nail down that one story, a naive but common notion held by those who do not understand the nature of historical knowledge. The manner that history is taught in schools perpetuates misconceptions about historical knowledge.

Students' Epistemic Stance

In contrast to historians, students often approach history classes with the idea that history is the past—simply what happened (VanSledright, 2002). And what happened is irrefutable, indisputable, and unquestionable. For instance, there is little doubt that the pope called for a mission against the Muslims in 1095, that Christian Crusaders gained control of Jerusalem in 1099, or that Muslims regained the city shortly thereafter, resulting in a series of crusades over centuries. For students, the whole of history is this type of string of unquestioned events. This way of thinking about historical understanding, the notion that history is simply what happened, is referred to as *objectivism* because students believe that learning history is a matter of gaining information about an objective reality, uncolored by human perception or interpretation. For them, learning history means accumulating information about what happened. They believe that any two individuals studying the same historical topic will eventually arrive at the same narrative. Differences in understandings or interpretations of historical events stem from someone not knowing the facts.

Where do students' ideas about the nature of history come from? VanSledright (2002) suggests that the importance of literal comprehension during the early years of learning to read creates the impression for young students that meaning resides in the text itself. He suggests that by focusing nearly exclusively on skills such as summarizing, retelling, and finding the main idea, students are implicitly taught to uncritically accept the information in texts. As children grow, history teachers, by the methods they use, reinforce an objectivist epistemic stance. When children encounter history textbooks, with their omniscient, voiceless tone, the "reality effect" is strengthened. Students accept that "all the words in the text map directly onto what's real" (VanSledright, 2002, p. 145). Additionally, when teachers exclusively assess students' factual knowledge rather than their ability to apply skills in historical inquiry, students continue to view learning history as a matter of remembering what the textbook or teacher told them. They believe that there is a single narrative and that their role is to remember the narrative long enough to answer questions about it on the test.

> *objectivism: the notion that history and the past are factual realities and that learning history is a matter of finding out and remembering what happened.*

One of Mrs. Hansen's goals for the school year is to help students begin to view historical understanding in more sophisticated ways—to help students reposition themselves epistemologically. In the inquiry that she has designed on the Crusades, she asks students an interpretive question, the kind of question a historian would ask, and gives them conflicting evidence, the types of resources historians would use. She wants students to recognize that history is not simply facts about the past but also includes interpretations, claims, and disputations.

Mrs. Hansen is aware of research that shows that students exposed to conflicting historical accounts often begin to reposition themselves, assuming a *subjectivist* epistemic stance (VanSledright & Maggioni, 2016). Students who view historical understanding from a subjectivist position recognize that multiple ways of interpreting past events exist. They understand that historical sources are extensions of imperfect individuals who have limited perspectives and biases. Because historical interpretation comes from imperfect sources, and multiple interpretations about historical events are possible, students who approach history from a subjectivist stance not only tolerate diverse opinions but accept any historical interpretation as equally valid as well. Because it is impossible to know what happened for certain, any version of the past is as good as any other. History becomes an unsubstantiated guess (Ashby et al., 2005). This way of viewing the past has also been referred to as naive or vicious relativism (Lee, 2005).

---

subjectivism: the notion that because history is interpretive, any opinion of what happened in the past is equally valid

---

The problems associated with subjectivism stem from students' inability to effectively cope with conflicting evidence—from their lack of any "criteria for managing bias" (Reddy & VanSledright, 2010, pp. 2–3). Subjectivism stems from their inability to use and make reasoned judgments about historical evidence. Research has shown that students have a difficult time distinguishing between more and less reliable sources (Ashby et al., 2005; Wineburg, 1991). Because of these challenges evaluating sources, and because students generally accept all information at face value, they experience frustration when exposed to conflicting accounts (Lesh, 2011; Wineburg, 1991). A typical reaction to this frustration is to uncritically accept one of the accounts and accuse the others of lying (Ashby et al., 2005). When pressed to justify their interpretation over others' conclusions, they cannot satisfactorily do so. Aware of their precarious position, they cannot critique interpretations that differ from theirs. They conclude that historical interpretations are simply subjective, with no way to evaluate alternative claims.

With repeated exposure to multiple text activities and with instruction on how to evaluate and use evidence, like Mrs. Hansen provided, students outgrow their subjectivist epistemic stance. However, even as students begin to mature in their historical thinking, they typically use unsophisticated strategies for defending historical interpretations. For instance, some young people tally the evidence for different interpretations and choose the interpretation that has quantifiably more support (Ashby et al., 2005). What is lacking in this approach is a critique of the sources. Historians know that the evidence found in a single reliable source outweighs a great deal of evidence from questionable sources. Although students' score-keeping strategy is flawed, it demonstrates that students are seeking criteria by which a historical interpretation can be evaluated. Given practice and strategy instruction on historians' critical reading strategies, they are poised to assume a *criterialist* epistemic stance—the stance taken by historians.

Historians' Epistemic Stance

> How is the epistemic stance that is assumed by historians different from the epistemic stance of mathematicians, artists, scientists, churchgoers, athletes, and so on?

Historians understand that the instant a pen strikes paper, or fingers hit the keyboard, historical writing is interpretive. Historians commence their research by making interpretive decisions about what is significant enough to study. They understand that there is no single, objective, agreed-on historical narrative that captures the whole of the past. Certainly, widely accepted historical facts do exist. But historical understanding is a work in progress, undergoing continuous reinterpretation and revision based on new evidence, new ways of considering old evidence, and new interests. Furthermore, historians do not accept all interpretations as equally valid. Much historical writing is argumentative, explaining and justifying how evidence has been used to reach conclusions. Historians know the accepted criteria that can be used to evaluate interpretations. They approach historical inquiry with a *criterialist* epistemic stance, judging evidence and interpretations using standards of evaluation—criteria—established by the community of historians. For instance, a historian would consider a number of questions:

- Has evidence that represents multiple perspectives has been used?
- Has the available evidence been carefully evaluated with particular attention paid to its origin?
- Has information found in each piece of evidence been cross-checked using evidence found elsewhere?
- Does the available physical evidence (artifacts), linguistic evidence, anthropological evidence, and scientific evidence corroborate interpretations made using written primary sources?
- How has the historian dealt with evidence that seems to contradict their interpretation?

- Has historical research been situated within the work that other historians have previously conducted?
- Has the historical evidence been contextualized within the period being studied?
- Have alternative, plausible interpretations been given serious consideration?
- Is the historical research fresh, interesting, and significant?

Historians' literacy strategies are keys to answering these questions satisfactorily, meeting the criteria required for establishing a valid and valued interpretation. Interpretations that meet disciplinary standards are superior to interpretations that do not. Yet multiple defensible interpretations are often possible to construct.

> *criterialism: the notion that historical interpretations must meet disciplinary norms based on generally accepted standards of evaluation, principally the manner that evidence has been used*

> What is the difference between an opinion (chocolate ice cream is better than vanilla) and an interpretation (the Crusades were primarily motivated by religious factors)? To what degree do history students need to understand the difference?

Using Multiple Text Activities to Foster a Mature Epistemic Stance

> What can teachers do to help students approach a historical inquiry with a criterialist epistemic stance?

Traditional history instruction does little to foster in students a mature epistemic stance. Overreliance on lectures and textbook reading promotes objectivism. Mrs. Hansen knew that for students to develop a criterialist epistemic stance, she had to engage them in nontraditional activities. Several features of her Crusades activity were designed to foster a criterialist stance. First, to show students that there are often multiple ways to perceive past events, she asked a question that could be answered in multiple ways. Second, she carefully selected the texts that contained disagreements, contradictions, and evidence that could be used to support conflicting interpretations. Her purpose in doing so was to create cognitive dissonance—a feeling of tension or uneasiness that exists when unresolved conflicting ideas are held simultaneously. The texts that she provided demonstrate that there is no simple textbook answer to her question. Furthermore, she chose texts that came from multiple perspectives, including Christian, Muslim, Jewish, and historian points of view, helping students see the effect of perspective on the content of a text.

> cognitive dissonance: a feeling of tension or uneasiness that exists when unresolved conflicting ideas are held in mind simultaneously

Third, knowing that the conflicting evidence might cause some students to adopt a subjectivist stance, Mrs. Hansen chose texts with easily recognizable evidence. She understood that one form of scaffolding is to simplify some aspects of an activity in order to allow deeper thinking about other aspects of the activity. She chose texts in which the evidence practically leapt off the page at students. And she modeled how to use evidence to support a claim, talking about the criteria for judging interpretations and claims. Thus, the activity was designed to help students recognize that although multiple interpretations are possible, not all interpretations are equally defensible. Historians must use evidence to construct and defend claims.

Fourth, the class discussion was laced with mini-lessons on appropriate ways of working with evidence. Students are unable to take a criterialist stance if they do not understand historians' reading strategies, and Mrs. Hansen's mini-lessons were designed to teach, reteach, model, and practice historians' ways of thinking critically about evidence.

Teaching Students Explicitly About Epistemology

> What are some specific ways teachers can help students understand epistemological issues in learning history and how to take a criterialist stance?

Students have a difficult time engaging in historical thinking activities when they do not take an appropriate epistemic stance. However, discussing with students the abstract idea of epistemology can be frustrating—it takes a great deal of time with limited productivity. However, simple means exist for helping students approach the learning of history from a criterialist stance. For instance, students are often familiar with the work of detectives, attempting to piece together the bits of evidence in solving a mystery. They have typically had enough exposure to detective work to assume an epistemic stance appropriate for solving a crime. By framing an activity as a historical mystery and positioning students as history detectives, they can, with relative ease, adopt an epistemic stance that more closely approximates that of a historian (e.g., see Gerwin & Zevin, 2010, and Zevin & Gerwin, 2010). Similarly, teachers can position students as jurors who

interact with evidence about a historical case in order to render a justifiable ver-
dict (Kuhn et al., 1994). In both cases, however, the students may approximate the
thinking that historians use, but they still might be searching for that single narrative that reflects reality. After all, television shows end with detectives or jurors
trying to reach the one correct conclusion. In contrast, historical inquiries may
end with students reaching different interpretations.

A history teacher might instead encourage students to assume a historian's
identity. This would first entail helping students understand the work of historians, what they do, how they search for evidence, and how they use it once they
find it. When students understand the basics of how historians search, analyze,
and write, they can be encouraged to work with evidence like historians do.
Even elementary-age students begin to identify the need for primary source
evidence in judging between alternative interpretations when they have been
taught to assume a historians' identity (Nokes, 2014).

Whether history teachers use the analogy of the detective, the juror, or the
historian, the key elements for promoting a mature epistemic stance must be
that students (a) are active in the process of historical thinking; (b) are allowed to
construct their own independent interpretation of the historical event that might
be different from that of their peers; (c) are aware of strategies that they can use
to effectively weigh evidence; (d) are expected to base claims on evidence; (e) are
supported throughout the process by interaction with peers and the teacher, by
graphic organizers, by teacher and peer modeling, and by checklists to remind
them of effective processes; (f) have regular opportunities to engage in historical
thinking; (g) are not overexposed to textbook accounts as objective information;
and (h) are assessed in a manner that values unique defensible interpretations and
not just knowledge of historical facts.

Teachers need to be aware that students may move back and forth between
epistemic stances, particularly students who are adept at playing the game of
school. During a lecture, they might assume a more objectivist stance, accepting
without question the information presented by the teacher. During a subsequent
document-based activity, they might assume a subjectivist or criterialist stance.
Students should be taught that history is always interpretive in nature, whether
the resources used to learn it are primary sources, the textbook, or the teacher's
lecture. After all, as soon as a teacher begins to lecture, they make decisions about
significance, content, word choice, tone, and perspective. They are not merely
giving "the facts" even during the most factual of lectures.

Assessing Students' Epistemic Stance

Teachers can assess students' epistemic stance along with their content knowledge
and historical thinking skills. Wineburg and his colleagues (2012) have created
a number of simple assessments. For instance, one asks students to evaluate how
helpful a 1932 painting of the "first Thanksgiving," would be in understanding

what happened at what is sometimes considered the first Thanksgiving that took place in Plymouth in 1621. Students who approach the problem from an objectivist stance value the painting and the details that it provides about the event. They view the painting as a conveyor of information ignoring the context of its creation. Students who approach the question from a more mature epistemic stance recognize that the painting reveals little about the original event, instead giving clues about the way the event was remembered in 1932 when it was made. They understand that the painting says more about the artist's purpose in creating it and the artistic styles of that later age. Without some background knowledge of the artist, their research, sources, purposes, and audience, the learner of history does not know how useful the image is in understanding the original event (Wineburg et al., 2012).

Ongoing, less formal assessments of students' epistemic stance can occur during multiple text activities as the teacher listens to and interacts with groups of students. Symptoms of an objectivist stance include looking for the one right answer or story; uncritically accepting the information presented in the sources at face value; experiencing frustration when dealing with contradictory sources; focusing cognitive resources on summarizing, finding the main ideas, gathering facts, and remembering information; expecting classmates to arrive at the same conclusions; and asking the teacher if their interpretation is right. Students approaching document-based activities with a subjectivist stance expend little energy in constructing or defending their interpretation; care little if others' interpretations differ from theirs; fail to justify their interpretation using evidence; discount evidence without valid reason simply because it disagrees with their ideas; change their mind with little resistance if peers suggest an alternative explanation; and wonder how their work with the documents will be assessed, failing to recognize that all interpretations are not equal in quality. In contrast, students who take a criterialist stance think deeply about the central question they are asked; spend significant time evaluating each source; use historians' strategies such as sourcing, corroboration, and contextualization to weigh evidence; defend their interpretations citing specific evidence; change their mind when a peer persuades them using evidence; appropriately discount unreliable information contained in the documents; and engage in argumentative historical writing, using evidence to substantiate their claims and to rebut alternative claims.

Activities for Helping Students Develop a Criterialist Epistemic Stance

What activities can a teacher do to help students understand that they should construct historical understandings from evidence and the thinking involved in doing so?

In my dissertation work, the first lesson taught by the teachers who were teaching students to analyze historical evidence was designed to help students think differently about the way historical knowledge is constructed. The teachers in my study gave students the imaginary scenario of a missing textbook. In the scenario a student's textbook went missing in a history class and the teacher wanted to help him find it. She asked students what they knew about its disappearance. She collected fragmentary and conflicting accounts from the students and tried to piece them together to figure out what had happened to the textbook. In my dissertation work, the teachers made a comparison between the teacher in the scenario and historians who try to reconstruct what happened in the past from the conflicting and fragmentary bits of evidence that have been left behind by those who lived through it.

The Stanford History Education Group created a much better scenario that teachers can use to help students think about the constructed nature of history (see Lunchroom Fight I and Lunchroom Fight II at https://sheg.stanford.edu/history-lessons?f%5B0%5D=topic%3A7#main-content#main-content). In this imagined event, a principal tries to get to the bottom of what happened when a fight broke out in the school cafeteria. In the scenario, the principal collects written statements from the fighters, eyewitnesses, and others. Students can then be given the written statements from the scenario and work like the principal to reconstruct what happened. Familiar with this context, students instinctively recognize the need to pay attention to the perspective behind the accounts of the fight. They identify some parts of some of the statements as exaggerations or outright lies and trust other parts of the same statements. They notice the details that some people leave out of their accounts. Although the term *epistemology* is not included in the lesson, students adopt a criterialist epistemic stance as they assume the identity of the principal. By encouraging students to approach historical inquiries with the same mindset that the principal would use, teachers advance students understanding of the way historians construct knowledge and prepare them to approach historical inquiry with a criterialist epistemic stance.

When I taught high school history, I would sometimes start the school year with an activity designed to help students think about the way historical knowledge is constructed. The activity also allowed the students to become better acquainted with me, their teacher. As class began, I would pull out a garbage bag filled with about 20 carefully selected items taken from my garbage can at home, things like a cold cereal box, two empty gallon plastic milk jugs, an empty gallon paint can, a worn-out pair of running shoes, and a broken toy. I would form students into small groups and have them construct what they could about my life from the evidence. At first their inferences would be basic—you eat cereal, you drink milk, you have children. If I pressed them through questioning, they would come up with more speculative inferences—because the garbage is taken every week and I had two empty gallon milk jugs, I either had a large family or I really like milk. After having them work with these items I would bring out additional items from my garbage can, this time things with writing on them directly related to my life: a to-do list with some items crossed out and others unmarked, a sales receipt from a clothing store, a note I had written to tell someone where I was going, and an electric bill. Students in small groups would use the new written evidence to flesh out the details of my life—not only could they infer that I had a room in the house that was red (from the paint can), but the new evidence revealed that I had painted the room myself and that it was my kitchen (from the to-do list). Throughout the school year, as students would engage in historical inquiries, I could remind them of the way they constructed interpretations about my life from evidence, and this would help them approach future inquiries with a criterialist epistemic stance.

Chapter Summary

Historical inquiries are rarely successful unless students understand that historical knowledge is constructed from evidence, with multiple interpretations possible. A prerequisite for students' historical literacies is that they approach the historical thinking task with the appropriate epistemic stance. The objectivist stance positions a learner to expect a single, objective, agreed-upon historical narrative. Elementary reading instruction, with its focus on the literal comprehension of texts, and traditional history instruction, with its focus on lectures and textbook reading, foster an objectivist stance. Unable to evaluate evidence or claims, the subjectivist stance positions the learner to accept any interpretation as valid. Exposure to multiple interpretations of historical events can lead students to assume a subjectivist stance where interpretations are merely opinions. The criterialist stance, the epistemic stance of historians, positions a learner to recognize that multiple interpretations are possible but that the skillful use of evidence allows one to evaluate interpretations. Frequently assigning document-based activities, providing historians' tools for sifting through evidence, and creating a setting where students can regularly engage in inquiry help them develop a criterialist stance. Teachers can and should assess students' epistemic stance in order to customize historical literacy lessons.

Questions for Consideration

1. Why can historical inquiries be frustrating and counterproductive for students who approach them with an objectivist epistemic stance? What are some of the symptoms of objectivism in history students?
2. To what degree do individuals assume different epistemic stances in different contexts, such as at church, when reading social media, or in different school classes? How might a history student's epistemic stance be different when listening to a lecture than when writing a research paper? Why should a student approach all history activities (lecture, textbook reading, historical inquiry) with a criterialist epistemic stance?

3. Have you had, or do you know of, history teachers who are particularly skilled in helping students develop a criterialist stance? What activities or instruction did they provide that helped students assume such a stance? How can a teacher structure a lecture to promote a criterialist epistemic stance?
4. How could you use professional learning community time to address students' epistemological issues in learning history?

Further Reading and Viewing

- For additional insights on epistemic stance see VanSledright, B., & Maggioni, L. (2016). Epistemic cognition in history. In J. A. Greene, W. A. Sandoval, & I. Bråten (Eds.), *Handbook of epistemic cognition* (pp. 140–158). Routledge.
- For a deep dive into the philosophy of history see Collingwood, R. G. (1993). *The idea of history*. Oxford University Press.
- For powerful lesson materials that help students understand the process of constructing historical understandings see the Stanford History Education Group's Lunchroom Fight I at https://sheg.stanford.edu/history-lessons/lunchroom-fight-i and Lunchroom Fight II at https://sheg.stanford.edu/history-lessons/lunchroom-fight-ii. A poster explaining "What Is History?" can also be found on this site at https://sheg.stanford.edu/history-lessons/what-history-classroom-poster.

References

Ashby R. A., Lee, P. J., & Shemilt, D. (2005). Putting principles into practice: Teaching and planning. In M. S. Donovan & J. D. Bransford (Eds.), *How students learn: History, mathematics, and science in the classroom* (pp. 79–178). National Academies Press.

Collingwood, R. G. (1993). *The idea of history*. Oxford University Press.

Finucane, R. C. (2002). Soldiers of the faith: Crusaders and Moslems at war. Cited in J. R. Mitchell & H. B. Mitchell, *Taking sides: Clashing views on controversial issues in world history, volume 1*. McGraw-Hill/Dushkin.

Gerwin, D., & Zevin, J. (2010). *Teaching U.S. history as mystery*. Routledge.

Halsall, P. (2021). *Internet medieval sourcebook*. Fordham University Internet History Sourcebooks Project. https://sourcebooks.fordham.edu/source/urban2-5vers.asp

Kuhn, D. Weinstock, M., & Flaton, R. (1994). Historical reasoning as theory-evidence coordination. In M. Carretero & J. E. Voss (Eds.), *Cognitive and instructional processes in history and the social sciences* (pp. 377–401). Lawrence Erlbaum Associates.

Lee, P. J. (2005). Putting principles into practice: Understanding history. In M. S. Donovan & J. D. Bransford (Eds.), *How students learn: History, mathematics, and science in the classroom* (pp. 31–77). National Academies Press.

Lesh, B. A. (2011). *Why won't you just tell us the answer? Teaching historical thinking in grades 1–12*. Stenhouse.

Levesque, S. (2008). *Thinking historically: Educating students for the twenty-first century*. University of Toronto Press.

Mayer, H. E. (2002). The Crusades. Cited in J. R. Mitchell & H. B. Mitchell, *Taking sides: Clashing views on controversial issues in world history, volume 1*. McGraw-Hill/Dushkin.

Mitchell J. R. & Mitchell, H. B. (2002). *Taking sides: Clashing views on controversial issues in world history, volume 1.* McGraw-Hill/Dushkin.

Nokes, J. D. (2014). Elementary students' roles and epistemic stances during document-based history lessons. *Theory and Research in Social Education, 42*(3) 375–413. doi:10.10 80/00933104.2014.937546

Perry, J., & Xue, L. (2001). Stephen, Count of Blois and Chartres letter to his wife, Adele. Hanover *Historical Texts Project.* http://history.hanover.edu/texts/lstcrusade2.html

Reddy, K., & VanSledright, B. (2010). *Epistemic change in history education* [Paper presentation]. *Annual conference of the College and University Faculty Assembly,* Denver, Colorado, USA.

Reilly K. (2007). *Worlds of history: A comparative reader* (3rd ed.). Bedford/St.Martins.

Reisman, A. (2012). Reading like a historian: A document-based history curriculum intervention in urban high schools. *Cognition and Instruction, 30*(1), 86–112. doi:10.10 80/07370008.2011.634081

Richard the Lionheart massacres the Saracens, 1191. (2001). *EyeWitness to History.* www. eyewitnesstohistory.com

VanSledright, B. (2002). *In search of America's past: Learning to read history in elementary school.* Teachers College Press.

VanSledright, B., & Maggioni, L. (2016). Epistemic cognition in history. In J. A. Greene, W. A. Sandoval, & I. Bråten (Eds.), *Handbook of epistemic cognition* (pp. 140–158). Routledge.

Wineburg, S., Smith, M., & Breakstone, J. (2012). New directions in assessment: Using Library of Congress sources to assess historical understanding. *Social Education, 76*(6), 290–293.

Wineburg, S. S. (1991). On the reading of historical texts: Notes on the breach between school and academy. *American Educational Research Journal, 28*(3), 495–519. doi:10.3102/00028312028003495

Zevin, J., & Gerwin, D. (2010). *Teaching world history as mystery.* Routledge.

6

EXPANDING HISTORICAL LITERACIES
Critically Reading Many Genres of Evidence

Authentic historical inquiries often require students to investigate multiple pieces of evidence from a wide variety of genres. By the time you finish reading this chapter you should have a better idea how a teacher can help students engage in historical inquiry and craft a historical argument by critically evaluating and synthesizing interpretations from a range of genres of evidence using a plethora of strategies. You should also be able to help students apply these same critical reading strategies during online reading and for responsible social media use.

> As you read this vignette think about the multiple levels of analysis required when engaged in historical inquiry, such as considering why a photographer may have cropped a photograph in a certain way, and why webpage designers may have used a specific photograph rather than other photos.

Mrs. Powell is planning a lesson on the spread of Islam for her 10th-grade world history course. She wants students to consider the ability of Islam to adapt to diverse global cultures as it spreads, a feature that has contributed to both its status as a world religion and its profound influence on world history. In addition to her content objectives, Mrs. Powell has several literacy objectives. Knowing that there is an aesthetic element of literacy, she wants to help students gain a deeper appreciation for the beautiful art and architecture of Islam. Furthermore, she wants students to use architecture, particularly architectural *function* and *form*, as historical evidence. Finally, she wants to help students become more skilled in internet research, with the ability to synthesize across hyperlinked multimodal online texts.

Mrs. Powell has been building up to this lesson all year. Some of her lessons have focused on working with photographs. Other lessons have taught individual

DOI: 10.4324/9781003183495-7

strategies such as sourcing or corroboration. Students have practiced perspective taking, have identified unique strategies for reading historical letters, and have been taught strategies for conducting online research. A lesson on mosques will give students a chance to apply a variety of strategies to study a range of genres of evidence during a single lesson. She believes that a good way to apply the literacy lessons taught all year would be to have students work online to explore mosques from around the world.

Mrs. Powell makes sure the class computers are charged, planning to spend about 45 minutes of the 90-minute period with students investigating mosque architecture using the internet. In order to illustrate Islam's adaptability, she decides to have students explore the features of mosques that are common across cultures as well as different features showing cultural distinctions. She thinks that students can learn about Islam by considering the functionality of the common features of mosques, such as minarets, courtyards, and arcades. She also thinks that the activity will dispel some stereotypes of Islam—such as that it is unyielding or backward. She creates a list of mosques that she will require students to study, but she also intends to give students some freedom to explore mosques of their own choosing.

Mrs. Powell's lesson will focus on the essential question: "In what ways did Islam remain consistent with its origins and in what ways did it evolve as it spread?" She creates a study guide that students will complete while working on their computers (see Figure 6.1). The study guide includes four columns. In the first, students will draw a sketch of the mosque or cut and paste an image they find online. In the second, they will write a brief physical and historical description of the mosque. In the third column, students will list the unique features of the mosque, with a special consideration of cultural influences on its *form*. In the fourth column, students will keep track of common features that they find across mosques from around the world, with a special consideration of the *function* of the common architectural elements. To model the thinking involved in "reading" mosques, Mrs. Powell decides to fill in the first row of the study guide for the students before making copies.

In preparation for class, Mrs. Powell browses the internet, finding images and descriptions of mosques that blend cultural and traditional elements of Islam. She decides to start the lesson by modeling an analysis of the Mosque of Sultan Ahmed in Istanbul, Turkey. She likes this mosque because it shows the influence of the Byzantine Empire, which her students have recently studied. She thinks that they will be able to make a connection between this mosque, built in the former Byzantine capital, and the Hagia Sophia, a Christian cathedral built during Byzantine times. She takes notes in the cells of the first row of the study guide to show students how they can use it to collect evidence. Continuing her online search, she finds several other mosques that she would like students to explore. As she browses, she discovers that Wikipedia provides information on many of the mosques. She spends some time considering how she can model the effective

Exploring Mosques from around the World

Your assignment is to consider the questions: "What do mosques suggest about the ability of Islam to adapt to different cultures? What impact would this have on the spread of Islam?" Before you can answer these questions you will need to explore some mosques from around the world. This study guide will help. On the study guide below, quickly draw a sketch of the mosque in the first column, give its name and write a brief physical and historical description in the second column, make a list of unique features of the mosque in the third column (trying to pay attention to how it captures the local culture), and make a list of common features of mosques from around the world in the fourth column. You will have to complete the third and fourth columns after looking at several of the mosques. When you run out of room on this side of the paper, make the same columns and continue on the back.

Sketch	Name/Description	Unique Features (function and form)	Common Features (function and form)
	Mosque of Sultan Ahmed: Istanbul Turkey, 1609-1616, built during the Ottoman Empire, called "Blue Mosque" because of tiled interior	Byzantine style flat domes and half domes—create spacious interior for large gathering	6 minarets for calling to prayer, rectangular courtyard with arcade for prayer and fountain to cool
	Great Mosque of Cordoba:		
	Ibn Tulum Mosque:		
	Great Mosque of Jenne:		
	Mashkhur Jusup Central mosque:		
	Cheng Hoo mosque, Indonesia:		

FIGURE 6.1 A graphic organizer to support studentsis' internet research on mosques.

use of sites like Wikipedia. Mrs. Powell also contemplates the sequence that she wants students to view the mosques, determining to have students view more traditional mosques first and to later view mosques that reflect a local culture in their architectural forms.

On the day of the activity Mrs. Powell explains the assignment before having students pick up a computer. She passes out the study guide, reads the instructions to students, and models how to conduct the online research. She points out that she has completed the first row of the study guide for the students and projects her computer screen, demonstrating her process for researching the mosque. With students watching and listening to her think-aloud, Mrs. Powell visits Wikipedia and several other sites, explaining how she decides what to write on the study guide as she works. Modeling the strategy of *click restraint* (McGrew et al., 2019), she scrolls down the page of search results and talks through her thought process in choosing which site to explore first. Once arriving on a relevant website, she shows how she identifies its source. Although she has practiced this search before, she thinks aloud as if this were her first time seeing these sites, even following some false leads to model how students might respond to websites that turn out to be irrelevant. She uses the term *lateral reading* to describe the strategy of investigating a website by opening new tabs and leaving the site to find out about its creator from an unaffiliated source (Breakstone et al., 2021). She demonstrates that it is appropriate to jump from pictures to written descriptions and video clips, with each source helping in different ways. Mrs. Powell recommends that they look at more than one picture before drawing the sketch because each photograph shows a different perspective. "Don't get in such a big hurry that you miss really looking at the pictures of the mosques and enjoying them. Some of the world's most beautiful buildings are mosques," she suggests.

Mrs. Powell expects that the last two columns of the graphic organizer will be the most difficult for the students to complete because they involve a synthesis of evidence across multiple mosques. She encourages students to attend to the *form* and *function* of the mosques in those last two columns, explaining that the form has to do with the style of the mosque and the function relates to the practical purpose of certain features.

The class enjoys having Mrs. Powell do their work for them—what she calls modeling—so the students ask her to model the process again with the second mosque on the study guide, the Great Mosque of Cordoba. With the class observing, she explores a few websites, looks at some of the pictures, and, leaving a particularly striking image on the screen, gives students a few minutes to sketch the mosque. As she continues browsing, she reads that after the Muslims were driven from Cordoba, a Christian cathedral was built in the courtyard of this mosque. As Mrs. Powell reads one of the written descriptions, she finds a few words that are unfamiliar to students. She models the use of an online dictionary to quickly learn that a *mihrab* is a niche in a mosque that points toward Mecca, the direction Muslims face when they pray.

After a few minutes of exploring, she finds some contradictory information across two sites. "Wait a minute," she says.

> I just read that the cathedral built in the middle of the mosque adds to its beauty and uniqueness. Now I read that it destroys the original purpose and beauty of the mosque. How am I going to deal with these disagreements? Why would two texts that are simply describing the mosque give different information?

She feigns confusion, jumping back and forth between the two sites until students help her discover that one webpage was created by a travel agency trying to attract tourists who might be interested in both Muslim and Christian edifices. The other celebrates Islam, speaking happily about the time when Spain was controlled by Muslims and criticizing the Christian takeover. From the tone of the writing, Mrs. Powell and the class infer that the second website was produced by a Muslim source. The students notice that the photographer picked angles to take unflattering photographs that make the cathedral an eyesore, very different from the pictures shown on the travel agency website. Mrs. Powell draws students' attention to the familiar strategies they are using—corroborating across multiple websites and sourcing—using the source of the website to understand and evaluate the site's content. She asks them to fill in the second row of the study guide then calls on a few students to share what they have written. She also models filling in the last two columns of the study guide now that she has studied two mosques and can make comparisons. Students add to their papers as they hear their peers' ideas and as they listen to Mrs. Powell talk through her thinking.

By now students are getting antsy to start working on their own. Mrs. Powell gives a few more instructions, then students form small groups and go to work. Mrs. Powell circulates and gives help. She watches as students jump from search engine to website and from picture to written description. A few of them discover videos related to mosques. She sees students looking at the same pictures of the assigned mosques: the Mosque of Ibn Tulun, the Great Mosque of Jenne, the Mashkhur Jusup Central Mosque, and the Cheng Hoo Mosque. Eventually she sees students looking at pictures of mosques that she has never seen before. Students alternate between browsing on the internet and working on their study guides. Occasionally, a student raises their hand and Mrs. Powell gives help. Some problems stem from their inefficient search strategies and the challenges of creating a brief summary that synthesizes, in their own words, information found in multiple pictures and written descriptions.

The students put their computers away with about 15 minutes left for debriefing. Mrs. Powell knows that this discussion is when much of the teaching and learning related to this activity will occur. She helps students reflect on the similar features of all the mosques, regardless of location, and draws from students' inferences that they have made about the importance of communal prayer within Islam, a practice facilitated by many of the architectural features. She also guides students as they reflect on the differences that they observed, helping them see the local cultural influences on the architectural styles. Through her questioning and their experiences researching online, students observe that the local cultures often influence the architectural forms. Students refer to and add to their study guides throughout the debriefing. Mrs. Powell returns to the original question that started their study: "In what ways did Islam remain consistent with its origins and in what ways did it evolve as it spread?" Mrs. Powell guides the students as they consider how the central tenets of Islam, such as prayer, remained constant as Islam spread to regions of the world as different as Mali, China, and Indonesia. However, peripheral elements of Islam were adapted by converts to increase local appeal. Introducing students to the vocabulary of *syncretism*, which they have already discovered conceptually, she talks generally about the tendency of world religions, such as Islam, to adopt local customs to appeal to people of diverse cultures.

> How does Mrs. Powell's lesson balance her guidance with students' exploration in a way that encourages them to actively construct their own interpretations of the spread of Islam?

Critical Intertextual Analysis With Multimodal Texts

> Why does critical intertextual analysis represent the gold standard of historical inquiry? To what degree are the critical reading strategies of historical literacy important outside of historical inquiry?

The dispositions and skills of historical literacy taught by Mrs. Powell and demonstrated by the students, preview many of the literacies described in the subsequent chapters of this book. Students worked with a wide variety of types of texts, such as photographs, videos, written descriptions, webpages, and architecture using a range of evaluative strategies, such as sourcing, corroboration, and close reading. VanSledright (2002) called this type of strategic work with multiple texts *critical intertextual analysis*. Critical intertextual analysis represents the gold standard of historical inquiry, a process only possible for most young people when they are given a great deal of support. In this chapter, I (a) define *critical intertextual analysis* in terms of online and historical reading, (b) review the distinction between general and historical literacies, (c) contrast intratextual with intertextual reading, and (d) reflect on the challenges of reading multimodal texts such as the Internet sites that blend and link written descriptions, images, video, and sounds.

Defining Critical intertextual Analysis

> Why is the ability to engage in critical intertextual analysis such a vital skill in the 21st century?

Twenty-first-century reading is unlike the reading of previous generations. The availability of information through the internet has created literacy experiences that are increasingly responsive to the reader, are richly intertextual, integrate reading and writing processes, and place unprecedented demands for critical reading on the reader (Nokes et al., 2020). Individuals have nearly immediate access to a vast array of resources. Online, one can move from written text to photograph to music to virtual field trip to video by scrolling down a page, clicking on a link, or opening a new tab. As Mrs. Powell demonstrated, unfamiliar terms, like mihrab, can be conveniently looked up in seconds, without distracting from the flow of study. Evidence found in one text can quickly be cross-checked against other sources. Biographies of "experts" can be verified by a few clicks of the mouse, streamlining sourcing. The nature of the internet creates a setting in which reading is not linear (i.e., the reader starting at the first word and proceeding to the last) but involves numerous jumps, side trips, backtracking, neglected opportunities, false leads, and distractions. In short, the internet makes it simple to move from text to text, which requires readers to make quick judgments about the relevance and utility of diverse sources—to engage in what some have called *click restraint* (McGrew et al., 2019).

So, in some ways, online reading is a completely new experience. However, in other ways the movement from text to text that occurs online is not very different from the way historians investigate the past—the internet just makes it occur more quickly and conveniently. Historians have always had to make judgments about the relevance and utility of different sources, with the accompanying jumps, side trips, backtracking, neglected opportunities, false leads, and distractions. Any historian would agree that none of these frustrations originated with the internet. Furthermore, historians have been observed to pause from reading one document, set it down, and pick up another, when confronted by discrepancies between texts (Wineburg, 1991). Thus, in the absence of hyperlinks, historians have always made their own hypolinks, forging less convenient connections across available resources. Checking and cross-checking evidence across multiple sources, referred to as corroboration, is a basic strategy employed by historians. So in some ways, the internet is a setting in which all readers can and should read more like historians, creating an even greater need for advancing students' critical reading abilities by building their historical literacies.

In his study of fifth-grade students, VanSledright (2002) identified characteristics of mature historical reading—or at least as mature as fifth graders could muster. He labeled students' most sophisticated historical reading and reasoning processes, which were rare, *critical intertextual analysis*. Internet reading makes the ability to engage in a critical intertextual analysis essential for all readers. It can be helpful to consider each of the components of critical intertextual analysis somewhat independently.

---

critical intertextual analysis: the evaluation of multiple pieces of evidence simultaneously, using each text to enhance the assessment of each of the other texts in the process of constructing an understanding or interpretation.

Critical Analysis

How does critical intertextual analysis differ from the kind of reading that is common in conventional history classes?

An analysis is *critical* when the reader approaches the task with an appropriate epistemic stance, understanding the nature of historical study and the historian's role. Critical students understand why contradictory accounts of an event exist, and they have cognitive tools to sift through contradictions. Critical analysis requires students to use sourcing, corroboration, contextualization, and perspective recognition to determine the reliability of various sources. Critical analysis requires a healthy skepticism. Students do not blindly accept information in the text as it is presented but view texts as accounts and traces representing human perspectives, imperfect evidence to be used according to their discretion and purposes. Similarly, students do not blindly reject a source, like Wikipedia or their textbook. When they approach any source with skepticism and the proper strategies for analysis, students can find utility in all kinds of texts, even Wikipedia. Critical thinking requires a sophisticated worldview, avoiding the oversimplification that is typical of textbooks and traditional history instruction. Critical analysis involves the strategies, dispositions, and habits of mind promoted in this book.

Intertextual Analysis

Furthermore, critical intertextual analysis is *intertextual* because the reader makes frequent connections across different texts, as Mrs. Powell's students did in their online reading. In intertextual analysis, the reader moves from text to text looking for agreement and disagreement that allows them to gain a more mature understanding or construct a more nuanced interpretation. Intertextuality requires exposure to multiple texts. Furthermore, it requires readers to use strategies to make connections between them. However, research suggests that students have a difficult time synthesizing across multiple texts. For instance, decades ago, Spivey and King (1989) found that instead of creating a synthesis, students tended to use a single source for the bulk of their writing, with little independent thinking. At best, they simply summarized, and at worst, they plagiarized the source. When pushed to include other sources, students threw in a token quote or two from other texts, but there was rarely a real synthesis of ideas across texts. Little has changed in the decades since their study. Stahl et al. (1996) made other discoveries about students' intertextuality in their observations of secondary students working with historical texts. They found that students noticed similarities across texts, and used the similarities to create strong summaries. However, discrepancies between the texts went unnoticed or were ignored. The researchers concluded that students have a difficult time dealing with conflicting evidence as they create syntheses from multiple sources. Making connections across texts is not a natural or easy process for most students.

Again, the reading of historians presents a model for history teachers to consider in supporting students' critical intertextual analysis. Historians do not simply search for a handful of sources to summarize and cite. They conduct exhaustive searches for evidence, leaving no relevant archive unexplored. They review every text that might inform their research. Although this type of exhaustive intertextual research is impractical in history classrooms, teachers can facilitate intertextuality by providing multiple texts or requiring the use of multiple sources for students' research. However, simply providing or requiring multiple sources does not guarantee intertextual reading—history teachers must support intertextuality.

Mrs. Powell included several measures that were intended to help students engage in critical intertextual analysis. First, students both compared and contrasted photographs and written descriptions of mosques found on websites. Students could not complete the assignment without considering mosques' common and unique characteristics, engaging in the thinking associated with intertextuality. She created a graphic organizer that required students to record the similarities and differences they noticed. Along with making students accountable for their work, the graphic organizer served as a reminder of the need to both compare and contrast across sources. Additionally, the study guide provided a place to record the physical description of mosques, allowing students to later move back and forth between the mosques, searching for similarities and differences.

Second, Mrs. Powell's selection of mosques was done purposefully to illustrate the concepts she was trying to teach and to facilitate intertextual analysis. Knowing that students have a harder time dealing with discrepancies than with similarities, she required students to study mosques with obvious differences. For example, the mosques in Mali and Indonesia that she assigned students to explore contrasted sharply with those in Spain and Turkey, making it easier for students to find differences. Third, Mrs. Powell modeled the kind of thinking that she wanted students to do. She modeled effective ways of verifying information found on Wikipedia with other sources. She revealed her thought processes in making judgments about which sites to enter and which links to select. She demonstrated the need to use multiple sites and how to identify and investigate the source of a site through lateral reading. Additionally, she had students model their thought processes for their peers. When a student made an insightful comment, her normal response was the question: "How did you figure that out?" Her purpose in doing so was to have those students who were skilled in their use of texts reveal for their peers the strategies that they used.

Fourth, Mrs. Powell gradually removed the scaffolding students received as the activity continued. She completed the first row of the study guide for students so that their attention could be focused entirely on her as she modeled her reading and reasoning processes. She made the students complete the second row of the study guide as she and other students modeled their reading and reasoning processes. Students then moved into small groups where they analyzed four other mosques that Mrs. Powell had purposefully selected. The graphic organizer continued to support their thinking. Finally, students ventured out on their own, finding and choosing mosques to explore, and creating their own graphic organizer on the back of their paper. Thus, as the assignment continued, Mrs. Powell withdrew the support that she had initially provided until students were comparing and contrasting mosques with relatively little support.

Analysis

In addition to being critical and intertextual, a critical intertextual analysis involves analysis. Historical analysis integrates several of the literacies described in the subsequent chapters of this book. Historical analysis revolves around the use of evidence to create reasoned, defensible interpretations. Texts serve as that evidence. Additionally, historical analysis calls for the making of inferences. During the class discussion, class members inferred that one of the websites was produced by a Muslim source based on the generous description of the mosque and the history of Muslim rule. Using texts as evidence and making inferences are key elements in historical analysis. Critical intertextual analysis is an application of each of the historical literacies described in greater detail in the subsequent chapters of this book. Students engaged in such analysis use a wide variety of genres of evidence, such as the architecture, web pages, and photographs used in the inquiry Mrs. Powell designed.

General and Historical Literacies

What have your former teachers done to prepare you to engage in critical intertextual analysis? What more could they have done?

In developing the notion of critical intertextual analysis, VanSledright (2002) tracked the progress of the fifth-grade students. One of the differences between less mature and more mature readers was their purposeful use of strategies. The poorest readers were not strategic in their reading or thinking. For example, some students unstrategically follow the rule, "never use Wikipedia," without recognizing Wikipedia's usefulness under the right conditions. In contrast, average readers used what VanSledright considered general literacies, such as using topic sentences to identify main ideas. Using general strategies to produce a summary is a useful strategy but it involves little critical analysis. In contrast,

VanSledright observed that the most skilled readers employed historical literacies. For instance, they use sourcing and corroboration in analyses that were evaluative, with students less likely to accept information without critical thought. With Mrs. Powell's guidance, students in the vignette applied historical literacies. For instance, they identified a website as coming from a pro-Muslim source based on the tone of the writing. They acknowledged the photographer behind the photographs, considering how the photographer's purpose influenced the content, lighting, and cropping of the picture. In order to engage in critical intertextual analysis, a student must employ critical reading strategies like those used in the study of history. General literacies, such as summarizing, are insufficient.

Intratextual and Intertextual Reading

> As you read this section consider your tendencies as a reader. Do you tend to make connections *without* texts, *within* texts, or *across* texts?

Several researchers have investigated the way readers make connections both within and across texts. One of the most interesting studies was conducted by Hartman (1995), who observed eight proficient readers think aloud as they read five texts. He paid particular attention to the links that they made as they read. Hartman found that readers approached a text, or series of texts, with certain attitudes about their role as a reader. Some readers resisted the author's meaning, instead imposing their own interpretation based on their background and expectations, which were sometimes only tangentially related to the reading at hand. They approached texts with their opinion firmly in place, discounting evidence that might suggest a different interpretation, and latching on to evidence that confirmed preconceived ideas. They made connections *without* the text. Other readers made numerous connections *within* the text in order to comprehend the author's meaning, removing themselves, their experiences, and other texts from the comprehension process. The connections they made between two or more elements within the same text, such as inconsistencies in the author's argument, are referred to as *intratextual*. And readers whose purpose is to merely comprehend the author's message tend to focus solely on intratextual connections.

Hartman (1995) found that the most skillful readers were less focused on merely comprehending the author's literal message but instead synthesized ideas from multiple texts. They considered several plausible interpretations based upon their own background knowledge and the content of other texts. He labeled these readers' connections, which most closely mirror those required in historical inquiry, as *intertextual*. In conclusion, Hartman suggested that the way a reader views their role influences their tendencies to make connections and interpretations without, within, or across texts. And it is the across-text intertextual connections that are valued in historical thinking.

In VanSledright's (2002) tracking of fifth-grade students' historical thinking, he used this same distinction between intratextual and intertextual reading. He suggested that some individuals progress through phases of intratextual reading, which involves general literacies used to comprehend individual texts, into intertextual reading, making connections across texts. Like Hartman, he suggests that intratextual analysis is a less sophisticated way of analyzing and evaluating text. In intratextual analysis, a reader focuses on a single text, comprehending, summarizing, and, to a lesser extent, evaluating its content. Judgments of the text are made based on its content, whether it makes sense, whether it is interesting, and its level of details rather than whether the source is reliable or by how it compares to other texts. In contrast, readers skilled in historical analysis engage in an intertextual analysis. To evaluate a text they use other texts, information about the source, and the content. Exposure to one text enlightens students' experience with subsequent texts. For instance, as strong readers encounter a piece of evidence, they gain a richer understanding of the context, and they use this contextual understanding to consider the sources and content of other pieces of evidence. At the highest levels of intertextual analysis, readers evaluate a text's validity based on its source and how it compares to other texts. VanSledright concludes that as students engage in critical intertextual analysis they systematically construct and revise their interpretation of the event they study based on evidence in multiple texts.

Challenges of Multimodal Texts

The students in Mrs. Powell's class did not gain their ability or tendency to engage in critical intertextual analysis in a single lesson on mosques. Rather, the development of such complex historical literacies is the result of regular opportunities to engage in historical inquiry accompanied by instruction on critical reading strategies. Students have worked with photographs and web pages before. Mrs. Powell has modeled sourcing and corroboration in many other lessons. She has taught students about the way historians build interpretations. She has explained to students that historians do not merely memorize history, but they build it using evidence, each adding their own unique perspective and interpretation, tempered by the standards of the discipline. Teachers like Mrs. Powell understand that the effort required to nurture students' ability to engage in critical intertextual analysis, practiced during historical inquiry, will prepare young people with the skills needed to thrive in the age of the Internet and social media.

Many literacy tasks—exploring the internet, skimming a textbook passage, and posting something on social media—involve learning with multiple genres of text. One of the themes repeated throughout this book is that each genre of text brings with it unique challenges for students in their roles as code breakers, meaning makers, text users, and text critics. Websites can represent particularly difficult reading because they often combine on a single page multiple genres such as written text, photographs, artwork, video, and audio texts. In addition, websites often bring together material from different sources that vary in reliability. Authors of web pages can produce attractive and entertaining sites that misrepresent, confuse, or distort historical events. Standards for publishing on the Internet are nonexistent, leaving internet readers vulnerable to the misinformation and disinformation that is a readily available online (Nokes, et al., 2020; Wineburg, 2018). The use of multimodal internet sites to answer historical questions requires students to use a variety of historical literacies and can better prepare young people to make sense of social media and online sites.

However, there is a growing body of research that suggests that experience with historical inquiry is inadequate for preparing young people to critically analyze websites related to current political controversies. For example, McGrew et al. (2018) compared the online reading of university students, academic historians, and professional fact-checkers as they evaluated websites dedicated to providing information about controversial topics. Most of the students, presumably intelligent digital natives who had been raised on the internet, used weak strategies for judging the credibility of webpages. Many of the historians, models of critical intertextual analytical thinking, struggled in a manner similar to the students. They had trouble finding and investigating the source of a website even when they were inclined to do so. Only the professional fact-checkers were able to efficiently discern and investigate the source of a website and use that information to evaluate its reliability.

What did professional fact-checkers do differently from the students and historians? Researchers labeled one of their strategies for investigating the level of bias in a website *lateral reading* (McGrew et al., 2018). Lateral reading involved gathering some information about the website's source from the website, then leaving the site, opening new tabs on the browser, and using a search engine to find out what they could about the people and sponsors and interests behind the webpage using unaffiliated webpages. They wanted to learn about the source of the website from someone other than the source of the website. Wikipedia proved to be one particularly useful resource for efficiently gathering information. With impressive efficiency, the professional fact-checkers could identify the special interest groups behind online information. They could then use that information the way historians use sourcing with documents to evaluate content. Few historians or university students used lateral reading, instead remaining on the page and using features as superficial as the text font to make judgments about the information they found (McGrew et al., 2018). Throughout a school year, a teacher like Mrs. Powell will model strategies, like sourcing, that are useful for reading primary source documents and model related strategies, such as lateral reading, that students can use for internet research.

At times a teacher might choose to provide explicit instruction on the decoding of a challenging genre of text. However, such instruction can be tedious and time-consuming. It would be a mistake to take a significant amount of class time during a single class period to provide explicit instruction on the decoding of multiple modes of texts, such as photographs, architecture, and blueprints. Mrs. Powell sensed this and chose to focus her instruction on the reading of the function and form of buildings. She purposefully chose not to focus much energy on students' struggles in reading photographs, blueprints, or videos found on webpages. Certainly, she took opportunities to model critical analysis of all texts when opportunities arose. And she celebrated students' critical analysis of photographs and the text on a webpage, asking them to make their thinking processes explicit for the class. However, her focus during this lesson was on teaching students to use architecture as historical evidence, and her explicit instruction focused on teaching those literacies. Mrs. Powell understands that the teaching of strategies for reading multiple modes of texts is a yearlong process and cannot yield expertise after a single lesson.

Chapter Summary

Internet literacies, like historical literacies, involve searching for sources, making judgments about their relevance and validity, seeking corroborating evidence, synthesizing across multiple genres of text, pursuing false leads, updating one's interpretation, and, in the end, constructing a defensible understanding of the topic of study. Both effective internet study and historical inquiry require a critical intertextual analysis of evidence. Critical intertextual analysis in history involves sifting through multiple pieces of evidence, synthesizing across different texts and using history-specific literacies to develop and defend an interpretation of a historical event. Critical intertextual analysis online involves cross-checking information found on one website with other sites, paying attention to similarities and differences, and seeking information about sources through lateral reading.

Questions for Consideration

1. Why do you think it is important for a teacher to model for students how to find and work with online historical sources? How can a teacher make a clear connection between historical literacies and online reading?
2. How are strategies like sourcing, corroboration, contextualization, and critical analysis different when working with different genres of evidence such as photographs, journal accounts, a sales receipt, prehistoric artifacts, song lyrics, or a feature film? What strategies are particularly important in online research?

3. How might teachers coordinate the teaching of historical literacies and online reading strategies for a school year and across multiple school years to maximize students' development of the vast range of literacies needed for historical inquiry and civic engagement?

Additional Reading and Viewing

- John Green has created a 10-episode "crash course" series to teach skills for online reading including *Navigating Digital Information* at https://www.youtube.com/watch?v=pLlv2o6UfTU&t=37s, *The Facts about Fact Checking* at https://www.youtube.com/watch?v=EZsaA0w_0z0&t=38s, *Check Yourself With Lateral Reading* at https://www.youtube.com/watch?v=GoQG6Tin-1E, *Who Can You Trust* at https://www.youtube.com/watch?v=o93pM-b97HI, *Using Wikipedia* at https://www.youtube.com/watch?v=ih4dY9i9JKE, *Evaluating Evidence* at https://www.youtube.com/watch?v=hxhbOvR2TGk, Evaluating Photos and Videos at https://www.youtube.com/watch?v=p7uvqb8fcdA, *Data and Infographics* at https://www.youtube.com/watch?v=OiND50qfCek, *Click Restraint* at https://www.youtube.com/watch?v=5tw44SkkXQg, and *Social Media* at https://www.youtube.com/watch?v=M5YKW6fhIss.
- The concept of critical intertextual analysis is introduced in VanSledright, B. (2002). *In search of America's past: Learning to read history in elementary school.* Teachers College Press.
- For an overview of the strategic reading process in history, see De La Paz, S., & Nokes, J. D. (2020). Strategic processing in history and historical strategy instruction. In D. L. Dinsmore, L. K. Fryer, & M. M. Parkinson (Eds.), *Handbook of strategies and strategic processing* (pp. 195–215). Routledge.
- For current research on students' struggles with online research see McGrew, S., Breakstone, J., Ortega, T., Smith, M., & Wineburg, S. (2018). Can students evaluate online sources? Learning from assessments of civic online reasoning. *Theory and Research in Social Education, 46,* 165–193. doi:10.1080/00933104.2017.1416320.
- For current research on students' struggles with social media see McGrew, S., Ortega, T., Breakstone, J., & Wineburg, S. (2017). The challenge that's bigger than fake news: Civic reasoning in a social media environment. *American Educator, 41*(3), 4–9, 39.

References

Breakstone, J., Smith, M., Connors, P., Ortega, T., Kerr, D., & Wineburg, S. (2021). Lateral reading: College students learn to critically evaluate internet sources in an online course. *The Harvard Kennedy School Misinformation Review 2*(1). doi:10.37016/mr-2020-56

De La Paz, S., & Nokes, J. D. (2020). Strategic processing in history and historical strategy instruction. In D. L. Dinsmore, L. K. Fryer, & M. M. Parkinson (Eds.), *Handbook of strategies and strategic processing* (pp. 195–215). Routledge.

Hartman, D. K. (1995). Eight readers reading: The intertextual links of proficient readers reading multiple passages. *Reading Research Quarterly, 30*(3), 520–561. doi:10.2307/747631

McGrew, S., Breakstone, J., Ortega, T., Smith, M., & Wineburg, S. (2018). Can students evaluate online sources? Learning from assessments of civic online reasoning. *Theory & Research in Social Education, 46*, 165–193. doi:10.1080/00933104.2017.1416320

McGrew, S., Ortega, T., Breakstone, J., & Wineburg, S. (2017). The challenge that's bigger than fake news: Civic reasoning in a social media environment. *American Educator, 41*(3), 4–9, 39.

McGrew, S., Smith, M., Breakstone, J., Ortega, T., & Wineburg, S. (2019). Improving university students' web savvy: An intervention study. *British Journal of Educational Psychology, 89*(3), 485–500. doi:10.1111/bjep.12279

Nokes, J. D., Draper, R. J., & Jensen, A. P. (2020). Literacy and literacies in the modern age. In J. Hartford, & T. O'Donoghue (Eds.), *A cultural history of education: Modern age.* Bloomsbury.

Spivey N. N., & King, J. (1989). Readers as writers composing from sources. *Reading Research Quarterly, 24*(1), 1–14. doi:10.1598/RRQ.24.1.1

Stahl, S. A., Hynd, C. R., Britton, B. K., McNish, M. M., & Bosquet, D. (1996). What happens when students read multiple source documents in history? *Reading Research Quarterly, 31*(4), 430–456. doi:10.1598/RRQ.31.4.5

VanSledright, B. (2002). *In search of America's past: Learning to read history in elementary school.* Teachers College Press.

Wineburg, S. (2018). *Why learn history (when it's already on your phone).* University of Chicago Press.

Wineburg, S. S. (1991). On the reading of historical texts: Notes on the breach between school and academy. *American Educational Research Journal, 28*(3), 495–519. doi:10.3102/00028312028003495

PART II

Strategies, Habits of Mind, Concepts, and Texts

Historians use a vast array of types of evidence to investigate the past. As described in Part I, they use written records as well as physical evidence. Depending on the questions they ask they may find evidence in television programs, magazine ads, video recorded speeches, music, artwork, photographs, diary entries, song lyrics, military uniforms, facial hair styles, modern nomadic societies, or just about anything. And while there are some historical thinking strategies that are useful in working with almost any type of evidence, each type of evidence also brings some unique challenges. The chapters in Part II of this book address the issues that students might face in working with different types of evidence.

Part I also introduced the reader to several strategies, habits of mind, and concepts that shape historians' reading, thinking, and writing while engaging in historical inquiry. To try to teach all these skills to students in a single lesson would be impossible. Instead, teachers often dedicate inquiry lessons to building a particular strategy or habit of mind, such as healthy skepticism. Other strategies are not excluded from the inquiry—students are encouraged to use historical literacies throughout all inquiries. However, a teacher might find it productive to provide explicit or implicit strategy instruction that focuses on a single strategy from time to time. Just as a basketball coach might diagnose a weakness in his players and design a drill to address that weakness, history teachers might plan instruction that addresses one needed strategy. But also like a basketball coach intersperses such drills with opportunities to scrimmage, history teachers do not overuse explicit or implicit strategy instruction.

The chapters in Part II of the book each focus on a specific strategy, habit of mind, or concept associated with historical inquiry. Each chapter also includes ideas for helping students work with a specific type of evidence. The pairing of strategies and evidence does not imply that certain strategies are only used with certain types of evidence. To the contrary, all the strategies discussed throughout the chapters of this book should be used flexibly, with all of the types of texts. Specifically, Chapter 7 describes methods for helping students use historians'

DOI: 10.4324/9781003183495-8

most basic strategies: sourcing, corroboration, and contextualization, while analyzing primary source evidence. Chapter 8 focuses on teaching students to use
observations and inferences using artifacts and physical evidence. In Chapter 9 I
present a list of metaconcepts, ways of thinking about historical methodologies
as I discuss helping students work with visual historical evidence. Chapter 10
is about historical empathy, including perspective recognition and caring, and
addresses the challenges for students in working with historical fiction. Chapter
11 focuses on healthy skepticism and academic humility, two habits of mind that
historians exhibit. The chapter also addresses instruction that helps students work
more skillfully with history textbooks and secondary sources. In Chapter 12 I
warn about the threat of reductionist thinking to historical inquiry and discuss
how a teacher might help students conduct inquiries that involve audio and
video recordings. Chapter 13 introduces instructional strategies that support students' argumentative historical writing and speaking, using numbers and statistics
as evidence. Finally, in Chapter 14 I remind readers that the strategies and texts
explored independently in Part II should be used in concert in historical inquiry.
I give some final advice about overcoming the barriers that might prevent teachers from applying the ideas presented in this book in their classrooms.

By the time you have finished reading the chapters of Part II you should be
able to do the following:

- Identify a range of "texts" that are useful as evidence in historical inquiry
  and consider the value of, and importance of teaching about different types
  of texts such as artifacts, numbers, journal entries, photographs, song lyrics,
  motion pictures, speeches, etc.
- Describe and demonstrate historians' strategies for working with evidence
  and accounts, particularly sourcing, corroboration, and contextualization.
- Explain why acceptance of the notion of "informational text" or expository
  text discourages historical thinking. Discuss how a teacher can nurture historical literacies with "informational texts" like textbooks and tradebooks.
- Distinguish between substantive concepts and metaconcepts (second-order
  concepts) and list and explain several important metaconcepts in historical
  thinking, including *account*.
- Describe instructional methods that can nurture students' ability to work
  with artifacts, visual evidence, and other "traces" (particularly the skills of
  observing and inferring).
- List forms of quantitative historical evidence and describe strategies that a
  teacher can use to help students think historically with quantitative evidence.
- List forms of visual/audio/video historical evidence, increasingly available
  during the 20th century, and describe strategies that a teacher can use to
  help students use it in historical inquiry.

- Describe strategies that a teacher can use to help students engage in historical thinking with historical fiction (novels, movies, picture books, etc.) and consider criteria for selecting appropriate historical fiction.
- Explain the characteristics of effective historical writing instruction (including supporting students' argumentative reading, appropriate writing prompts, mentor texts, scaffolding, feedback, etc.).
- Anticipate the potential barriers to teaching in a way that nurtures historical literacies and develop a plan for overcoming these barriers.

Of course my ultimate objective is having readers prepared to nurture students' historical literacies as they engage in historical inquiries.

7

USING CRITICAL READING STRATEGIES WITH PRIMARY SOURCES

How do you know whether to believe something that you read on social media? How can a person verify what they hear on the news? In this chapter, you will read about strategies that are useful for analyzing primary source historical evidence and for thinking critically about the messages you receive on social media and the things you read online.

As you read this vignette think about how Mr. Dunn's lesson follows the steps of explicit strategy instruction. Think about the other steps Mr. Dunn takes to support students' work with primary sources.

Mr. Dunn is teaching a unit on the European colonization of North America in an 11th-grade U.S. history course. He wants to show students the way many cultures from Europe, America, and Africa blended in the colonies. He thinks that students have misconceptions about the relationship between individuals from the three continents. He wants students to understand that Europeans, Native Americans, and Africans were all active agents of change. He thinks about the best possible texts that he might use. He could show a clip from the Disney movie *Pocahontas* to illustrate the interaction, but he is afraid that it might reinforce stereotypes and misunderstandings. The textbook has a long section about the English colonies, but it doesn't portray Native Americans or Africans as meaningful contributors to colonial life, merely as victims. He wonders whether primary sources exist that students could work with that illustrate the complex relationships. He researches online and discovers John White, a Nipmuck Indian, who died in London, England, in 1679 (Pulsipher, 2018). He decides that John White, formerly known as John Wampus, has an interesting story that is intertwined with major colonial events such as King Philip's War. He finds relevant, interesting primary and secondary sources on John White and determines that

DOI: 10.4324/9781003183495-9

White's story will provide an engaging case study through which students can explore Native American and English relationships in the early colonies. He will bring the story of Africans into the narrative in a different lesson.

Mr. Dunn establishes the following objectives for a pair of lessons on John White and Native American/English relations in the British colonies:

1. Students will explore the complex, continuously changing relationship between Native Americans and European colonists in North America, considering examples of both cooperation and conflict and viewing both groups as active agents of change.
2. Students will differentiate between primary and secondary historical sources and develop strategies, including sourcing and corroboration.

Mr. Dunn prepares a collection of documents that includes several primary and secondary sources: records of court proceedings, a petition by a Native American group, a letter written by King Charles II, and carefully selected excerpts from a historian's analysis of John White's life. He creates a legible transcript of one document that is particularly challenging to read. He notices the difficult vocabulary in another and writes the definition of unfamiliar terms in the margins of the text for students to refer to. He rewrites a third document, simplifying the language so that students will be able to comprehend it.

Mr. Dunn spends two 45-minute class periods investigating this topic with students. On the first day, he assesses students' prior knowledge. He begins class by engaging students in a short writing activity and discussion of the Indigenous people and English settlements of New England. He asks students to write about the possible ways that Indigenous peoples might have reacted to the arrival of colonists. He uses the writing and subsequent discussion to discover students' background knowledge, their misconceptions, and their ideas about the 17th-century American colonial frontier.

Once he has a sense of students' background knowledge, Mr. Dunn lectures for several minutes on the human and physical geography of colonial New England. He points out, for example, that there were many different Indian nations living in the region, some of them allied with each other and some of them enemies. He also teaches that nations varied in size and strength, with some posing a grave threat to the fledgling colonial settlements and others more vulnerable to the aggression of colonists and rival nations. He reminds students that there were different reactions within Native American groups to the arrival of the colonists, just as there were differences in opinion among the colonists about the best ways to interact with Native Americans. As his lecture ends, he informs students that they are going to do a case study of one Nipmuck Indian who viewed the arrival of the colonists as an opportunity to build his own personal wealth, adopting a dual Native American/English identity to negotiate the sale of much Native American land to English colonists. In the end, he was viewed as a traitor by both groups.

Mr. Dunn introduces students to John White, by giving some basic facts and by revealing a few puzzling pieces of historical evidence that directly confront students' misconceptions. Students are told, for instance, that his original name was John Wampus (sometimes spelled Wompowess or Wompas), but it was later fully anglicized to John White. Students are surprised to hear that he attended Harvard and later resided in a house in Boston. Mr. Dunn clarifies that a handful of Native Americans were admitted into Harvard in the 1660s and 1670s in hopes that they would become Christian ministers who would convert their people to both Christianity and to English culture. Mr. Dunn tells students about one of John White's schoolbooks from Harvard. The inscription "John Wompowess his booke" appeared on the front inside cover. On the opposite page near a sketch of a meetinghouse in different handwriting was written, "John Savage his meeting-house the king of it I say." Mr. Dunn explains,

> You probably thought vandalizing textbooks was a new activity, but it appears that it has been going on for a long time. It looks like John White wrote his name in his book, and someone else wrote an insult on the opposite page. There's a story in these two sentences that might help us to understand John White's life within the context of Native American and colonist interaction.

Mr. Dunn brainstorms with students the people who might have written this insult and what they meant by calling John Wampus "John Savage." A few students voice their opinions. Mr. Dunn leaves the question unanswered, acknowledging the plausibility of several of the students' ideas, including the speculation that it might have been written by a colonist or an Indigenous person, either of whom could have been disgusted with John White's efforts to live in both the White and the Indigenous world.

Mr. Dunn explains that students will look at evidence to reconstruct a better picture of John White, his life, and his context. As Mr. Dunn lectures, he continues to ask questions.

> Why might a Native American have taken an English name? How did he gain admission to Harvard? Why was he in London at the time of his death? Why did his own people, in 1677, petition the Massachusetts magistrates not to allow him to represent them in future land dealings? What did his life suggest about general trends in Native American/English relations?

Students add to the list of questions:

> Did other Native Americans feel like he was selling out his people? How did the White people feel about Native Americans like him, who adopted English lifestyles? Did they welcome them into their society? Did the English ever marry Native Americans?

As students speak, Mr. Dunn writes their questions on the board. After creating a list of questions, Mr. Dunn announces that he has gathered documents that they will use to explore their questions.

Before Mr. Dunn gives students a text set, a collection of documents related to a historical topic gathered and prepared by a teacher to be used by students during an inquiry, he talks to them about historical evidence.

> Imagine that you observed a traffic accident on your way home from school today, and police officers took your name and phone number and said they might call later to find out exactly what happened. Imagine that you went home from school and told your mother about the accident. Later, a police officer calls your home. Would the officer want to talk to you or your mother?

In the discussion that follows, Mr. Dunn helps students distinguish between primary and secondary sources. He introduces students to perspective by asking,

> What if one of your friends was the driver of one of the cars involved in the accident. Would the police officer want to talk with you or your mother? Does the perspective of the source of the information matter?

Mr. Dunn makes a connection between investigating an accident and investigating historical controversies. He points out that in both cases, the investigator must sift through evidence that might be incomplete or contain contradictions. He discusses with students what an investigator might do when faced with contradictory evidence, talking explicitly about historians' strategies of sourcing and corroboration. After discussing each strategy briefly, he passes out the text sets and says,

> Let me show you what I mean. Take a look at the first document. Historians always start by looking at the source. It's called sourcing. Down at the bottom of the first page I can see that it was written by Jenny Pulsipher in 2018. What do I know about it immediately?

When students flounder a little, he restates the question, "Is this a primary or a secondary source?"

After students acknowledge that it is a secondary source, one suggests that it must not be very reliable—less reliable than a primary source. Mr. Dunn agrees that primary sources have some advantages over secondary sources but explains that secondary sources can also be valuable if they come from a dependable source.

"How can we find out about this source? Can we trust that Pulsipher is an expert?" he asks. Eventually, with Mr. Dunn's guidance, the students do an

Internet search to find out about Pulsipher. They discover that she is a history professor who specializes in English and American Indian relations during colonial times, recently publishing a book on Wompas (Pulsipher, 2018). After reaching the conclusion that the text comes from a reliable secondary source, students express confusion. Are secondary sources a good way to study a topic or not?

Mr. Dunn talks about the messy process of historical inquiry, helping students understand why historians and history books sometimes disagree with each other. He explains that historical inquiry involves a great deal of interpretation even after careful investigation. Even if Pulsipher's interpretations make sense, when others look at the evidence, they might reach different conclusions or might be able to build on her ideas. So it is still worthwhile to investigate primary sources even after looking at a reliable secondary source. He explains that by finding out about the author of primary or secondary sources they can have a better idea of how they can use the text. He reminds them that paying attention to the source is called sourcing. He explains that another way they can evaluate a text is by comparing what it says to other documents, a strategy known as corroboration.

Mr. Dunn passes out a graphic organizer that he designed that has a place to record source information, a brief summary of the source, and how the source compares to other sources students have investigated (see Figure 7.1). He encourages students to make notes in the cells related to the first text and to continue filling it out as they evaluate the other texts. He points out that also included in the graphic organizer is a place to take notes on evidence as it relates to their original research questions, and space to record new questions that arise as the sources are explored. The notes students take will help them keep track of the evidence they have found and where it came from, a process that would otherwise become unmanageable after students have looked at several pieces of evidence.

Mr. Dunn models the process of sourcing and corroboration with one more text before class ends. The students examine together a petition written by John Wampus to Charles II, king of England, explaining his plight. Mr. Dunn reminds students to first consider the source. He spends the rest of the period leading the class in a discussion of the source, corroborating the story it tells with the first text they read, and reflecting on the context. As the bell rings, he collects the text sets and dismisses the class.

The next day Mr. Dunn forms students into small groups and assigns them to take most of the class exploring their text set, which includes a variety of primary sources and carefully selected excerpts from secondary sources. He reminds them to use sourcing and corroboration to make sense of the texts. While students work, he circulates, listens to their discussions, makes suggestions, and asks questions.

With about 10 minutes left in class he calls for the students' attention and leads the class in a discussion of the answers they found to the questions they asked the day before. He reminds students about some of their misconceptions and asks

Name _____

John Wampus Inquiry

Instructions: You will receive several primary sources and secondary sources related to John Wampus. Choose one of the following questions, or come up with your own, and use this graphic organizer to manage the evidence you find in the texts you analyze. On the back of this form write your interpretation of the answer to the question and explain your interpretation using evidence from the texts. Circle one of the following questions that you will focus on or write your own:

- Why was Wampus in London at the time of his death?
- Why did his own people, in 1677, petition the Massachusetts magistrates not to allow him to represent them in future land dealings?
- What did his life suggest about general trends in Native American/English relations?"
- "Did other Native Americans feel like he was selling out his people?
- How did the White people feel about Native Americans like him, who adopted English lifestyles? Did they welcome them into their society?
- Your own question: _____

Doc	Source Information	Summary	Comparison to other texts
1			
2			
3			
4			
5			

FIGURE 7.1 A graphic organizer for supporting students' work with primary sources.

them to use evidence from the primary and secondary sources to correct those misconceptions. During the discussion some students point out that some of the Native Americans, like John White, may have been glad that the colonists were there. White took advantage of the colonists to become wealthy.

After a brief discussion of their other misconceptions, Mr. Dunn encourages each group to report on what they found about one of their original research questions. As the bell rings, students leave class with a more sophisticated understanding of Indigenous and White colonial relations, and they have had an opportunity to evaluate primary and secondary sources using historians' strategies of sourcing and corroboration. Mr. Dunn understands that this has been only one chance to practice and that he will need to continue to remind students about these important historical literacies and provide opportunities to practice throughout the school year.

> Teachers can cover more content in a lecture than they can in a document-based lesson like Mr. Dunn's lesson on John White. What are the other disadvantages and advantages of lessons like Mr. Dunn's? Do the advantages outweigh the disadvantages?

Helping Students Learn With Primary Sources

As described in the introductory chapters of this book, written records provide the foundation of historical inquiry, and primary sources, such as those gathered by Mr. Dunn, are historians' preferred format of written record. However, as also reported in previous chapters, students have a difficult time working with primary sources the way historians do. They typically view texts—all texts, of any format—as conveyors of information. Their focus is on reading, remembering, and regurgitating. In contrast, Mr. Dunn wanted students to adopt a criterialist epistemic stance, using documents as evidence in building historical understanding. Mr. Dunn knows that familiarity with historians' strategies would give students the tools needed to evaluate documents as evidence. This chapter discusses (a) historians' strategies of sourcing, corroboration, and contextualization and how they can be taught; (b) helping students read primary sources; (c) how a teacher can help students critique and use primary sources to construct historical interpretations; (d) ideas for selecting appropriate primary sources; (e) supporting students writing with primary sources; and (f) assigning students to produce primary sources.

Historians' Strategies of Sourcing, Corroboration, and Contextualization

Even in inquiry driven classroom settings students are not likely to be able to work well with primary sources unless they have the strategies to do so. Fostering debate and discussion without giving students tools for working with evidence creates a potentially chaotic environment where unsubstantiated claims, voiced with passion, overwhelm reasoned, evidence-based interpretations. In Chapter 3, I introduced historians' strategies and habits of mind for working with historical sources. As described there, historians' approach all sources with skepticism, consider the source of each text, determine the reliability of various sources through corroboration, maintain an openness to alternative interpretations, place themselves in the physical and social context of the document's creation, and fill in gaps in the evidence with reasonable speculation. Mr. Dunn's lessons included instruction on two of these strategies: sourcing, and corroboration, which, when added to contextualization, make up the three most basic of historians' strategies (Baron, 2012; Leinhardt & Young, 1996; Nokes & Kesler-Lund, 2019; Shanahan, et al., 2011; Shanahan & Shanahan, 2008; Wineburg, 1991).

Sourcing

Why is sourcing, finding out where the information came from, important not only for reading primary sources but also for reading online material and social media?

Students must be taught that when they begin to explore an unfamiliar text, they should look first at its source. A reader cannot comprehend, critique, or use a text as historical evidence without establishing where it came from. When sourcing, students should identify the type of document they are working with and adjust their reading accordingly. For instance, after identifying a document as a letter, a student should attend to the signature, to identify who wrote it; the greeting, to identify the recipient; and the date, to see when it was written. Other types of texts elicit different reading procedures. Students should always consider whether the author had firsthand knowledge of the event. If investigating an event that pits two sides against each other, such as a battle, a political campaign, a sporting event, or a trial, the position of the author is important. The author's social standing, educational background, and even physical location during an event can influence the content and value of an account. For example, a person holding public office may have more to gain or lose by the way an event is portrayed. Students should think about the intended audience and its impact on a text. For instance, a letter John Wampus wrote to King Charles II would have a very different tone from the graffiti in the textbook. Much of this difference is a result of the intended audience. Students should consider the purpose of a text and look at the timing of its creation. Was it produced immediately following an experience, or years later, when some of the details might have been forgotten but a broader perspective of the event might have been gained?

When considering the source, there are few absolute rules that can be taught to students. The value of the record is based on the questions being asked, the range of sources available, and the content of the text. At times, private writing, such a journal entry, is more valued than public records, such as a sworn deposition, and sometimes it is not. At times, close personal involvement in an event yields the richest resources, and sometimes distance creates a more valuable perspective. In spite of the flexibility required in sourcing, all historians demonstrate that the use of any evidence should begin by considering its origins (Wineburg, 1991). Mr. Dunn recognizes the challenges of sourcing for young students. Whereas students want firm rules, such as "primary sources are always more reliable than secondary sources," he suggests that the evaluation of multiple texts is a messy business and that multiple strategies must be used flexibly.

Some researchers promote what they call a *sourcing sequence* that teachers guide students through in order to thoroughly consider the creator of a piece of evidence (Reisman & Fogo, 2016). The sourcing sequence involves *closed sourcing*, finding out basic facts about the source from the information provided in the document or by conducting a quick internet search. During closed sourcing, the reader identifies the author's name, the date the evidence was produced, what genre of evidence it is, where it was published, who the intended audience was, and any other relevant information about the circumstances surrounding its creation. Information needed for closed sourcing is often included before or after the document. Next, readers engage in *open sourcing*. During open sourcing, the reader uses the information gathered during closed sourcing to make inferences about the strengths and limitations of the source. The reader anticipates what the document might include, even before reading it. The reader reflects on the author's potential biases, strengths, and the unique insights they bring to the historical question. During open sourcing, the reader starts to consider how much they will trust and use the document as they prepare to defend their interpretation of the event they study.

> *sourcing sequence: a technique taught to students to evaluate a piece of evidence by first engaging in* closed sourcing—*noticing and gathering information about the author, then engaging in* open sourcing—*making inferences about the strengths and weaknesses of the evidence based on what is known about the author and the circumstances surrounding the creation of the evidence*

Corroboration

The graphic organizer that Mr. Dunn prepared not only reminds students to pay attention to the source of the text but also encourages them to use corroboration to consider multiple pieces of evidence in the light of each other. Corroboration, which some teachers call cross-checking, helps students determine the validity and reliability of sources. Texts with descriptions that are substantiated by other sources are deemed more reliable. Texts with content that is contradicted by other sources present a greater challenge. Differences between texts might include *omissions* of specific details by one or more source, *unique inclusions*, or outright *factual disagreement*. Students must be taught to notice and seek explanations for discrepancies, which can often be found through sourcing. A simple explanation for discrepancies might be discovered, such as the different physical locations of eyewitnesses. In such cases, two divergent accounts might both be judged reliable. At times, the differences between accounts might require students to make judgments between opposed texts. In such cases, sourcing can help. Mr. Dunn's graphic organizer is intended to help students corroborate by asking them to record similarities and differences between the content of texts.

Contextualization

Students must learn to consider the physical and social context of a document's creation to help them comprehend, critique, and use it as evidence. This strategy of imagining a historical setting has been labeled *contextualization*. Important things to be kept in mind when engaged in contextualization include the *geography* surrounding an event; the *time of day* or *season of the year* that the event occurred; the cultural and *social setting* of the event, such as traditions or etiquette; a *biographical awareness* of participants, such as the tendencies of a military commander or politician; a *linguistic awareness* of the changing meaning of words across time; and a *historiographic awareness* of how an event has been perceived by different historians at different times. Some research suggests that students have a harder time using contextualization than they do sourcing or corroboration (Nokes et al., 2007; Reisman, 2012), which is not surprising given their lack of background knowledge. Not wanting to overwhelm students with too many new ideas in a single day, Mr. Dunn did not provide explicit instruction on the strategy of contextualization during this lesson. However, he used the story of John White to help students understand the complex social context of the interaction between Indigenous people and colonists—an example of implicit strategy instruction. He will spend time explicitly teaching about contextualization later in the school year.

One instructional method used to support students' thinking about the context of an event is a graphic organizer with a small circle within a larger circle (see Figure 7.2). The larger circle represents the *big-c context*—long range events and conditions that influenced an event. Social values, common ideas about race, technological resources, governmental structures, and scores of other contextual factors make up the big-c context of an event. The inner circle represents the *little-c context*, events and conditions that had a more immediate impact on an event. The time of day, weather conditions, the people present, specific government policies, events immediately preceding an event, and many other factors are part of the little-c context. Students can use the graphic organizer to reflect and take notes on the way both long-range factors and immediate factors created a context that influenced an event and the evidence associated with it.

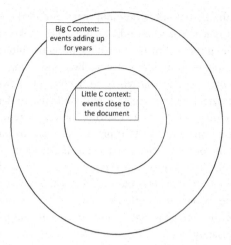

FIGURE 7.2 A graphic organizer for students to record the Big-C context and the Little-C context.

Other researchers have found additional instructional methods that help students engage in contextualization. For example, van Boxtel and van Drie (2012) found that providing background knowledge and explicitly teaching students about contextualization yielded better results than just explicit instruction. Background knowledge was required to imagine historical contexts. And Baron (2016) found that if students' background knowledge related to different time periods was leveraged appropriately using visual images, students imagine historical contexts better. Specifically, images related to clothing styles, means of transportation, and home styles shown on the top of a study guide or document helped students imagine the historical period during which the document was created.

Teaching Historians' Strategies

In spite of historians' nearly universal use of these three strategies, Mr. Dunn understands that history students do not instinctively engage in sourcing, corroboration, or contextualization. It is up to him to help them develop these historical literacies as part of his overall goal of helping them develop critical reading strategies. He understands that teachers can increase students' ability to work well with primary sources by explicitly teaching these strategies (Nokes et al., 2007), so he frequently builds historical literacy mini-lessons into his curriculum.

Mr. Dunn provided explicit strategy instruction on sourcing and corroboration. He openly discussed the strategies with students, naming them, elaborating on the processes used in implementing them, and suggesting why the strategies were effective and important. He modeled both sourcing and corroboration for the students. He thought aloud as he questioned one of the sources in the text set—pointing out that it was a secondary source. He walked them through the process of researching the authority of a source using the internet. He also modeled how two strategies, sourcing and corroboration, could be used together. Additionally, he provided a setting where students could practice with support. The graphic organizer provided a gentle reminder that students needed to pay attention to the source and facilitated corroboration by reminding students to make direct comparisons across texts. It provided a place to summarize the content of each text in order to create a record that students could cross-check against other sources. Furthermore, working in groups allowed students to think aloud, get feedback on their ideas, and observe others use strategies. His circulating during group work allowed him to support the use of sourcing and corroboration, further use the language of these strategies, and praise students who used them appropriately.

In addition to explicit instruction on sourcing and corroboration, Mr. Dunn provided implicit strategy instruction on contextualization. Although not mentioning the strategy by name, his questions prompted students to immerse themselves in the context of the time and his short lecture gave students background knowledge that was useful in doing so.

Types of Primary Sources

As you read this section consider why it matters whether a piece of evidence is categorized as an account or a trace?

Researchers categorize primary sources as either *accounts* or *traces*, suggesting that different reading strategies take on increasing importance when working with one or the other type of evidence (Seixas, 2016). The following breakdown can help students analyze evidence. *Accounts* are intentionally produced narratives of an event. Accounts are primary sources when a person tells a story of an event that they observed directly. Accounts are secondary sources when someone retells about an event they did not witness. Textbook accounts are not primary sources, but they are accounts nonetheless because textbook authors intentionally produce narratives of events. Accounts can take on a wide variety of formats, such as a telephone conversation, during which someone tells a friend about an event; a sketch drawn by someone who wants to remember the geographic setting of an event; a diary entry or letter describing something that happened; a National Park ranger giving a tour of a historic site; a painting depicting an event; a textbook passage; a historian's monograph; a website dedicated to an event; a Hollywood-produced movie "based on actual events"; or a range of other formats.

account: an intentionally produced narrative that tells about an event, created in one of a wide range of formats

In contrast to accounts, *traces* are pieces of evidence that give clues about historic events or conditions but were not produced for that purpose. For example, a sales receipt might help a historian make inferences about a person's activities. A popular feature film provides clues about an audience's tastes within a certain context. Artifacts left behind at a prehistoric garbage dump help archaeologists reconstruct the material culture of people in the past. Depending upon the inquiry, traces might include a recipe, a president's appointment book, an advertisement in the newspaper, a fashionable hat from the 1920s, a science-fiction novel from the 1960s, a building, a speech, or scores of other types of evidence that help historians understand past events and conditions. In thinking about the way history is reconstructed, Collingwood (1993) explained that almost anything could be considered evidence if a historian approached it with the right question in mind, and most of this evidence would be considered traces rather than accounts. Some historical evidence, such as a photograph, straddles the artificial line that distinguishes accounts from traces.

trace: artifacts and other remains of human activity that give evidence of historic events and conditions that were not produced intentionally to tell about the past

The distinction between accounts and traces is important because historians think differently and interrogate each using different strategies. For example, sourcing proceeds differently when working with a journal entry, an account, than when working with a prehistoric pottery shard, a trace. Those conducting an inquiry need to know who produced the journal entry in order to work with it effectively. The creator of the pottery shard is impossible to know and unimportant when answering the kinds of questions archaeologists ask about it. Questions about the trustworthiness of accounts require a different investigation than traces. For example, during an inquiry on the impact of the Cold War on American society, it is not productive to investigate whether the Cold War–era movie *Red Dawn*, a trace, is trustworthy. However, if the producer of *Red Dawn* gave an account describing the enormous impact of the movie on American society, questions about that account's trustworthiness would apply. Because historical inquiry often involves solving ill-defined problems (Ferretti et al., 2001), students need to be prepared to use historical thinking strategies flexibly depending on their research context. The nature of the evidence—whether account or trace—is one factor that can help students know which analytical tools to employ.

Helping Students Read Primary Sources

When working with primary sources, students often need support in each of their four roles as readers: code breakers, meaning makers, text users, and text critics described in Chapter 4. These roles suggest that working with texts is an active process. Teachers can promote students' active engagement by encouraging them to ask questions and seek plausible interpretations using primary sources. Additionally, they can help students view primary sources as evidence rather than as conveyors of information. I consider each of these notions in this section.

Code Breakers and Meaning Makers of Primary Sources

What are some specific things that a teacher could do to help students in their roles as code breakers and meaning makers when working with a faded, difficult-to-read primary source written in cursive using challenging 18th-century English?

Before students can reason with historical evidence, they must be able to decode and construct meaning with primary sources—to "read" them. Teachers should be aware that basic comprehension of primary sources can present challenges for students for a number of reasons. First, decoding is difficult when texts are age-worn or written in illegible handwriting, as primary sources often are. The reading of old texts can be so challenging that historian specialists called palaeographers focus on the decoding of old handwriting. Students who must work hard to decode a text (i.e., read it) have fewer remaining cognitive resources with which to conduct an analysis (Nokes, 2011). Mr. Dunn compensated for this challenge by preparing a transcript of one document, which he presented beside the original so that students could use both.

Second, comprehension is difficult when texts are written using challenging language, unfamiliar vocabulary, or terms that have a different historical meaning. Mr. Dunn addressed this problem by choosing some simple texts, one being only a single sentence in length, and by defining difficult vocabulary in the margins of another text. Researchers have suggested that teachers also help students understand the evolving or contextualized meaning of some words and, in some cases, even translate documents into simpler language that students can comprehend (Wineburg & Martin, 2009). Additionally, allowing students to work as a class or in small groups to read texts, as Mr. Dunn did, can provide scaffolding for students as the more able readers decode for their less capable peers. The graphic organizer he prepared had a place for students to summarize their understanding of each text—allowing Mr. Dunn to assess their comprehension of the documents and providing them a place to refer back to when corroborating across texts. In summary, students cannot engage in the analysis of documents that they cannot comprehend. Mr. Dunn took measures to help students decode and comprehend the primary source materials he provided.

Figures 7.3 through 7.5 illustrate how a teacher might prepare a primary source for students to use in an inquiry. Figure 7.3 shows one page of a letter written by Confederate General Hood to Union General Sherman during Sherman's troops' siege of Atlanta, a city defended by Hood's troops. The letter might be a great piece of evidence for in inquiry related to Sherman's controversial tactics during the Civil War. However, in its original format it presents challenges for most young readers that would render it nearly useless in an inquiry. Unfortunately, some teachers who are urged to use primary sources with their students throw a document like this in front of them, and when the activity flops, they conclude that students cannot work with primary sources. Instead, there are several steps a teacher can take to help students have success with primary

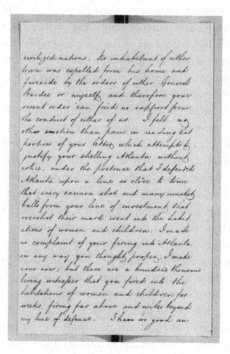

FIGURE 7.3 One page of a letter written from General Hood to General Sherman in its original format (Hood, 1864).

I felt no other emotion than pain in reading that portion of your letter which attempts to justify your shelling Atlanta without notice, under the pretense that I defended Atlanta upon a line so close to town that every cannon shot and many musketballs from your line of investment that overshot their mark went into the habitations of women and children. I made no complaint of your firing into Atlanta in any way you thought proper. I make none now; but there are a hundred thousand living witnesses that you fired into the habitations of women and children for weeks, firing far above and miles beyond my line of defenses. I have too good an opinion, founded both upon observation and experience, of the skill of your artillerists to credit the insinuation that they for several weeks unintentionally fired too high for my modest field-works, and slaughtered women and children by accident and want of skill....

You say "let us fight it out like men." To this my reply is, for myself, and I believe, for all true men, aye and women and children in my country, we will fight you to the death. Better to die a thousand deaths than submit to live under you or your government and your negro allies.

Source information: *Parts of a letter written by Confederate General J.B. Hood to William T. Sherman on September 12, 1864. Found in the William T. Sherman Papers: General Correspondence 1837-1891; 1864, Apr 8-Oct. 11., images 225, 226, and 232 at https://www.loc.gov/item/mss398000017*

FIGURE 7.4 Transcript of letter from General Hood to General Sherman.

sources. First, rather than giving students the entire multipage letter, the teacher can select a brief passage that gets at the heart of the inquiry. Second, the hand-written cursive script, though beautifully composed, will present a code-breaking challenge for many students. If a reader stumbles through decoding they will be less likely to comprehend what they read. Figure 7.4 shows the same letter transcribed, eliminating code-breaking issues for most students.

But the document continues to present meaning-making challenges for most young readers who might struggle to make sense of vocabulary like *artillerists* and phrases like "under the pretense" and "line of investment." Students who struggle to comprehend a document have few cognitive resources remaining to think deeply about it. Pausing to look up the meaning of unfamiliar words or seeking an explanation on challenging phrases slows the reading process in a manner that might make it difficult for students to remember why they were reading the passage in the first place. Some historians might cringe with the idea of translating a primary source into simpler language, but in my experience, doing so is often a necessity for an inquiry to proceed smoothly. I feel no more discomfort translating a passage written in 19th-century military commander jargon into 21st-century eighth-grader English than I would translating something from Swedish to English for students to read. If a document is written in language that students cannot comprehend it is of no use to them. Figure 7.5 shows the same letter translated into language that students are more likely to understand, allowing them to use the letter as evidence in an inquiry. Notice that the source information informs students that the language has been simplified. Also note that the word *artillerist* is defined in the passage rather than translated. I suggest giving students access to the original letter (because some students like to see what the original looked like) and the transcribed but untranslated letter (so that skeptical readers can check my translation or so that I can differentiate the activity by assigning gifted readers to read it). Preparing documents in this way can turn a botched lesson with impossible primary source documents into an engaging historical inquiry.

I felt no other emotion than pain when I read that part of your letter which tries to justify your bombing of Atlanta without warning by a lie. You pretend that I defended Atlanta with my line of soldiers so close to the city that every cannon shot and many musketballs from your soldiers that were aimed too high went into the homes of women and children. I did not complain about you firing into Atlanta any way you thought proper. I do not complain now. But there are a hundred thousand living witnesses that you fired into the homes of women and children for weeks, firing far above and miles past my line of defenses. From what I have seen and experienced, I have too good of an opinion of the skill of your artillerists [people who fired cannons] to think that for several weeks they mistakenly fired too high for my small defenses, and slaughtered women and children by accident and because they were not skilled....

You say "let us fight it out like men." To this my reply is, for myself, and I believe, for all true men, and women and children in my country, we will fight you to the death. Better to die a thousand deaths than submit to live under you or your government and your [mild racial slur] allies.

Source information: Parts of a letter written by Confederate General J.B. Hood to William T. Sherman on September 12, 1864. [Changed for easier reading]. Found in the William T. Sherman Papers: General Correspondence 1837-1891; 1864, Apr 8-Oct. 11., images 225, 226, and 232 at https://www.loc.gov/item/mss398000017

FIGURE 7.5 Simplified transcript of letter from General Hood to General Sherman.

Critiquing and Using Primary Sources

Mr. Dunn has created a classroom where students are expected to evaluate texts and use them as evidence to answer questions related to historical inquiries. He has carefully structured his classroom to promote historical literacies. During the lesson, he uses the analogy of a witness at an accident scene to help students understand their role as investigators of the past and the use of accounts as evidence. The purpose of his lecture is not simply to transmit information but to help students understand the context of historical questions. The explicit instruction that he provides is intended to help students critically evaluate texts, using sourcing, and corroboration. The structure of his activities promotes questioning, contextualization, a search for answers to questions, and further questioning. His assessment in this case, the graphic organizer, is meant to evaluate students' ability to engage in historical thinking processes rather than their arrival at a predetermined conclusion. Thus, Mr. Dunn's lesson facilitates the critique and use of documents in authentic ways by creating an environment where students ask questions and seek plausible interpretations using documents as evidence.

Asking Questions and Seeking Plausible Interpretations

Mr. Dunn has found puzzling resources, the types of texts that historians would use, in order to promote students' spontaneous and authentic questioning. He poses questions that allow multiple interpretations. But more important, classroom activities revolve around not only his questions but also authentic questions that students develop under his guidance. His lesson is an example of structured historical inquiry during which students pursue answers to authentic questions they have within parameters established by the teacher. At the outset of the case study on John White, Mr. Dunn is uncertain how students will interpret the texts or which questions they will consider. He is quite confident, though, that he has selected resources that will promote students' learning of concepts central to the required curriculum—Indigenous and White relations.

It is possible for teachers to use primary sources without promoting historical inquiry or historical literacies. As I mentioned in Chapter 2, when I observed several history lessons, the most common way teachers used primary sources was to present short one- or two-line quotes in order to illustrate a point made during a lecture. The teachers typically read and explained the primary source to students with few opportunities for students to interpret (Nokes, 2010). In the worst cases, the primary sources were used for the same purpose that textbooks and lectures are typically used—to convey information to students. In the best cases, teachers used primary sources as evidence of a point they were trying to make. But even when primary sources were used under these circumstances, there was no explicit discussion of strategies like sourcing or corroboration, no distinction made between primary and secondary sources, and no critique or questioning of the source.

Thus, exposure to primary sources does not build students' historical literacies unless teachers create the appropriate conditions. These conditions include introducing inquiries that do not have an agreed-on interpretation; allowing students to semi-independently develop original interpretations based on evidence; bringing in multiple contradictory texts that provide room for differences of interpretations; permitting students to disagree with their peers, the teacher, textbooks, and even historians; and encouraging students to explore their own interests using both teacher-provided text sets and their own independent inquiry. There is little opportunity for historical thinking when teachers simply offer, as factual, their interpretations of primary sources, expecting students to remember rather than to question and seek plausible alternative interpretations. In contrast, classrooms that not only tolerate but also appreciate diverse interpretations help students feel safe in positioning themselves in historical debates. Students in settings that appreciate independent inquiry and allow alternative evidence-based interpretations are more likely to work with primary sources in a discipline-appropriate manner.

Viewing Primary Sources as Evidence

As part of the process of helping students understand the nature of history and the role of historians, students must consider documents evidence rather than repositories of facts or conveyors of information. The vandalism in the textbook is not comprehended literally—suggesting that John Wampus was the king of his own meetinghouse. Instead, Mr. Dunn's students use it as evidence of the attitudes of others toward an Anglicized American Indian. In the process of working with historical evidence, students must acknowledge that primary sources were typically not written for the purpose they are now being used. As a result, the author may assume background knowledge that students and historians lack.

Some knowledge of the historic and geographic context may be necessary to comprehend the text. Aware of this, Mr. Dunn lectured briefly on the human and physical geography of New England in order to build the necessary background knowledge before expecting students to comprehend and evaluate the texts as evidence.

To illustrate further, I sometimes use a note Eisenhower wrote prior to the D-Day invasion to teach students that the Allied victory in World War II was not inevitable, help students understand the risk of the landing, help them understand the personality of Eisenhower, and help them comprehend the nature of historical evidence (see Figures 7.6 and 7.7). If students read the text with the attitude that they are gathering information, they learn that D-Day was an American failure, that the Allies fell short in their attempt to establish a foothold in France, and that the attack occurred in early July. All these "facts" that could be gathered from the document are untrue. In order to learn with this text, students must understand the context and purpose of its creation: that it was written as a potential press release that could be used in case the invasion failed, that Eisenhower had written an incorrect date on the note, that he discarded

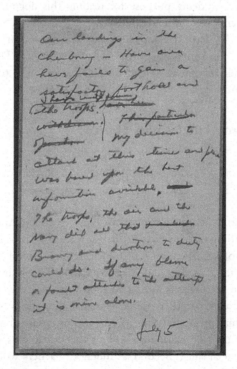

FIGURE 7.6 Eisenhower's unreleased press release of the Normandy Invasion (Eisenhower, 1944. Courtesy of the Dwight D. Eisenhower Presidential Library National Archives and Records Administration, Abilene, Kansas).

> Our landings in the Cherbourg-Havre
> area have failed to gain a
>   I have
> satisfactory foothold and
> withdrawn
>   the troops. ~~have been~~
> ~~withdrawn. This particular operation~~
> My decision to attack at this time and
> place was based upon the best
> information available. The troops, the
> air and the navy did all that
> ~~(undecipherable)~~ bravery and
> devotion to duty could do. If any
> blame or fault attaches to the
> attempt it is mine alone.
>   July 5

FIGURE 7.7 A transcript of Eisenhower's unreleased press release of the Normandy invasion.

the note after the invasion succeeded, and that an aide retrieved the note from the trash as a relic. Students' purpose for reading this document is drastically different than Eisenhower's intended purpose for creating it. Students use it to answer questions *they* have developed—what kind of person was Eisenhower, for example—and not simply to gather facts about D-Day. Thus, in historical inquiry, when using documents as evidence, the student or historian determines how the document is used.

Selecting Appropriate Primary Sources

> What kinds of primary sources are appealing and useful for young people?

As teachers help students engage in historical inquiry, in addition to creating an investigative classroom climate and nurturing critical literacy strategies, teachers must choose appropriate primary sources. Mr. Dunn's careful selection of texts is an important factor in the success of his activity. There are several criteria that he used. First, the content should be appropriate for the age and maturity of the students. Violent or otherwise questionable content in some documents, particularly informal, private writing, may be inappropriate in some educational contexts. I generally edit racial slurs out of the documents, leaving in their place the note "[racial slur]." Second, as much as teachers would like students to analyze some difficult texts, the fact remains that if a student cannot read it, they cannot reason with it. Thus, teachers should choose primary sources that are at or below students' reading abilities, adjust instruction to support students' reading, or modify the texts in order to facilitate students' comprehension as illustrated in Figures 7.3 through 7.5. Third, selected primary sources should promote instructional objectives. Mr. Dunn's lesson planning began with a consideration of objectives, for which appropriate texts were uncovered. With the nearly inexhaustible supply of texts available, including primary sources, teachers should ask themselves, "Is this the best possible text to use to reach my instructional objectives?"

Teachers should be purposeful in their selection of texts for document-based activities. Students are more likely to engage in sourcing when there is variety in the perspectives of the sources. When possible, text sets should contain documents with conflicting information so that students can have a voice in interpreting the evidence and so that students reach diverse interpretations. Text sets might include both accounts and traces to require students to use strategies more flexibly. And texts should vary in their reliability so that students can begin to distinguish between more and less trustworthy sources and feel empowered to make judgments about credibility. Additionally, providing texts that represent multiple points of view can expose students to alternatives to the canonized historical narrative to which they have become accustomed. I found that students were not as likely to engage in sourcing or corroboration or to question the reliability of texts if they were given only one text or multiple texts with a common point of view and similar content.

As teachers prepare text sets it is vital that they include the perspectives of individuals from groups that are sometimes marginalized in the historical record. Doing so may present challenges because of a tradition in historical inquiry that favors cultures that maintain written records over those who maintain their histories orally. To be frank, history as a discipline has not been equitable in its consideration of the perspectives of Indigenous people, enslaved individuals, or victims of colonization. Fortunately, this oversight is being corrected by modern historians who have expanded the types of resources they consider primary sources and who investigate questions associated with marginalized groups. Today, digital archives provide greater access to the range of primary sources produced by people of color than ever before. Texts from non-White, female, and LGBTQ individuals carry greater appeal with students of color, young women, and students who identify as LGBTQ. Text sets must include evidence that has been produced by individuals whose voices have been silenced or marginalized in the traditional textbook narrative. For instance, oral histories produced by Indigenous people or individuals formerly enslaved represent important perspectives in many inquiries. Inquiries related to difficult histories such as slavery, racism, genocide, or ethnic cleansing, which include primary source evidence that represents multiple perspectives have the potential to heal long-standing wounds in societies when carried out with sensitivity (Barton & McCully, 2012). This healing is maximized as students work in diverse groups with documents that match the diversity of the students (Goldberg, 2013).

Mr. Dunn intentionally chose a wide variety of genres and perspectives for students to evaluate. Doing so allowed students to practice recognizing the subtle differences, strengths, and weaknesses of various forms of evidence. Without exposure to various text types such as diaries, written on a daily basis, and memoirs, written after a lifetime of experiences, students might fail to acknowledge the subtle differences between genres. However, as students work with new genres of historical evidence they have the opportunity to discover the unique characteristics of each. Mr. Dunn provided students with both primary sources and a secondary source including a petition, graffiti, court proceedings, a letter, and excerpts from a monograph.

The following is a list of some written primary source documents that I have used with students. Creative teachers will be able to create an endless list of accounts and traces, useful to historians and, thus, for students:

- Letters, notes, and emails (both informal, private letters and more formal, public letters)
- Official government documents such as laws, state constitutions, or treaties
- Audio or video recorded speeches or speech transcripts
- Diaries, memoirs, personal histories, and autobiographies
- Newspaper articles, obituaries, want ads, letters to the editor, and political cartoons
- Accounts written by contemporary non-witnesses
- Historic local phone books
- Court records including indictments, transcripts, and depositions
- Historical magazine articles, advertisements, and magazine covers
- Graffiti and defacing
- Reports from medical examiners
- Novels written in historic settings (such as a novel written in 1920 used as evidence about life in 1920)
- Ship passenger logs
- Family histories and genealogical records
- Manuscript and published census records
- Transcripts of oral histories
- Property inventories, deeds, wills, or other personal documents.

These types of resources are increasingly available through the World Wide Web.

In addition to choosing a variety of genres, teachers should select texts with particular appeal to students. The adolescents I worked with were drawn to issues of oppression, particularly the oppression of groups with which they felt some association (young people, people of color, women). Primary sources that include surprising content create curiosity and stimulate research questions. Texts that are shocking or disgusting are appealing to students. The tender relationships that are often revealed in primary sources, particularly letters, can be especially appealing to young people. And humor and satire are often engaging for students—particularly when historical humor continues to be appreciated as funny. In the vignette, Mr. Dunn's selection of texts included some that were intended to catch students' attention by providing unexpected and puzzling content.

Helping Students Create Primary Sources

> How might producing primary sources change the way students think about analyzing them?

In addition to working with primary sources, students can learn about the nature of history by creating primary sources themselves. Students' personal reflections on national, world, or even personal events, written in a history class, create a source that can be used by future historians, or by the students themselves, as they learn how to do history. For example, Bain (2005) assigned his students to write about their experiences on the first day of school. In a subsequent class session he asked students to analyze the various diverse accounts of that day. As students compared the accounts they had created, they recognized the profound effect of point of view on the content of primary sources. Additionally, students, realizing the impossibility of constructing a complete record of the first day of school, gained a better understanding of the work of historians in determining what to include and what to omit in their determination of historical significance.

When historical events occur during the course of a school year, such as the inauguration of a president or a national emergency, teachers can have students write descriptions and reactions to the events in order to create a historical record. Students' records can be compiled into a book or on a web page documenting important events and providing a record for future historians. Production of such records puts students on the other side of history—creating evidence—giving them a new perspective that can improve their understanding of the work of historians who interpret the past based on the types of records students will have produced. Students can also create oral histories by interviewing individuals with connections to historical events such as the civil rights movement or the Vietnam War. For a similar purpose, some teachers assign students to build time capsules with written record and artifacts to create a record that individuals might use at some future date to understand current conditions. By carefully selecting items for inclusion, students gain a different perspective on the role of evidence, particularly primary sources, in the construction of understandings about the past. For examples of activities during which students produce primary sources in a structured way, see the Covid 19 Memory Project at https://history.utah. gov/covid-19-memory-project/ and the Library of Congress' Veterans History Project at https://www.loc.gov/vets/.

Chapter Summary

Primary sources provide a foundation on which the discipline of history is built. However, students face several challenges in working with primary sources. Teachers can help students overcome these challenges by supporting their comprehension of texts by creating transcripts of hard-to-read documents and by simplifying the language in primary sources. Teachers help students read more critically when they teach them historians' strategies for interrogating primary sources—particularly sourcing, corroboration, and contextualization. History teachers promote the effective analysis of primary sources by creating safe classrooms that honor questioning, encouraging students to view documents as evidence, and providing them with regular opportunities to semi-independently develop original interpretations of historical events throughout the school year. Producing primary sources helps students understand the nature of evidence in the study of history.

Questions for Consideration

1. How can a teacher design historical inquiries that have personal relevance for students? Which types of documents have personal relevance for them?
2. Sourcing and corroboration are both vital for online reading, as internet users should find out who is behind a webpage and corroborate information found on a single site. Does contextualization also have application for online reading, or is it important solely when working with historical texts?
3. What are the advantages and disadvantages of using graphic organizers to help students gather evidence from primary sources? To what degree would teaching students to annotate documents serve the same purpose as the graphic organizer? What additional alternatives exist for supporting students as they work with multiple texts?

Additional Reading and Viewing

- A video produced by the Stanford History Education Group explaining how a teacher can modify a primary source to make it more comprehensible for students can be found at https://sheg.stanford.edu/history-assessments/morale-after-fredericksburg.
- A book, written by a teacher with extensive classroom experience with lessons illustrating how to teach students to work with primary sources is Lesh, B. A. (2011). *Why won't you just tell us the answer? Teaching historical thinking in grades 7–12*. Stenhouse.
- A book with several document-based lessons that can be used to nurture students' ability to engage in critical reading strategies is Wineburg, S. S.,

Martin, D., & Monte-Sano, C. (2012). *Reading like a historian: Teaching literacy in middle and high school history classrooms.* Teachers College Press.

• Numerous resources to support teachers who teach with primary sources can be found at the Library of Congress website at https://www.loc.gov/programs/teachers/about-this-program/.

• A short webinar on finding primary sources developed by the website DocsTeach can be viewed here https://www.youtube.com/watch?v=VUYT5ydABeQ&goal=0_c35d12af24-522d06b1bb-54105381&mc_cid=522d06b1bb&mc_eid=58e2a51c6d.

References

Bain, R. B. (2005). "They thought the world was flat?" Applying the principles of *How people learn* in teaching high school history. In M. S. Donovan & J. D. Bransford (Eds.), *How students learn: History, mathematics, and science in the classroom* (pp. 179–213). National Academies Press.

Baron, C. (2012). Understanding historical thinking at historic sites. *Journal of Educational Psychology, 104*(3), 833–847. doi:10.1037/a0027476

Baron, C. (2016). Using embedded visual coding to support contextualization of historical texts. *American Educational Research Journal, 53*(3), 516–540. doi:10.3102/0002831216637347

Barton, K. C., & McCully, A. W. (2012). Trying to "see things differently": Northern Ireland students' struggle to understand alternative historical perspectives, *Theory & Research in Social Education, 40,* 371–408. doi:10.1080/00933104.2012.710928

Collingwood, R. G. (1993). *The idea of history.* Oxford University Press.

Eisenhower, D. D. (1944, June 5). [Untitled memo.] Dwight D. Eisenhower Presidential Library National Archives and Records Administration. http://www.archives.gov/education/lessons/d-day-message/

Ferretti, R. P., MacArthur, C. D., & Okolo, C. M. (2001). Teaching for historical understanding in inclusive classrooms. *Learning Disabilities Quarterly, 24*(1), 59–71. doi:10.2307/1511296.

Goldberg, T. (2013). "It's in my veins": Identity and disciplinary practice in students' discussions of a historical issue. *Theory & Research in Social Education, 41*(1), 33–64. doi:10.1080/00933104.2012.757265

Hood, J. B. (1864, September 12). [Letter to William T. Sherman]. *William T. Sherman Papers: General Correspondence, 1837–1891; 1864, Apr. 8–Oct. 11.* Library of Congress. https://www.loc.gov/item/mss398000017

Leinhardt, G., & Young, K. M. (1996). Two texts, three readers: Distance and expertise in reading history. *Cognition & Instruction, 14*(4), 441–486. doi:10.1207/s1532690xci1404_2

Nokes, J. D. (2010). Observing literacy practices in history classrooms. *Theory and Research in Social Education, 38*(4), 298–316. doi:10.1080/00933104.2010.10473438

Nokes, J. D. (2011). Recognizing and addressing barriers to adolescents' "reading like historians". *The History Teacher, 44* (3), 379–404.

Nokes, J. D., Dole, J. A., & Hacker, D. J. (2007). Teaching high school students to use heuristics while reading historical texts. *Journal of Educational Psychology, 99*(3), 492–504. doi:10.1037/0022-0663.99.3.492

Nokes, J. D., & Kesler-Lund, A. (2019). Historians' social literacies: How historians collaborate and write during a document-based activity. *The History Teacher, 52*(3), 369–410.

Pulsipher, J. H. (2018). *Swindler Sachem: The American Indian Who Sold His Birthright, Dropped Out of Harvard, and Conned the King of England.* Yale University Press.

Reisman, A. (2012). Reading like a historian: A document-based history curriculum intervention in urban high schools. *Cognition and Instruction, 30*(1), 86–112. doi:10.10 80/07370008.2011.634081

Reisman, A., & Fogo, B. (2016). Contributions of educative document-based curricular materials to quality of historical instruction. *Teaching and Teacher Education, 59,* 191–202. doi:10.1016/j.tate.2016.05.018

Seixas, P. (2016). Translation and its discontents: Key concepts in English and German history education. *Journal of Curriculum Studies, 48*(4), 427–439. doi:10.1080/002202 72.2015.1101618

Shanahan, C., Shanahan, T., & Misichia, C. (2011). Analysis of expert readers in three disciplines: History, mathematics, and chemistry. *Journal of Literacy Research, 43*(4), 393–429. doi:10.1177/1086296X11424071

Shanahan, T., & Shanahan, C. (2008). Teaching disciplinary literacy to adolescents: Rethinking content-area literacy. *Harvard Educational Review, 78*(1), 40–59. doi:10.17763/haer.78.1.v62444321p602101

van Boxtel, C., & van Drie, J. (2012). "That's in the time of the Romans!" Knowledge and strategies students use to contextualize historical images and documents. *Cognition and Instruction, 30*(2), 113–145. doi:10.1080/07370008.2012.661813

Wineburg, S., & Martin, D. (2009). Tampering with history: Adapting primary sources for struggling readers. *Social Education, 73*(5), 212–216.

Wineburg, S. S. (1991). On the reading of historical texts: Notes on the breach between school and academy. *American Educational Research Journal, 28*(3), 495–519. doi:10.3102/00028312028003495

8

HELPING STUDENTS MAKE INFERENCES WITH ARTIFACTS

When you look at a photograph on social media can you tell whether the photograph was spontaneous or staged? Can you tell whether it was photoshopped? What can you guess about the person who posted the photograph by their decision to post it? What can you infer about the person who took the picture? In this chapter you will read about the strategies of observing and inferring, important processes for analyzing artifacts and visual texts like photographs.

As you read the following vignette identify the elements and strategies of historical thinking that students use to analyze the memorial.

Mrs. Dahl is planning a unit on World War II for her 10th-grade U.S. history classes. She recently visited Washington, D.C., and was impressed by the National World War II Memorial that was constructed in 2004. She contemplates how she might have her students analyze the memorial as part of their study of the war. In her reflection, she realizes that a memorial is an unusual type of artifact and not only because of its enormous size. Most artifacts are traces, not created to be a source of historical information for future generations. They are often intentionally discarded, such as a flawed brick or broken piece of pottery thrown into a garbage dump; are lost by accident, such as a coin or an arrowhead; or abandoned for various reasons, such as the ruins of an ancient village. Some continue to be used, such as a feature film or a vehicle. Their use as historical evidence was not intended during their production or placement. In contrast, a memorial is an account, built for the express purpose of helping future generations remember a historical character, event, or accomplishment. Similarly, counter-memorials, such as the National Memorial of Peace and Justice in Montgomery, Alabama, which memorializes the victims of racially driven lynching and ongoing injustices, force

DOI: 10.4324/9781003183495-10

FIGURE 8.1 A photograph of the *Lend Lease Act*, a sculpture on the National World War II Memorial.(Photograph printed with permission of Matthew Richardson). Source: Kaskey (2004).

visitors to remember and confront traumatic and difficult histories. Memorials and counter-memorials are artifacts that are produced as accounts to help future generations remember or learn about the past. As such, they are a source for learning not only about the event they commemorate but about the people who produced them as well.

Mrs. Dahl considers how the National World War II Memorial represents not only the events of World War II, but shows how modern society chooses to remember or forget those events. The various quotes, sculptures, symbols, and reflecting pool provide numerous resources that she could draw from to support students' learning about the war. She decides to use photographs of a series of bas-relief sculptures at the memorial, created by Ray Kaskey, that depict different events of the war, such as shipping war materials to Great Britain following the passage of the Lend Lease Act (see Figure 8.1). She remembers that 24 bas-relief sculptures adorn the walkway into the memorial, 12 depicting events associated with the war in the Pacific and 12 representing events from the war in the Atlantic. She decides to have students either individually or with a partner analyze one of the sculptures and report on their analysis to the class. She will assign them to make inferences about the way events of the war are remembered and the way the current generation would like future generations to remember the war. She decides to use these sculptures at the end of the unit as a review, allowing students to apply the knowledge they have gained during the unit.

Additionally, she recognizes an opportunity to have students review the important events that they studied that are not depicted in the sculptures to consider why some significant events were omitted from the bas-relief panels. By considering the choices made by the designers of the memorial, students will not only review the important events of World War II, but they will become more skilled in making inferences, will practice sourcing, and will become more literate in constructing historical interpretations with artifacts. As she researches, she finds an interview conducted of the artist, which she will assign students to read to help them understand the process of designing and creating the monument, including the bas-reliefs (Gurney, 2004).

To introduce her students to the process of analyzing a sculpture, she models her thinking in an analysis of the bas-relief that depicts the Lend Lease Act (see Figure 8.1). Her modeling with this sculpture will leave 23 others for the students to analyze and report on. She spends a few minutes thinking aloud in front of the students, considering the source, making observations and inferences about the story shown in the sculpture and making inferences about the artist's message and what it says about the people who designed the monument. Projecting a picture of the sculpture in front of the class, she begins the lesson by thinking out loud to the students, helping them observe her code-breaking and meaning-making processes.

"Like with all other historical sources I want to start by thinking about the source," she begins.

> The article we read helped me learn about the artist, Ray Kaskey, and I know that the monument was constructed in 2004. I know who the intended audience is: the American people and foreign tourists and officials who might visit the nation's capital. I was there a few months ago so I know the physical context: it sits between the Lincoln Memorial and the Washington Monument near the Vietnam War Memorial on the National Mall. I understand that the purpose of these monuments is to celebrate great accomplishments and to remember those who made sacrifices, sometimes even giving their lives, to win the war. I remember that the monuments are visited by individuals, families, and school children who often have an emotional or even spiritual experience while there. I know that the memorial has been built at a time when the generation of Americans who experienced World War II is growing old and passing away. I wonder whether it was created in 2004 to honor that generation before they are all gone.

Mrs. Dahl helps students see that she is modeling the same process that she has taught students to engage in when analyzing a document. Before starting to read they think about the source and context. She has done that with the monument—thinking about who made it, who it was made for, and where, when, and why it was made. She reminds them that it does not matter what type of historical evidence they are using—documents, artifacts, music, a building, or a monument like this—they always want to consider its origin and the historical context of when it was made.

After modeling sourcing, Mrs. Dahl thinks aloud through an analysis of the content of the sculpture. She acts as though this is the first time she has seen it, even though she has thought carefully about what she will say.

> I can tell right away that this does not look like a scene from war, except that there is an army jeep. This sculpture must depict something happening on the home front. Sometimes it is hard to catch the details if I look at the whole image at once so I am going to start on the left side and move slowly

toward the right. On the left I see a man. What I notice about him is that his hand is stretched out toward a boy. I cannot really tell what he is doing but he looks like he is holding something small. His other hand is in his pocket. Oh, now I see what is happening. I think he is buying a newspaper.

Mrs. Dahl continues:

It looks like the newspaper headline says something about Germany, but I cannot read the second word. Maybe it says "declares." I cannot tell for sure. Now, looking behind the man and boy I see boxes marked "Great Britain." Now I think I am figuring out what is happening—this must be at a shipyard. The boxes and the jeep are being shipped to Great Britain. There is a man sitting on the boxes with a newspaper in one hand with his other hand at his face. He seems to be in deep thought, maybe worried. I wonder what he is thinking about—maybe he wonders what the future will bring or whether the United States is making the right choice shipping these things to Great Britain. Now I am starting to make a connection to one of the things we studied in class: the Lend Lease Act, when the U.S. became involved in the war by sending war supplies to Great Britain. How do I know what is in the boxes?

she asks herself.

That is an inference. I have to read between the lines using my background knowledge of the war, the evidence on the sculpture, and the context of the bas relief as part of the World War II memorial to infer that these are war supplies rather than other goods.

Mrs. Dahl pauses to allow students to think about what she has done.

Do you see how I worked to comprehend this sculpture? I did not understand what it was showing at first. I started by looking over the whole thing. Then I looked at details, focusing on small parts of the sculpture at a time. Gradually, I started to piece together what it represented using the background knowledge that I had about the war. You are going to have to go through this same process with your assigned sculpture to try to figure out what it is showing. Once you have a feel for the basic representation you can begin to think more deeply about the artist's, Ray Kaskey's, intended message. For example, I notice that there is one man who appears to be African American and the others appear to be White. I wonder what kind of meaning Mr. Kaskey intended with that. Looking at the whole sculpture I think that he is trying to show that Americans were working together to support the

Lend Lease Act, represented by the African American and White workers lifting together. Now I observe that the man sitting and thinking and
staring off into the distance is a young man. I think he is probably
thinking about his future—another inference. I see this as a tribute to
the young men who ended up fighting in the war. I think Kaskey is
trying to show the nervousness of an uncertain future. Now the final
question for us to think about has to do with how this event is remembered by the current generation. In the sculpture it appears that most
people, Black and White, were united behind the Lend Lease Act. This
idea of unity does not match what we learned about in class, though,
when we studied the controversy surrounding the passage of the Lend
Lease Act. Nor does the sculpture show that supplies were sent to the
USSR along with Great Britain. I wonder why Kaskey chose to present
the Lend Lease Act in this way,

she ponders. Answering her own question, she continues to model her thinking:

I think it makes sense for a memorial like this to celebrate unity and
cooperation rather than to reflect the reality of the time when the Lend
Lease Act was being debated. And it makes sense to ignore the controversy of shipping goods to help the dictator Stalin. Leaving out this
content would help the memorial fit in with the context of the National
Mall and the other memorials there that present a clean and patriotic
history,

she concludes.

After modeling an analysis of the bas-relief depicting the Lend Lease Act, Mrs.
Dahl has students draw numbers for their assigned sculptures. She informs them
that when it is time for them to present, she will display an image of the sculpture for the class. They will need to describe what they observe in the sculpture,
including details that agree with and disagree with things they studied in class.
She lets them know that they will not need to model all their thinking, like she
just did, but they should explain what some of the details in the sculpture mean.
They will start by talking about what the sculpture shows, what events it represents, and how it represents them. Then they will talk about Kaskey's message
and what it shows about how the current generation wants to remember that
aspect of the war. She has created a study guide (see Figure 8.2) to help students
analyze their assigned sculpture and to keep a record of the presentations on the
other sculptures. During their preparation time, they should complete numbers
one through five on the back of the study guide. During the presentations, they
will complete the front. After the presentations, the class will work together on
numbers six through nine. Students can use a textbook, notes from class, or a
computer to prepare.

Name _____

Date _____

Analysis of the bas-relief sculptures on the National World War II Memorial.
Complete this chart as the class reports on the 24 bas-relief sculptures depicting events from World War II. After listeningtoall of the reports, complete questions 6-9 on the back of this paper.

Atlantic Panels	Description of panel	How we remember	Pacific Panels	Description of panel	How we remember
Lend Lease			Pearl Harbor		
Bond Drive			Enlistment		
Women in military			Embarkation		
Rosie the Riveter			Shipbuilding		
Battle of the Atlantic			Agriculture		
Air war/B-17			Submarine warfare		
Paratroopers			Navy in Action		
Normandy Beach landing			Amphibious landing		
Tanks in combat			Jungle warfare		
Medics in the field			Field burial		
Battle of the Bulge			Liberation		

FIGURE 8.2 A graphic organizer and study guide for supporting students' work with World War II Memorial sculptures.

Mrs. Dahl passes out the study guide and circulates as the students go to work. Most of them work on their own, but she assigns pairs of students to some of the sculptures. As Mrs. Dahl moves around the room, she engages students in conversations to support their work. For instance, she helps one pair see that their assigned sculpture is vague enough that it could be a scene from many battlefields. The sculpture becomes a more inclusive memorial for the whole war and all the jungle warfare rather than one specific battle.

Russians meet Americans			V-J Day		

Use the following questions <u>to prepare</u> to report to the class:
1. Summarize the things shown on your assigned panel.

2. What are some of the interesting details shown on your panel? What is the significance of their inclusion?

3. What, if anything, is missing from the way your sculpture depicts the event? (Can you find the original photo it was based upon and how does it compare?)

4. What was Mr. Kaskey and the Site and Design Committee's message in creating the panel?

5. What does the panel suggest about the way we remember World War II?

Complete the following <u>after listening</u> to all of the presentations:
6. What patterns do you see across the panels?

7. What events are missing from these panels?

8. Why do you think these events were not included in the memorial?

9. What do these omissions suggest about the way the Site and Design Committee's would like us to remember World War II?

FIGURE 8.2 (Continued)

Later in class, the students make presentations on their assigned bas-relief. Most of them capture the main idea of what the sculpture represents. Some of them do an excellent job of considering what the message of the sculptor was, and some even talk about what it suggests about the way modern Americans want to remember the war. For example, one team talks about the sanitized version of D-Day depicted on one bas-relief. They suggest that the designers of the memorial might have considered the families and school children who might look at the sculpture and decided that it would be better if children did not see a more graphic depiction of the beaches of Normandy.

The richest discussion of the day takes place after all of the groups have presented. Mrs. Dahl leads students in a discussion of the patterns they see across the panels. Students express surprise by the eight panels that have to do with the home front, including one showing farmers in a field working. As the discussion progresses students theorize that the memorial was designed to make visitors feel good about what they, their parents, or their grandparents did to help, even if they were not on the front lines. The memorial shows that everyone sacrificed to secure an Allied victory. During the discussion the students also consider the events that the designers chose to leave out, such as the atomic bomb, the internment of Japanese Americans, and the Holocaust. The class concludes that these are events that many Americans would prefer to forget. They go against the general themes of unity and victory depicted throughout the memorial and across most of the National Mall.

The discussion continues as students use the account shown in the bas-reliefs of the memorial to make inferences about how Americans want to remember World War II. In the process, students review the major events of the war and analyze the memorial as an artifact created for the unique purpose of remembering a historical event.

> How are students better prepared to view memorials, monuments, and counter-memorials after having participated in this lesson? Why should controversial memorials, such as Civil War memorials, be evaluated based on the events they depict, the time period during which they were constructed, and how they are viewed today?

Helping Students Make Inferences With Artifacts

> How can artifacts be used to investigate both prehistoric periods, times when there was no writing, and historic periods, times when written records exist?

The memorial that Mrs. Dahl's students studied represents only one of a wide array of types of artifacts that might be used to study history. Archaeologists and historians more commonly use items produced *by* the people they intend to study rather than produced *about* the people they study, such as the World War II Memorial. Still, many of the strategies that Mrs. Dahl taught her students reflect the tools archaeologists use to learn about people of the past. Although archaeology is often associated with the study of prehistoric people who had no written records, historical archaeologists study the material remnants of societies that also produced written records. In historical archaeology, the material record is used as corroborating evidence for the written record or to study those groups within a historical society that left few written records, such as members of lower economic classes and enslaved individuals. Thus archaeology and history provide two lenses for understanding the past, each considering unique types of evidence. In this chapter, I explore the use of archaeological evidence in history classrooms to foster historical thinking in general and inference making specifically. I consider inference making, including the role of inferring in historical thinking, the sister strategies of observing and inferring, the role of background knowledge in inference making, and criteria for judging inferences. I also consider the use of artifacts in secondary classrooms, including the challenges students have in working with artifacts, and support teachers can provide to help students use artifacts as evidence. The chapter concludes with practical advice about bringing artifacts or virtual artifacts into classrooms.

---

artifact: material remains made and left behind by people, used by archaeologists and historians to study prehistoric and historic people.

---

historical archaeology: the study of a historic people's material remains—artifacts—to corroborate the written evidence used to study them.

Inference Making and Historical Thinking

Why is inferring one of the most important skills in both history and archaeology, as well as many other fields?

To infer is to use evidence to reach a probable, but uncertain, conclusion. Inference making has been described as "reading between the lines," using what *is* in the text to imagine what *is not* there. Whether working with primary source documents, secondary sources, or artifacts, historians' work requires them to make inferences. For example, inference making is involved in historians' strategies of sourcing, corroboration, and contextualization. When considering the source of a document, for instance, the historian might infer the author's intent in producing the document using knowledge of the author, the historical context, and the intended audience. When working with artifacts, the archaeologist or historian might infer the purpose of an artifact based on its shape, the location where it was found, and the artifacts that were found around it. Historians use anthropological research on modern hunter hunter-gatherer societies to make inferences about prehistoric societies that left behind no written records and few material remains. And inferences are used to explore causation, such as when scientific research dates climate change at the same time that a society experienced cultural change. There is no literacy strategy that cuts across more elements of historical thinking than inferring.

---

infer: to make defensible conjectures based on evidence and background knowledge

---

Inference making is a general literacy strategy that is not exclusive to historical thinking. A great deal has been written about teaching methods that help students improve their ability to make inferences. In many texts, inferring is essential in comprehension. In fact, in their review of reading comprehension research, Afflerbach and Cho (2009) list "attempting to infer information not explicitly stated in a text when the information is critical to comprehension of the text" (p. 77) as one of 15 essential strategies for reading traditional texts. In addition, they list inferring as one of a handful of strategies necessary for reading multiple texts and internet hypertexts. Across genres and content areas, including history, the ability to make inferences is essential in literate activity. Literacy research makes it clear that appropriate instruction can improve students' ability to make inferences (Paris & Hamilton, 2009). Furthermore, literacy research provides specific guidelines that are useful for fostering inference making in historical thinking, including the connection between observing and inferring, the connection between background knowledge and inferring, and criteria for judging inferences.

Observing and Inferring

How are observing and inferring related, and why are both skills essential in historical thinking and in civic engagement?

Good inferences must be based on evidence. And an effective evaluation of archaeological evidence begins with careful observations. Observation involves collecting information through the five senses. Scientific instruments, such as microscopes or thermometers, increase what humans can observe. Because observation revolves around the use of senses, some students think that it is easy and automatic. However, not all individuals are equally adept in their ability to observe, with those who are unusually gifted at observing being labeled *observant*.

Observations	Inferences

FIGURE 8.3 A T-chart used to record observations and inferences.

Teachers can help students become more observant. Mrs. Dahl understood that before students could make inferences about the sculptures, they had to look at them carefully, making observations. In order to help her students become more observant, she gave them a specific strategy, recommended starting at one side of the sculpture and moving slowly across it, thinking aloud about what they observed. In addition, she recommended looking at the sculpture holistically in order to observe the relationship among its different parts. She understood that collaboration with peers would increase the quantity and quality of observations, so she assigned teams of students to work together with some sculptures.

Observing is an important strategy not only for working with artifacts but also for analyzing all types of visual evidence, such as photographs and paintings. Several educators have developed instructional strategies for helping young people work with visual evidence. For example, a simple T-chart, with students listing observations on the left and inferences on the right, can help students be more thoughtful about these processes (Nokes, 2008). Using the chart, students can draw arrows connecting observations with inferences to make explicit the way that inferences are based on observations (see Figure 8.3). A similar instructional approach was developed by Richards and Anderson (2003) to help young children analyze images in picture books. Students use a three-columned study guide to record what they *see* (observe), what they *think* (infer), and what they *wonder* (see Figure 3.1, page 38, for example). Whether using the terms *observe* and *infer*, or the simpler terms of *see*, *think*, or *wonder*, such study guides can simplify the process of making inferences from visual evidence.

Background Knowledge and Inferring

How can teachers use lectures to build students' background knowledge in preparation for an inquiry without giving them the impression that history is transmitted rather than constructed?

In addition to evidence, inferences are based on the reader's background knowledge. Research on literacy has shown that students' ability to make inferences increases when they or their teachers "make a conscious effort to draw relationships between text content and background knowledge" (Pearson, 2009, 16). Mrs. Dahl knew that the best time to engage students in the analysis of the bas-relief sculptures was at the end of the World War II unit after they had deeper knowledge of the war. She knew that rich and accurate background knowledge improves the quality of inferences. Furthermore, as she modeled the desired thought processes, she made explicit to the students that she was drawing on her background knowledge of the war to construct understanding. She was implicitly teaching the students that a thorough review of the evidence combined with accurate background knowledge leads to plausible inferences.

Of importance, background knowledge should not overshadow or replace the use of evidence in making inferences. Researchers have found that poor readers rely too much on background knowledge and not enough on the evidence in a text when making inferences. It is easy to understand why. Students who lack basic decoding and comprehension skills cannot access the evidence in the text. In the absence of evidence, they are left with their background knowledge alone, leading them to make inferences that are unwarranted given the textual evidence. An overreliance on background knowledge may serve as an indication to a teacher of a student's struggles to understand written, visual, or physical evidence.

The opposite problem also occurs in history classrooms. Given an artifact or document, students who lack historical background knowledge are unable to stray far from the evidence. Their analysis often represents a summary of what the document says with little contextualization, sourcing, or other acts of reading between the lines. Teachers can improve students' ability to make inferences by building their background knowledge prior to having them engage in historical thinking activities. Lectures hold greater importance when the purpose is not simply to transmit information to students so that they can regurgitate it on a test but so that they can apply it while working with historical evidence. For instance, acknowledging the role of background knowledge in historical thinking, each lesson developed by the Stanford History Education Group (2012) dedicates a short amount of time to build students' background knowledge before conducting the historical thinking activity (Wineburg et al., 2011).

Evaluating Inferences

What criteria can be used to distinguish a strong inference from a weak one?

It has been established that good inferences are a synthesis of background knowledge and evidence. Teachers can improve students' ability to infer by reflecting with them on their inference-making processes. Questions such as "What evidence in the text leads to that inference?" require students to think about and justify their inferences. Furthermore, asking students to review the specific background knowledge that led to a conclusion enhances their ability to judge inferences. Conversely, inaccurate background information can lead to poor inferences.

In addition, good inferences generally follow the principle of *parsimony*, which suggests that the hypothesis that requires the fewest assumptions is usually correct. Stated plainly, the simplest explanation is usually best. Inferring that the crates stamped for shipment to Great Britain contained war goods is easier to explain than is the inference that they contained party supplies. Good inferences account for background knowledge, all text-based evidence, and do so in logical and simple terms.

Teaching With Artifacts

> How could integrating artifact analysis activities into the curriculum on occasion strengthen history classrooms?

Artifacts, particularly ancient and strange items, can spark curiosity. Teachers and students may wonder: Who made this? Why did they make it? What does it represent? Which parts possess important meaning? How was it used? Many artifacts carry with them engaging mysteries that students enjoy considering. Artifacts produced more recently, such as items found in grandparents' attics or museum exhibits, also provide evidence about the culture and values of the people who produced, consumed, and preserved them. Countless artifacts exist that a history teacher might use as evidence to ponder historical questions. Working with artifacts can provide students with opportunities to think historically, consider historical contexts, corroborate interpretations across artifacts and written texts, and contemplate the role of evidence in the construction of historical interpretations. Because students who struggle with traditional reading may excel in their ability to make observations and inferences with artifacts, using artifacts can bring struggling readers into conversations about evidence. Artifacts represent an important genre of historical "texts," requiring students to use historical literacies.

Mrs. Dahl's lesson shows that artifacts provide clues about the people who produced them, whether they were made a few years ago or thousands of years ago, and whether they were intentionally buried or placed where millions would see them. Furthermore, her lesson shows that the literacies useful in constructing meaning with artifacts include a range of strategies, such as observation, inference making, sourcing, corroboration, and contextualization. And as in working with other forms of historical evidence, students must engage in the four roles of a reader, acting as a code breaker, meaning maker, text user, and text critic. Mrs. Dahl modeled each of these roles, showing students both how she decoded and comprehended the images in the sculpture and how she thought critically about its source and context, making inferences about the society that produced the monument. The study guide she created provided additional scaffolding as students worked through all four roles. She knew that helping students engage in these roles required scaffolding because reading artifacts presents unique challenges for students.

Challenges in Working With Artifacts

One challenge of using artifacts in history classrooms is finding them and making them available to students. Certainly any human-produced item, from a cave painting of Lascaux, France, to a modern tool, is an artifact, useful in discerning the values and cultures of the people who produced it. Any classroom is full of modern artifacts. However, artifacts associated with a historical era under investigation, such as Classical Greece or the Trail of Tears, might be difficult to procure. Furthermore, many of the most insightful observations require instruments that are unavailable to students or that require specialized training that students and history teachers lack. For instance, in looking through a microscope at bones that were stirred in rough stoneware pots, archaeologists have detected a trait they call pot polishing. Rubbing against the rough edges of the pot smoothed the exposed edges of bones. Based on pot polishing, archaeologists are able to establish the meats, including at times human, that prehistoric people stirred in pots and presumably ate. Pot polishing is an observation that students, without scientific training and tools, are unable to make. In other cases, DNA testing has revealed traces of blood or flesh of a variety of species of megafauna, such as mammoths and giant camels, on the same hunting implements, allowing archaeologists to make numerous inferences about the culture of prehistoric Americans. Obviously, students do not have opportunities to engage in DNA testing or other advanced scientific analysis of evidence.

Additionally, students face epistemic issues when working with artifacts. Historians readily admit that constructing a historical understanding from artifacts requires some conjecture, particularly when there is little written evidence to corroborate interpretations. To illustrate, in the first chapter of a popular college world history textbook describing Ice Age societies, of whom there is but scanty artifactual evidence, there are over a dozen admissions of uncertainty (Armesto, 2010). Armesto (2010) acknowledges "perplexing problems," "puzzling" bits of evidence, and at one point admits "we have no idea — beyond guesswork" about the most ancient migration patterns (pp. 12–13). Although students can gain insight into historical processes and, perhaps, develop a more mature epistemic stance from such admissions, there is also a risk that students will think that artifacts invite wild speculation. They might assume that any artifact-based interpretation is as plausible as any other. By admitting that we do not know *everything* about the origins or meaning of certain artifacts, some students might incorrectly assume that we cannot know *anything* about the cultures that produced them. However, as with all historical inquiry, standards exist for evaluating artifacts that prevent unwarranted guesswork.

Supporting Students' Use of Artifacts as Evidence

What are some specific teaching strategies you can use to support students' work with artifacts?

As with all other historical literacies, experience working with artifacts in a simplified and supportive context is valuable for students. As described in Chapter 5, a teacher might bring in several items from their own garbage can, such as empty pizza boxes, packaging from a new purchase, or a discarded toy that is broken or no longer used. Students could then be asked to list what they can infer about the teacher based on these artifacts. Within this context, the teacher could help students explore the process they use to make observations and inferences. It may be helpful for students to practice the literacies of working with artifacts within a context that is familiar and for which they have rich background knowledge (like a modern garbage can) before engaging with artifacts from unfamiliar eras (like a prehistoric cave in France).

Mrs. Dahl's lesson included several measures designed to improve students' analysis of the monument. As mentioned, she knew that students would have a difficult time analyzing the sculptures until they had rich and accurate background knowledge of the war so she planned the activity at the end of the unit on World War II. History teachers can facilitate students' analysis of artifacts by building students' background knowledge prior to exposing them to the artifacts. She gave students explicit instruction on observing, pointing out that she liked to start at the left and work her way slowly to the right, focusing on the details of the artifact. She pointed out that good observations also required a holistic look at the artifact, paying attention to the relationship between the different parts. In addition to explicit instruction on observations, she modeled inference making for the students. Furthermore, during group work, she asked students to justify their interpretations, requiring students to engage in metacognition by vocalizing and making explicit their thought processes. Explicit and implicit strategy instruction, teacher and peer modeling, and metacognitive interactions nurture students' ability to work with artifacts and other types of historical evidence.

Nurturing students' ability to think creatively and critically using artifacts as evidence requires multiple exposures to them. As with working with primary sources or any other type of evidence, students need opportunities to practice in a variety of contexts, with different research questions, and with a range of types of artifacts. For instance, the curriculum of most history classes includes opportunities to engage with both prehistoric artifacts from people who produced no written records and historic artifacts from people who had writing. In lessons dealing with prehistoric people, students can use corroboration across artifacts to test and retest their hypotheses. In lessons dealing with historic people, students can similarly corroborate across artifacts and written records. With repeated exposure to artifacts, teachers can reduce the amount of time dedicated to explicitly teaching literacy strategies, such as observing and inferring, and increase the amount of time students are actively engaged with texts and artifacts.

Teachers support students' development of skills in working with artifacts and other types of historical evidence by giving them space to construct their own interpretations. These interpretations can and should be subject to peer and teacher review and feedback. As explained in Chapter 2, history classrooms are often places where students simply listen to others' interpretations of the evidence, stated in unquestionable terms. In traditional classrooms, teachers introduce students to historical evidence, but it is usually done simply to illustrate the content presented during a lecture (Nokes, 2010). Instead, teachers can provide students with artifacts and give them the freedom to construct, test, revise, and share their independent interpretations. Constructing interpretations involves some measure of creative thinking, as students discover unique explanations for evidence. The process further involves critical thinking, as students test and revise their interpretations based on corroborating evidence. Furthermore, as students share their insights with peers, their ideas are subject to peer review and feedback. Students who have been taught explicitly the elements of effective inferences are more able to evaluate their peers' ideas. Students serving as reviewers might be prompted to ask questions such as "What evidence do you base this interpretation on?" or "What background knowledge helped you develop this interpretation?" or "Is this interpretation the simplest explanation that accounts for all of the evidence?" Developing independent interpretations and engaging in the critique of interpretations made by others provides students with opportunities to engage in historical thinking.

As part of efforts to teach students to work with artifacts, history teachers might allow students to observe the work of archaeologists as they engage with artifacts. This can be done by bringing in an archaeologist to describe their work to students, showing a video clip that describes an archaeologist's work with evidence, exploring websites that show archaeologists working at excavations, or through virtual field trips to archaeological sites. Observing the work of archaeologists provides a model for students to emulate as they work with artifacts in the classroom.

Bringing Artifacts Into the Classroom

As mentioned, one of the challenges of having students work with artifacts is procuring them for the classroom. Teachers have limited access to traveling exhibits and few resources for field trips to archaeological sites, museums, or artifact labs (e.g., see https://www.penn.museum/sites/artifactlab/). However, with the advent of the internet, all types of historical evidence, including images of artifacts, have become increasingly accessible. Often, photographs of artifacts, easily available online, are sufficient to allow students to make inferences about a culture or event. Teachers might prepare digital or physical folders containing photographs depicting different aspects of a society, such as homes, tools, art, toys, weapons, and floral and faunal remains (as Mrs. Francis did with the lesson on the Ancestral Pueblo described in Chapter 3). Small groups of students can work together to make observations and inferences about a culture based on an artifact folder made up of photographs of one type of artifact. Their inferences can then be tested and expanded as different artifact folders are circulated between groups.

Furthermore, some websites provide an opportunity for students to engage in a virtual archaeological dig or to observe the evidence in an artifact lab. Virtual field trips to museums offer additional online access to artifacts. Although not as intimate as holding the artifact in one's hand, online resources provide enough engagement with artifacts to allow teachers to involve students in artifact-related historical literacies.

Questions about the more recent past can be considered by having students collect everyday artifacts at home and bring them to class. For instance, students in a U.S. or local history class might address the question, "What did young people do for fun before television?" Investigating such a question might involve several historical literacies, as students gather and analyze historical evidence. For instance, students might interview grandparents or older neighbors, creating a historical record. In addition, they might be assigned to bring to class artifacts or photographs of artifacts that could be analyzed to corroborate the historical evidence they collect. Figure 8.4 is a graphic organizer that could be used to help students analyze artifacts brought to school by students as part of an inquiry on what young people did for fun prior to the invention of television.

School yearbooks are valuable and accessible artifacts that provide evidence of the daily lives of teenagers in recent decades. Teachers might guide students through a historical inquiry that addresses questions such as "What was teenage life like in the 1980s?" or "To what degree is the stereotypical image of a 1960 teenager as a hippy accurate?" or "How have school activities changed in the past 30 years and how have they remained unchanged?" or "How did bussing programs increase the integration of schools in the 1970s?" Students could be assigned to try to find a yearbook they could bring to class on a given day; then, on that day, in small groups they could look at several yearbooks to collect evidence that answers their question. Yearbooks are also available online for students

Name _____

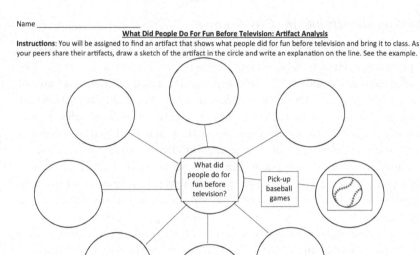

What Did People Do For Fun Before Television: Artifact Analysis

Instructions: You will be assigned to find an artifact that shows what people did for fun before television and bring it to class. As your peers share their artifacts, draw a sketch of the artifact in the circle and write an explanation on the line. See the example.

FIGURE 8.4 A graphic organizer used to analyze artifacts during an inquiry.

to use to supplement those that have been brought to class. Students' work with yearbooks might be corroborated by inviting a panel of individuals from the community to visit class and answer questions related to the historical inquiry.

Chapter Summary

Mrs. Dahl's review of the World War II unit involved students working with sculptures representing historical events. In a way, the images that the students studied as evidence are not very different from prehistoric pictographs that celebrated a successful hunt or other event. In both cases, the art was created to memorialize an important event. Artifacts, ancient and modern, are a valuable source of evidence about the past. Working with artifacts requires students to make inferences about the people who produced them. Good inferences are simple and are based on observations of evidence merged with accurate background knowledge. Explicit instruction on inference making, and repeated practice in settings that allow independent interpretations, build students' ability to work with artifacts. The internet makes photographs of artifacts and virtual visits to archaeological sites increasingly accessible to history classrooms.

Questions for Consideration

1. How does daily life require a person to make inferences? How do you make inferences as you have conversations with friends, work on social media, or

interact with others? How are inferences required in reading? Why can it be valuable to understand where inferences come from?

2. How is the process of making inferences in real-life settings similar to and different from making inferences when engaging in historical inquiries? What are the challenges involved in making inferences in both settings?

3. If someone were to study your life, which artifacts would you want them to use to make inferences about you? Which artifacts would you want them to avoid?

4. Who do you know that is particularly observant? What do they do that makes them more observant than others?

Additional Reading and Viewing

- Ford's Theatre, the site of Abraham Lincoln's assassination, has created a resource for teachers related to teaching with monuments and memorials, especially Civil War memorials, available at https://www.fords.org/blog/post/monuments-and-memorialization-a-resource-guide/.

- As an example of the way background knowledge and careful observations come together to make inferences you might show this video clip from the Disney movie, *Great Mouse Detective* to students: https://www.youtube.com/watch?v=K-q8FHq4bKk

- For a more detailed description of the process of teaching students about observation and inference using the Observation/Inference T-chart see Nokes, J. D. (2008). The observation/inference chart: Improving students' ability to make inferences while reading non-traditional texts. *Journal of Adolescent and Adult Literacy, 51*(7), 538–546.

- An article that describes an activity that converts "show and tell" into an artifact analysis activity can be found at Alber, R. (2017). Updating an Age-Old Class Activity. *Edutopia* at https://www.edutopia.org/blog/updating-age-old-class-activity-rebecca-alber.

References

Afflerbach, P., & Cho, B.Y. (2009). Identifying and describing constructively responsive reading strategies in new and traditional forms of reading. In S. E. Israel & G. G. Duffy (Eds.), *Handbook of research on reading comprehension* (pp. 69–90). Routledge.

Alber, R. (2017). Updating an age-old class activity. *Edutopia*. https://www.edutopia.org/blog/updating-age-old-class-activity-rebecca-alber

Armesto, E. E. (2010). *The world: A history* (2nd ed.). Prentice Hall.

Gurney G. (2004). Sculpting the World War II Memorial: A conversation with Raymond Kaskey. *American Art, 18*(2), 96–105. doi:10.1086/424792

Kaskey, R. (2004). *The lend lease act [sculpture].* World War II Memorial. .

Nokes, J. D. (2008). The observation/inference chart: Improving students' ability to make inferences while reading non-traditional texts. *Journal of Adolescent and Adult Literacy, 51*(7), 538–546. doi:10.1598/JAAL.51.7.2

Nokes, J. D. (2010). Observing literacy practices in history classrooms. *Theory and Research in Social Education, 38*(4), 298–316. doi:10.1080/00933104.2010.10473438

Paris, S. G., & Hamilton, E. E. (2009) The development of children's reading comprehension. In S. E. Israel & G. G. Duffy (Eds.), *Handbook of research on reading comprehension* (pp. 32–53). Routledge.

Pearson, D (2009). The roots of reading comprehension instruction. In S. E. Israel & G G Duffy (Eds.), *Handbook of research on reading comprehension* (pp. 3–31). Routledge.

Richards, J. C., & Anderson, N. A. (2003). What do I see? What do I think? What do I wonder? (STW): A visual literacy strategy to help emergent readers focus on storybook illustrations. *The Reading Teacher, 56*(5), 442–444.

Stanford History Education Group (2012). *Charting the future of teaching the past.* http://sheg.stanford.edu/

Wineburg, S., Martin, D., & Monte-Sano, C. (2011). *Reading like a historian: Teaching literacy in middle and high school classrooms.* Teachers College Press.

9

TEACHING HISTORICAL CONCEPTS WITH VISUAL TEXTS

People are constantly bombarded with visual images. Social media, internet sites, and memes display visual texts that young people must decipher. Yet little time is generally spent helping students learn how to make sense of and think critically about the images they see. This chapter will give you ideas for teaching young people strategies for working with historical visual texts—strategies that can be transferred to young people's visually rich world.

> In the following vignette, what are the strategies that Ms. Jensen teaches students to use when analyzing propaganda?

Ms. Jensen, an 11th-grade U.S. history teacher, is planning a lesson on the home front during World War I. She wants students to learn about such trends as shortages, voluntary rationing, the sale of war bonds, and the general war hysteria that engulfed the nation during the war. She brainstorms, producing a list of texts that might be used to teach these concepts: there might be transcribed oral histories of individuals from the local community, the textbook chapter has a section that gives an overview of life on the home front, and the school has in its collection a video series on World War I, which certainly includes appropriate clips. When she asks other U.S. history teachers at the school what they use, Mrs. Wade tells her that she uses propaganda posters produced by the U.S. government. Ms. Jensen researches and finds propaganda posters used to advertise war bonds, encourage home production, promote enlistment, encourage conservation, and vilify the enemy. She decides that propaganda posters are good evidence that students can use to study home-front trends.

Ms. Jensen understands that using propaganda posters as historical evidence will require students to have specialized literacies, including the ability to identify propaganda in its various formats, the disposition to consider the sources of

DOI: 10.4324/9781003183495-11

propaganda, and skills in analyzing the use of color, visual imagery, and language intended to produce emotional responses. Furthermore, she wants students to recognize the role of propaganda in moving people from an attitudinal state to a behavioral state. She wants them to assess the effectiveness of propaganda posters from World War I. She sees this as an opportunity to review the concept of *evidence*, an important element of historical thinking. In the process of working with the posters, she wants students to be immersed in home-front issues during the war.

Ms. Jensen decides to dedicate one class period to working with propaganda posters as evidence of home front trends. She intends to teach explicitly about the purpose of propaganda, having students explore the characteristics of visual-oriented propaganda using the posters. She considers teaching explicitly about the strategies of observing and inferring but decides to try implicit strategy instruction instead, guiding students as they use the strategies but without talking about the strategies directly. Ms. Jensen searches the internet and finds numerous examples of propaganda posters from World War I. She chooses examples associated with the selling of war bonds, enlistment drives, and home food production and preservation. She creates PowerPoint slides to display them. She prepares a graphic organizer to structure the class discussion, with a place for students to sketch or cut and paste an image of the poster, identify the emotion being manipulated, describe characteristics that intensify the emotion, and summarize what the poster suggests about life on the home front (see Figure 9.1).

During the first part of class, Ms. Jensen projects the image of a propaganda poster from the war (see Figure 9.2). She asks a student to come up to the whiteboard and record observations; then she calls on students to list things they see on the poster. At first, they describe the most obvious items: a gorilla monster, a woman being attacked, a club with something written on it. Students continue to call out what they see and their comments are recorded on the board. Eventually they notice more subtle elements of the propaganda: a helmet with a weird spike on it, the monster standing on the word *America*, a body of water, a city in ruins in the background.

#	Sketch	Target emotion and elements of the propaganda that intensify it	What the poster suggests about life on the home front
1			
2			

FIGURE 9.1 The top two rows of a graphic organizer for supporting students' work with propaganda posters.

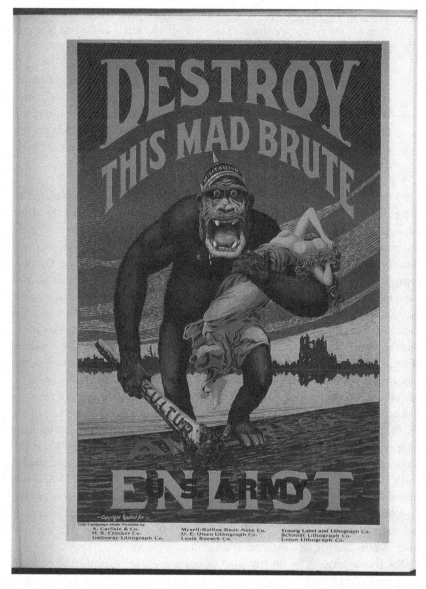

FIGURE 9.2 A World War I propaganda poster.
Source: Hopps (1917).

After a few minutes, Ms. Jensen gives the class a brief explanation of propaganda. "Propaganda is designed to motivate people to take some type of action," she explains.

Propaganda is intended to intensify a target emotion and promote an active response. In other words, it makes you feel so angry, sad, proud, or guilty that you will run out and do something. You decided that the target emotions for the poster we analyzed were anger and fear. The desired action is written explicitly on the bottom of the poster—'enlist.'"

She continues,

Propaganda is generally not intended to change a person's mind but to intensify what someone is already feeling to get the person to do something. If a person was already inclined to think of Germans as monsters, the propaganda poster might motivate them to enlist. So propaganda posters are good evidence about what many people were thinking about and feeling at the time the poster was created.

Ms. Jensen continues by reminding students about the concept of *evidence*, something that has been discussed on occasion throughout the school year. Students remember from prior lessons that evidence is a clue that helps historians figure things out, like a detective trying to solve a crime. Historians look for evidence and make interpretations of what it tells them about the past. She explains that the propaganda posters that they will look at during the lesson are not primarily to give them information. They cannot take what they say literally. For instance, the poster the class analyzed did not show what was happening. Germany had not invaded and did not invade America and Germans were not apelike monsters. The information on the poster required a critical analysis. The way historians use evidence like the propaganda posters is to try to answer their questions—in the case of the propaganda posters, to interpret the attitudes of Americans on the home front.

After this brief reminder about the role of evidence, Mrs. Jensen returns to a discussion of the propaganda poster. "So what can we infer about Americans on the home front from what we observed in the poster?" she asks. Students offer many suggestions: Americans did not like Germany. They were afraid the Germans might invade America. They thought Germany was strong and threatening. They were more concerned about what Germany might do to America than they were about what Germany was doing in Europe. They questioned the morality of the Germans. They thought Germans threatened American liberty. In the end, the class concludes that the poster was primarily playing on a fear that many Americans had of the threat of a German invasion.

Ms. Jensen reviews for students the cognitive processes they used to evaluate the poster as evidence:

Do you see how we used the poster as evidence of what people were feeling on the home front? The poster was not made for this purpose, and it does not just give us information, but we are using it to answer a question that *we* came up with. This is the way historians use evidence. They ask questions and then seek evidence to answer their questions. These propaganda posters give us clues about what Americans were feeling during a particular part of World War I. They serve as evidence.

She discusses with students other types of evidence a historian might use to answer this same question, such as newspapers from the time period, letters and journals written by people on the home front, photographs taken in the 1910s, and other evidence.

Ms. Jensen passes out the graphic organizer (Figure 9.1) and helps the class members fill out the first row related to the poster they have just analyzed. She then projects a second propaganda poster and asks students to go through the same process with a partner, using the poster as evidence about life on the home front. The remainder of the class period, Ms. Jensen alternates between partnered work and whole-class discussions analyzing each of the posters she projects. Students take notes on their graphic organizers as they work. At the end of class, Ms. Jensen conducts a short debriefing. Among other questions, the students consider how propaganda posters can serve as evidence to help us answer other historical questions: whether other countries made propaganda posters that made Americans look like monsters, whether common elements of propaganda posters cut across different cultures, and how effective the posters were.

As the bell rings ending class, Ms. Jensen commends the students for their good thinking. Most of them seem to grasp the concept of *evidence*, which she was trying to teach. They have also been active in identifying home-front trends—she thinks that the visual images of the posters will help them understand what was going on at home. And she is quite confident that students have a better understanding of the nature of propaganda.

How can understanding how to think critically about propaganda prepare students to deal with politicized news sources, advertising, social media, and other common sources of information in the 21st century?

Metaconcepts and Visual Evidence

In this chapter, I explore two elements of Ms. Jensen's lesson. First, I consider important historical metaconcepts, such as *evidence*. I define *metaconcept* and list and describe several historical metaconcepts. I subsequently discuss the use of visual texts, like the propaganda posters in Ms. Jensen's lesson.

Metaconcepts

As you read this section, consider why metaconcepts are rarely taught to young people in history lessons in spite of their importance? How can a knowledge of metaconcepts improve a student's ability to engage in historical inquiry?

Metaconcepts, also known as second order concepts, are ideas, notions, or tools that are related to the methods historians use to study the past. Lee (2005) lists the following metaconcepts, the understanding of which is essential to historians' work: *time, change, empathy, cause, evidence*, and *accounts*. Limon (2002) describes additional metaconcepts such as *explanation, space, source, fact, description*, and *narration*. Other metaconcepts include *significance* and *context*. Metaconceptual understanding is vital to the work of historians—they perceive some historical *accounts* to be *evidence* and others not, for instance. To write effectively they must understand the differences between *description, explanation, argumentation*, and *narration* and know when to employ each. However, because historians use metaconceptual understanding with little conscious thought, a shroud of mystery hides metaconceptual knowledge and use. As Gaddis (2002) explains, "[o]ur reluctance to reveal our own [structures] . . . too often confuses our students—even, at times, ourselves—as to just what it is we do" (p. XI). Most history teachers rarely devote class time to building students' metaconceptual understandings.

---

metaconcepts: historical ideas that have to do with the process of studying history, cutting across all historical fields of study, themes, and topics.

Metaconcepts should not be confused with *substantive concepts*, the structures, phenomena, persons, and periods of history (Lee, 2005; van Drie & van Boxtel, 2008). Substantive concepts have been categorized as *inclusive concepts*, concepts that transcend any given historical period or topic, such as democracy, compromise, or economic depression; *unique concepts*, concepts that describe a specific person, place, or event, such as Franklin D. Roosevelt, Athens, and Gettysburg; and *colligatory concepts*, hierarchical classifications that bring order to history such as Persian Empire, Progressive Movement, or Great Awakening (Nokes & McGrew, 2021; van Drie & van Boxtel, 2008). Most history instruction revolves around substantive concepts. However, without metaconceptual understanding of ideas like *change* and *time*, students might fail to understand the subtleties of substantive concepts. For instance, without a correct understanding of the concept of *change*, a student might think that the concept of *king*, an inclusive concept, remains stagnant throughout history, when, in fact, a 15th-century king was very different from an 18th-century king, which is very different from a 21st-century king (Lee, 2005). It is rare for teachers to address metaconcepts, the subject of this chapter. Without an understanding of key metaconcepts, historical literacy is impossible. To illustrate the importance, I consider several metaconcepts.

---

substantive concepts: ideas that make up the substance of historical content, sometimes divided into inclusive concepts that represent abstract ideas

> important within multiple fields of study (democracy), unique concepts that are important within a single field (Battle of Lexington), and colligatory concepts that create hierarchical order (Roman Empire).

Evidence

Because history is the evidence-based study of the past, without evidence there is no history. Most history students spend little time considering how we know what we know about the past. As described in Chapters 5 and 11, they typically accept the authoritative historical narrative they receive from the textbook and teacher without question. However, students who understand the metaconcept of evidence are prepared to take on a different role in learning history. They can assume the task of semi-independently constructing their own understanding of historical events using texts as evidence. Ms. Jensen wants students to consider how a researcher might know what people on the home front were thinking and feeling during World War I. Rather than merely read a textbook author's interpretation and accept it as fact, students use propaganda posters as evidence to piece together their own understanding. The propaganda posters serve as evidence through which they answer this question. In Ms. Jensen's class, the posters serve as clues about the past rather than as conveyers of information. Students, with the continual prodding of Ms. Jensen, view them as evidence. As described in Chapter 7, historical evidence can be classified as either *accounts* or *traces*. Accounts, described in more detail next, are the intentional retelling about a historical event. Traces are other pieces of evidence that serve as clues about a historical question. Traces include a wide range of evidence, not originally intended to explicitly give information about an event or condition but merely a product of the past, such as a sales receipt, a blueprint, a song, a speech, a shoe, and scores of other clues that might be useful to historians.

Accounts

An account is a historical narrative—an intentional retelling of something that happened. Each account represents a particular point of view, with contents that are filtered through the author's decisions of what to include or omit, which words to use, and the tone of the narrative. The bas-relief sculptures of the World War II Memorial described in Chapter 8 give an account of the war, created for the purpose of retelling what happened. Like all accounts they include some details and leave other things out. Textbooks give a different account of the war. And primary sources provide other unique accounts. No account is complete or untainted by its creator's purposes. Accounts are influenced by many things besides just what happened. For example, a young person, telling about a party they attended, might give a completely different account to their mother than the account that they give to their best friend. Events at the party have not changed, though the account of it differs. So among other factors, the audience influences an account. Accounts come in a wide variety of formats, some primary sources, others secondary or tertiary, and some fictional, as described in Chapter 10. Textbooks provide tertiary accounts, intentionally retelling what happened but not from an eyewitness perspective. As described earlier, accounts of past events can also be found in a phone call, a letter, a diary entry, an interview, a tour of a historical site, a sketch, and a painting. Accounts provided by eyewitnesses are primary sources. Primary source accounts serve as evidence about the past, resources historians sift through as they reconstruct past events. Approaching each narrative with the understanding that it is an account leads the historian or student to consider the source, read critically, and accept or reject each idea it includes. No more important metaconcept exists for promoting critical thinking than the concept of account.

Significance

The process of historical inquiry requires historians and others to determine when an event, person, era, or society is worth studying. Determining historical significance is one of the main roles of historians and history teachers. For instance, there is little interest in what Ms. Jensen ate for lunch on December 11, 1973. And without interest there is no significance and thus no history. On the other hand, a biographer of Abraham Lincoln might devote a great deal of energy trying to uncover what Abraham Lincoln ate the evening of April 14, 1865, his final meal. The biographer creates historical significance by his interest in and investigation of this topic. Determining significance is a highly subjective process. For instance, Paul Revere's famous ride has entered America's collective memory, gaining significance, while William Dawes's more successful ride that same night has largely been forgotten. A poem written decades later about Paul Revere by Henry Wadsworth Longfellow is the primary reason for Revere's historical significance today. Alexander Hamilton gained unprecedented significance in Americans' collective memory in the 2010s when the musical, *Hamilton* was produced, not because of new evidence discovered about his contributions to American society but because of the popularity of the Broadway play.

Perhaps the most compelling case for considering historical significance is that of the Indus River society, a civilization that flourished 3,500 years ago in a large region near the Indus River in modern Pakistan. For many years, even after the British occupation of India, there was little interest in Indus ruins, besides scavenging building material for use in the construction of railroad lines. Eventually, after the discovery of their unique writing system, interest began to grow and a new civilization was "discovered" in the early 20th century. A more accurate description of this "discovery" would be that historians began to place significance on a society that had been known of for ages. Significance relates to topics as large as a civilization or as small as a grandson's search for records of his grandmother's life.

Ethical Judgment

Ethical judgment is an important element of historical thinking and one of the "big six" historical thinking strategies defined by Seixas and Morton (2012). Ethical judgment involves evaluating the actions of historical characters and identifying them as good, right, and fair; or bad, wrong, and unfair. This process is complicated by the fact that today's values and understanding of the world differ from the values and understandings of people in the past. The fact that values were different in the past does not absolve historical characters from responsibility for immoral actions. However, knowing the context surrounding the actions of people in the past helps the current generation explain why they acted as they did. Based on Seixas and Morton's (2012) research, I suggest that several questions should guide students' judgment of former generations' actions (Nokes, 2019, p. 83):

- Were a person's actions reasonable given their understanding of right and wrong?
- What did people know or think at the time that influenced the person's actions?
- Were the person's choices limited because of laws, policies, or expectations?
- Does evidence show that a person believed that they acted ethically?
- How does a person's actions reveal what they thought was ethical?
- What are current ethical controversies that are related to historical events?
- What ethical action can we take today to make amends for mistakes made in the past?

Time

It is difficult to study history without a grasp of the metaconcept of time. Time is particularly helpful in establishing sequence and duration. And an understanding of duration is critical in distinguishing between a single event and a long-term process (Lee, 2005). However, students sometimes have distorted views of time. For instance, students often fail to comprehend the important distinction between long eras, such as the tens of thousands of years of the Ice Age, and shorter eras, such as the years of the New Deal. Lee (2005) contends that "the attempt to transfer common-sense ideas about time from everyday life to history may pose problems" (p. 42). For instance, although the development of the first agriculture evolved over thousands of years, students may view the change to farming as being an invention of a single generation or even the choice of a single individual. Furthermore, students are often literal and inflexible in their understanding of time, basing it on clocks and calendars. Historians, on the other hand, think of time in terms of processes or patterns. For instance, a historian might refer to the "greater 20th century" in order to link events of the late 1800s with similar 20th-century trends.

Change and Continuity

Many students have distorted views of the metaconcept of change as well. For instance, young people often confuse the notion of event and change (Lee, 2005). Although events are not, in and of themselves, change, patterns of events can mark changing conditions. Some events are deemed to cause such far-reaching changes that they are called *turning points*. Historians recognize that the absence of change is not the absence of events but acknowledge, instead, the notion of *continuity* (Lee, 2005). Additionally, students tend to view change as perpetual progress, failing to understand that progress is not inevitable and that changes sometimes result in regression.

Cause and Effect

Without an understanding of causation, history becomes "one damn thing after another" (Toynbee, 1957)—simply a parade of events. Causes and effects are what link events into historical narratives. Much of the work of historians involves identifying the causes of observed phenomena. In doing so, they impose a sense of order on the past. Thus chronology is not simply a time sequence but also involves causes and effects. Nor should chronology be considered a simple chain of causes and effects but instead should be viewed as a complex network of causes and potential and actual effects, with both predictable and unanticipated outcomes (Gaddis, 2002). Historians often make a distinction between *long-range causes*, conditions that build up over months, years, or even longer, and *immediate causes*, events that trigger a direct outcome. Likewise, historians think about *immediate effects*, outcomes that occur soon after an event, and *long-range effects*, the far-reaching changes that carry more permanence. An understanding of cause and effect, as well as change, time, significance, account, evidence, and other metaconcepts, lays the groundwork for students to engage in historical literacies. Ms. Jensen's lesson on the home front during World War I was designed to help students understand the metaconcept of evidence.

Building Historical Literacies With Visual Text

Why is it important to teach students strategies for working with visual texts?

In the remainder of this chapter, I consider the building of historical literacies, including the building of metaconceptual understanding, using visual texts. The focus is on teaching with visual texts, understanding the challenges students face in working with visual texts, and methods of building students' historical literacies with visual texts. I provide case studies of four types of visual texts: maps, political cartoons, paintings, and photographs. I conclude the chapter with a consideration of students using visual texts in argumentation.

Teaching With Visual Texts

Today's students live in a visual-oriented world. They are regularly exposed to images through internet sites, social media, movies, iPods, and television. Interestingly, they typically receive very little formal instruction on how to construct meaning with visual texts, relying instead on their instincts (Callahan, 2015). Their intuition may be sufficient to comprehend, critique, and use some types of visual texts, such as a video of a group of friends on TikTok. However, many of the texts that are useful in historical inquiry require in-depth analysis using unique strategies—visual literacies. History classrooms provide a suitable context for building students' visual literacies because visual texts serve as valuable evidence for historians.

Visual texts may be primary or secondary sources depending on the historian's questions and the source of the text. Some of the oldest evidence used by archaeologists and historians are visual primary sources. Cave paintings at Lascaux, France, for example, are over 17,000 years old. Human forms of art, from prehistoric times to the present, offer a glimpse into values, attitudes, and cultures, and serve as invaluable evidence—particularly when studying cultures that did not produce written records. Since the invention of the camera, photographs have added a new genre of historical primary sources. Individuals involved in historic events make sketches or draw maps. Political cartoonists capture public opinion in their work. Governments sponsor propaganda posters. Corporations pay for ads in magazines and newspapers. The list of visual texts that historians use as evidence is nearly endless. Imaginative history teachers have an inexhaustible supply of visual primary sources from which to choose.

In addition, secondary and tertiary visual sources are important in learning history. Paintings often reveal how past events were viewed by later generations, and, thus, serve as both secondary sources of the events they depict and as primary sources of the time period during which they were produced. Modern textbooks are filled with colorful images, both primary and secondary sources, that illustrate the events described in the writing. Historians produce maps to help others visualize the geographic setting of events. Illustrators support the narrative in magazines and children's books. As with all other texts, visual texts have a human source, and history students should think differently about primary and secondary visual texts, just as they do with other types of evidence.

Historical thinking can be fostered with visual texts. For instance, Ashby et al. (2005) observed students trying to make sense of paintings as historical sources. Through a teacher's coaching, eventually a student acknowledged, "You would need to know about the painter who actually painted it. You need some background information." Through continued dialogue, another student wanted to know, "What period of time it was painted and whereabouts it was painted" (Ashby et al., 2005, p. 99). These students demonstrate the strategy of sourcing applied during an analysis of visual texts. Furthermore, their statements suggest that they understand the metaconcepts of evidence.

The Challenges of Reading Visual Texts

What are some of the challenges students face in working with visual texts? How can teachers help students overcome these challenges?

Students face several challenges in working with visual texts. First, there are often subtle, or not-so-subtle, symbol systems in visual texts that may be difficult to decode. For example, in topographical maps the elevation is shown using lines drawn to indicate certain altitudes (i.e., at 5000′, 5500′, 6000′; see Figure 9.3). A person who understands the symbol system can break the code of lines and construct meaning, visualizing the layout of a landscape. Topographical maps have many applications in teaching history. For example, a topographical map of the

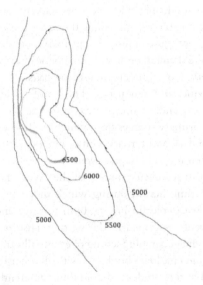

FIGURE 9.3 A topographical map.

Battle of Gettysburg can show how the lay of the land was influential in determining the outcome of the battle. But the usefulness of topographical maps is based on the ability of the reader to construct meaning with them. Such is also the case with other visual resources: their usefulness is based on the reader's ability to decode, comprehend, critique, and use the text in constructing interpretations.

Some visual texts use symbol systems that are more subtle and difficult to decode than topographical maps. For instance, artists use colors, symmetry, movement, and theme to convey a message more subjectively to the viewer. In negotiating meaning with art, students may lack the background knowledge necessary to decode or comprehend the artist's intended meaning. Because a painting often says as much about the artist as it does about its subject, the historical context for the creation of art is extremely important. Additionally, students often experience an initial reaction to a work of art that may interfere with their ability to effectively negotiate meaning (Gabella, 1996). They might confuse realism with historical accuracy, for instance. Compounding the difficulties, students often feel quite confident in their ability to break the code and construct meaning with many visual texts in a mere glance. This creates the dangerous combination of incompetence and confidence as students engage with art. Thus, artwork presents a particular literacy challenge.

Students face a different challenge in working with photography. They often assume that photographs are isomorphic with historical "reality," forgetting that photographs always have a source, were created for a purpose, and sometimes have been manipulated to achieve that purpose. For example, during the Great Depression, photographers working for the Farm Security Administration were commissioned to build public support for government programs that aided poor farmers. Their photographs of dust-bowl farms, immigrant farmworkers, poor farming families, and wealthy bankers were not simply produced to document events but were politically motivated. Nor did the photographs always capture naturally occurring situations, but they were sometimes manipulated. Historians, for example, have discovered what they call the "perambulating skull," a cow's skull used as a prop that was moved from location to location to add emphasis to the desolation of dust-bowl farms. Like their work with textbooks, students often view photographs as being sourceless snapshots of reality and thus exempt from the criticism that they would use in analyzing other sources. To summarize, students face particular challenges in working with visual texts, namely, unfamiliar symbol systems that present challenges in code breaking; overconfidence in their ability to construct understanding at a glance; and overestimation of the reliability and validity of photographs.

Building Students' Visual Literacies

Because different formats of visual text use different symbol systems, learning with unique visual texts requires unique literacies. Depending on the research questions, visual texts that are important in building historical meaning might include propaganda, maps, political cartoons, paintings, photographs, cartograms, flags, billboards, organization or corporation logos, product packaging, and countless other genres. It is impossible to elaborate on all forms of visual text in this volume. Instead, I consider four types of visual texts in some detail: maps, political cartoons, paintings, and photographs, providing a few specific resources for teachers. Effective teaching with all visual texts requires students to engage in the four roles of the reader described earlier: code breaker, meaning maker, text user, and text critic. Students must be able to *break the code*, which sometimes requires explicit instruction on unfamiliar symbol systems. They must *construct meaning* with the text, and *critically evaluate* the image, which involves strategies of sourcing, contextualization, and corroboration. With these skills, students can *use visual texts* as historical evidence.

Maps

Historians acknowledge that geography has a profound influence on many historical events. So maps serve as important primary and secondary sources in the study of history. Historians can trace, for instance, changing knowledge of and attitudes about the land or bodies of water through historical maps, using them as primary sources. For example, a lesson found on the Stanford History Education Group's website uses early colonial maps to study colonists' evolving attitudes toward Indigenous people (Stanford History Education Group, 2012, at https://sheg.stanford.edu). Through sourcing, contextualization, and corroboration across several maps that were produced within a few decades, students can make interpretations about increasing racism in colonial attitudes toward the Indigenous inhabitants of the land. The maps serve as evidence in this process. Historical maps can be useful evidence in a wide range of historical inquiries.

Maps are also used as secondary sources to illustrate the connection between geospatial context and history. Historians often produce maps to clarify and substantiate their claims. For instance, a historian might produce a map showing colonial settlements to argue the importance of rivers to colonists. Often the details of physical locations of an event are important for purposes of contextualization. Students should understand that maps produced by historians do not simply contain the facts of a location but are constructed for particular purposes and with audiences in mind. For example, a historian who was making the argument about the spread of Islam within certain latitudes might use a cartogram that demonstrates the Muslim population of nations by the size of the country on the cartogram (e.g., see https://worldmapper.org/maps/religion-muslims-2005/). This map does not simply present the facts, although it is factually accurate. Instead, it presents the facts in a way that bolsters the historian's argument. Many maps are used for this same purpose, to substantiate a historian's claim.

Teachers can facilitate students' learning with maps by providing explicit instruction on map-reading skills. As with all sources, students should consider the source and purpose of each map and become familiar with their common features. Students should know that a wide variety of maps exist, each having a unique function. The features of a map suit its particular purpose. To facilitate meaning making, students should be taught to look at the title, the legend or key, and the scale. They should be aware of an index on road maps, which can narrow down the search for a town to one small section of the map, thus improving students' facility with the map. Decoding the map involves traditional decoding, identifying words; symbolic decoding, recognizing the meaning of different symbols (i.e. green lines representing interstate highways and broken parallel lines representing dirt roads); and structural decoding, using the index and coordinates to locate details.

Although the decoding and constructing meaning with maps require unique skills, the critique and use of maps as evidence require more familiar historical literacies. For instance, knowing the source of a map can help a historian infer things about the context of its creation. Furthermore, the purpose of the map-maker and the attitudes of the time can often be inferred by the decisions made about inclusions on the map, as in the case of the colonial maps in the lesson mentioned earlier.

Political Cartoons

Political cartoons, depicting both current and historic events, present a particular challenge to students. In the age of the internet, memes and social media have replaced print newspapers as the primary means of remaining informed, and political cartoons are becoming increasingly unfamiliar and incomprehensible to many young people. Unlike their work with other types of visual texts, students often recognize and acknowledge that they "do not get it" after their initial glance at a political cartoon. Furthermore, students are often unwilling to put forth the effort to decode and construct meaning with political cartoons because of the challenge of doing so. However, political cartoons are an important part of America's political culture and a valuable historical resource. They provide evidence of popular and unpopular opinions associated with politics and events, both currently and in the past.

Breaking the code of political cartoons is sometimes tricky for students. They are often very literal in decoding, failing to understand that each image and inter-action in a political cartoon symbolizes a metaphorical event or idea. Students' ability to decode political cartoons is aided when teachers talk explicitly with students about their purpose. To aid with decoding, students can be shown that political cartoonists often give hints of what symbols represent, sometimes going so far as to label the symbol. For example, in Dr. Seuss's 1941 cartoon (see Figure 9.4), some symbols are labeled with words, such as the names of countries written on the trees; some symbols are labeled by other symbols, such as the black woodpecker with the Nazi symbol or the eagle with the starred and striped hat;

FIGURE 9.4 A political cartoon.
Source: Seuss (1941).

and some symbols are not labeled at all, such as the eagle's closed eyes, smile, and twiddling thumbs. The process of breaking the code requires students to identify the symbolic meaning of the various images. Additionally, the process of breaking the code requires students to figure out the meanings implied in the relationships between images. For example, the American eagle's back is turned to the Nazi woodpecker and, as noted, its eyes are closed. So, students' ability to break the code rests in their identification of the symbolic images in the cartoon and clarification of the relationships between the images. In many instances, decoding and comprehending also require students to understand rhetorical devices such as irony, sarcasm, forced connections, and exaggeration. For example, in Dr. Seuss's cartoon, the eagle's foolish optimism is exaggerated in the sarcastic quote. Dr. Seuss did not believe those words he wrote.

As students break the symbolic code they can work to construct meaning with the cartoon. The construction of meaning with political cartoons is facilitated by whole-class or small-group discussions as students brainstorm, suggest interpretations, and critique each other's ideas. As with the analysis of other types of visual texts, a synergy develops as students work together, play off one another's ideas, and collaboratively construct meaning. Additionally, when teachers require students to make explicit their thinking processes, students model literacies for each other. For example, when a student puts forward an evidence-based interpretation, the teacher can demand that they cite the evidence upon which the interpretation is based, using the question, "How did you figure that out?" Teachers demonstrate the need to rely on evidence when they have proficient students reveal to struggling students the manner of thinking that constitutes proficiency.

Early on, teachers can facilitate students' comprehension of political cartoons by creating checklists, worksheets, or posters that prompt students to (a) activate or build background knowledge needed to comprehend the cartoon; (b) consider the source and context of the cartoon; (c) identify and decode word-labeled, symbol-labeled, or unlabeled symbols; (d) describe important relationships among symbols; (e) find instances of irony, sarcasm, forced connections, or exaggeration; and (f) help students summarize the message the cartoonist is trying to send. Figure 4.3 (page 76) serves as an example of such a poster. Over time and with practice, as students gain proficiency in decoding and comprehending political cartoons, teachers can remove the posters and prompts and provide less support.

Once students understand the meaning of a political cartoon, they must critique it and can use it as historical evidence. Working specifically with the Dr. Seuss cartoon shown in Figure 9.4, the teacher might ask students what this cartoon reveals about Dr. Seuss. Questions should be raised whether his opinion reflected a majority or minority opinion in the United States at the time. Why might he have advocated this position? What were the flaws in his logic in this cartoon? Who might have opposed his ideas? A search could be conducted for political cartoons that show alternative points of view. Teachers can support students as text critics and text users by asking questions, such as "When was the cartoon produced?" "What do we know about the cartoonist?" "Is the tone of the cartoon humorous or serious?" "How well did the artist do in presenting their message?" "How popular was this cartoon?" "Who would be likely to agree with this message?" "Who would be likely to disagree?" and "What other evidence is needed to fully comprehend and critique this cartoon as historical evidence?" As with all literacies, with practice many students become more proficient in using political cartoons as evidence in the development of historical interpretations, and, in the process, become more literate with current political cartoons.

Paintings and Sculptures

Students' tendencies in constructing meaning with paintings contrast sharply with the challenges they face in reading political cartoons. Instead of quickly admitting an inability to comprehend, with paintings students often believe that they have achieved complete comprehension at a glance. Frequently the challenge in working with paintings is to get students to slow down and think more deeply about what they see, what it might represent, and what it suggests about the artist and his/her time — in other words, to engage in the close reading of paintings and to use them as evidence.

One way to help students think deeply about historic paintings is through the use of the Observation/Inference (O/I) chart (Nokes, 2008), introduced in Chapter 8. The O/I chart is a graphic organizer that breaks down the process of analyzing paintings into the stages of observing and inferring (see Figure 8.3, page 159). The O/I chart is a basic T-chart with two columns. In the left column, students keep a record of the things they observe in a painting. In the right column, students record inferences they make about the painting and the author's intended message. In connection with the use of the graphic organizer, teachers can provide explicit instruction on strategies that make students more observant and more skilled at making inferences. For instance, students can be encouraged to take their time, in essence, to slow their reading speed, to look at the details of the painting quadrant by quadrant, to look at each of the images included in the painting in isolation, and to look at the relationships between images. Additionally, allowing students to work together increases and improves the quality of their observations. One student's discovery often stimulates a flurry of new observations.

The metaconcept of *evidence* comes into play when working with the O/I chart to analyze paintings. Students keep a record of observations, evidence on which to base inferences. For each inference they list on the chart, students should be able to identify the evidence on which it is based. Arrows linking observations to inferences can be drawn on the O/I chart to explicitly demonstrate the connection between evidence and inference. The O/I chart is effective for several reasons. It provides scaffolding by reminding students about the process of making observations and inferences. It gives them a place to record their thoughts, thus freeing up cognitive resources and allowing them to return to their thinking later. It helps them be metacognitive by requiring them to slow down and think about their cognitive processes in making inferences. The O/I chart promotes self-critique because students must justify their inferences. It allows students to record their thinking processes on paper, allowing others to observe their thought processes. It creates a record for the teacher to use to assess and provide feedback on their analysis (Nokes, 2008).

Art provides a useful resource for helping students explore difficult histories, such as racism, slavery, and genocide. For instance, paintings and sculptures record the racism inherent in the westward expansion of the United States and could be used in an inquiry on that topic. For example, a statue titled *The Rescue* (Greenough, 1850) was displayed on the east façade of the U.S. Capitol building until 1958 (see Figure 9.5). The sculpture, offensive to both Indigenous people and to women, shows a larger-than-life Daniel Boone constraining a much smaller American Indian man who wields a tomahawk. A woman holding a baby cowers to the side. The sculpture

FIGURE 9.5 Sculpture titled *The Rescue* by Horatio Greenough (1850), displayed in the US Capitol building until 1958.

reinforces stereotypes of Indigenous people as savage, women as weak, and White men as superior to both. A historical inquiry might include consideration of the message being sent by the presence of this statue in the U.S. Capitol building. The inquiry might also include paintings such as John Gast's (1872) *American Progress*, which shows Indigenous people side by side with the wild animals that are being chased out by civilizing, angelic Columbia (see Figure 9.6). The equestrian statue of Theodore Roosevelt at the American Museum of Natural History is an additional sculpture that might be used in the inquiry. Because of its racist presentation of an African American and American Indian, museum representatives asked city officials to remove it, which they agreed to do (Pogrebin, 2020). The teaching of difficult history through inquiries involving art can help students confront racism and can help them be more informed in ongoing conversations about racism including the removal of statues from public spaces.

FIGURE 9.6 Painting titled *American Progress* by John Gast (1872).

Photographs

Lewis Hine, a Progressive-era photographer, explained, "[Y]ou and I know that this unbounded faith in the integrity of the photograph is often rudely shaken, for, while photographs may not lie, liars may photograph" (Dimock, 1993, p. 39). What do you think he meant by this?

Since the mid-19th century, photographs have become a useful resource for studying the past. Students should be taught how to use them as historical evidence. As mentioned, students should acknowledge that photographs have a source, do not represent an objective reality, are created with a purpose in mind—sometimes to document, sometimes to persuade — and can be manipulated to exaggerate or distort their subject. In working with photographs, students should seek to find the source and its sponsorship. With the source in mind, students can analyze photographs in much the same way recommended in analyzing paintings. The O/I chart works equally well with paintings and photographs (as well as other types of nonprint texts such as artifacts or movie clips). In preparing to help students work with a particular photograph, a teacher should reflect on the following questions: (a) What basic background knowledge do students need to effectively read this picture? Without the necessary background knowledge, students are not likely to be able to construct appropriate meaning with the photograph. However, teachers should not do the analysis for students (except during modeling), which can happen if they provide too much background knowledge. (b) How can students' attention be drawn toward important details in the photograph? Teachers might suggest that students analyze specific sections of the photograph in addition to analyzing the photo as a whole. (c) What challenges might students face in dealing with the details in the photograph? For example, are objects, people, or activities shown that students are not likely to accurately identify? (d) How can students be led to consider the photographer's purposes in taking a picture? For instance, why did they choose a certain perspective, certain lighting, and so on? And (e) how can this picture be used as evidence in the development of historical interpretations? In other words, how does this photograph help us understand the past?

Students can have opportunities to engage in historical inquiries that use photographs as evidence. For example, students might explore questions such as "What tactics did the Farm Security Administration photographers use to build support for New Deal programs?" "How did Lewis Hine and other Progressive-era photographers build support for child labor reforms?" and "How did the silent sentinels work to promote women's suffrage?" Such questions lead naturally into a discussion of the way cell phone cameras have been used to promote police reform.

Researchers have found that photographs carry an important role in the teaching of difficult histories. Photographs can capture trauma and violence in a way that can arouse strong feelings in students (Simon, 2011). For example, Miles (2019) found that viewing images of Indigenous youth who had attended Indian Residential Schools in Canada made Canadian youth confront this difficult history, although their reactions were mixed. Most students felt the traumatic or "dark atmosphere" (Miles, 2019, p. 485) in the image. They felt sympathetic for the suffering of the children. But conversations around the photographs soon changed, as the students began to deny wrongdoing and imagine happiness in the images. In the end, most students were able to skirt the emotional trauma of confronting the difficult past. Miles concluded that without adequate scaffolding, simply providing the photographs that depicted events that carry emotional trauma was not enough to disrupt dominant narratives that avoid difficult history. Greater success is likely when a teacher uses photographs as part of a text set that includes other genres when studying difficult histories. Teachers must take an active role in helping students manage their thoughts, emotions, and interactions because of the power of photographs as historical evidence.

Finally, modern technology and the increasing use of "photoshopping" places a greater demand on viewers of photographs to maintain healthy skepticism and to investigate a photograph's origins. Furthermore, photographs are often misidentified in blogs or other social media, with the error being repeated by scores of people who repost information without evaluating its accuracy. Seeing can no longer be believing. The use of reverse image searching allows an internet user to explore the online presence of a photograph and detect errors in its identification or use. Students should be taught to use reverse image searches before they use photographs in historical inquiry and before they repost an image that gives misinformation.

Using Visual Texts as Evidence

Because visual texts can be useful evidence during historical inquiries, they should also be used in students' argumentative writing and speaking. Just as a student would cite or paraphrase a written text to bolster an argument, students should be encouraged to use visual texts to substantiate claims. Images can be pasted directly into a presentation or argumentative paper. Alternatively, students can provide written descriptions of the image. The purpose of the inclusion of visual evidence in argumentative work is not merely to add color or to take up space but to strengthen a claim by providing evidence to back it up. The argumentative writing process is explored more thoroughly in Chapter 13.

Chapter Summary

Metaconcepts are concepts that cut across all historical study, the understanding of which is vital in historical thinking. Metaconcepts include ideas like *evidence*, *account*, *change*, and *time*. Evidence includes visual texts. History teachers can help students increase their visual literacy by helping them learn the unique symbol systems of various genres of visual texts, such as propaganda, maps, political cartoons, paintings, and historical photographs. Students have different literacy needs when working with different types of visual texts. Teachers can help students critique and use visual texts as evidence in constructing historical interpretations. As is the case with all forms of historical evidence, students should use visual texts in their argumentative writing and speaking to substantiate their claims.

Questions for Consideration

1. Why does working with visual historical evidence like photographs or paintings feel less like work than analyzing written historical evidence? How does the inclusion of visual texts invite struggling readers into historical inquiries?
2. In what ways are the strategies for working with visual historical evidence similar to the strategies for working with written evidence? In what ways are the strategies unique?
3. Some people would argue that there are certain documents like the Declaration of Independence, the Constitution, and the Gettysburg Address

that every U.S. history student should study. Do iconic photographs, paintings, sculptures, and buildings also exist that every student should study?

4. How do the internet and social media place greater demands on individuals to critically evaluate the images and videos that they view online?

Additional Reading and Viewing

*   The United States National Archives provides a study guide for analyzing historical photographs at this site: https://www.archives.gov/education/lessons/worksheets/photo
*   The artist Ken Gonzales-Day blends photography and art by erasing the victims from lynch photographs using Photoshop in order to draw attention to the crowd in an excellent resource for teaching difficult history at https://kengonzalesday.com/projects/erased-lynchings/.
*   In a TED Talk, artist Titus Kaphar asks, "Can art amend history?" and discusses the depiction of racism in art and ideas for amending this at https://www.ted.com/talks/titus_kaphar_can_art_amend_history?language=en.
*   Ideas for teaching with iconic historical photographs can be found at Lindquist, D. H. (2012). The images of our times: Using iconic photographs in developing a modern American history course. *The Social Studies, 103*(5), 192–197.
*   An interactive website called Image Detective that walks students through the process of analyzing photographs is located at http://cct2.edc.org/PMA/image_detective/index.html.
*   John Green has produced a "crash course" video with suggestions for analyzing the photographs and videos they find online at this site: https://www.youtube.com/watch?v=p7uvqb8fcdA

References

Ashby R. A., Lee, P. J., & Shemilt, D. (2005). Putting principles into practice: Teaching and planning. In M. S. Donovan & J. D. Bransford (Eds.), *How students learn: History, mathematics, and science in the classroom* (pp. 79–178). National Academies Press.

Callahan, C. (2015). Creating or capturing reality? Historical photographs of the Progressive Era. *The Social Studies, 106*(2), 57–71. doi:10.1080/00377996.2014.973013

Dimock, G. (1993). Children of the mills: Rereading Lewis Hine's child labor photographs. *Oxford Art Journal, 16*(2), 37–54.

Gabella, M. S. (1996). The art(s) of historical sense. *Journal of Curriculum Studies, 27*(2), 139–163. doi:10.1080/0022027950270202

Gaddis, J. L. (2002). *The landscape of history: How historians map the past.* Oxford University Press.

Gast, J. (1872). *American progress [Painting].* Autry Museum of the American West. Los Angeles, CA. Wikimedia commons (2018). Retrieved from https://commons.wikimedia.org/wiki/File:American_Progress_(John_Gast_painting).jpg

Greenough, H. (1850). *The rescue [Sculpture]*. Formerly East Façade US Capitol Building (in storage), Washington, DC. https://commons.wikimedia.org/wiki/File:GreenoughRescue.jpg

Hopps, H. R. (1917). Destroy this mad brute [Poster]. USA: A. Carlisle & Co. Found in H. D. Laswell. (1971). *Propaganda technique in World War I*. MIT Press.

Lee, P.J. (2005). Putting principles into practice: Understanding history. In M. S. Donovan & J. D. Bransford (Eds.), *How students learn: History, mathematics, and science in the classroom* (pp. 31–77). National Academies Press.

Limon, M. (2002). Conceptual change in history. In M. Limon, & L. Mason (Eds.) *Reconsidering conceptual change: Issues in theory and practice* (pp. 259–289). Kluwer.

Lindquist, D. H. (2012). The images of our times: Using iconic photographs in developing a modern American history course. *The Social Studies, 103*(5), 192–197. doi:10.1080/00377996.2011.606437

Miles, J. (2019). Seeing and feeling difficult history: A case study of how Canadian students make sense of photographs of Indian Residential Schools. *Theory and Research in Social Education, 47*, 4, 472–496. doi:10.1080/00933104.2019.1626783

Nokes, J. D. (2008). The observation/inference chart: Improving students' ability to make inferences while reading non-traditional texts. *Journal of Adolescent and Adult Literacy, 51*(7), 538–546. doi:10.1598/JAAL.51.7.2

Nokes, J. D. (2019). *Teaching history, learning citizenship: Tools for civic engagement*. Teachers College Press.

Nokes, J. D., & McGrew, S. (2021). The psychology of learning history. In A. O'Donnell, J. Smith, & N. Barnes (Eds.), *The handbook of educational psychology*. Oxford University Press.

Pogrebin, R. (2020, June 21). Roosevelt statue to be removed from Museum of Natural History. *New York Times*. https://www.nytimes.com/2020/06/21/arts/design/roosevelt-statue-to-be-removed-from-museum-of-natural-history.html

Seixas, P., & Morton, T. (2012). *The big six: Historical thinking concepts*. Nelson Education.

Seuss, Dr. (1941, May 22). Ho hum! When he's finished pecking down that last tree he'll quite likely be tired. *PM Magazine. Dr. Seuss Collection, MSS 230*. Mandeville Special Collections Library, UC San Diego.

Simon, R. I. (2011). A shock to thought: Curatorial judgment and the public exhibition of 'difficult knowledge'. *Memory Studies, 4*, 432–449. doi:10.1177/1750698011398170

Stanford History Education Group (2012). *Charting the future of teaching the past*. http://sheg.stanford.edu/

Toynbee, A. J. (1957). *A study of history*, Vol. 2. Oxford University Press.

van Drie, J., & van Boxtel, C. (2008). Historical reasoning: Towards a framework for analyzing students' reasoning about the past. *Educational Psychology Review, 20*(2), 87–110. doi:10.1007/s10648-007-9056-1

10

SEEING OTHERS' PERSPECTIVES THROUGH HISTORICAL FICTION

In politically polarized societies opponents can often be framed as evil, immoral, and stupid. In this chapter you will be introduced to historical empathy, a strategy that helps you understand others' points of view, even though you may still disagree with them. This strategy is vital when seeking the common good in polarized societies. You will also see how historical fiction might help someone understand the perspectives of people in the past.

As you read this vignette, consider why it is easier to acknowledge the perspective of people you agree with than those you disagree with. Also consider why it is important to understand the perspectives of both.

In a few weeks, Miss Anderson will start a unit on the civil rights movement in her eighth-grade U.S. history class in her Midwest suburban school. She wishes there was a way to help students experience the conditions across America at the outset of the civil rights movement. She's heard of teachers doing simulations that re-create feelings of anger over discrimination, but she is afraid that a simulation might trivialize the realities of the period. She would not think of doing a simulation on the Holocaust or the Middle Passage and, for the same reasons, is hesitant to do a simulation related to the civil rights movement. In former years, she has started the unit by telling the story of Emmett Till, a 14-year-old African American boy from Chicago who was murdered while visiting his cousins in Mississippi. White men tortured and brutally killed Till because he was accused of whistling at a white woman. His killers, who later confessed to the murder, were acquitted by an all-White jury despite overwhelming evidence against them. Eighth-grade students can relate to Emmett Till. They are about his age. And most of them have committed a prank, have taken a dare, or said something dumb. It is shocking for them to imagine that such a minor offense could be used

DOI: 10.4324/9781003183495-12

to justify murder in the segregated South in 1955. She tells the story because it draws students into a world very different from current conditions, a world that seems remarkably foreign to students despite its closeness in both time and space.

As Miss Anderson begins to research Emmett Till's story, she discovers a historical novel that was written about him, *Mississippi Trial, 1955* (Crowe, 2002). She checks it out from the library and reads it over the weekend. She finds a story that she believes would appeal to her predominantly White students and will immerse them in the culture and conditions of Greenwood Mississippi at the time of the Emmett Till murder. She finds in the novel the story of relatively normal people who are so invested in a culture of segregation that they commit heinous acts to "preserve their Southern way of life." Pooling her annual supply money with some resources from the school's Social Studies Department, English Department, and school library, she has the school secretary put in a rush order for a classroom set of novels.

The books arrive a few days before her civil rights unit is scheduled to begin. In the meantime, she has spoken with some of the language arts teachers at her school about what they do to motivate students to read, make them accountable for reading, and assess their learning with the novel. She creates a reading schedule for the students, expecting them to read two or three chapters for homework each evening. To monitor and assess their comprehension and to motivate students to read, she assigns them to create a double-entry journal (see Figure 10.1), a T-chart for recording elements of the story particularly relevant to history or to them in the left column and reactions, questions, or connections in the right column. She intends to give a short reading quiz in class each day before forming students into discussion groups that will reflect on issues, themes, and questions about the book.

In addition to the quiz and discussion groups, instructional methods designed to help students comprehend the text, Miss Anderson wants to help students critique the novel—to think about it not just as an average reader would but to also read it as a historian might. She wants students to understand the genre of historical fiction and to be able to distinguish between historically accurate elements of the story, both events and conditions, and fictional and literary elements of the

Parts of the story that talk about historical conditions, events, people, or places	Your reaction, complaints, connections, questions, or predictions

FIGURE 10.1 A double-entry journal to support students' work with a historical novel.

story. She understands that historical fiction is not typically used as evidence by historians, nor is it generally produced by professional historians. But nonetheless, it is a genre of historical writing that her students will be exposed to throughout their lives. What better place to learn how to deal with historical fiction than in a history classroom? She gathers primary sources on the Emmett Till case for students to use to assess the accuracy of the book. She builds several document collections on topics addressed in the novel including segregated schools, African Americans' working conditions, White Citizen Councils, Jim Crow laws, the murder of Emmett Till, and the trial of those who committed his murder.

Students are surprised when she passes out the books at the end of class one day. Miss Anderson has not had them read an entire book before. She gives them the reading schedule and, amid groans, explains that they will have a short quiz to start class each day to assess their comprehension of the chapters from the evening before. She also tells them that she will give them a few minutes in class each day to discuss what they have read with their classmates, to ask questions, and to consider some questions she will ask them. "I think that reading and talking about this book will be a good experience for you," she explains.

After passing out the books, Miss Anderson discusses with students the characteristics of historical fiction. She reminds students that historical novels are based on something that really happened but that some parts of the story are not true. She spends a few minutes previewing the novel.

> This book is the story of Hiram Hillburn, a boy from Arizona who goes to Mississippi to spend a summer with his grandpa in 1955. Hiram and his grandpa are made-up fictional characters, but some of the people Hiram meets, and some of the events he witnesses, really happened.

She explains:

> What is most important for you to learn as you read this book are the conditions Hiram finds in the South, in the Mississippi Delta in 1955. The main reason that I want you to read this book is so that you can get a sense of the relationships between African Americans and White people in the South during the 1950s. I want you to go with Hiram to a place that might seem foreign to you to experience what people were feeling and thinking at the time. So as you are reading, I want you to focus on race relations—what do people say and do that helps you understand how the races interacted in the South?

Using a term students have heard in previous lessons, she continues: "I want you to experience the historical context of one part of the deep South in the early years of the civil rights movement. I think this novel will help you with *contextualization*."

Miss Anderson continues:

> I could tell you about events that might help you understand some aspects of the context, but you know how reading a novel, or watching a well-made movie, can help you experience an unfamiliar time or place in a way that I cannot just tell you about. It can also help you understand why people made some of the choices that they did that seem crazy to us today. Historical fiction can help you see the world from other people's perspectives—to engage in what is called *historical empathy.*

She writes the phrase on the board as she says it.

A week or so later, the civil rights unit is well underway. The students have read through Chapter 11 in the novel, and Miss Anderson has planned an activity that will immerse students more fully in the context of the civil rights movement. Students are used to the routine by now. Class starts with a five-question quiz on Chapters 10 and 11 with questions that assess their comprehension of the story. After the quiz is corrected, students form groups where they discuss the chapters they read. Miss Anderson has prepared questions for the discussion groups: "What is your reaction to Grandpa's involvement in the 'White Citizens' Council'?" "Do you agree with the editorial 'A Just Appraisal'? Why or why not?" Some of the questions are intended to promote historical empathy: "Did good people participate in White Citizen Councils? Why or why not?" "Why didn't Mr. Paul do something when he realized the Black students were attending inferior schools?" Students spend a few minutes talking informally about these and other questions they have. Miss Anderson does not care whether they get through all her questions, skip some of them, or if they discuss their own questions about the book. The questions, the time, and the format of the discussion groups are to stimulate authentic conversation about the book—an opportunity for students to think more deeply about the issues surrounding the origins of the civil rights movement.

Miss Anderson wants students to consider the context of the civil rights movement including the segregated school system, African American working conditions, White Citizen Councils, and Jim Crow laws. She has collected sets of primary sources on each of these topics. For most of the remainder of the class period, students form groups and collaboratively critique the novel's depiction of one topic. Students begin by reading an excerpt from the novel related to their study and then search for evidence in the primary sources that supports or contradicts it. One group, for instance, reads a passage in the novel that shows Hiram Hillburn, the visitor from Arizona to the Mississippi Delta, seeking to understand segregated schools. Hiram asks, "But don't Negroes want their own schools just like we do?" (Crowe, 2002, p. 73). Mr. Paul, another fictional character in the novel, then paints the picture of the inequities between White and Black schools for Hiram and for the reader. After reading the passage from the novel the group of students turns to the primary sources to answer Miss Anderson's question, "Does the novel accurately portray the segregated schools of the South?" Her lesson plan calls for students to spend about 30 minutes exploring one of the four text sets and then take a few minutes to report to the class, critiquing the book's accuracy in its portrayal of schools, working conditions, social attitudes, or legal discrimination.

For a different day, Miss Anderson has created another document collection that all students will use to analyze the Emmett Till murder, trial, and national response. This collection features the transcript of an interview with Emmett Till's accused murderers, during which they brazenly describe the night of the murder (Huie, 1956). Other texts include trial transcripts, an autopsy report, photographs, and letters sent from around the country in reaction to the Emmett Till murder and to the killers' published confession. These letters paint a picture of an America deeply divided by the murder. Miss Anderson is hopeful that these texts, which all the students will review, will help them experience a different America, one in which many people condoned the killing of a teenage boy for crossing the lines of segregation, an attitude unfathomable to most people today. Together with the novel, Miss Anderson is confident that the texts will help students contextualize the civil rights movement and, perhaps, experience historical empathy for both the whites who stubbornly clung to traditional, oppressive race relations, and the Americans of every background that fought for change. For the remainder of the class period, students will work in small groups with a copy of this text set.

Just before allowing students to get into groups to work through the documents, Miss Anderson asks them to try to feel historical empathy for the characters involved in this struggle. She points out that doing so will be easier when considering the perspective of those who were fighting for change than it will be when trying to understand the perspective of those fighting for tradition and segregation. "To be able to understand their perspective does not mean that you support their racist ideas or actions," she explains.

> It means that you are trying to understand the social context that would produce people who viewed African Americans as inferior and who saw the world around them changing, threatening their way of life. They viewed the quality of their children's schools being threatened as resources might be diverted toward other schools—or, even worse, from their perspective—their children might be sent to a run-down school with African American children. I know it will be difficult to understand their thinking, but consider people like Grandpa in the novel—these are not people like the villains in Disney movies who sing about how great it is to be evil. They are people who are fighting for what they think is best—even willing to kill to preserve their way of life.

Students struggle with the idea of trying to understand the worldview of the racists who murdered Emmett Till and the community that acquitted them in spite of overwhelming evidence of their guilt. So Miss Anderson continues:

> Do not get confused about what *historical empathy* means. It is not the same thing as feeling sorry for someone or having empathy in the traditional sense. It does not mean agreeing with them and does not involve justifying horrific acts that have been committed in the past. *Historical empathy* means to be able to explain why people behaved the way they did. It is an effort to understand their motivations without rationalizing their actions. It is based on the idea that people's behavior generally makes sense to them, given their perspective. A historian assumes that people are not inherently evil, stupid, or crazy but that they live in cultures with values, standards, and priorities that may be very different from ours. Again, think of Grandpa Hillburn in the novel—he's a pretty lovable guy other than his racist attitudes? I told you this was not going to be easy, but hopefully it will give you a better understanding of the context during which the civil rights movement emerged. The civil rights movement was not about politically overpowering a handful of extremists or lunatics in the South. That would have been easy. The civil rights movement was about changing an entire nation—every region—where millions of otherwise sensible people viewed traditional segregated society as a good and natural thing. That was, and is, extremely difficult.

Some of the students are starting to understand what Miss Anderson is talking about as they form groups and explore their text sets. They take notes on a study guide (see Figure 10.2). Miss Anderson has prepared a place for them to list the justifications that some people put forward for the murder and a place for the arguments raised by those who opposed the murder. She again makes it clear to the students that she could not be in greater disagreement with those who supported the murder, and they should be too. "But in order to understand the time period, we have to understand their ways of thinking," she explains.

> We've got to try to see the world from their perspective. We need historical empathy. Once a person understands the thinking of the people who opposed equality for African Americans, the accomplishments of the leaders of the civil rights movement become even more heroic.

What can teachers do to give students the freedom to explore ideas without interference while preventing students from developing interpretations that are unwarranted, inaccurate, or otherwise inappropriate?

Name _____

Historical Empathy and the Civil Rights Movement

Instructions: In order to understand what a monumental success the Civil Rights Movement was, people today must try to understand the extreme racism of the time period. The evidence that you review will be disturbing, but will help you understand how people felt about the races in1955. Today reasonable people universally condemn the murder of Emmett Till. But in 1955 there were many who defended his murderers. On the left side of the diagram, summarize the statements people made in defense of the murderers. On the right side of the diagram summarize the statements people made that condemned the murderers. Below the diagram record the insights that you gained about the social context of the Civil Rights Movement.

Summaries of statements made in defense of the murderers	Summaries of statements made to condemn the murderers

What insights do these documents give you about the social context of the Civil Rights Movement?

FIGURE 10.2 A study guide used to support students' historical empathy.

Historical Empathy and Historical Fiction

Why is historical fiction especially appropriate for helping students develop skills in contextualization and historical empathy? What other types of resources would help students develop these skills?

Miss Anderson wanted her students to show historical empathy, and she thought that using the novel with the supplemental primary sources would help them do so. In the remainder of this chapter, I explore two ideas: the notion of historical empathy, and methods of teaching with historical fiction, children's books, poetry, and song lyrics. I first explore historical empathy and perspective taking as historical literacies. I then consider the advantages, disadvantages, and challenges of using historical fiction. I continue with the exploration of the use of children's books, poetry, and song lyrics as both accounts and artifacts. The chapter concludes with ideas for helping students develop historical empathy by producing historical fiction.

Historical Empathy as a Historical Literacy

Historical empathy, as Miss Anderson explained to her students, is the ability to comprehend a historical individual's actions as a logical effect of their world-view. Historical empathy involves two processes—*perspective recognition* and *caring*

(Barton & Levstik, 2004; Endacott & Brooks, 2018). Perspective recognition is the ability to imagine the point of view of another person in an attempt to understand their actions. It is in part a cognitive activity as the historian imagines the historical context, explores evidence, and makes inferences about motivation. In addition to the cognitive elements of perspective recognition, historical empathy also involves caring—an emotional reaction to past events. Historians take into consideration the emotions of historical characters, explaining past actions as not just the outcome of their rational thought but also of their emotion. But caring goes beyond a consideration of others' emotions. It involves an emotional reaction on the part of the person studying history, fostering interest and compassion for those in the past and inspiring action in the present to prevent or resolve injustices. Thus, historical thinking and historical literacies require students to engage in the two elements of historical empathy: perspective recognition and caring (Barton & Levstik, 2004; Endacott & Brooks, 2018).

> *perspective recognition: the ability to imagine the way another person, particularly a historical character, views the world, imagining their values, priorities, knowledge, and understanding of morality, in an effort to understand their actions*

> *caring: feeling an emotional attachment to historical characters, including an understanding of the emotions that shaped their behaviors, leading to a desire to take action to correct former wrongs and eliminate present and future injustice*

Because of the way people learn, no other element of historical literacy presents a greater challenge than developing historical empathy. Most modern learning theories acknowledge and highlight the role of background knowledge and personal connections in the learning process. For instance, schema theory proposes that factual knowledge is stored in nodes and links and that learning something new requires the learner to link new nodes of information within their existing network of knowledge (Alba & Hasher, 1983). Constructivist theories suggest that a learner's new experiences are filtered through their prior experiences, and so perceptions, conclusions, and learning depend on background knowledge (Anderson et al., 1977). These models of learning present a dilemma for history teachers. If all learning is dependent on the learners' prior knowledge and experiences, and learning history involves trying to understand actions, values, and events from times and places that are foreign to us, then it follows that learning history involves a distortion of the past to fit our experiences. When we understand the actions of historical characters through the lens of our own experiences—and it is difficult to learn in any other way—we do not really understand their actions. In response to this dilemma, Wineburg (2001) called learning history an "unnatural act."

Historians forge ahead through this dilemma using the strategy of contextualization, introduced in Chapter 3, and by developing historical empathy, the ability to understand an individual's actions in light of *their* experiences, context, values, priorities, and perspective, rather than ours. Fostering historical empathy and nurturing students' ability to view the world from multiple perspectives are vital elements of building historical literacies. Historical empathy, as Miss Anderson's students found out, is among the most difficult of skills to develop, because it requires unnatural thinking. For instance, current theories of reading comprehension focus on the readers' interaction with a text. Instead, to fully comprehend historical resources, it is more important to focus on the writer's interaction with the text. What were they seeing, hearing, feeling, and thinking as the text was produced? In historical inquiry, the reader's as well as the writer's background knowledge, values, perspective, and reaction assume great importance. In addition to focusing on what *we* feel and think as we investigate the evidence, we must consider what the creator of the evidence was feeling and thinking as they produced it.

Furthermore, teaching in a manner that discourages unrestrained personal connections and reactions, cuts against the grain of traditional learning theories and, as a result, often clashes with the instincts of good teachers who want students to make powerful personal connections with texts. However, such a reaction decreases the likelihood that they will understand the context of the event they study. Unrestrained connections and reactions, while highly valued in many teaching situations, become problematic when learning history. What on the surface appears to be good teaching, might actually promote *presentism*, the tendency to view historical events through the lens of the present and judge historical characters by modern sensibilities rather than by their context. Presentism interferes with historical literacies.

---

presentism: the natural tendency to project current values, perspectives, priorities, and contexts onto people of the past, creating a distorted understanding of their choices and behaviors, interfering with historical thinking

---

The experiences of Miss Anderson's students suggest that historical empathy comes easier in some circumstances than others. Her students had an easier time assuming the perspective of Emmett Till, Hiram Hillburn, and the writers of letters that called for reform than they did of Grandpa and the individuals who praised the murder. It is not surprising that students find it easier to see the world from the viewpoint of people who were similar to them in age, beliefs, interests, and motives than to assume the perspective of those who held dramatically different beliefs. However, a rigorous appraisal of historical events requires historians to attempt to observe the event from diverse perspectives. Miss Anderson worked hard to help students feel historical empathy for both those who held beliefs similar to theirs and those who held loathsome opposing viewpoints. The historical novel and other resources that she brought into the classroom served that purpose.

Historical Fiction

Some researchers suggest that one of the keys to building historical empathy is providing students with opportunities to immerse themselves in historical contexts through detail-rich historical fiction (Nokes, et al., 2012; Tomlinson et al., 1993; Tunnell & Ammon, 1996; VanSledright & Frankes, 1998). They argue that through fiction, students can vicariously experience conditions and events that occurred in distant times and places in a manner that is impossible with textbooks (Schwebel, 2011). Contextualization and historical empathy require the ability to immerse oneself into the physical, social, economic, and historic conditions of an event. Doing so is extremely difficult for students, who often lack background knowledge of the details of historical times and places (Nokes, et al., 2007; Reisman, 2012; Wineburg, 1991). The elaborate descriptions and imagery included in well-researched historical novels and movies may hold a key to building the background knowledge students need to engage in historical empathy.

Because historical fiction is a popular genre in young-adult publishing, history teachers have an increasingly large selection of novels to choose from, with books available dealing with diverse time periods and themes. However, a variety of types of historical novels exist. Some, often referred to as costume novels, are set in a historical time and place but do not describe historical events or people. Others have a historical setting with a plot that only tangentially involves noteworthy historical events. Some historical fiction, like *Mississippi Trial, 1955*, weaves significant historical events into the plot line, with fictitious characters interacting with historical characters. Still other historical novels describe actual events, filling in details with creative reconstructions, such as dialog between characters. Each of these types of fiction might serve a purpose for history teachers, depending on their objectives. Furthermore, historical fiction varies significantly in its historical accuracy, depending, to a great degree, on the research conducted by the author.

Advantages

Well-written historical fiction has several advantages over other types of text. As mentioned, a novel's detailed dialogues, setting descriptions, character development, and depiction of events can transport students to historical settings, facilitating contextualization and historical empathy. Furthermore, many students enjoy reading novels more than they do textbook passages or even primary source documents. The phrase "I could not put it down" is used more often with novels than textbooks. Additionally, historical fiction, as all good literature does, presents truths that run deeper than historical facts. The 19th-century novelist Stephen Crane contended that historical fiction

> makes us feel . . . what otherwise would be dead and lost to us. It transports us into the past. And the very best historical fiction presents to us a truth of the past that is not the truth of the history books, but a bigger truth, a more important truth—a truth of the heart.
>
> (quoted in Brayfield & Sprott, 2014, p. 28)

Historical fiction can introduce students in a powerful manner to significant historical themes and concepts, such as the clash of cultures, the quest for freedom, surviving hardship, or correcting societal ills.

Disadvantages

Historical fiction carries with it several disadvantages. Admittedly, the ease with which Miss Anderson procured her classroom set of novels was exaggerated in the vignette—schools typically devote fewer resources to purchasing novels (for the History Department) than they do textbooks. However, an ambitious history teacher will find English teachers, media specialists, grant adjudicators, and principals who are extremely supportive of efforts to gather historical novels. Additionally, reading a novel takes a great deal of time that otherwise could be devoted to other assignments or classroom activities. As with all curricular decisions, there is an opportunity cost associated with taking time to read historical fiction. Furthermore, students' diverse reading abilities and interests make it impossible to find historical fiction that is universally appropriate or appealing. However, this same argument could be made about any text or topic studied in a history class and has rarely been applied to rule out the use of textbooks, which appeal to few students and snub certain perspectives. Finally, teaching with novels is an unfamiliar process for most history teachers, presenting challenges in motivation, assessment, and instruction. Miss Anderson sought advice from language arts teachers. Such collaboration, combined with experience, can help history teachers develop satisfactory methods for working with novels, a genre outside of traditional disciplinary reading and writing.

Challenges

Simply providing students with historical fiction is not guaranteed to help them develop historical empathy or the ability to contextualize historical events.

Students first need to recognize that historical novels and feature films, as historical fiction, represent *accounts* but they generally do not represent *evidence* of the
time period they depict. Rather than a primary account or a secondary account,
historical fiction represents a *fictional account*. Like other accounts, fictional
accounts are intentional retellings of historical events, created for a particular
audience and for particular purposes—primarily to entertain. Just like any other
type of account, the reader or viewer must consider the source, the audience, the
purpose, and the context in order to fully understand and think critically about
the text. Fictional accounts pose unique challenges for students.

Research on students' work with movies, one genre of historical fiction, is
illustrative. Seixas (1993) showed history students two movies related to 19th-
century Indigenous and White relations. Students judged the movie that showed
characters acting and reacting according to modern values and conditions to
be more "realistic." The movie that captured the context with greater accuracy was considered less "realistic" by students because the characters did not
respond to conditions the way one would expect given current conditions. Seixas
expressed concerns that students were looking for realism rather than accuracy
in Hollywood's accounts of historical eras (a tendency also common in students'
work with historical novels and art). His research suggests that students have a difficult time distinguishing between fictional accounts that accurately present historical settings and fictional accounts that twist the past to attract modern patrons.

One of the biggest challenges students face in learning history with historical
fiction is distinguishing fictional from accurate elements of the story. "Based on
actual events" can mean many different things. However, the challenges students
face in sifting the historical from the fictional in historical fiction are similar to
the challenges they face in distinguishing evidence from claims in secondary
sources, or relevant from irrelevant material in primary sources. In fact, the process of learning to work with historical fiction may facilitate general historical
thinking. For instance, historians are hesitant to accept information that is found
in only one source, remaining skeptical until they find corroborating evidence.
To give students the opportunity to engage in corroboration, Miss Anderson provided them with collections of primary sources that gave eyewitness accounts of
conditions. Passages from the novel were compared and contrasted with primary
sources. Using these text sets, students could not only make judgments about the
research that went into writing the novel but also further immerse themselves
into the context of the civil rights movement, her objective for using the novel
in the first place.

Teaching With Historical Fiction

As with any other type of text, history teachers need to consider their objectives
to identify when historical fiction would be a wise choice. In Miss Anderson's
case, she wanted students to experience the effects of segregation on southern

society in the years leading up to the civil rights movement. She did not believe that students could understand the significance of the movement or the bravery of civil rights leaders without knowing and feeling the context. And the novel *Mississippi Trial, 1955*, which detailed an outsider's attempts to understand southern society within the context of the Emmett Till murder and trial, seemed to be an appropriate text to reach her objectives. One of the first issues Miss Anderson faced was finding a way to motivate her students to read. She established a reasonable reading schedule, replacing homework assignments with a small amount of reading each night. She developed quizzes and discussion questions that were intended to make students accountable for reading and to support and assess their comprehension of the novel, with a particular focus on those elements that were relevant to the civil rights unit. Most significantly, she created collections of documents that would engage students in historical thinking related to the novel. As part of her instruction, she allowed students to make their own evidence-based judgment of the accuracy of the novel, using evidence she supplied. At the conclusion of the unit, students were knowledgeable not only of the Emmet Till case but also of general conditions that led to the civil rights movement. Furthermore, they were more informed about the nature of historical fiction, more skilled in sifting between fictional and historical elements of a story, and more able to engage in historical thinking.

Miss Anderson stumbled onto the novel quite by accident. But systematic ways exist that history teachers can use to search for appropriate historical fiction. For instance, each year, the Scott O'Dell Award for Historical Fiction is given to an outstanding historical novel written for children or young adults. Reviewing the list of O'Dell Award recipients, a teacher would find novels on a great variety of U.S. history topics including colonist and Indigenous relations, the Revolutionary War, slavery, the Civil War, Reconstruction, the settlement of the Midwest, the Depression and dust bowl, the World War II home front, and the development of the atomic bomb. Fewer titles relate to world history events. Other young-adult book awards, although not dedicated to historical fiction, include additional titles. Furthermore, the National Council for the Social Studies publishes an annual list of notable trade books for young people, with a large collection of titles of young-adult fiction and children's books going back to 1972. Archived lists of prior winners are available online at https://www.socialstudies.org/notable-social-studies-trade-books. Recommended titles from the current year are available to National Council for the Social Studies members in an annual publication. Other awards honor books written about African American experiences, (Stone Book Award); Latin American themes (Pura Belpré Award), American Indian perspectives (American Indian Youth Literature Award), and the experiences of others. In addition, local libraries often published lists of recommended titles in historical fiction annually, as do many bookstores and publishing companies on Internet sites (e.g., see https://www.goodreads.com/genres/young-adult-historical-fiction).

Miss Anderson sought advice from language arts teachers as she prepared for instruction with the novel. Other history teachers have formed even stronger collaborations with English teachers. In many cases, language arts teachers will coordinate their instruction so that they teach the literary elements of a novel as a history teacher teaches about its historical features. Such cooperation can split the time commitment between two courses, making the use of historical novels more feasible.

Children's Books, Poetry, Graphic Novels, Song Lyrics, and Feature Films

In addition to historical novels, short stories, plays, picture books, and feature films have been produced that blend fictional and historical elements, paint vivid pictures of historical settings, and present memorable and moving depictions of the past. These genres hold many of the same advantages, disadvantages, and challenges as historical novels, providing opportunities for teachers to immerse students in historical contexts and to teach historical thinking. Through the creation of multigenre text sets that include images, fiction, primary sources, picture books, and video or audio clips related to the same topic, teachers can foster historical thinking while differentiating their curriculum.

For instance, a teacher might build text sets relating to any number of incidents that occurred as part of the civil rights movement, in addition to or in place of the activities Miss Anderson planned. A text set on Jackie Robinson, who was the first African American to play in all-White Major League Baseball, might include books such as *A Picture Book of Jackie Robinson* (Adler, 1997), *Testing the Ice: A True Story About Jackie Robinson* (Robinson, 2009), *The Story of Jackie Robinson: Bravest Man in Baseball* (Davidson, 1996); primary sources such as a handwritten note containing a death threat to Robinson, the transcript of an interview of Robinson's wife, a letter that Robinson sent President Eisenhower; photographs; video clips; and the lyrics from the song "Did You See Jackie Robinson Hit That Ball?" (Johnson, 1948); among others. Students, in small groups, could be assigned to explore Jackie Robinson's contributions to the civil rights movement. With the teacher's guidance, a student who struggles with reading might explore the children's book and the threatening note, while those more proficient at reading would search other texts written in more challenging prose. The group could collaboratively analyze the photographs, song, and other sources. Similar text sets could be created exploring Rosa Parks and the Montgomery Alabama bus boycott, the Freedom Riders, the Little Rock Nine, the Woolworth's lunch counter sit-in, the Birmingham antisegregation protests and violence, voter registration in Mississippi, the Black Panthers, and numerous other topics. Thus, text sets, particularly those including children's books, photographs, and music, provide an opportunity for teachers to differentiate the curriculum based on both students' interests and abilities. Text sets with many different genres of accounts and evidence allow teachers to engage even struggling readers in historical inquiries.

Of importance, resources such as children's books or song lyrics might be used as primary or secondary source accounts. In the example in the preceding paragraph, the books listed would be considered secondary accounts, recently produced interpretations of historical events. However, the song "Did You See Jackie Robinson Hit That Ball?" serves a different function as a primary source produced by Robinson's contemporaries. As such, it corroborates other accounts of Jackie Robinson and provides clues as to how he was perceived by others during his lifetime. Thus, as teachers search for resources they should seek modern secondary source accounts that might be particularly appealing to students (such as the slide show/video of the song at http://www.youtube.com/watch?v=r-7Ac2LVVYU) and primary source evidence that provides insight on people's thinking at the time, such as the lyrics and music of the song.

In recent years graphic novels set in historical contexts have become a resource for studying past events. Graphic novels, with the appearance of comic book pages, have the potential to motivate some young readers who are less interested in traditional writing. For instance, the story of civil rights leader John Lewis is told in an autobiographical graphic novel trilogy, *March*, that uses engaging writing and pictures to tell a story of the civil rights movement (Lewis & Aydin, 2016). Not only do graphic novels tell interesting stories, but they can also promote historical thinking in many of the same ways that historical novels and feature films do. For example, Clark (2013) found that graphic novels set in historical contexts helped young readers think about the agency of historical characters and the constraints on that agency. People of the past became more real to readers as they understood historical individuals as active agents in the construction of their lives, rather than merely victims or passive recipients of others' actions.

The Importance of Using Historical Fiction

Some may question the use of historical fiction, picture books, and feature films in history classrooms. Why would a teacher use resources that blend accurate information with fictional historical information? One reason for doing so has to do with the preparation of young people for life as an adult. Once students leave secondary classrooms, they may never enroll in another history class. But they will continue to learn history. One of the main resources for lifelong learning of history are feature films and historical novels—fictional accounts. Students who learn how to analyze fictional accounts in history classrooms are more likely to learn appropriately with fictional accounts throughout their lives. Those who do not learn strategies for learning with historical fiction may end up suffering from an ailment I call "*Gone with the Wind* Syndrome." This occurs when an audience member of a film set in a historical context fails to understand the nature of fictional accounts and accepts the movie as the unadulterated truth. These audience members confuse the claim "based on actual events" as a claim that the film is an accurate portrayal of historical events as they occurred, which may or may not be true. In reality, the history lessons taught by movies like *Gone with the Wind* (as entertaining as they may or may not be) are fraught with inaccuracies, distortions, oversimplifications, and exaggerations. This novel and movie portray enslaved African Americans as happy and loyal members of kind and loving families, a misunderstanding so widely observed by moviegoers that it perpetuated racist stereotypes for a generation and continues to confound people's understandings today.

Jerry Bruckheimer, the producer of the feature film *Pearl Harbor*, explained the process he used to produce that movie:

> You research the subject, you talked to survivors, you read, you listen to old radio broadcasts, and watch other films and documentaries. You educate yourself. And then you do your best to come up with a screenplay that's . . . entertaining . . . and shows the tragedy that so many families went through. We tried to be accurate, but it's certainly not meant to be a history lesson.
> (cited in Nokes & Ellison, 2017, p. 135)

One valuable resource for evaluating feature films about historical events can be found at the History vs. Hollywood website at https://www.historyvshollywood.com. Researchers on this site compare movie depictions of events with the actual history behind the movie. Students who understand that historical fiction blends accurate information with fictional elements and is produced primarily for entertainment and who have strategies for evaluating accuracy are prepared for a lifetime of learning through feature films and novels. Students who do not have opportunities to learn these strategies are at risk of suffering from *Gone with the Wind Syndrome* throughout their adult lives.

Students Developing Historical Empathy by Producing Historical Fiction

> Why must a teacher be cautious when assigning students to produce historical fiction? How might such a writing assignment discourage historical thinking?

In addition to reading historical fiction, writing historical fiction can help students engage in perspective recognition, can promote historical empathy, and can allow teachers to assess students' historical thinking skills. Language arts teachers often assign students to produce "realistic fiction" to extend students' thinking.

Although the term *realistic* might ruffle some historians' feathers, the notion that students can write fictional descriptions of historical settings has applications for teaching history. However, some researchers warn that assigning students to create fictional historical accounts promotes *presentism*, the projection of current conditions, values, perspectives, and contexts onto historical characters. Students who engage in presentism create characters who think, speak, and behave like 21st-century teenagers (Monte-Sano & De La Paz, 2012) This tendency is magnified when teachers assign students to write in first person, as if they were the historical actor (De Leur et al., 2017). These potential pitfalls can be avoided when history teachers assign students to produce carefully researched fictional accounts. Depending on the instructional objective, teachers could focus students' writing on a dialogue, a perspective, a character, a setting, or an event. In each case, careful research involving primary source evidence is a key to avoiding presentism.

Dialogue

Teachers might assign students to write a dialogue between fictional or actual historical characters in a historic setting. For example, a teacher might build a writing activity around the Norman Rockwell painting *New Kids in the Neighborhood* (1967), created a year before the Fair Housing Act was passed, which shows the African American children of a family that has moved into a suburban neighborhood meeting the children of their White neighbors. Students could write the dialogue that they believe might have transpired in this hypothetical event. In order to prepare students to write the dialogue, the teacher could spend some time analyzing the painting, considering Norman Rockwell and what he might have been thinking and showing as he painted. Students can further prepare to write the dialogue by discussing historical events that were occurring at the time the painting was created, such as the passage of the Civil Rights Act of 1964 a few years earlier, but a year before the passage of the Fair Housing Act of 1968. What were the children thinking and how would their thoughts play out in a dialogue? After writing, students could assess their peers' ability to accurately capture the context as they read their dialogues to each other.

Perspective Recognition

Teachers might have students write fictional reactions to historic events from alternative perspectives. For instance, after teaching about the Louisiana Purchase the teacher might have students write the fictional reaction of Jefferson, Napoleon, a Native American woman living along the Missouri River, a French plantation owner living outside of New Orleans, the wife of an American farmer living along the Ohio River, a justice of the Supreme Court evaluating its constitutionality, a Spanish ambassador to the United States, or other historical or made-up characters. Students could read their peers' fictitious reactions in order to consider multiple contrasting perspectives of the event. Teachers can use writing assignments that require perspective recognition to assess students' ability to engage in historical empathy. As with other fictional writing activities, careful research using primary source evidence can help students overcome the tendency to project present values and conditions onto people in the past.

Character Development

Students' research on a historical person could be presented in the format of rich character description such as that found in novels. For instance, students could write a description of Ferdinand Magellan, Mary Wollstonecraft, Sundiata Keita, Sitting Bull, Ida B. Wells, George Patton, Ruth Bader Ginsburg, or any other historical character. In order to explore classes of people, students could write a vivid description of a Christian crusader, an Irish immigrant to the United States, a 12th-century Chinese merchant, a sodbuster, a suffragette, or another class of person. After conducting research, looking at primary source descriptions, students could blend what is known about people with reasonable, research-based conjectures. Furthermore, drawings of the character could supplement written descriptions. Such writing can help students position themselves in historical contexts.

Setting Descriptions

Instead of writing about individuals, students could be assigned to write about the physical or social setting of a historical event. For instance, an in-depth understanding of the physical context of Valley Forge, Jamestown, Gettysburg, the Acropolis, King Tut's tomb, Mecca, or Omaha Beach might help students contextualize historical events. In these and countless other settings, physical geography affected an event. In other cases, the social context was more significant than the physical context. For instance, the social context of Jackie Robinson's entry into Major League Baseball, John Hancock's signing of the Declaration of Independence, Kristallnacht, or the Black Death's arrival in Egypt in 1347 could be explored by creating rich written descriptions of the social context. Miss Anderson was hopeful that reading the novel would immerse her students in the social context of the Emmett Till murder and subsequent trial. Writing a rich research-based description of the social context could have served the same purpose. As with the other examples, students' written descriptions of physical and social contexts would allow a teacher to assess their understanding of historical contexts.

Event Depictions

Instead of focusing on characters or settings, students could be assigned to write rich descriptions of historical events. The process of writing these descriptions could involve students in historical research, historical thinking, and creating research-based conjectures to fill in the details. Like the other examples of fiction writing described earlier, teachers can use writing about events to promote and assess contextualization.

Chapter Summary

Well-researched historical fiction may foster students' ability to engage in historical empathy and contextualization. Historical empathy is the ability to understand the actions of historical characters, with two elements: perspective recognition and care. Historical empathy is related to contextualization. Historical empathy involves recognizing that individuals' actions, although sometimes hard to understand by modern standards, made sense to them given their conditions, values, and understanding of the world. Historical fiction includes details that can immerse students in the physical and social context of unfamiliar historical eras and, by doing so, can promote a greater awareness of historical contexts and historical empathy. Children's books, poetry, literature, and many feature films set in historic contexts hold the same potential to help students develop historical empathy. Writing carefully researched historical fiction based on primary source evidence can support the development of historical empathy as well as allow teachers to assess this element of historical literacy.

Questions for Consideration

1. How can popular feature films manipulate society's collective memory? Can you think of a recent movie that may have had a detrimental effect on people's understanding of a historical event?
2. How might a teacher help students transfer historical empathy to political empathy in order to prepare young people to work together with political opponents to achieve the common good?
3. Why is it important to recognize the perspective of historical characters whose actions are surprising, offensive, or worse? How can a person try to understand terrible actions without rationalizing them?

Additional Reading and Viewing

- Several websites provide updated reviews of novels including historical novels. One can be found at http://readinginaction.org/bookcasts/friendship-today. Check "historical fiction" to filter the search results.
- Research on nurturing historical thinking with graphic novels can be found in Clark (2013) Encounters with historical agency: The value of nonfiction graphic novels in the classroom. *The History Teacher*, *46*, 4, 489–508. Available at http://www.societyforhistoryeducation.org/pdfs/A13_Clark.pdf

- The lists of notable trade books reviewed by the National Council for the Social Studies in former years can be found at https://www.socialstudies. org/notable-social-studies-trade-books. Members of the NCSS have access to the list for the current year.
- A teacher's blog produced by fifth-grade teacher Tarry Lindquist (1995), titled *Why and How I Teach With Historical Fiction*, gives advice on using historical fiction. You can find it at http://www.scholastic.com/teachers/ article/why-and-how-i-teach-historical-fiction.

References

Adler, D. A. (1997). *A picture book of Jackie Robinson*. Holiday House.

Alba, J. W., & Hasher, L. (1983). Is memory schematic? *Psychological Bulletin, 93*(2), 203–231. doi:10.1037/0033-2909.93.2.203

Anderson, R. C., Reynolds, R., Schallert, D. L., & Goetz, E. T. (1977). Frameworks for comprehending discourse. *American Educational Research Journal, 14*(4), 367–382. doi:10.3102/00028312014004367

Barton, K. C., & Levstik, L. S. (2004). *Teaching history for the common good*. Lawrence Erlbaum.

Brayfield, C., & Sprott, D. (2014). *Writing historical fiction: a writers' and artists' companion*. A&C Black.

Clark (2013) Encounters with historical agency: The value of nonfiction graphic novels in the classroom. *The History Teacher, 46*(4), 489–508.

Crowe, C. (2002). *Mississippi trial, 1955*. Penguin.

Davidson, M. (1996). *The story of Jackie Robinson: Bravest man in baseball*. Gareth Stevens.

De Leur, T., Van Boxtel, C., & Wilschut, A. (2017). 'I saw angry people and broken statues': Historical empathy in secondary history education. *British Journal of Educational Studies, 65*(3), 331–352. doi:10.1080/00071005.2017.1291902

Endacott, J. L., & Brooks, S. (2018). Historical empathy: Perspectives and responding to the past. In S. Metzger & L. Harris (Eds.), *International handbook of history teaching and learning* (pp. 203–225). Wiley Blackwell.

Huie, W. B. (1956). The shocking story of approved killing in Mississippi. *Look, 20*, 46–50.

Johnson, W. B. (1948). *Did you see Jackie Robinson hit that ball? [Recorded by the Count Basie Orchestra]*. Victor. July 13, 1949). http://www.youtube.com/watch?v=r-7Ac2LVVYU

Lewis, J., & Aydin, A. (2016). *March trilogy*. Top Shelf Productions.

Lindquist, T. (1995). *Why and how I teach with historical fiction*. Scholastic.

Monte-Sano, C., & De La Paz, S. (2012). Using writing tasks to elicit adolescents' historical reasoning. *Journal of Literacy Research, 44*(3), 273–299. doi:10.1177/1086296X12450445

Nokes, J. D., Crowe, C., & Bausum, A. (2012, March 23). *Finding the story in history: Teaching with stories of diversity*. Paper presented at the National Council for History Education Annual Conference. Kansas City, MO.

Nokes, J. D., Dole, J. A., & Hacker, D. J. (2007). Teaching high school students to use heuristics while reading historical texts. *Journal of Educational Psychology, 99*(3), 492–504. doi:10.1037/0022-0663.99.3.492

Nokes, J. D. & Ellison, D. (2017). Historical films: An essential resource for nurturing historical literacy. In S. Waters & W. Russell (Eds.), *Cinematic social studies: A resource for teaching and learning social studies with film* (pp. 131–156). Information Age Publishing.

Reisman, A. (2012). Reading like a historian: A document-based history curriculum intervention in urban high schools. *Cognition and Instruction, 30*(1), 86–112. doi:10. 1080/07370008.2011.634081

Robinson, S. (2009). *Testing the ice: A true story about Jackie Robinson*. Scholastic.

Rockwell, N. (1967). *New kids in the neighborhood [Painting]*. Norman Rockwell Museum

Schwebel, S. (2011). *Child-sized history: Fictions of the past in U. S. classrooms*. Vanderbilt University Press.

Seixas, P. (1993). Popular film and young people's understanding of the history of Native American-White relations. *The History Teacher, 26*(3), 351–370. doi:10.2307/494666

Tomlinson, C. M., Tunnell, M. O., & Richgels, D. J. (1993). The content and writing of history in textbooks and trade books. In M. O. Tunnell & R. Amnion (Eds.), *The story of ourselves: Teaching history through children's literature* (pp. 51–62). Heinemann.

Tunnell, M. O., & Ammon, R. (1996). The story of ourselves: Fostering multiple historical perspectives. *Social Education, 60*(4), 212–215.

VanSledright, B., & Frankes, L. (1998). Literature's place in learning history and science. In C. Hynd (Ed.), *Learning from text across conceptual domains* (pp. 117–138). Routledge

Wineburg, S. S. (1991). On the reading of historical texts: Notes on the breach between school and academy. *American Educational Research Journal, 28*(3), 495–519. doi:10.3102/00028312028003495

Wineburg, S. S. (2001). *Historical thinking and other unnatural acts: Charting the future of teaching the past*. Temple University Press.

11
FOSTERING HEALTHY SKEPTICISM USING TEXTBOOKS AND SECONDARY SOURCES

Many students have a natural tendency to challenge authority—except when it comes to the authority of textbook authors, which many students trust without question. In this chapter, you will consider how you can and why you should encourage students to approach authoritative texts, like textbooks, social media, and internet sites, with a little skepticism and with academic humility.

> As you read this two-part vignette, consider how you might respond to parents, colleagues, and administrators who expect you to build your course around the textbook narrative.

At a parent–teacher conference, Mr. Johnson is confronted by a father who wants to know why his daughter Sandra is not using a history textbook. "I have not seen her bring it home all year," he complains, not certain whether Sandra is being lazy or whether her excuses are legitimate. "She says that you did not even assign them textbooks, but I find that hard to believe." Mr. Johnson is not sure how to respond. He has spoken before with parents and colleagues like this who think that if students are not reading lengthy selections from textbook chapters for homework every night, their history class lacks rigor. "Sandra is telling the truth about the textbook," Mr. Johnson replies.

We have a classroom set that we use occasionally, but I do not assign students a lot of reading from the textbook. She should bring home from time to time collections of documents or other resources that she will use to try to build her own interpretations of historical events. And you might see her working online, searching digital archives for historical documents. She should be doing some historical writing at home, putting the finishing

DOI: 10.4324/9781003183495-13

touches on the work we have been doing in class. We spend a lot of time doing case studies related to important events, with students figuring out what happened and developing their own interpretations.

Sandra's father does not understand:

I thought people have already figured out what happened and wrote it in textbooks. These kids do not need to figure it out—they just need to learn it. When I was in school my history teacher gave me one hour of reading from the textbook every night, and I hated it at the time, but now I have learned to love history.

Most parents and students appreciate the way Mr. Johnson teaches, history but there are a few, like Sandra's dad, who do not understand why he does not rely heavily on the history textbook as the main source of information for the students. Mr. Johnson reflects on his attitude about the textbook. One of the goals of his class is to help students understand the textbook's place as *a* text rather than *the* text. He wants them to acknowledge that the textbook, like all *accounts*, has human sources. Textbook authors must make interpretive choices about what to include and what to omit, where to begin the historical narrative, how to integrate the histories of diverse groups, how to address historical controversies such as slavery and American imperialism, and whether to raise questions about the flaws of heroes and heroines. Mr. Johnson wants students to understand that textbooks targeted to large markets are published with their audience in mind, changing content for conservative- and liberal-leaning states (Goldstein, 2020). Mr. Johnson would like to help students develop a healthy, historian-like skepticism toward all texts, including textbooks, viewing them as the products of imperfect individuals with limited perspectives and specific purposes for producing them. Luckily, he has an entire school year to do this with his students, much more time than the few minutes he had to try to explain his rationale to Sandra's father.

To help achieve these objectives and to help his 10th-grade world history students learn about the Mongols, Mr. Johnson decides to conduct an activity giving students numerous descriptions of the Mongols from Chinese, European, Muslim, Mongol, and contemporary perspectives. In preparation, he creates a digital archive of primary sources. He decides to assign students to compare and contrast the different documents, consider the source of each text, and then write on one of a number of questions that he poses. He brainstorms questions that might promote authentic inquiry, such as "How do you explain the patterns in the way the Mongols were viewed by people from a wide variety of backgrounds?" "How did the Mongols use psychological warfare to subject their enemies?" and "How did religion play a role in the expansion of the Mongol Empire?" The answers to these questions cannot be found in any single text but in a synthesis of the documents. In addition, Mr. Johnson decides to assign

Expository Account 1: The Textbook   Expository Account 2: My Account

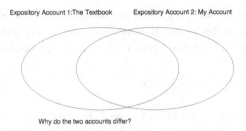

Why do the two accounts differ?

FIGURE 11.1 A Venn diagram for comparing a textbook account with a student's account.

students to write a textbook-like summary of Mongol warfare based on the documents that he gives them and other primary sources they find.

On the day of the lesson he moves around the classroom as students, in small groups, work with their document packets seeking answers to various questions. At the end of class, he assigns students to use the resources in the text set, and other primary sources they can find online to write a two-paragraph description of the Mongols' war tactics. He emphasizes that they should write something original that sounds like what they might read in a textbook—just a summary of the most important characteristics of their war practices.

When class starts the next day, Mr. Johnson projects for the students a textbook account of Mongol warfare. He asks them to create a Venn diagram comparing and contrasting the content of their paragraphs with the textbook account (see Figure 11.1). Additionally, he asks students to write a few sentences explaining why their account differs from the textbook, justifying the choices they made about what to include. After students have a chance to work on their own for a while, he leads the class in a discussion of their experience comparing the texts.

"I assume that your account was not identical to the textbook account. Why do you think differences exist?" Mr. Johnson begins the discussion. Students describe how their accounts differed from the textbook and trying to explain why. Some are critical of omissions in the textbook. Some have doubts about the account they wrote, thinking they might have made errors. Others explain why the textbook included information that was missing from their accounts. Mr. Johnson asks questions like

> Do you think that the textbook is wrong if it differed from your account? Do you think that your account is wrong if it differed from the textbook account? How is it possible that differences can exist in textbook accounts if textbook authors are just trying to give basic factual information?

Students consider how different authors might disagree about what is most important to include, how the sources they look at to get their information shape their accounts, and how their word choice influences the tone of their accounts.

The conversation continues for a while, before Mr. Johnson summarizes his class's findings:

> I think it is important to understand that textbooks are like other historical accounts. They are written by authors who have purposes in writing. The authors have to make tough decisions about what to include and what to leave out. The authors also have opinions that are sometimes shown in the choice of words or the tone of the writing. In the future, as you use the textbook in this class and in other history classes, you need to remember to read it with the same critical eye that you use when you read other types of historical sources.

How might this lesson have been strengthened by having students contrast the account they wrote with three or four different textbook accounts rather than just one?

Healthy Skepticism, Textbooks, and Secondary Sources

Why is it important to help students consider the text, the context, and the subtext when analyzing a historical text?

One of the characteristics that distinguish historian readers from history students is that they approach every text with healthy skepticism. They do not accept the content of a text at face value. Instead, historians understand that each text has a context, which includes its historical and physical setting—the occasion of its creation. Furthermore, every text has a subtext, which includes the author's proximity to the event in time, space, and emotion; the intended audience; the author's perspective; and the author's motives (Lesh, 2011; Merkt et al., 2017; Wineburg, 1994). Any text represents an extension of an individual, blending the value of unique insights with the flaws that characterize human perception and communication. Historians do not simply collect information from texts; they also use texts as evidence, rationally and strategically choosing how to interpret the text's content. Wineburg (2001) put it well when he explained that to historians "what is most important is not what the text says, but what it does" (p. 65). Healthy skepticism is the filter through which text content is evaluated, allowing a text to serve as evidence rather than as a conveyer of information.

healthy skepticism: the tendency to be mildly resistant to the information that one finds, questioning the source, cross-checking the facts, and seeking alternative perspectives

> *subtext: the purposes behind the production of a text including the author's motives, the author's background, the intended audience, and the social context during which the text was created—all influencing the content of the text*

Unfortunately, most students display a remarkable lack of skepticism. Because this is particularly true when they work with textbooks (Paxton, 1999), I discuss skepticism within the context of history textbooks and secondary sources. I explore (a) skepticism and historians' thoughts about textbooks, (b) skepticism and students' and teachers' thoughts about textbooks, (c) supporting students' historical thinking with textbooks and other expository texts, (d) introducing students to the role of secondary sources and historiography, and (e) helping students develop historical literacies by producing expository texts.

Skepticism and Historians' Thoughts about Textbooks

> How do students typically read textbooks? How does this contrast with the way historians interrogate accounts?

Textbooks are not a source historians typically use in their original research. However, the few studies of historians' reading of textbooks show that historians approach them with the same healthy skepticism that characterizes their work with other historical accounts. They understand that textbooks, like other forms of historical writing, have a source, context, and subtext. Wineburg (1991) tested this notion by observing historians' reading of a textbook excerpt as part of his study of historians' and students' reading of historical sources related to the Battle of Lexington. Not only did historians, using evidence found in primary sources, point out factual errors in the textbook account, but they also engaged in an analysis of the context of the textbook's creation and its subtext. Fred, for instance, suggested that phrases such as "swift riding" and "stood their ground" celebrated American heroism—something completely absent in primary source accounts, even those representing patriot perspectives (Wineburg, 2001). Another historian, after seeing the source information and publication date, but before reading the textbook passage, began to anticipate what she would find. "[Textbooks] tend to be a little bit patriotic," she predicted, adding that textbooks reduce historical complexity in order to prepare students to answer multiple-choice questions (Wineburg (1991)). Interestingly, the historians, as a whole, rated the textbook excerpt as the least reliable of the sources that they considered, even lower than a fictional account from a historical novel.

Students' and Teachers' Thoughts About Textbooks

> Why do students place such great trust in textbook accounts? What is the harm in doing so?

One of the great ironies of history teaching is that textbooks, a resource that historians find little use for, are the staple for many teachers and students (Bain, 2006). And the traditional use of history textbooks is a barrier to students thinking like historians (Nokes, 2011). Students, unlike historians, have a difficult time thinking critically about textbook passages. In fact, in Wineburg's (1991) study, the same textbook account that was rated least reliable by the historians was selected as the most reliable text by the students—more trustworthy than eyewitness accounts that painted a remarkably different picture from the textbook account. Derek, one of the students, whom Wineburg (2001) praised for his general literacy skills, trusted the textbook because, as he explained, it was "just reporting the facts" (p. 68). In Derek's mind, the textbook lacked the bias present in the minutemen's sworn deposition and a British officer's journal, two accounts that were highly valued by the historians. Research suggests that students' struggles to think critically about their history textbook stem from the way textbooks are written and the way textbooks are used (Paxton, 1997, 1999).

Paxton's research focused on the way textbooks were written. He suggested that anonymous, authoritative textbook authors present what seem to be objective historical facts through an omniscient third-person voice that is above question (Paxton, 1997). To students, textbooks appear to be nearly sourceless. Paxton suggests that students who read traditional textbook accounts are unlikely to give independent thought to the information presented, rarely asking questions, making connections, or offering criticism. Instead, he complains that textbooks facilitate "mindless memorization" (Paxton, 1999, p. 319). Most students do not understand, as the students in Mr. Johnson's class were finding out, that as soon as a textbook author begins to write, they make interpretive decisions about where to start, what to include and omit, and how to handle historical controversies. Furthermore, textbooks often portray claims, theories, and even uncertainties as historical facts— facts that students, and much of the public, accept without question.

Still, textbooks remain a staple in many history classrooms. Teachers use textbooks for several reasons. Textbooks help teachers address the constant concern of coverage by providing what policymakers, parents, and the public mistakenly believe is *the* comprehensive narrative. Those who understand the nature of history know that history includes so much more than the textbook narrative. Textbooks help teachers organize history into manageable chronological and thematic units, often based on textbook chapters. Supplemental material that accompanies teachers' editions of textbooks provides support in lesson planning and the writing of exams. These materials often include primary sources, although these documents are typically used to reinforce or illustrate themes in the textbook—a far different use than providing an opportunity for students to engage in historical inquiry. Textbooks might make history teachers' work a little easier but if used in traditional ways decrease opportunities for historical inquiry and negatively impacts students' engagement and long-term learning.

In addition, the way textbooks have traditionally been used interferes with the building of historical literacies. My dissertation research investigated, among other things, the use of textbooks and other historical sources. As mentioned in Chapter 1, I spent 72 hours observing eight history teachers, paying particular attention to the texts they used and the way that they had students work with texts (Nokes, 2010). I found that students rarely had opportunities to develop their own interpretations of historical events or to critique the content of textbooks. Instead, when textbooks were used, and they were the most commonly used resource in seven of the eight classrooms, the accompanying assignments were intended to help students summarize, find main ideas, or answer factual questions using information from the book. Unlike Mr. Johnson in the vignette, teachers did not ask students to question or critically examine the content of textbook passages. Instead, they promoted students' memorization of information from their book, without a critical thought. Thus, the way textbooks are written and the way they are used makes it unlikely that students will treat textbooks as interpretive historical accounts that have contexts and subtexts (Lesh, 2011; Paxton, 1999). What is missing from students' work with textbooks is the healthy skepticism that historians display. As Wineburg (2001) concluded, "[b]efore students can see subtexts, they must first believe they exist" (p. 76). This is particularly true when students use textbooks (Bain, 2006).

However, students' lack of skepticism is not isolated to textbook reading. As I illustrated in Chapter 6, studies of students' online reading show that they experience the same difficulties in reading informational websites (Leu, et al., 2007; McGrew et al., 2018) and social media (Brookfield, 2015), that they have in working with a history textbook. They typically accept information uncritically, focusing on remembering or reposting rather than critiquing what they read. Students are often seduced by detail-rich text, colorful pictures, and formal language, characteristics of modern textbooks and many webpages.

Supporting Students' Historical Thinking With Textbooks and Expository Texts

Teachers can help students think historically about textbooks when they understand the nature of so-called *informational texts*, when they design activities that promote skepticism, when they value academic humility, and when assessments measure more than basic factual knowledge. I consider each of these ideas in this section.

"Informational Texts"

> Why does thinking about texts as "informational" discourage students from assuming an appropriate epistemic stance for historical thinking?

Textbook accounts and other so called "informational texts" are referred to as expository texts. Expository texts, such as essays, encyclopedia entries, Wikipedia and other websites, and magazine articles, are designed primarily to convey information. However, this classification of *informational text*, which is common in literacy research and instruction, should be troubling to history educators who know that all texts, in spite of how factual they might seem, include a context and a subtext. In the study of history there is no such thing as informational text. Instead, all texts that purposefully retell stories of the past—primary sources, secondary sources, movies, and textbooks—should be considered *accounts*. Accounts are constrained by perspectives and biases. Their production involves interpretive decisions about significance and tone. And each of these factors influences the development of textbooks, just as they influence the writing of a diary entry. Teachers can help students become more skeptical about informational texts by designing activities that remind students that all texts have authors, and by encouraging them to think critically about the choices authors make. In Mr. Johnson's class, students went through a process of constructing expository text similar to that which a textbook author might go through. They experienced the challenge of deciding what to include in their accounts. Their analysis at the end of the lesson, contrasting their accounts with that of the textbook author, helped them think more deeply about the interpretive choices that writers, themselves included, make.

> *informational text: a classification of nonfiction frequently used in English language arts to distinguish a thematic text from a narrative, a classification potentially confusing to history students who should view texts as accounts rather than as bearers of unadulterated information. Sometimes also called expository text.*

Promoting Skepticism

> What are some of the conditions during which a person is less likely to be skeptical about the information that they find? When does a person tend to be more skeptical?

Mr. Johnson wanted students to search for the subtext in history textbooks and the other documents they read. He was determined to help students understand that all historical sources, including textbooks, should undergo a critical review. He wanted students to approach primary source documents with a measure of skepticism, considering contexts and subtexts. The students' study of the Mongols helped them think critically about the textbook as well. Instead of having students find main ideas, summarize, or outline the textbook passage, as teachers often do, Mr. Johnson had students question the textbook content. Students' role was not that of managing information by reading, summarizing, and taking notes but more historian-like, critiquing and synthesizing historical accounts. Students noticed and wondered why certain things were included or omitted from the textbook account of the Mongols' warfare. They began to see that textbooks do not simply contain "the facts" but that the authors of the textbook put their own personal spin on their description of the Mongols both by selecting the story to tell and by choosing the words with which to tell it.

Modern technology has elevated the role of skepticism in reading and consuming information (Nokes et al., 2020). The internet has removed the traditional gatekeepers of publishing, allowing anyone to publish whatever they want in a digital format. These changes have led to a proliferation of fake news posted and reposted through social media. Perhaps more dangerous are the objective sounding and professional appearing web pages that distort the facts to promote the goals of special interest groups. Just as the unbiased language of textbooks discourages critical thinking, professional looking webpages, humorous memes and catchy one-liners promote political ideologies without critical review. Even emotional rants and unsubstantiated claims shared through biased news sources and on social media are accepted without question. People are rarely skeptical about things they hear that they want to believe (Rose, 2020). And evidence exists that increased exposure to social media does not promote critical media literacy skills—in fact, the opposite may be true (Powers et al., 2018). Young people who possess the greatest confidence in working with social media may be the least careful in analyzing the information they find before forwarding it to their digital network (Dharmastuti et al., 2020). Democratic societies are placed at risk when the people who live there lack the skills and dispositions needed to research political issues. Healthy skepticism is one of the dispositions most essential for informed civic engagement in the 21st century.

Valuing Open-Mindedness and Academic Humility

How might academic humility be one of the most important antidotes to the toxic political polarization of the 21st century?

One element of critical thinking that is often overlooked is maintaining an open mind. As described in Chapter 3, historians tend to be open-minded, understanding that historical interpretations are works in progress, in need of constant updating based on new evidence or new ways of considering old evidence. In recent research, a colleague of mine and I found that historians challenged their own ideas as frequently as they challenged their peers' ideas when engaged in historical inquiry (Nokes & Kesler-Lund 2019). Their interpretations were subject to ongoing review, and they frequently changed their minds as new evidence was encountered or as discussion with peers led them to more nuanced ways of understanding events. Historians' willingness to revise their thinking when compelled to do so by evidence is called academic humility.

> *academic humility: the tendency to recognize one's understandings as tentative and subject to change as a scholar encounters compelling evidence, better arguments, or other reasons for revision.*

Ironically, students' unsophisticated understandings are often more resistant to change than historians' mature views. For example, some students uncritically reject certain sites, such as Wikipedia, as historical sources, without investigating them. However, students can be shown the usefulness of textbooks, Wikipedia, and other expository texts in providing a basic understanding of an event that can be corroborated by and integrated with the contents of other resources. Researchers have found that professional fact-checkers, who are among the most skilled internet readers, effectively employ Wikipedia to evaluate other webpages through lateral reading (McGrew, et al., 2018). Expository texts, despite their imperfections, can be useful as one of many types of resources employed to solve historical problems. They are, perhaps, the most useful sources when trivial information is needed quickly and when the stakes for accuracy are low. History teachers can model for students how to synthesize material from multiple sources, including expository texts, to build a coherent understanding. When students are skillful at critically evaluating all sources, they need not avoid or fear expository texts like Wikipedia or the textbook.

Assessing More than Basic Factual Knowledge

> How do traditional history tests that assess students' recall of trivial information promote an unsophisticated epistemic stance, distort students' views on the nature of history, and discourage historical thinking?

Teachers undermine their efforts to help students think critically about textbook passages when they give students traditional assessments that focus solely on remembering the historical facts presented in textbooks. History tests are notorious for assessing obscure tidbits of information that have little relevance to the lives of students, facts that are quickly forgotten shortly after, or even before, the test is given. When teachers assess students solely on their ability to remember basic facts, they imply that facts, rather than interpretations, the use of evidence, or the processes of historical literacy, are of primary importance. The literal comprehension of the textbook gains preeminence over the ability to think critically about its content. Most students do not have the cognitive resources to focus on memorizing details from their textbooks at the same time they are critiquing what the author has chosen to include, analyzing the tone the author uses, or considering how to wisely use textbook information. However, when students use the details in the text to question the author's motives and perspective, they are more likely to remember what they have read, even without trying to do so (Beck et al., 1997; Reisman 2012). Teachers must be certain that their assessments are aligned with their instructional objectives. When their instructional focus is on building students' historical literacies, their assessments must not measure the management and memorization of historical information rather than historical thinking. Under the label *Beyond the Bubble*, the Stanford History Education Group provides practical assessments a teacher could use to evaluate students' ability to engage in sourcing, corroboration, and contextualization (see https://sheg.stanford.edu/history-assessments).

In summary, history teachers play an important role in helping students learn how to think critically about textbooks, websites, and other expository sources. They can do so by designing activities that require a critical analysis of the textbook rather than focusing solely on remembering the information it contains. They should help students approach expository texts with a healthy skepticism and academic humility. Furthermore, teachers can facilitate historical thinking by designing assessments that measure students' ability to use evidence to build and defend interpretations rather than simply assessing students' ability to remember historical facts.

Exposing Students to Secondary Sources and Historiography

> Why should teachers include not only primary sources but secondary sources, such as excerpts from historians' writing, in their classroom activities?

Historians begin their study of any topic by considering what other historians have already written about it. Their historical inquiries are grounded in the work that others have done (Graff et al., 2015). They become familiar with the writing of those historians who have established themselves as authorities and learn the theories and interpretations that are most accepted in the field. Often the study of a historical topic changes over time, in the specific areas of interest, the types of evidence used, and the lenses through which evidence is evaluated. Historians refer to the way a historical topic has been studied as historiography. They immerse themselves in the historiography of their specialty area because, in order to be successful, a historian must produce original scholarship that complements and contributes to the work of others. To do so, they must become familiar with the history and trajectory of research on their topic—with historiography.

In contrast, students rarely have exposure to the published work of historians (Nokes, 2010). Presenting the notion of historiography to young people is not central to most history teachers' ideas for classroom activities (Brown & Hughes, 2018). Should history students be introduced to the notion of historiography as part of a general effort to build historical literacies? Bain (2005), a history teacher and researcher, suggests that they should and models how it can be done. He includes historiography in a lesson that he teaches on Christopher Columbus, during which students are exposed to shifting interpretations of Columbus in historical texts. Students start with the traditional, widely accepted, story of Columbus pioneering the notion that the world was round and of his attempts to sail west in order to reach the Far East. Students read a series of excerpts from textbooks published between 1830 and 1997 that suggest that the conception of a flat earth was the primary obstacle to Columbus's success. With impeccable timing, Bain then introduces new texts that claim that "virtually all major medieval scholars affirmed the earth's roundness," and he shows images of a sculpture of Atlas holding the globe on his back—a representation of a round earth produced around 150 CE (Bain, 2005). Students begin to see that the idea of Columbus pioneering the belief that the earth is round represents an evolving public conception rather than the realities of Columbus's time. Students are introduced to a simplified notion of historiography when Bain asks, "How have stories about Columbus changed since 1492?" The purpose of a lecture that follows is not simply to provide information on Columbus but to describe how interpretations of Columbus have changed over time. Students begin to see that historical understandings evolve as a result of changing interests, purposes, and evidence.

Other researchers have suggested that teachers provide students with conflicting secondary sources, particularly the work of historians, side by side with conflicting primary sources. For instance, at the Stanford History Education Group website (2012), one suggested lesson provides students with two conflicting primary source accounts of Pocahontas's rescue of John Smith, ironically both from John Smith, and two conflicting interpretations written by scholars. Students are asked to assess each of the historians' interpretations and develop their own interpretations based on the conflicting primary and secondary source accounts. Such activities help students understand the interpretive nature of historical thinking and help them become more skeptical of accounts—even those produced by authorities. Simply put, students cannot accept two accounts at face value when they offer antithetical interpretations. Students must critically evaluate both accounts and search for reasons for disagreeing interpretations. In summary, exposure to the writing of historians can be used to help students understand historiography and, when given opposing historians' interpretations, to develop a healthy skepticism toward secondary sources.

Helping Students Transfer Historical Literacies to Online Reading

Social media has become a leading source of news information for the majority of people, especially young people (Khan & Idris, 2019). Their immersion in social media makes it difficult for them to critically evaluate the information they find. As Brookfield (2015) eloquently explained,

> when you swim in an ocean of socially mediated information it is hard to levitate out of the water, jump to the beach, and observe the big picture of wave movements, changing colors, tidal advances, and retreats. Immersed in the ocean you are not even aware that multiple other realities—land and air—exist.

(p. 49)

History teachers, as outsiders of students' social media world have the potential to help students step back from social media to think critically about what they read.

The key to helping students apply critical thinking skills to online reading is to model the transfer of the strategies important in historical inquiries, particularly sourcing and corroboration, to the authentic inquiries that students might engage in. For instance, a teacher might discuss the need to engage in sourcing with information found online and model this process while gathering information about a current controversial topic. The teacher can project their computer screen for the class to observe as the teacher engages in lateral reading—the act of opening new search tabs and leaving a website to gather information about its source (McGrew et al., 2019). The teacher might model the process of corroboration by cross-checking information found on one website with information found on websites that represent diverse interests. Furthermore, a teacher might provide explicit instruction on the nature of newsfeeds, warning about the *echo chamber* that an individual resides in when they merely consume the ads and news that is targeted to them. Teachers can issue warnings about people's tendency to be less skeptical of information they want to believe, encouraging students to think about the alternative perspectives that might help them not only verify information but think about issues in more sophisticated ways as well.

Students Creating Expository Texts

Mr. Johnson assigned students to create a textbook-like account of Mongol warfare. On the surface, his assignment was not unlike traditional writing assignments in history classrooms. Teachers often ask students to write summaries or reports on historical people, events, or eras. However, there were two noteworthy distinctions in Mr. Johnson's assignment. First, students were composing their accounts from multiple primary source documents. Often, when students are assigned to write a history essay or report, they simply recast information found in one expository text into their own expository text in a process some researchers call *knowledge telling* (Scardamalia & Bereiter, 1987). At best, the process consists of general literacies, such as finding the main idea, summarizing, composing with a logical organizing scheme, writing a topic sentence, and so on. At worst, the process entails plagiarizing a single, original source. Students engaged in such writing do little historical thinking. In contrast, Mr. Johnson's class composed from multiple primary sources. To successfully complete the assignment, they had to sort through the sources, evaluating the reliability of each source, corroborating patterns found across multiple texts, determining significance, and writing. Composing their paragraphs involved many elements of historical thinking and was an example of what researchers call *knowledge transforming* (Scardamalia & Bereiter, 1987).

---

knowledge telling: a writing process, such as summarizing, that involves repeating back the information found in sources

---

knowledge transforming: a writing process that includes synthesis and critically evaluation and results in original ideas, distinct from the sources used to research the topic

---

Second, Mr. Johnson had students use their expository writing to critique a textbook account. Students' experience writing gave them insight into the process that the textbook author might go through in selecting material for inclusion and in the word choices that they made. Students' experience in writing expository text gave them expertise that allowed them to be more critical of the textbook authors, questioning their decisions about what to include or omit from the textbook account. Students' experience helped them see that textbook narratives do not simply contain the facts and that information in textbooks should not be accepted at face value but that like all other historical accounts, textbooks have a context and a subtext and should be subject to the same evaluation that all historical texts undergo. Their use of the textbook was tempered by a healthy skepticism.

Chapter Summary

Historians approach textbooks with the same healthy skepticism with which they approach all historical texts. In contrast, students trust textbooks, primarily because of the way textbooks are written and the way they are used. Teachers can facilitate students' critical analysis of textbooks and other expository texts by helping them understand the nature of expository texts, by shifting the focus of assignments from remembering information to questioning why authors have included what they have, and by helping students consider the context and subtext of expository texts. Teachers must carefully design assessments to avoid the uncritical acceptance of the historical facts that textbooks contain. Furthermore, the writing of historians can be used to introduce students to historiography and to foster a healthy skepticism. Teachers can help students critique expository texts by drafting alternative expository texts.

Questions for Consideration

1. How can a history teacher foster healthy skepticism and critical thinking when using textbooks or lecturing? How can the format of lectures be changed to make them less informational and more interpretive?
2. How might a teacher help students transfer the disposition of healthy skepticism to online reading and to social media use? Why is healthy skepticism so important in an age of fake news and the loss of objectivity in news media?
3. How might the presence of academic humility change the political landscape in polarized societies? How might teachers nurture academic humility in students?

Additional Reading and Viewing

*   A book that shows how U.S. history textbooks have changed over time is Ward, K. (2010). *Not written in stone: Learning and unlearning American history through 200 years of textbooks.* The New Press.
*   An anthology of how foreign textbooks describe events that involve the United States is Lindaman, D., & Ward, K. (2006). *History lessons: How textbooks from around the world portray US history.* The New Press.
*   Bruce Lesh describes in greater detail how to teach students about the text, subtext, and context in Lesh, B. A. (2011). *" Why won't you just tell us the answer?": Teaching historical thinking in Grades 7–12.* Stenhouse Publishers.
*   Assessments of sourcing, corroboration, and contextualization can be found on the Stanford History Education Group's website under the label "Beyond the Bubble" at https://sheg.stanford.edu/history-assessments.
*   For a thorough discussion of new assessments to measure historical thinking, see Nokes, J. (in press). Using Library of Congress resources in purposeful

social studies assessment. In S. Waring (Ed.), *Inquiry and teaching with primary sources to prepare students for college, career, and civic life*. National Council for the Social Studies.

• A library of lesson plans and resources for helping students transfer historical literacies to civic online reasoning are available at https://cor.stanford.edu/

References

Bain, R. (2006). Rounding up unusual suspects: Facing the authority hidden in the history classroom. *Teachers College Record, 108*(10), 2080–2114. doi:10.1111/j.1467-9620.2006.00775.x

Bain, R. B. (2005). "They thought the world was flat?" Applying the principles of *How people learn* in teaching high school history. In M. S. Donovan & J. D. Bransford (Eds.), *How students learn: History, mathematics, and science in the classroom* (pp. 179–213). National Academies Press.

Beck, I. L., McKeown, M. G., Hamilton, R. L., & Kugan, L. (1997). *Questioning the author: An approach for enhancing student engagement with text*. International Reading Association.

Brookfield, S. D. (2015). Teaching students to think critically about social media. *New Directions for Teaching and Learning, 144*, 47–56. doi:10.1002/tl.20162

Brown, S. D., & Hughes, R. L. (2018). "It's not something we thought about": Teachers' perception of historiography and narratives. *Social Studies Research and Practice, 13*(1), 16–30. doi:10.1108/SSRP-09-2017-0054

Dharmastuti, A., Wiyono, B. B., Hitipeuw, I., & Rahmawati, H. (2020). Adolescent critical thinking prior to social media information sharing. *International Journal of Innovation, Creativity and Change, 13*(10), 1195–1213.

Goldstein, D. (2020, January 12). Two states. Eight textbooks. Two American stories. *New York Times.* https://www.nytimes.com/interactive/2020/01/12/us/texas-vs-california-history-textbooks.html

Graff, G., Birkenstein, C., & Durst, R. (2015). *They say, I say: The moves that matter in academic writing*. W. W. Norton & Co.

Khan, M. L., & Idris, I. K. (2019). Recognise misinformation and verify before sharing: A reasoned action and information literacy perspective. *Behavior and Information Technology, 38*, 12, 1194–1212. doi:10.1080/0144929X.2019.1578828

Lesh, B. A. (2011). *Why won't you just tell us the answer? Teaching historical thinking in grades 1–12*. Stenhouse.

Leu, D. J., Zawilinski, L., Castek, J., Banerjee, M., Housand, B. C., Liu, Y., & O'Neil, M. (2007). What is new about the new literacies of online reading comprehension? In L. S. Rush, A. J. Beagle, & A. Berger (Eds.), *Secondary school literacy: What research reveals for classroom practice* (pp. 37–68). National Council of Teachers of English.

Lindaman, D., & Ward, K. (2006). *History lessons: How textbooks from around the world portray US history*. The New Press.

McGrew, S., Breakstone, J., & Ortega, T. (2018). Can students evaluate online sources? Learning from assessments of civic online reasoning. *Theory & Research in Social Education, 46*, 165–193. doi:10.1080/00933104.2017.1416320

McGrew, S., Smith, M., Breakstone, J., Ortega, T., & Wineburg, S. (2019). Improving university students' web savvy: An intervention study. *British Journal of Educational Psychology, 89*(3), 485–500. doi:10.1111/bjep.12279

Merkt, M., Werner, M., & Wagner, W. (2017). Historical thinking skills and mastery of multiple document tasks. *Learning and Individual Differences, 54,* 135–148. doi:10.1016/j.lindif.2017.01.021

Nokes, J. D. (2010). Observing literacy practices in history classrooms. *Theory and Research in Social Education, 38*(4), 298–316. doi:10.1080/00933104.2010.10473438

Nokes, J. D. (2011). Recognizing and addressing barriers to adolescents' "reading like historians." *The History Teacher, 44* (*3*), 379–404.

Nokes, J. (in press). Using Library of Congress resources in purposeful social studies assessment. In S. Waring (Ed.), *Inquiry and teaching with primary sources to prepare students for college, career, and civic life.* National Council for the Social Studies.

Nokes, J. D., Draper, R. J., & Jensen, A. P. (2020). Literacy and literacies in the modern age. In J. Hartford, & T. O'Donoghue (Eds.), *A cultural history of education: Modern age.* Bloomsbury.

Nokes, J. D., & Kesler-Lund, A. (2019). Historians' social literacies: How historians collaborate and write during a document-based activity. *The History Teacher, 52*(3), 369–410.

Paxton, R. J. (1997). "Someone with like a life wrote it: "The effects of a visible author on high school history students. *Journal of Educational Psychology, 89*(2), 235–250. doi:10.1037/0022-0663.89.2.235

Paxton, R. J. (1999). A deafening silence: History textbooks and the students who read them. *Review of Educational Research, 69*(3), 315–337. doi:10.3102/00346543069003315

Powers, K. L., Brodsky, J. E., Blumberg, F. C., & Brooks, P. J. (2018). Creating developmentally-appropriate measures of media literacy for adolescents. *Proceedings of the Technology, Mind, and Society* (pp. 1–5). doi:10.1145/3183654.3183670

Reisman, A. (2012). Reading like a historian: A document-based history curriculum intervention in urban high schools. *Cognition and Instruction, 30*(1), 86–112. doi:10.1080/07370008.2011.634081

Rose, J. (2020). To believe or not believe: An epistemic exploration of fake news, truth, and the limits of knowing. *Postdigital Science and Education, 2*(1), 202–216. doi:10.1007/s42438-019-00068-5

Scardamalia, M., & Bereiter, C. (1987). Knowledge telling and knowledge transforming in written composition. In S. Rosenberg (Ed.), *Cambridge monographs and texts in applied psycholinguistics. Advances in applied psycholinguistics, Vol. 1. Disorders of first-language development; Vol. 2. Reading, writing, and language learning* (pp. 142–175). Cambridge University Press.

Stanford History Education Group. (2012). *Charting the future of teaching the past.* http://sheg.stanford.edu/

Ward, K. (2010). *Not written in stone: Learning and unlearning American history through 200 years of textbooks.* The New Press.

Wineburg, S. S. (1991). On the reading of historical texts: Notes on the breach between school and academy. *American Educational Research Journal, 28*(3), 495–519. doi:10.3102/00028312028003495

Wineburg, S. S. (1994). The cognitive representation of historical texts. In G. Leinhardt, I. Beck, & C Stainton (Eds.), *Teaching and learning in history* (pp. 85–135). Erlbaum.

Wineburg, S. S. (2001). *Historical thinking and other unnatural acts: Charting the future of teaching the past.* Temple University Press.

12

EXPLORING HISTORICAL COMPLEXITY WITH AUDIO AND VIDEO TEXTS

With technological breakthroughs of the late 19th and 20th centuries, a wide range of new genres of evidence has become available to historians. In this chapter, you will consider how you might enhance students' historical inquiries by using audio-recorded music, movies, and a range of other audio and video texts in connection with more traditional historical evidence. You will also consider why presenting history in its complexity encourages students to make independent interpretations during historical inquiry.

In the vignette that follows, how does Miss Chavez help students decode jazz music? How does she introduce the concept of reductionist thinking?

Ms. Chavez is planning a lesson on social trends of the 1920s for a U.S. history class. She will focus on the clash between traditional rural society and dynamic urban culture. She feels like this clash between tradition and change is an ongoing phenomenon in American history—something that students can relate to today. She wants to help students recognize the problems that can arise from clinging to some traditions or abandoning others. She knows that high school students have a great interest in music, so she decides to use jazz music as a medium through which students can explore the clash between tradition and change in the 1920s. She finds recordings of several jazz songs, intending to play short clips for students. She also gathers recordings of popular songs from the 1920s that would not be considered jazz. As she collects resources, she finds other primary sources created during the 1920s and 1930s, voicing various opinions about jazz. She decides to spend time with the students helping them discover the unique characteristics of jazz and then have them investigate why many people opposed this revolutionary art form. She determines that this might be a good time to

DOI: 10.4324/9781003183495-14

introduce students to the problems of oversimplistic thinking by talking about the flaws of historical labels like the "Jazz Age."

Ms. Chavez establishes the following objectives for her lesson on "the Jazz Age."

1. Students will identify the characteristics of jazz music, including the types of musical instruments commonly used; the role of improvisation and individual interpretation; the combination of a soloist's melody and the rhythm section's countermelody; and its origins with African American musicians.
2. Students will use the varied reactions to jazz in the 1920s to explain the clash between tradition and change, investigating why many people opposed jazz.
3. Students will evaluate the use of historical labels, such as the "Jazz Age," considering forms of popular music of the 1920s that provided an alternative to jazz.

Ms. Chavez finds on YouTube and other internet sites examples of jazz music and other popular songs of the 1920s that she will use as counterexamples. In addition, she makes copies of magazine articles criticizing jazz music (Faulkner, 1921) and defending the flappers' lifestyle (Page, 1922). She also finds a short animated movie produced in 1936 that captures the conflict between classical and popular music and jazz (Schlesinger & Avery, 1936).

Ms. Chavez starts class with a *concept attainment* activity, a way for students to inductively discover some of the defining characteristics of jazz music. She explains to students that she is going to play examples of a certain type of music, each example followed by a counterexample. She tells them that she is not merely looking for a name of the type of music but also for the common characteristics found in all the examples and missing from all the counterexamples. The students must try to figure out what all the examples have in common and how they differ from the counterexamples. She starts by playing 1 minute of Louis Armstrong's "When the Saints Go Marching In" (1968), while the students listen. She then plays the counterexample of Gene Austin's "Carolina Moon" (Burke & Davis, 1928). After playing the second audio clip she asks students to identify the differences between the first and second recording, making a list on the board as students point out the lively beat and the use of different musical instruments.

She plays a minute-long clip of two additional songs, "When You're Smiling" by Louis Armstrong (Shay et al., 1929) and "I'll Be With You in Apple Blossom Time" by the Andrew Sisters (Tilzer & Fleeson, 1920) and then opens the discussion again for students to compare, adding students' observations to the ideas already listed on the board. Students point out the presence of nonsense lyrics (scat singing) and the prominence of African American singers.

Ms. Chavez continues to alternate between playing an example and a counterexample, pausing for more discussion after each pair. Eventually students become certain that the examples are all jazz. And they identify many of the traits of jazz including the common musical instruments, the free flow, the improvisation, the cooperation among musicians, an unconventionality, and the role of African American artists. Once the characteristics of jazz have been identified, Ms. Chavez asks the class to see if they can identify each characteristic as she plays a video recording of the first jazz song students listened to in the lesson, "When the Saints Go Marching In." She projects the video of the musicians and singers, which makes the characteristics more obvious. Through this concept attainment activity, Ms. Chavez has helped students begin to *break the code* of jazz, seeing it as a free, spontaneous, rebellious art form.

After showing the video, Ms. Chavez transitions into the larger issue of the clash between tradition and change. She asks students how they think people responded to jazz. During the discussion that follows many students are surprised to learn that there was a great deal of opposition to jazz. Most students like it better than the alternative popular music style they heard in the counterexamples. Erroneously applying presentism, they project that people in the 1920s had a similar reaction to theirs. The discussion leads directly into the inquiry activity Ms. Chavez planned. She explains that students will work in small groups to analyze several pieces of evidence from the 1920s and 1930s that reveal opposing viewpoints about jazz. She reminds them to consider the source and context of each item. After working in small groups, they will each write an interpretive, argumentative paragraph explaining whether the nickname, "the Jazz Age," is an appropriate label for the era.

Ms. Chavez passes out the materials and circulates as students analyze them. When one group of students has questions about the source of one essay that is critical of jazz (Faulkner, 1921), she encourages them to use their phones to find out what they can about the author, Anne Faulkner. She helps another group understand the context of a photograph that shows musicians in lively poses—an action common today but a major break from tradition at the time. Using a graphic organizer that Ms. Chavez prepared (see Figure 12.1) students spend most of the class period looking at various texts and gathering evidence of why people opposed jazz. After students have had a chance to investigate the evidence, she conducts a debriefing with them. Students list several reasons for opposition: racism, fear that jazz harmed people morally or intellectually, and the rebelliousness that accompanied it. After each response she asks students to cite their evidence.

Ms. Chavez concludes the discussion by asking whether *Jazz Age* is an appropriate label for the era. Students debate the question with peers representing both sides of the issue. Some contend that there were other forms of popular music and that many people hated jazz. Others respond by suggesting that since people who liked it and disliked it were all talking about jazz, the name suits the era. As the discussion winds down Ms. Chavez points out that the label *Jazz Age*, like most labels, while useful in capturing some trends, oversimplifies a complex

Jazz Document Analysis Graphic Organizer

Name _____

Use the following graphic organizer to prepare to make an argumentative about why there was opposition to jazz music.

Doc	Who is speaking and what is the situation (SOURCING)	What do they say? (SUMMARIZING)	What does this make you think about why there was opposition to jazz? How can you use this to make an argument?
Doc 1: Article Excerpt	Anne Shaw Falkner, head of music dept. leader of women's organizations. White??? Upper class??? Traditional??? Writing for a conservative magazine and audience	Jazz is responsible for moral decline among youth. More permissiveness in outrageous dances. Strange tones and rhythms	Older generation saw jazz as contributing to moral decline. This is a woman who is representative of older viewpoints and holds a position of power.
Doc 2: Quote 1			
Doc 3: Quote 2			
Doc 4: Political Cartoon			

FIGURE 12.1 A graphic organizer for students to take notes on the evidence of reasons for opposition to jazz.

Doc	Who is speaking and what is the situation (SOURCING)	What do they say? (SUMMARIZING)	What does this make you think about why there was opposition to jazz. How can you use this to make an argument
Doc 5: Article Excerpt			
Doc 6: Photo			
Doc 7: Ad			
Doc 8: Cartoon			

1. Why do you think there was opposition to jazz music?

2. How did jazz musicians respond?

3. Now think about how this relates to the larger context of history. How was opposition to jazz a symptom of the cultural clash of the 1920s

4. Now make a connection to today. What are some areas today where there is a clash between tradition and change?

FIGURE 12.1 (Continued)

history. She points out that historical labels are a form of *reductionist thinking* that people often engage in. She writes the words *reductionist thinking* on the board. She explains that reductionist thinking oversimplifies the past, noting that sometimes students of history forget about how diverse people's taste in music was during the 1920s because historians use the label *Jazz Age*. Historical labels like *Jazz Age* are useful for helping people make sense of a time period, but they are also flawed because they oversimplify things. Calling the 1920s the *Jazz Age* might give the impression that jazz was the main form of music in America during the time—which they had learned was not true.

Continuing the lesson on reductionist thinking, she explains that historical labels that oversimplify history can cause other problems. Labels sometimes cause students of history to forget the point of view of marginalized groups, or, in the case of jazz, to ignore other interesting trends in music. She teaches the students that historians create labels for time periods, like the Jazz Age or the Stone Age; for groups of people, like the Robber Barons or the Mound Builders; and places, like the Dust Bowl or Bible Belt. She points out that the key thing to remember about labels like these is that there are almost always exceptions to general trends.

"Do you remember the Mound Builders we studied at the start of the year?" she asks. "They did not wander around all day making piles of dirt. The most noticeable features of their civilization for us today are the large mounds of earth they built. So we sometimes refer to them as the Mound Builders, but mounds were only a small part of their culture." She concludes her mini-lecture on reductionist thinking by reminding students that historical labels help us make sense of a time period but that they can cause us to forget or ignore things that do not fit in with the label. Historical labels are one type of reductionist thinking, and they will talk about more throughout the year.

At the end of class she shows the animated movie, *I Love to Singa*, which captures the clash between traditional music and jazz (Schlesinger & Avery, 1936). Before showing it, she asks students to consider the source and whether the producers of the cartoon were more inclined to listen to jazz music or to traditional music.

> How does Ms. Chavez use modeling, direct instruction, and small-group work at different times during this lesson? What are some of the advantages of using a variety of teaching methods during a lesson?

Patterns in Reductionist Thinking

In this chapter, I explore two elements that were addressed in Ms. Chavez's lesson. First, I consider reductionist thinking, warning about specific examples that are common in secondary history classrooms. Second, I discuss the use of video and audio resources, like the music and the video clips that Ms. Chavez used. I explore potential audio and video resources, three different purposes for showing movies, challenges students face in working with audio and video texts, and ways that teachers can promote historical thinking by having students create audio and video texts.

Reductionist Thinking

What are the advantages of using reductionist thinking to simplify history for students? What are the disadvantages of doing so? How does reductionist thinking discourage historical thinking?

Reductionism is an effort to explain complex processes in terms of the interaction between simpler, fundamental parts. There is something appealing about explaining history in simple terms. For instance, in his extremely popular book *Guns, Germs, and Steel,* amateur historian Jared Diamond (1999) explains the economic inequalities between modern societies as a result of relatively simple geographic factors such as the north–south or east–west alignment of continents. Many academic historians have criticized his popular work as reductionist, while the public appreciates it for the same reason. True historical literacy requires the ability to understand and appreciate a complexity that is absent from his analysis. For purposes of this chapter, and, ironically, in simplifying this element of historical literacy for working with students, *reductionism* is defined as any effort to simplify historical content, including causation, in order to avoid historical complexity. Reductionism is the tendency to reduce history to a single narrative such as that contained in textbooks by eliminating the disorder that is inherent when alternative viewpoints, exceptions to rules, and multiple interpretations are acknowledged. One of the challenges of building students' historical literacies is helping them understand the complex nature of historical causation, changes, trends, and events (Gaddis, 2002), without overwhelming them.

reductionism: an effort to simplify historical content or causation in order to avoid the complexity inherent in historical inquiry

Reductionist traps must be avoided in building students' historical literacies for many of the same reasons that teachers must address students' epistemic stance. If history is viewed as a single narrative to be remembered, then explaining it in simple chains of cause and effect and dividing it up into clean categories with clear labels make the task more manageable. However, since history is constructed through the skillful use of multiple pieces of evidence, with diverse perspectives being recognized, then historians and students must consider multiple narratives and contrasting interpretations. Categories and labels must be open to critique, the perspectives of marginalized groups must be included, and exceptions to general trends should be acknowledged. Building students' historical literacies requires teachers, like Ms. Chavez, to introduce increasing complexity into their history classrooms. For her, the "Jazz Age" continues to serve as a framework around which to build an understanding of the 1920s. However, the students' analysis of 1920s music (both popular and jazz) gives them a more complete picture of the clash of culture that developed during the era.

In traditional history classrooms, teachers frequently oversimplify historical complexity. This statement is not meant to be critical of teachers—in fact, considering the emphasis on learning historical facts in many educational settings, wise teachers have found ways to simplify, categorize, and label in order to help students manage an otherwise overwhelming volume of historical facts they are expected to remember. However, as teachers shift the emphasis of history teaching away from the exclusive learning of historical facts toward historical inquiry, they must also expose students to the greater complexities of thinking historically. If building historical literacy is an objective of a history class, then the perspectives of marginalized groups such as people of color, women, Indigenous people, and people in lower economic classes, must be included in evidence sets, even when their story clashes with a patriotic narrative. Exceptions to general trends must be acknowledged, and historical assumptions must be critiqued.

Common Examples of Reductionist Thinking

> Which of the following types of reductionist thinking have you seen teachers use during your experience as a student? Why might each example of reductionist thinking interfere with historical inquiry or historical thinking?

In the vignette, Ms. Chavez pointed out to her students one example of reductionist thinking—historical labeling. Other examples of reductionist thinking that often occur, and are sometimes promoted, in history classrooms include categorization, stereotyping, stagnation, viewing outcomes as inevitable, dualism, single or simplified causation, looking for *the* answer (Lesh, 2011), group personification (Barton, 2010), the expectation of linear narrative of progression toward the present (Barton, 1996), and disregarding counter-viewpoints. Each of these is considered.

Historical Labeling

Historians are adept at giving labels to historical eras, for example, "Jazz Age" or "Stone Age"; locations, for example, "Fertile Crescent" or "Balkan Powder

Keg"; and groups of people, for example, "Robber Barons" or "Mound Builders." While doing so, historians understand the dangers of such labels: reducing complex trends, places, and people to a single prominent attribute. Historians remain open-minded about the characteristics of eras, places, and people who carry such labels. For example, the Stone Age is so named because most of the artifacts that remain from that time period are made of stone. However, historians understand that this is a trick of evidence rather than the realities of the era. They recognize that societies' technologies changed over the tens of thousands of years and the thousands of miles of peoples' migrations. Stone Age humans used cords, textiles, baskets, ceramics, animal skins, bone, and stone tools in different locations at different times. Few non-stone artifacts remain, but the stone artifacts give clues as to the other technologies that people possessed (Angier, 1999). Aware of the risk of historical labels, Ms. Chavez's lesson plan explores the label the "Jazz Age" to help students appreciate the diverse forms of popular music at the time. Ms. Chavez helps students see that traditional music continued to be popular even as a new type of music gained fans. By having students question the label, she prepares them to think deeply about the clash between tradition and cultural change during the 1920s as well as in the 21st century.

Categorization

Categorization is another way teachers help students manage historical information. Just as combining bits of information into "chunks" can serve as a memory aid, creating categories as an organizational framework can help students understand and remember historical content. For instance, many teachers help students manage the factual overload associated with Franklin D. Roosevelt's New Deal, using *the three Rs*—relief, recovery, and reform—as a framework for understanding the scores of alphabet agencies. Students categorize a sample of alphabet agencies based on their purpose: to provide relief, to help the economy recover, or to make needed reforms to avoid future economic calamities. Yet historians and economists understand that most alphabet agencies served more than a single purpose. Thus, while categorization is a helpful way of thinking about the New Deal, teachers should help students see that the categories do not capture the complexity of the agencies. Like most categorization systems, *the three Rs* oversimplifies historical complexity.

Stereotyping

One particularly dangerous way of categorizing is through stereotyping, assuming that all individuals within a group possess the same characteristics. Often history teachers address stereotyping by attempting to replace negative stereotypes with positive stereotypes rather than addressing the real issue—stereotyping reduces the complexity of the spectrum of individual personalities into a distorted understanding of people. In the vignette in Chapter 7, for example, Mr. Dunn helped students see that not all Indigenous people—even within the same nation—reacted the same way to the arrival of European colonists. Often, stereotypes include racist or sexist notions that lead to discrimination. Stereotyping can interfere with historical thinking. For example, Wineburg (2001) found that students misidentified an image of a peace protester during the Vietnam War because he did not fit the stereotypical *hippie* image. Pop culture creates simplistic images of racial groups, women, soldiers, pioneers, Pilgrims, hippies, and countless others, which misrepresent and oversimplify the complexities of people in the past.

Stagnation

One specific type of stereotyping is viewing a group of people as unchanging over time. History teachers often present an oversimplified account of history by failing to consider the changes that occurred within societies, presenting instead the story of stagnant, unchanging peoples. They do this by focusing on groups at a particularly interesting time and failing to acknowledge the lifestyles of peoples at different times. Egyptians were always building pyramids and mummifying their pharaohs. American Indians rode horses and hunted buffalo. The Europeans built castles, wore armor, and erected cathedrals. The Romans watched gladiator fights and sent their legions to battle barbarians and rebellious subjects. When teachers fail to acknowledge how cultures changed over time, students get a distorted view of history. Instead, when studying America's Indigenous people, for example, a teacher must encourage students to consider not only *where* they lived but also *when* they lived. Indigenous cultures changed significantly over time due to technological development, the spread of agriculture, climate change, the rise and fall of Indigenous empires, the spread of European diseases, access to horses and other European livestock, and numerous other factors. People's culture generally changes over time and history teachers must avoid presenting snapshots of stagnant, unchanging people.

Viewing Outcomes as Inevitable

Approaching historical events with hindsight creates the illusion that the outcomes of historical events were inevitable. However, the constant interplay of diverse causal factors makes most outcomes uncertain—a concept referred to as *contingency*. Patriots did not know whether the United States would win its struggle for independence. Many pioneers in the fight for women's rights did not see women vote in their lifetime. Muhammad probably had no idea when he led a handful of followers to Medina that his teachings would change the world. Dr. Martin Luther King could not foresee a Black president. And Susan B. Anthony could not have foreseen a woman becoming president of the United States. Part of the valor of historic heroes is that they persevered in the face of uncertainty. Historical thinking, including contextualization, showing historical empathy, and taking a historical perspective, requires students to understand that historical characters faced uncertain outcomes. Students sometimes forget about contingency—that events did not have to turn out the way they did. It is common for people with hindsight to find fault with historical actors, forgetting that they did not know how events would unfold like those who study history do.

---

contingency: the fact that outcomes are uncertain and that the interplay of many causal factors, including human agency and chance, create uncertainty in how events will unfold

---

Dualism

Students, particularly young students, tend to see the world in dualistic terms of right or wrong, good or evil, and helpful or harmful (Nokes, 2011). They have a difficult time acknowledging that men like George Washington, who many Americans revere, enslaved men and women, or that Hitler's economic policies improved Germany's depressed economy for millions of people. In an effort to categorize policies as good or bad, students fail to see that programs that benefit one group often harm other groups. It is difficult to find policies that are universally beneficial. And it can be cognitively debilitating for students who think in dualistic terms to understand that people who do monumental acts of good can also make serious mistakes. How could the same person who wrote the Declaration of Independence claiming that all men are created equal hold men and women in race-based bondage. The Reconstruction period following the Civil War is an ideal time to help students face the problems of dualistic thinking. For instance, during the early years of Reconstruction, Lincoln's policy of leniency toward former Confederates might be praised by students. They appreciate the words from Lincoln's (1865) second inaugural address, "with malice toward none, with charity for all." However, students fail to understand that mercy toward wealthy southerners disadvantaged those formerly enslaved. Lincoln's proposed policies left in dire economic conditions most of those people who had been held in bondage. When exposed to these ideas, students begin to understand the complexity of Reconstruction. The issues the government faced were not about whether to have mercy but to whom they would show mercy. Decisions during Reconstruction are one of many opportunities to confront dualistic thinking by showing students that policies and people are rarely absolutely right or wrong or exclusively good or bad.

Single or Simplified Causation

Often students, with the aid of their history teacher, identify a causal chain, that is, a single cause leading to a single event, which then causes a new event, and so forth. Most teachers know that causal chains create a logical system for remembering the relationship between historical events, much superior to memorizing a random list of facts (Bransford et al., 2000). However, causal chains oversimplify the complexity of relationships between historical events. Instead of a chain, historians would be more likely to use the metaphor of a causal network to represent the multiple interlinked causes that lead to multiple interlinked effects. The notion of a network creates more room for individual interpretation and debate about the relative strength of diverse causal strands and the relationship between effects. Furthermore, the image of a network leaves room for students to consider potential effects that were unrealized—counterfactual histories (Gaddis, 2002). Avoiding the reduction of a complex network of related events into a single causal chain sets the stage for students to use historical literacies in argumentative speaking and writing.

Looking for the Answer

Lesh (2011) suggests that another way teachers reduce historical complexity is by laying out a curriculum that directs students to a single correct answer. Instead, he suggests that teachers allow students to interact with evidence in a way that promotes questioning and diverse interpretations. He acknowledges that initially students feel frustrated when placed in a situation that requires them to develop original interpretations. But he describes how teachers can ease students into a position where they ask questions themselves and contemplate multiple possible answers. For instance, he describes an activity during which he gives students a series of straightforward questions about the Nat Turner slave rebellion and then gives small groups of students a different text with which to answer the questions. As students come together as a class they find that their peers have different answers, at first perceived to be "wrong." He then provides the groups with source information of the texts that they originally read, a process that helps them understand why conflicting accounts exist. Lesh shows that it is questions rather than answers that should drive the history curriculum. He concludes that this and other similar activities, which give students a degree of agency in choosing how to interpret the past, "changed the atmosphere in [his] classroom" (Lesh, 2011, p. 50), energizing both his students and him, increasing students' content knowledge, and building students' historical literacies. Students need to be weaned away from the expectation of a single, textbook-driven historical narrative assessed by factual questions with right or wrong answers.

Group Personification

Barton (2010) discovered that students often adopt simplistic notions of historical agency, projecting the traits of individuals onto groups or nations. For instance, during a unit on World War II he found that students in New Zealand commonly made statements, such as "New Zealand feared Japan." When questioned, they began to realize that they did not know what this meant. Certainly not all the people of New Zealand feared all the people of Japan. Did they mean that individuals within the government of New Zealand feared Japanese military aggression? Or did they mean that the majority of the people of New Zealand were afraid? Can a nation feel fear or other human emotions? Barton found that students' language repeatedly demonstrated a distorted view of agency by describing individuals' actions as a nation's. Barton suggests that students should be questioned when they make comments such as "Europeans were becoming curious . . ." or "America was upset over the tax on tea . . . ," which reduce the range of reactions that typically exist on any issue into a single continentwide or nationwide response.

Progress

Students often understand history as a linear progression from less civilized times through increasingly enlightened societies, culminating in the present. For Americans, the United States is viewed as the crowning achievement of this constant and consistent progress. The manner that Western civilization courses have been taught through the years perpetuates this reductionist view of progress: civilization was born in Mesopotamia, nurtured in Egypt, flowered in Greece and Rome, and, after a short medieval period, during which barbarians attempted to destroy it, was reborn during the European Renaissance, eventually being transplanted to America where it reached its full potential. Cultures appear and disappear in this story in a manner that suits the narrative. During each era, earlier technologies were improved upon and more enlightened ideas were developed. Achievements in non-Western societies were primarily failed attempts at being Western and are relegated to the fringes of the tale. In contrast, historians understand that history includes many more rises and falls, false starts, wrong turns, and enlightened ideas being replaced by less enlightened ideas. Although there are certainly patterns, and even global patterns at times, the trajectory of diverse societies often lies in different directions, some of which would be considered progress and some of which, including some modern changes, would be considered regression. Students with the distorted view of history-as-progress are less likely to be able to engage in historical empathy, an important element of historical literacy described in Chapter 10.

Disregarding the Viewpoints of Marginalized Groups

"Balboa was the first person to see the Pacific Ocean." Although students might say this, they will quickly admit their error when reminded that people lived throughout the Pacific Islands millennia before Balboa was born. Such a statement, even offered at times by history teachers, ignores the perspectives of those outside the traditional historical narrative. Unfortunately, more subtle ways exist for eliminating some groups' perspectives from students' study. For example, most U.S. history teachers include a unit on "westward expansion," failing to acknowledge that such a title ignores the perspective of Indigenous people of western North America or the Spanish living in the West—for them, the unit would be called "eastern encroachment." Ms. Chavez, in the vignette, attempted to expose students to the perspective of Americans who embraced jazz as well as those who opposed it. Her purpose was to help students explore alternative perspectives that might be ignored in a typical unit on the 1920s. Research shows that students of color notice when the perspectives of people who look like them are absent from the historical narrative. They become understandably indifferent or contemptuous toward history that excludes them (Bostick, 2021; Epstein, 2000; Peck, 2018).

I have described several reductionist traps that history teachers and students might fall into. Each one diminishes the perceived need for historical inquiry and discourages historical thinking by reducing history to a single simple story that has already been written. When students understand the complex nature of history as a discipline, they are more likely to assume a mature epistemic stance and understand their role in interpreting historical events. I now consider the use of audio and video recordings as historical evidence during historical inquiry.

Using Audio and Video Texts as Evidence

> How can the technology-driven products of the late 19th and 20th centuries, including recorded music, movies, television programs, radio and television ads, recorded news events, social media posts, and so on, add life and energy to the written evidence that students use during historical inquiries?

Potential Audio and Video Resources

Today's young people grow up in a visual world (Lesh, 2011). Many young people are immersed in social media that includes images, videos, music, and memes. Never in world history has sound, particularly music, been more accessible on demand to a wider range of people. The internet makes available diverse audio texts that can be used as evidence in constructing and defending historical interpretations. Historical inquiry assumes a new look in the 21st century. Not only are more written primary sources accessible through digital archives, but new forms of evidence that have only existed for a century or two are also available to help historians understand the recent past. Ms. Chavez felt that jazz and other popular music of the 1920s—not the lyrics but the music itself—was useful evidence in analyzing the clash between tradition and change during the Jazz Age.

There is something exciting and engaging in working with audio texts. For example, although the words used in Dr. Martin Luther King's "I Have a Dream" speech demonstrate his genius, his masterful delivery, which can be shown through audio or video recordings, reveals a force that students might miss if simply analyzing a transcript of the speech. Twentieth-century historical evidence includes a wealth of recorded speeches, radio broadcasts, music, debates, and historical sounds. Video recordings, furthermore, make available similar evidence with the added resources of clothing styles, body movements, facial expressions, and the like. Audio and video texts, as well as other visual texts, can supplement traditional written texts in ways that make primary source collections come to life.

A wide range of audio and video texts are available to students as they engage in historical inquiry. For example, students might view video clips from popular television shows from each decade since the 1950s to investigate how perceptions of humor, the portrayal of families, or the experiences of women have evolved in the 20th and 21st centuries. Television commercials marketing domestic products in the 1950s might be shown as part of a collection of documents to answer questions about the lives of married women during that era. Clips from newscasts reporting important events might be included in collections of documents to help students imagine the context surrounding events. Important speeches are often video- or audio-recorded. Music, like jazz, can provide insights into the tastes of people at different times. And song lyrics are useful primary sources given the right question. Popular trends can also be found in the cartoons of different eras. Training videos, such as the 1952 "Duck and Cover" Civil Defense film (Rizzo, 1952), provide evidence of the concerns of people at the time they were produced.

Recorded music, too, provides evidence that is useful in a wide range of historical inquiries. For example, students might study evolving public opinions of World War I by analyzing the lyrics of popular songs of the time such as "I Didn't Raise My Boy to Be a Soldier," "Over There," "Oh It's a Lovely War," "How Ya Gonna Keep 'Em Down on the Farm," and "Your Lips Are No Man's Land but Mine." Students might consider the counterculture movement of the 1960s and 1970s by analyzing the lyrics to songs like "Respect," "Good Vibrations," "Pleasant Valley Sunday," "Say it Loud, I'm Black and I'm Proud," "My Generation," "Masters of War," "People Got to Be Free," "I Fought the Law," "Lucy in the Sky with Diamonds," "Age of Aquarius," and "Okie from Muskogee" with the last song an example of the push back against the counterculture. A long list of songs could be used in an inquiry on opposition to the Vietnam War. Inquiries that use popular music from different eras are engaging for students (Burroughs & Hare, 2008). They may have heard these songs before but never considered them evidence of what people were thinking during different time periods.

These types of audio and video resources are engaging for most students. Furthermore, students who struggle with traditional reading can often decode and comprehend audio and video texts. Incorporating audio and video sources can invite poor readers into historical thinking activities.

Three Different Purposes for Showing Videos

Why is it important that a history teacher is clear in their own mind about their purpose for showing a movie in class?

Showing movies has been a common instructional practice in history classrooms since the time when teachers used projectors and reels of film (Ravitch & Finn, 1987). With the dawn of the VCR, feature films "based on true events" were added to teachers' library of movies. Today, the internet provides teachers with a wide range of video resources unavailable in the past. With the ease of using different kinds of movies, teachers should be very clear in their own minds about their purposes for showing a video. Three content-related purposes for showing films in a history classroom correspond roughly with the traditional purposes of using textbooks, historical fiction, and historical evidence (Nokes & Ellison, 2017).

Videos as Expository Teaching

How are documentary videos similar to history lectures or textbooks? How might a teacher help students engage in historical thinking using a documentary?

First, documentary videos, which history teachers are notorious for showing, are typically used for expository teaching. Documentary videos are typically used to convey information to students in a way that is similar to other methods of expository teaching: lecture and textbook reading. Teachers sometimes give students a worksheet or other assignment to help them manage the information presented in the video—similar to what they would do to help students manage the information presented in a lecture or during a textbook reading assignment. Commonly, students' role in working with documentary videos is to receive and remember information and to prepare to regurgitate it during assessments. In most classrooms, this is the most common use of videos and the least helpful in nurturing students' historical literacies. Instead, teachers might foster critical thinking about the content of documentary videos in a similar manner to the methods recommended for critiquing textbooks in Chapter 11. Students might be asked to consider the producer's purpose in making the documentary, evaluate the decisions made about what to include and what to leave out of the narrative, imagine the intended audience, think about how images, music, and words are used in coordination (such as ominous or cheery music being played while certain content is discussed), and compare the documentary's account with accounts contained in other sources.

> expository instruction: the sharing of information directly to students, often through a lecture, a documentary video, or an expository text like a textbook, with the intent that they will remember the information

Videos as Historical Fiction

> How are feature films that are "based on actual events" like historical fiction? How can a teacher help students think historically with feature films?

Teachers sometimes show Hollywood-produced feature films. These types of movies, like historical fiction, can be a good way to help students engage in contextualization by immersing them in a historical era (Marcus et al., 2018; Russell III & Waters, 2017). However, the utility of entertainment movies depends on the quality of research that went into the production of the movie as well as the preparation that teachers give students to learn with them. Similar issues arise in the use of entertainment movies as develop when students are exposed to historical fiction (see Chapter 10). Research has shown that students have a difficult time critically analyzing historical movies. For example, students may be unable to distinguish accurate from fictitious elements of the story. They may evaluate characters' actions based upon modern standards rather than by the standards used at the time the film portrays. As mentioned previously, Seixas (1993) found that students mistakenly judged a movie more *realistic* when the characters in the movie reacted to situations in a manner similar to the way the students would react, rather than in a way that reflected the values and standards of people within the historical context being portrayed. Unsurprisingly, students are drawn to characters who are more like them than to characters who accurately reflect the traits of historical people.

Teachers can help students think critically about entertaining feature films using many of the same techniques described in Chapter 10 for working with historical fiction. Doing so is of vital importance. For example, Wineburg (2007) found that a generation of students' understanding of the Vietnam War was shaped more by the movie *Forrest Gump* than by the instruction they received in high school history classes. Many adults continue to view movies related to historical events throughout their life. For some, watching movies is their primary ongoing exposure to historical events. It is essential that history teachers help students understand the nature of feature films that are "based on actual events" by helping students view them as accounts, produced to entertain, with elements of fiction integrated with accurate events in a manner intended to attract a large audience. The teacher can help students develop research skills to cross-check the narratives they are exposed to in the movies with trusted primary and secondary sources. They can help students watch movies with some skepticism, understanding that the phrase "based on actual events" is employed liberally as movie producers use their poetic license to craft entertaining films.

Videos as Historical Evidence

In contrast to using videos to convey information or to immerse students in a historical context, Ms. Chavez used the recording of Louis Armstrong's band playing "When the Saints Go Marching In" as historical evidence, part of a collection of resources on jazz music. Such use of video texts requires students to use many of the same strategies they use in working with other artifacts (see Chapter 8) and primary sources (see Chapter 7). Using video texts as evidence presents a challenge to students because they might be inclined to believe that a video, like a photograph, simply captures a moment of reality. However, video texts, like all other texts, have a source, an intended audience, a purpose, and a context, all of which are useful in interpreting their content. It is possible to corroborate across texts and use the other skills and habits of mind associated with historical thinking when working with video texts.

For example, when I taught about the psychological effects of the Cold War on the American people, I showed excerpts from the movie *Rocky IV* (Brubaker & Stalone, 1985) as an artifact from 1985 America. Students could make observations as they watch clips from the movie and then make inferences about American attitudes about the Soviet Union using the movie as evidence. What was the message that the producers of the movie were trying to send? What can historians infer about an American (and a global) audience that was drawn to the movie? As with the use of more traditional texts, I provided scaffolding to help students with their analysis. At times I would show still images from the film to allow students to engage in something akin to "close reading." Students could then pay attention to details, decoding such things as the color in the background or the facial expressions of secondary characters, that they might otherwise miss if the movie was being played at normal speed. I allowed students to discuss their ideas in groups and provided students with a graphic organizer, the Observation/Inference (O/I) chart described in Chapter 8, with a place to record observations and inferences. I provided other documents for students to use to corroborate their movie-based interpretations.

The use of videos for this third purpose, as historical evidence, is rare in history classrooms. Providing students with multiple opportunities to work with video artifacts in connection with other genres of evidence, coupled with explicit reminders about strategy use, can foster historical thinking and make the history content more memorable. Using videos as evidence is a much nobler purpose than simply to convey historical information to students, as they are normally used. They can be used to build students' historical literacies. Ms. Chavez recognized the appeal of movies as evidence and included a cartoon produced in 1936 as one of the texts students analyzed.

Overcoming Challenges in Using Audio Texts

Students face unique challenges in learning with audio texts. In some instances, they might have trouble decoding or comprehending the literal meaning of texts. Old recordings might be poor in quality or the recordings might capture people talking quickly or with distracting background noise or, as with any text, using unfamiliar vocabulary or subtle, unnoticed symbols. As with all texts, if students cannot decode or comprehend the literal meaning of an oral or video text, they cannot analyze it. Students for whom English in not their native language experience particular difficulty in listening to muffled recordings of spoken English or song lyrics, or, as with any text, cultural references of which they have no background knowledge. A teacher can support students' code breaking and meaning making by building background knowledge, providing vocabulary instruction, and giving students a transcript of the dialogue to read as they listen.

A teacher can do several other things to help students get more out of their use of oral and video texts. Ms. Chavez, for example, provided multiple opportunities to learn with the texts. Much of her lesson was designed to help students "decode" jazz music, identifying its defining features. If students could not distinguish the elements of jazz after the first recording, they might do so after the second, third, fourth, or fifth example. She exposed students to one song twice— once early in the activity and once at the end—to reinforce key points. Like Ms. Chavez, teachers can play a song or a recorded speech multiple times, with students focused on different elements—perhaps the words the first time and the delivery the second time. There is often a need for students to hear oral texts multiple times in order to fully decode and comprehend, just as they sometimes need to read and reread written texts to fully grasp the meaning. Additionally, teachers can provide students with written transcripts of speeches or song lyrics. Both the students for whom English in not their native language and those for whom English is their first language benefit from being able to follow along with the words on a printed transcript. Depending on instructional objectives, a teacher might play a recording once to try to recreate the context, with students listening as individuals would have at the time that the speech was delivered, then play it a second time after giving students a written transcript, with students listening as a historian.

With oral texts or video texts teachers can pause the recording from time to time to allow students to summarize, discuss details, or offer critique, much as a teacher might have students pause while reading a written text. In the vignette, Ms. Chavez interspersed exposure to the audio recordings with opportunities for students to discuss what they were hearing. She knew that as with analysis of most historical resources, students need time to think deeply and to make interpretations with audio texts.

Promoting Historical Thinking With Student-Produced Audio and Video Texts

The increasing availability of digital technologies, combined with students' increasing experience producing digital and audio recordings, creates a setting in which history teachers can assign students to produce oral and video texts. Almost any assignment that students can record, revise, and edit in traditional, written format can be produced in a video format that might be more appealing to create and easier to publish with peers. For instance, currently, the National History Day competition includes a category for documentary video and webpage design (see https://www.nhd.org). Students' interpretive and argumentative videos are judged based on many of the same criteria with which historical writing is evaluated, such as students' use of primary source evidence, critique of sources, and historical analysis. With the expanded notion of texts used throughout this book, it follows that the literate act of writing should also be expanded to include the creation of the genres of texts valued by 21st-century teens, including audio and video recordings, social media posts, and webpages.

Chapter Summary

Because historical inquiry is messy and complex, teachers sometimes simplify historical periods, people, and events using reductionism. Reductionist thinking includes stereotyping, ignoring contingency, categorization, dualism, imposing stagnation, simplifying causation, and disregarding the counter-perspectives of marginalized groups. Teachers can advance students' ability to engage in historical inquiry by helping them appreciate the complexity of the study of the past. As historical evidence, recorded audio and video texts present a complex representation of the past. Music, movies, recorded speeches, television programs, television and radio ads, and newscasts provide evidence that is engaging for students and valuable in historical inquiry. As with other types of evidence, teachers can enhance students' ability to work with audio and video texts by considering their needs as code breakers, meaning makers, text users, and text critics. They can encourage students to produce argumentative video presentations to defend their interpretations.

Questions for Consideration

1. Why does analyzing music and video recordings feel less like work than analyzing written texts, even though doing so requires many of the same thinking strategies? How might integrating audio or video texts within a text set enhance students' engagement?
2. Why are reductionist tools such as labels or causal chains often used in traditional, information-focused history classrooms? How can reductionist thinking hinder historical thinking? Is simplification of complex historical ideas ever justified when working with young people?
3. What are additional 20th- and 21st-century technology-based resources not mentioned in this chapter that students might use as evidence during historical inquiry. How has the nature of historical evidence changed in the digital age?

Additional Reading and Viewing

- An edited volume that provides numerous ideas for teaching with films is Russell III, W. B., & Waters, S. (Eds.). (2017). *Cinematic social studies: A resource for teaching and learning social studies with film*. Information Age Publishing.
- A book that provides numerous instructional strategies for teaching students with historical films is Marcus, A. S., Metzger, S. A., Paxton, R. J., & Stoddard, J. D. (2018). *Teaching history with film: Strategies for secondary social studies*. Routledge.
- The webpage "History vs. Hollywood" is a good place to find reviews of the historical accuracy of feature films, found at https://www.historyvshollywood.com.
- Ideas and examples for teaching about social issues with music of the late 20th and early 21st centuries are provided in the article White, C., & McCormack, S. (2006). The message in the music: Popular culture and teaching in social studies. *The Social Studies, 97*, 3, 122–127.
- The online application *edpuzzle* found at https://edpuzzle.com/ provides a resource for teachers to embed discussion or comprehension questions into videos.

References

Angier, N. (1999, December 15). Furs for evening, but cloth was a Stone Age standby. *New York Times*. https://www.nytimes.com/1999/12/14/science/furs-for-evening-but-cloth-was-the-stone-age-standby.html

Armstrong, L. (1968). When the saints go marching in. In *On when the saints go marching in [Record album]*. Delta Entertainment.

Barton, K. C. (1996). Narrative simplifications in elementary students historical thinking. In J. Brophy (Ed.), *Advances in research on teaching vol. 6: Teaching and learning in history* (pp. 51–84). JAI Press.

Barton, K. C. (2010, May 1). *There'd be a coup if people knew they were scammed: New Zealand students and historical agency* [Paper presentation]. Annual meeting of the American Educational Research Association, Denver, CO.

Bostick, D. (2021). The classical roots of White supremacy. *Learning for Justice, 66.* https://www.learningforjustice.org/magazine/spring-2021/the-classical-roots-of-white-supremacy

Bransford, J. D., Brown, A. L., & Cocking, R. R. (2000). *How people learn: Brain, mind, experience, and school.* National Academy Press.

Brubaker, J. D. (producer), & Stalone, S. (director). (1985). *Rocky IV [Film].* 20th Century Fox Home Entertainment.

Burke, J., & Davis, B. (1928). *Carolina moon. [Recorded by G. Austin]. On Gene Austin: Voice of the Southland [Record album].* Victor.

Burroughs, S., & Hare, D. (2008). Music and messages from the past: Tuning into history. *Social Studies Research and Practice, 3, 2,* 68–78.

Diamond J. (1999). *Guns, germs, and steel: The fates of human societies.* W.W. Norton & Co.

Epstein, T. (2000). Adolescent's perspectives on racial diversity in U. S. history: Case studies from an urban classroom. *American Educational Research Journal, 37*(1), 185–214. doi:10.2307/1163476

Faulkner, A. F. (1921). Does jazz put the sin in syncopation? *Ladies Home Journal, 38,* 16–34.

Gaddis, J. L. (2002). *The landscape of history: How historians map the past.* Oxford University Press.

Lesh, B.A. (2011). *Why won't you just tell us the answer? Teaching historical thinking in grades 1–12.* Stenhouse.

Lincoln, A. (1865). Second inaugural address, endorsed by Lincoln April 10, 1865. March 4, 1865. Found in Series 3, General Correspondence, 1837–1897; *The Abraham Lincoln papers.* Library of Congress, Manuscript Division. http://memory.loc.gov/ammem/alhtml/alhome.html

Marcus, A. S., Metzger, S. A., Paxton, R. J., & Stoddard, J. D. (2018). *Teaching history with film: Strategies for secondary social studies.* Routledge.

Nokes, J. D. (2011). Recognizing and addressing barriers to adolescents "reading like historians". *The History Teacher, 44* (*3*), 379–404.

Nokes, J. D., & Ellison, D. (2017). Historical films: An essential resource for nurturing historical literacy. In S. Waters & W. Russell (Eds.), *Cinematic social studies: A resource for teaching and learning social studies with film* (pp. 131–156). Information Age Publishing.

Page, E.W. (1922, December 6). A flapper's appeal to parents. *Outlook.* http://faculty.pitt-state.edu/~knichols/flapperappeal.html

Peck, C. (2018). National, ethnic, and Indigenous identities and perspectives in history education. In S. Metzger & L. Harris (Eds.), *International handbook of history teaching and learning* (pp. 311–333). Wiley Blackwell.

Ravitch, D., & Finn, C. E. (1987). *What do our 17-year-olds know: A report on the first national assessment of history and literature.* Harper & Row.

Rizzo, A. (Director). (1952). *Duck and cover [Motion picture].* Archer Productions.

Russell III, W. B., & Waters, S. (Eds.). (2017). *Cinematic social studies: A resource for teaching and learning social studies with film.* Information Age Publishing.

Schlesinger, L. (Producer), & Avery, T. (Director). (1936). *I love to singa [motion picture].* USA: Warner Brothers and Vitaphone. http://www.youtube.com/watch?v=akAEIW3rmvQ.

Seixas, P. (1993). Popular film and young people's understanding of the history of Native American-White relations. *The History Teacher, 26*(3), 351–370. doi:10.2307/494666

Shay, L., Fisher, M., & Goodwin, J. (1929). *When you're smiling. [Recorded by L. Armstrong].* On *Louis Armstrong's greatest hits [Record album].* MCA Music Media Studios.

Tilzer, A. V., & Fleeson, N. (1920). I'll be with you in apple blossom time. [Recorded by The Andrews Sisters]. In *The Andrews Sisters 20 greatest hits* [Record album]. MCA. (1940).

White, C., & McCormack, S. (2006). The message in the music: Popular culture and teaching in social studies. *The Social Studies, 97*(3), 122–127. doi:10.3200/TSSS.97.3.122-127

Wineburg, S. S. (2001). *Historical thinking and other unnatural acts: Charting the future of teaching the past.* Temple University Press.

Wineburg, S. S. (2007). Forrest Gump and the future of teaching the past. *Phi Delta Kappan, 89*(3), 168–177. doi:10.1177/003172170708900305

13

BUILDING AN ARGUMENT WITH HISTORICAL NUMBERS

What do numbers have to do with history? In this chapter, you will find out that statistics can be useful evidence in reconstructing the past. Like historians, students can use numbers as historical evidence with the right support. You will also be exposed to ways that history teachers can help students engage in argumentative writing and speaking.

> As you read this vignette pay attention to how Mr. Erickson supports students in their roles as code breakers, meaning makers, and text users. What more could he do to help students as text critics?

Mr. Erikson is planning a unit on industrialization, immigration, and urbanization for his 11th-grade U.S. history course. He realizes that historians frequently use statistical records in historical inquiry. He wants to introduce students to some of these resources. As he discusses his ideas with one of the other history teachers, his colleague recommends that he look at a census from the early 1900s. She is certain that he will be able to find census figures that have to do with immigration. As Mr. Erikson explores, he finds a table from the 1910 census showing the number of foreign-born people living in the United States (Durand & Harris, 1913). The table breaks down the number of immigrants by their native country and region or state of residence. Students can find, for example, how many German immigrants lived in New York in 1910 and whether that number had increased or decreased since 1900 or 1890. Browsing the table, he realizes that a nearly limitless number of possible comparisons exist that students could make to explore immigration trends (see Figure 13.1).

Mr. Erikson has found a great text for discovering immigration trends. Next, he considers the support that students will need to decode, comprehend, critique, and use it. He realizes that the layout of the table might be difficult for some

DOI: 10.4324/9781003183495-15

	DIVISION OR STATE AND CENSUS YEAR.	Total foreign born.	Northwestern Europe.							
			Eng-land.	Scot-land.	Wales.	Ireland.	Ger-many.¹	Nor-way.	Swe-den.	Den-mar
	MIDDLE ATLANTIC.									
	New York:									
1	1910	2,748,011	146,870	39,437	7,464	367,889	436,911	25,013	53,705	12,
2	1900	1,900,425	135,685	33,862	7,304	425,553	499,820	12,601	42,708	8,
3	1890	1,571,050	144,422	35,332	8,108	483,375	498,602	8,602	28,430	6,
	New Jersey:									
4	1910	660,788	50,375	17,512	1,202	82,758	122,880	5,351	10,547	5,
5	1900	431,884	45,428	14,211	1,195	94,844	121,414	2,296	7,337	3,
6	1890	328,975	43,785	13,163	1,069	101,059	106,181	1,317	4,159	2,
	Pennsylvania:									
7	1910	1,442,374	109,115	32,046	29,255	165,109	195,202	2,320	23,467	3,
8	1900	985,250	114,831	30,386	35,453	205,909	226,796	1,393	24,130	2,
9	1890	845,720	125,145	32,081	38,301	243,836	230,516	2,238	19,346	2,
	EAST NORTH CENTRAL.									
	Ohio:									
10	1910	598,374	43,347	10,705	9,377	40,062	175,095	1,110	5,522	1,
11	1900	458,734	44,745	9,327	11,481	55,018	212,829	639	3,951	1,
12	1890	459,293	51,027	10,275	12,905	70,127	235,668	511	2,742	
	Indiana:									
13	1910	159,663	9,783	3,419	1,498	11,266	62,179	531	5,081	
14	1900	142,121	10,874	2,805	2,083	16,306	77,811	384	4,673	
15	1890	146,205	11,200	2,948	888	20,819	84,900	285	4,512	
	Illinois:									
16	1910	1,205,314	60,363	20,755	4,091	93,455	319,199	32,913	115,424	17,
17	1900	966,747	64,390	20,021	4,364	114,563	369,660	29,979	109,147	15,
18	1890	842,347	70,510	20,465	4,138	124,498	338,382	30,339	86,514	12,
	Michigan:									
19	1910	597,550	42,737	9,952	786	20,434	131,586	7,638	26,374	6,
20	1900	541,653	43,839	10,343	833	29,182	145,292	7,582	26,956	6,
21	1890	543,880	55,388	12,068	769	39,065	135,509	7,795	27,366	6,
	Wisconsin:									
22	1910	512,865	13,959	3,885	2,507	14,049	233,384	57,000	25,739	16,
23	1900	515,971	17,995	4,569	3,356	23,544	268,384	61,575	26,196	16,
24	1890	519,199	23,633	5,494	4,297	33,306	259,819	65,696	20,157	13,
	WEST NORTH CENTRAL.									
	Minnesota:									
25	1910	543,595	12,139	4,373	1,023	15,859	109,628	105,303	122,428	16,
26	1900	505,318	12,022	4,810	1,288	22,428	125,191	104,895	115,476	16,
27	1890	467,356	14,745	5,315	1,470	28,011	116,955	101,169	99,913	14,
	Iowa:									
28	1910	273,765	16,788	5,162	2,434	17,756	98,759	21,924	26,763	17,
29	1900	305,920	21,027	6,425	3,091	28,321	123,277	25,634	29,875	17,

FIGURE 13.1 A portion of a table from the 1910 census. *Source:* Durand & Harris (1913).

students to read. It even takes him a few minutes of reflection to realize that the numbers on the census do not indicate the number of new immigrants during a 10-year period but instead show a cumulative figure. The same people were counted and recounted if they continued to live in the same location over the decades when multiple censuses were conducted. As he struggles to decode and comprehend the meanings of the numbers, Mr. Erikson realizes how difficult it is going to be to help students decode the census and use it as historical evidence. He determines that during the first part of his lesson he will need to provide explicit instruction on how to decode it.

Mr. Erikson decides to spend the first part of class guiding students through the code-breaking and meaning-making processes as they talk about the patterns of *old immigration* and *new immigration*. With so many numbers on the page, he anticipates that students' attention might be scattered or misdirected, or the students might just feel overwhelmed. The challenge during the first part of the lesson will be to help students attend to those numbers that represent the important trends. After working together as a class to see the trends of old and new immigration, and once he is confident that students can make sense of the numbers on the table, he will help them develop research questions related to census figures and use the internet to search for evidence to answer their questions. He creates a study guide (see Figure 13.2) that will give students practice decoding and comprehending, draw their attention to numbers that reveal patterns of old and new immigration, allow students to raise their own questions, and provide a space for students to record and substantiate their claims, both with census figures and with other historical evidence.

Mr. Erikson prints the study guides and makes copies of the census table for his class. On the day of the activity, he passes a copy of the table and study guide to each student and reads the background information with the class. He explains to students what the census is, and how they are going to use it. Mr. Erickson plans to use the first items on the study guide under the heading "I. Practice reading the census" to do just that—to help students practice code breaking and meaning making. These questions will be used flexibly, depending on how quickly students understand the meaning of rows and columns and can comprehend what the numbers are showing. Mr. Erickson models with the first question, projecting a copy of the census on the screen in front of the students and pointing out where he looks to find out what the columns and rows mean. Students work more independently on the other four items, with Mr. Erickson using each question as a formative assessment to see which students have figured out how to read the census and who needs more support. For instance, on the second question on the study guide, "How many people born in Wales lived in the United States in 1870?" he asks them to look over the census and raise their hand when they know the number. After most hands are up, he asks those who are still looking to get help from someone they are sitting near. Still projecting the table on the screen in front of the class he asks for a volunteer to come to the screen and demonstrate how they figured out the number. Mr. Erickson asks the student to elaborate on how they knew what the column and rows represented. Sending the student back to their seat, he has students work through the remaining questions on the study guide in a similar way, making sure all the students can decode and construct meaning with each number on the table. Mr. Erikson knows that this first part of the lesson will be a little tedious, especially for those who are confident in their use of the table, but he wants to be certain that everyone in the class will be able to read it. It is worth the few minutes at this slow pace at the start of the lesson.

Name _____

Exploring Immigration Trends

Background: The Constitution requires the federal government to conduct a census every 10 years. During a census, surveys or interviewers are sent to each home in an effort to count the number of Americans. Through the years censuses have collected information about farming, industry, poverty, education, and immigration. You are going to use a table from the 12th census, conducted in 1910, to explore immigration trends at the turn of the century.

I.   Practice reading the census
   a. How many people were living in the USA in 1910 who had been born in another country?
   b. How many people born in Wales lived in the USA in 1870?
   c. Is this number higher or lower than the number in 1900?
   d. How many people born in Italy lived in New Hampshire in 1900?
   e. Which geographic division had the most Irish immigrants living in it in 1890?

II. Discovering trends with the census
   a. In 1870, which five foreign countries were represented by the greatest number of immigrants? (Rank in order from first to fifth.)
      i.
      ii.
      iii.
      iv.
      v.
   b. Where are all of these countries located geographically?

   c. In 1910, which five foreign countries were represented by the greatest number of immigrants? (Rank in order from first to fifth.
      i.
      ii.
      iii.
      iv.
      v.
   d. Which new countries have joined this list?

   e. Which other countries experienced the most dramatic increase in numbers between 1890 and 1910?

   f. Where are all of these countries located geographically?

   g. What general statement could you make about changing trends in immigration at the turn of the century based on your observations?

FIGURE 13.2 A study guide to support students' work with the 1910 census table.

Name _____

III. Exploring the census data
    a. Identify a trend, surprising statistics, or some other characteristic of immigration, and complete the following:
        i. Write a brief description of the trend, surprise, or characteristics that you notice giving specific numbers:

        ii. Write a question that you have based on this trend:

        iii. Research your question and report here your interpretation of the trend you see in the form of a claim.

        iv. Make a list of the evidence that you found that supports your claim:

IV. **Extension activity:** On a piece of graph paper or using an online bar graph maker, construct a bar graph that demonstrates the trend or characteristics that you based your claim on. Below the graph give a written explanation telling how the data on the graph supports your claim.

FIGURE 13.2 (Continued)

Mr. Erickson designed the second part of the study guide, under the heading "II. Discovering trends in immigration," to help students discover the patterns of old and new immigration. The questions on the study guide prompt students to compare the nations from which most of the immigrants had come prior to 1870, with the nations from which immigrants came between 1870 and 1910, the year this census was taken. Students are given time to work on their own with Mr. Erickson spending most of his time helping a handful of students who are still struggling with a basic comprehension of the census numbers. As students answer the questions on the study guide that prompt them to look for the patterns, they should be able to identify the shifting immigration trends from the old immigration that originated in northern and western Europe to the new immigration from southern and eastern Europe. Furthermore, as students work, they gain fluency with the census and are better prepared for the inquiry activity that will follow. After students have completed the second part of the study guide, Mr. Erickson calls for the class's attention and leads the class in a brief discussion of the patterns they found, eventually helping students define *old immigration* and *new immigration*.

Mr. Erickson designed the activities up until this point in the lesson to help students become fluent with the census table. After a short discussion of old and new immigration, Mr. Erikson explains the third part of their assignment, which students will do independently. It requires them to look for an interesting trend, a surprising statistic, or a region with personal significance and develop a related research question. They will need to research the question looking for historical evidence that helps them construct an interpretation, then make a claim, and defend that claim with the evidence they found.

Knowing that this inquiry activity might present challenges for students, Mr. Erikson models the process for them. He explains to students that his ancestors immigrated to Minnesota from Sweden in the 1890s, so he is curious about that area. He projects the census page that contains information about Minnesota and discovers that many Swedes moved to Minnesota. He projects a different page and sees that there were only 729 Swedish immigrants living in Florida in 1910 compared to more than 122,000 in Minnesota. From this observation he formulates his research question: Why did so many Swedes immigrate to Minnesota rather than to other states? He talks about the features of his question that make it strong: it is open-ended, people might disagree about the answers, and he really wants to know. He contrasts his research question with a poor question: Were there more Greeks in Illinois or New York in 1910? He talks with the class about the characteristics that make his question better.

Next, Mr. Erickson models how to search for evidence to answer the research question. With the class observing and with him thinking aloud, he does a "Google" search using the search phrase "Swedish Immigration to Minnesota." The search yields several potential websites that might be useful. Modeling *click restraint* (McGrew et al., 2019), he scans the entire page of search results finding many, written in Swedish, might be difficult to use. He returns to the first item on the search result page, https://www.mnopedia.org/swedish-immigration-minnesota, and selects it, which takes him to a page that he soon discovers is sponsored by the Minnesota Historical Society, an organization that he trusts to provide accurate information and legitimate sources. Modeling *sourcing*, he finds the name of the person who wrote the article, Joy K. Lintelman, opens a new tab, and searches her name, finding that she is a university professor in a history department who has published several books on Swedish immigration. He concludes that Lintelman sounds like an expert on the topic. On the right side of the MNOpedia page, Mr. Erickson finds several images that appear to be primary sources. He selects the primary sources one by one. Some prove useful and others less so. He uses an online translation site to translate the cover of a document written in Swedish to find that it is a pamphlet, distributed free of charge, that was designed to encourage immigration. It includes information about the climate, forests, lakes, and rivers of Minnesota designed to encourage immigration. He also finds that a Swedish-language newspaper was published in Minneapolis at the turn of the 20th century. From the evidence, Mr. Erickson concludes that Swedes, including his ancestors that arrived in Minnesota in the late 19th century, came primarily for two reasons. First, the geography and climate of Minnesota were like Sweden's. Second, the growing Swedish community in Minnesota encouraged new immigrants to come and made them feel at home when they arrived.

After modeling his inquiry, Mr. Erickson dedicates most of the rest of the class period to students conducting their own inquiries related to a trend or statistic they observe in the census. He keeps busy during the class period helping individual students formulate good research questions, find reliable internet sites to gather information, and look for primary sources in digital archives. The study guide serves as a place for students to take notes as they research. Some students complete the assignment quickly. Mr. Erickson has designed an extension activity for them—he encourages them to use an online bar graph maker to create a bar graph that highlights the trend they have researched. For example, he shows them how he could create a bar graph showing Swedish immigration to Minnesota, Illinois, and Michigan, states with a climate like Sweden's, compared to Swedish immigration to Florida, Georgia, and South Carolina, states with a climate much hotter than Sweden's. The bar graph would serve as evidence that the climate of Minnesota was part of the reason Swedes immigrated there.

With about 5 minutes left of the class period, Mr. Erickson calls for the students' attention. He projects an argumentative paragraph he wrote as a model for students' argumentative writing (see Figure 13.3). He reads the paragraph to the students, pausing to point out his claim and the evidence he has used as substantiation. He shows them that he has included direct quotes from primary source evidence as well as some paraphrasing of evidence. He encourages them

In 1910, 122,428 people who had been born in Sweden lived in Minnesota. By comparison, only 10,547 lived in New Jersey and only 729 lived in Florida. Why did so many Swedes immigrate to Minnesota rather than to other states? Evidence suggests that part of the reason was that Minnesota's climate, forests, lakes, and rivers reminded Swedes of their native land. A brochure published in 1867, written in Swedish, told potential immigrants of Minnesota's history, geographic location, government, cities, rivers, lakes, forests, and climate inviting them to come. It was distributed free of charge. Once Swedes arrived in Minnesota, they created an environment that appealed to future Swedish immigrants. Minneapolis published a newspaper in Swedish. And want ads were placed in newspaper seeking Swedish employees. It is not surprising that Swedish immigrants would want to live in a place that looked and felt so much like home.

FIGURE 13.3 A model argumentative paragraph.

to take home the census records and their notes and complete the argumentative paragraph as homework.

> What were some of the instructional strategies Mr. Erickson used in this vignette? What more could he have done to support students who struggled with the activity?

Argumentation and Quantitative Historical Evidence

Historians' writing blends narration, description, and argumentation. In order to publish cutting-edge historical research historians must interpret events in new ways and defend interpretations through the skillful use of evidence. Much of their writing, then, consists of a justification of their use of resources and an explanation of how their interpretations flow from evidence. Visual aids such as tables, graphs, and maps serve not only to clarify historical concepts but also to persuade readers that claims are substantiated by evidence. In this chapter, I focus on the historical literacy of argumentation, with an emphasis on the use of numerical data, such as census records. The connection between argumentation and numerical data is not meant to imply that quantitative data is the only evidence which historians use in argumentation. On the contrary, numerical data is only one type of the vast array of evidence historians use. Every possible genre of evidence can be used in argumentation. In this chapter, I explore (a) argumentation and historical thinking, (b) teaching argumentation, (c) finding numerical data, (d) helping students interpret numerical historical data, and (e) helping students use numerical data in constructing historical arguments.

Argumentation and Historical Thinking

> Why are historians required to engage in argumentation? Why is approaching history with the right epistemic stance—a criterialist stance—a prerequisite for historical argumentation?

Because history is constructed by humans using evidence produced by humans, it is influenced by human perceptions, interests, and interpretations. As discussed throughout this book, history is not the past but is the study of the past, with people determining significance, interpreting causation, and evaluating evidence. Historians have established criteria that guide disciplinary practice. As historians share their interpretations with peers, they must convince them that their research was needed, their topic was significant, and their methodologies and conclusions were sound. Doing so requires historians to engage in argumentative writing and speaking. To begin, historians must argue that their research is needed, substantiating this claim by showing that other historians' work inadequately or inaccurately covers their topic. Then, in addition to telling a story, they must convince their audience that their story is not only plausible but makes the most sense given the evidence. The most graceful historical writing seamlessly blends a story of the past with the story of how the evidence was used to reconstruct it.

Historical argumentation does not begin when a historian starts to write, but when a historian begins to research their topic. Like Mr. Erickson, historians start with a question. Then, in what I have called *argumentative reading* (Nokes & Kesler-Lund, 2019), historians interrogate evidence with the understanding that they are going to need to use that evidence to craft an argument. They evaluate evidence, distinguishing strong sources from weak because they know that an argument can only be as powerful as the evidence that substantiates it. Argumentative reading requires the orchestrated use of numerous historical literacies such as sourcing, corroboration, healthy skepticism, inference making, contextualization, and historical empathy. Researchers and teachers working with students likewise understand that the foundation of a student's strong written argument starts with the interrogation of the evidence that will be used in the writing (Monte-Sano et al., 2014). Of importance, historians construct an interpretation and prepare to defend their interpretation simultaneously as they explore evidence and as their understanding of the past takes shape. Much of their planning for writing (Hayes, 2006) occurs as they evaluate the evidence (Nokes & Kesler-Lund, 2019). They do not approach an inquiry with predetermined interpretations in mind, although they may have some hunches.

argumentative reading: the process of purposeful, critical analysis of evidence that prepares a writer to substantiate claims with solid evidence in order to craft a strong argument

Those who study argumentation have identified several elements that make up a strong argument. An argument focuses on a *claim*, a debatable, defensible, specific, interpretive statement about a historical event. The writer or speaker must "go out on a limb" taking one of multiple plausible, debatable interpretations.

Statements of fact are not claims because they do not invite a critical response. For instance, "the number of Greek immigrants to America increased between 1900 and 1910" is not a debatable claim but a statement of fact. However, the statement "Greek immigrants reshaped U.S. labor unions to reflect Greek fraternal orders" would be a debatable claim. Claims must also be specific enough to be contestable. "Greek immigrants were important in U.S. history" is too vague to be a debatable claim. Vague statements are easy to defend because they can be interpreted flexibly to fit any evidence.

> *claim: a debatable, defensible, specific interpretation of evidence*

Claims are substantiated through *evidence* and *warrants*. Evidence includes indisputable facts that support a claim. For example, Mr. Erickson used the fact that a Swedish newspaper was being published in Minneapolis to support the idea that Swedes felt at home in Minnesota. That a Swedish newspaper was being published in Minneapolis is an indisputable fact. That a pamphlet was being published in Swedish in 1867 giving a description of Minnesota's climate, forests, lakes, and rivers is a historical fact that serves as evidence that Swedes were attracted to Minnesota's climate and geography. Evidence must be used in a manner that is generally accepted by historians. Sources must be carefully evaluated, multiple perspectives must be represented, and an exhaustive search for evidence must be completed. Written evidence can be cited verbatim or paraphrased. Visual evidence can be described or displayed in argumentative writing. Warrants explicitly link evidence to claims. Evidence does not speak for itself, but the reader must be shown how the evidence supports a claim. The warrant makes that connection, showing how a pamphlet or a Swedish newspaper, the evidence, supports the claim that Swedes felt at home in Minnesota.

> *substantiate: to provide evidence that supports a claim*

> *evidence: indisputable facts that are used to support a claim*

> *warrant: an explanation of how evidence supports a claim*

In argumentation, writers anticipate opposition from a mildly skeptical audience. Evidence often exists that contradicts or raises doubts about a claim, evidence that must be accounted for. Skillful writers anticipate criticisms of their claims and, through reasoned explanations and evidence, rebut counterarguments before they are raised. Historians' argumentative writing must not only show how evidence supports their interpretations but also how other interpretations are not supported.

---

rebut: to anticipate arguments that go against a claim and to explain evidence in a manner that discredits these counterarguments

---

Mr. Erickson's modeling could help students recognize the distinct role of questions, claims, warrants, and evidence. Argumentation typically begins with an authentic research *question*. As phenomena are observed, historians ask why? In Mr. Erikson's case, he wondered why so many Swedes immigrated to Minnesota. Within the discipline of history, *claims* are explanations for historical phenomena. Mr. Erikson claimed that geography, climate, and chain migration all played a part in Swedish immigration trends. *Warrants* include logical support for a claim. For instance, Mr. Erikson argued that immigrants would be drawn to a region that friends and family had already settled. *Evidence* includes the primary sources, artifacts, and, in this case, numbers that support a claim. Mr. Erikson's evidence included the numbers of Swedes in Minnesota, the free brochure, and the existence of a Swedish language newspaper.

Teaching Argumentation

What can teachers do to support students' argumentative writing and speaking? How can they support students' cognitive and social argumentative processes?

The Common Core State Standards for writing in social studies, history, and science suggest that students should be able to engage in and evaluate argumentation (2010). The standards for 12th grade include the ability to

> a. Introduce precise, knowledgeable claim(s), establish the significance of the claim(s), distinguish the claim(s) from alternate or opposing claims, and create an organization that logically sequences the claim(s), counterclaims, reasons, and evidence. b. Develop claim(s) and counterclaims fairly and thoroughly, supplying the most relevant data and evidence for each while pointing out the strengths and limitations of both claim(s) and counterclaims in a discipline-appropriate form that anticipates the audience's knowledge level, concerns, values, and possible biases. c. Use

words, phrases, and clauses as well as varied syntax to link the major sections of the text, create cohesion, and clarify the relationships between claim(s) and reasons, between reasons and evidence, and between claim(s) and counterclaims. d. Establish and maintain a formal style and objective tone while attending to the norms and conventions of the discipline in which they are writing. e. Provide a concluding statement or section that follows from or supports the argument presented.

(Common Core State Standards, 2010, p. 64)

Building on the Common Core State Standards, the C3Framework, developed by the National Council for the Social Studies (NCSS, 2013), further promotes student inquiry. Through an "inquiry arc," teachers are encouraged to help students develop questions and plan inquiries, use disciplinary concepts and tools, gather evidence to construct and defend claims, communicate their claims to others through a variety of written and spoken media, and take informed action. Argumentative speaking and writing are a basic part of the inquiry arc. The Inquiry Design Model that has grown out of the C3 Framework helps teachers put into practice the ideas central to current reforms in history teaching (Grant et al., 2017). Students answer compelling and supporting questions using historical evidence and historical thinking strategies. Teachers are increasingly expected to teach history students the skills needed to engage in historical inquiry including argumentative historical writing. As a result of these reforms, there is growing interest among history teachers in teaching argumentative writing and speaking that reflects disciplinary norms. In other words, new curricular standards ask history teachers to teach students to argue like a historian.

Teachers can support students' argumentative writing when they consider ways to help them during three cognitive processes described in Chapter 4: planning, composing, and revising (Hayes, 2006). Teachers can aid students in their planning by teaching them explicitly about the interpretative nature of history, helping them assume a criterialist epistemic stance. As teachers help students use the strategies of sourcing, corroboration, and contextualization to evaluate historical evidence, they are helping students engage in argumentative reading, a vital part of planning for writing (Monte-Sano et al., 2014). In addition, teachers can frame writing or speaking prompts in a manner that requires students to make a claim and defend it using evidence. Research shows that prompts that demand an argument elicit better thinking than prompts that ask students to write as if they were a historical character (De Leur et al., 2017).

For instance, when considering Manifest Destiny, including its inherent racism, a teacher might give the following writing prompt associated with Emanuel Loetz's 1861 painting *Westward the Course of Empire Makes its Way*. "What does Loetz's 1861 painting suggest about American attitudes about the West during westward expansion? What evidence in the painting leads you to this interpretation?" Responding to this prompt requires the writer to go beyond simply

Claim (Make a debatable statement about your topic that you will have to defend)	
Evidence (Describe, paraphrase, or cite the evidence that supports your claim)	**Warrant** (Explain how the evidence supports your opinion)

FIGURE 13.4 A graphic organizer designed to help students structure an argument.

retelling what they see in the image by considering the artist and his attitudes about the West within the historical context of 1861 when the painting was created.

The second stage of argumentative writing is composing, sometimes referred to as translating because the writer must translate their thoughts into written text (Hayes, 2006). Teachers can help students with composing by lightening their cognitive load. Teachers can scaffold writing assignments by providing structure as students plan. For example, a teacher might divide an inquiry lesson over two class sessions, the first dedicated to the analysis of evidence, argumentative reading, and the second dedicated to students' argumentative writing. On the second day of the inquiry, students might reorganize the notes they compiled on a graphic organizer from the first day into a different graphic that lays out an evidence-based argument (see Figure 13.4). This new graphic organizer becomes an outline from which they could compose an argumentative essay.

Instead of providing additional structure, a teacher might provide support for students by suggesting the wording of key elements of their argument. For instance, the teacher might tape to each desk in the classroom a paper with sentence stems such as the following:

- The _____ (letter, diary entry, etc.) written by _____ (author's name) shows that _____ (the part of the claim supported by the quote.)
- _____ (author's name) wrote " _____ " (a direct quote from the source)

- _____ (author's name) claimed that _____ (a paraphrase from the source)
- This quote supports my claim by showing that _____ (tell how the quote supports your claim).
- _____'s (author's name) _____ (letter, diary, etc.) is reliable because _____ (explain why you think the quote or paraphrase is reliable)
- The author's account can be trusted because _____ (explain why the account is trustworthy).
- Both _____ (one author) and _____ (another author) give a similar account of the incident.
- Although _____ (one author) claims _____ (explain what one author says), another witness, _____ (a second author) claims _____ (explain what another author says that is different).
- _____ (author's name) explains that _____ (paraphrase). However, their account is less reliable than other accounts because _____ (explain why this account is not reliable).

As students begin to use the phrases of argumentation appropriately, this type of scaffolding should be removed.

Rather than generic sentence starters such as these, teachers could provide sentence starters designed for a specific inquiry. As occurs with generic sentence starters, rather than thinking about the specific words students need to use in their claim or when introducing evidence, they can focus on their ideas. For example, a teacher might give students the following sentence starters to help them with their composition of an argumentative paragraph about Loetz's 1861 painting.

- CLAIM: "Emanuel Loetz's 1861 painting *Westward the Course of Empire Makes its Way* shows that Americans . . ." [explain how they felt about the West]
- EVIDENCE 1: "Loetz shows that Americans felt this way by . . ." [describe one of the things shown in the painting that helped you know how Loetz felt about the West]
- EVIDENCE 2: "This idea is also supported by Loetz's use of . . ." [describe one other thing in the painting that shows how Loetz felt]

The translation of students' ideas to writing is facilitated when teachers provide them with the words of argumentation as shown in these sentence stems.

Alternatively, a teacher might lighten students' cognitive load during argumentative writing by providing them with alternative claims to choose between rather than having to come up with their own interpretation completely independently.

For instance, students might be asked to identify what George Caleb Bingham's 1851 painting *Daniel Boone Escorting Settlers through the Cumberland Gap* suggests about American attitudes about the West in 1851? The teacher might also ask for the evidence in the painting that leads the students to their interpretation. The teacher might then give students a list of interpretations to choose from, interpretations that they might be able to support with evidence from the painting, such as the following:

- The West was a dangerous place.
- The West was good for Americans.
- Americans were good for the West.
- Westward expansion was God's work.
- Westward expansion was difficult but worthwhile.
- Americans should stay out of the West.

In addition to these possible interpretations, the students might come up with one of their own. Such a list of possible alternative claims models for students what claims look like, simplifies the writing process, and reduces the cognitive load that students carry during inquiries that involve argumentative writing.

The third stage of writing is revision, during which expert writers modify and refine their ideas and edit their prose. In contrast, students tend to focus solely on editing during the revising stage, correcting errors in writing conventions but doing little to improve their argument. One of the challenges young people face when revising is that they may have had few opportunities to read argumentative writing. This lack of exposure leaves them without a clear understanding of what strong argumentative writing looks like. Providing students with opportunities to read argumentative historical writing prepares them to make substantial revisions to their writing to improve their ideas (Applebee & Langer, 2006). Mr. Erikson's sample paragraph that includes a claim, warrants, and evidence illustrates for students what argumentative writing looks like.

In addition to the cognitive processes of planning, composing, and revising, argumentative historical writing also involves social processes (Nokes & De La Paz, 2021). The social nature of argumentation involves researching what others have said about the issue. Historians and history students can construct a stronger argument when they know what others have written about the topic. Historical argumentation includes listening with an open mind to what peers say, crafting a thoughtful response to others' ideas, altering ideas based on others' strong evidence, finding commonalities and differences between one's ideas and those of others, and exhibiting academic humility by acknowledging the "unforced force of a better argument" (Habermas, 1991, p. 103). Historians interact with other historians who research within the same subfield of history. Students' peer group is made up of other students. Argumentation involves working collectively and deliberatively toward consensus, the common good, or respected and

understood differences of interpretations. Teachers can promote the social interactions essential in historical argumentation by encouraging students to provide
feedback on one another's ideas and by giving them instruction on appropriate
ways for doing so.

Mr. Erikson's approach to teaching argumentation is authentic to the discipline of history. Historians do not start with a claim and then search for evidence to support it. Instead, they start with historical or modern observations,
develop questions, and then seek evidence to answer their question. Gaddis
(2002) explains that historians notice a current or historical condition and then
seek a historical explanation for the condition. Questions spring out of observations, and claims flow from evidence. Like historians, students' exploration of
census figures raises questions. After a period of exploration, the censuses, along
with other evidence that students have collected, help them construct interpretations. That same evidence helps them substantiate their claims about immigration
trends. The bar graph that Mr. Erikson assigns to some students is an element
of argumentative writing and speaking. It does not simply present facts but is
designed to persuade. A bar graph would substantiate the claim that Swedish
immigrants were attracted to Minnesota and other states with Scandinavian-like
climates. Other evidence that he gathers further substantiates his claim. Modeling
a historian's thinking and writing process is an important part of Mr. Erikson's
teaching. And based upon research, he knows that one lesson on argumentative
writing is not likely to nurture the skills in every student. Instead, they will need
repeated opportunities to practice writing with a variety of evidence, including
statistics and more traditional written evidence.

Finding Numerical Data

> Why is it important that history students learn how to work with quantitative
> evidence during historical inquiry?

One of the challenges of helping students work with historical numerical data
is finding sources that are accessible to young people. An experienced coworker
directed Mr. Erikson to the census records that he found so useful in exploring
immigration. U.S. census records could be used to study a great many topics
and to explore trends at various locations across decades. For instance, census
records include statistics on the number of enslaved people; trends in farming, industrial, and mining production; trends in ages, family size, and other
social issues; and immigration trends. The U.S. Census Bureau's webpage at
http://www.census.gov/ includes links to a wide range of resources for teachers including lesson ideas (though these ideas primarily focus on current rather
than historical data). Other government agencies provide statistics on a wide

range of historical trends. For example, the Bureau of Labor Statistics' website at http://www.bls.gov/home.htm provides data on unemployment rates; the consumer price index; earnings by occupation, race, and sex; and numerous other statistics over the past decade. Using these types of websites, teachers can find data that students could use to explore historical topics related to a variety of course objectives.

Additionally, websites sponsored by historical organizations often provide links to numerical data. For instance, The Friends of Valley Forge Park have made available the muster rolls from Valley Forge through the winter of 1777 to 1778 (The Friends of Valley Forge Park, 2011). These rolls include statistics on the monthly strength of divisions, brigades, and regiments including the number of soldiers who were fit for duty, who were assigned, who died, who deserted, who were discharged, and who enlisted. A student could use these statistics to assess a claim made on an introductory page of that website that "the encampment experience [at Valley Forge] could be characterized as 'suffering as usual' for privation was the continental soldier's constant companion." The website goes on to suggest that the misery ascribed to Valley Forge is exaggerated to create a "parable to teach us about American perseverance." The number of deaths compared to the number of enlistments could be used, along with other primary sources such as diary entries or letters, to evaluate the website's claims of a romanticized notion of Valley Forge.

Teachers who spend time searching the internet will find a wealth of historical numerical data—compelling texts around which to build lessons on topics as diverse as the spread of AIDS in Africa, World War I or American Civil War battle casualties, global population trends, urbanization trends in America and the world, global literacy rates, and countless other topics. Teachers can also use graphs and tables to explore historical statistics. Graphs are persuasive texts that show historical trends, such as income inequality and U.S. tax policy (Crocco et al., 2011), global urbanization trends, disease rates, population trends, or historic gas prices. The internet has made available a wide range of historical sources, including historical numerical data, tables, and graphs.

Helping Students Interpret Numerical Historical Data

How can a teacher provide explicit instruction on code breaking and meaning making in a manner that is not too tedious but is engaging for students?

Whether using census records, charts or graphs, or other numerical data, working with quantitative evidence presents some unique challenges for students. As explained in Chapter 4, a history teacher must help students in each of their four roles as readers: code breaker, meaning maker, text user, and text critic. Mr. Erikson's lesson was designed to help students in three of these four areas, including a few opportunities for students to critique the census as evidence. First, Mr. Erikson formatted his study guide and his lesson to support students' development as code breakers and meaning makers. As with many tables and graphs, the census figures were organized within a structure that was difficult for some students to comprehend. Mr. Erikson taught students explicitly about the structure of the table, particularly the meanings of columns and rows. He supported students' code breaking by asking them to help each other, showing each other how to use the structure of the table to find the data they wanted. Furthermore, he modeled the process involved in constructing an argumentative paragraph and provided an example for them to see. Mr. Erikson's work with the students involved a great deal of instruction on decoding and comprehending tables.

Furthermore, Mr. Erikson modeled for students how to use quantitative data to discover historical trends and as evidence to substantiate a historical argument. Mr. Erikson's study guide drew students' attention to features of the census that would allow them to "discover" the distinction between old and new immigration. The census numbers served as a springboard into research, inspiring a research question, and providing evidence. Throughout the lesson students could see how a historian might use quantitative data in historical argumentation.

Mr. Erikson did not do much to support students in their role of text critic. He did little to critique the census as a source, nor did he suggest to students the need to be skeptical about the census data. The numbers on the census were accepted as being accurate without question. Students did not consider the methods used to conduct the census, whether it might under- or overrepresent certain groups, or why some countries were not included in the columns of the table. For Mr. Erikson, it was a conscious decision not to question the reliability of census data during this lesson. He thought that the thinking that he required was sufficiently challenging without introducing more complexity. However, his lesson was not completely void of the notion of the reader's role as text critic. He raised questions with the students about other sources that should be used as evidence to support his claim. His search for additional evidence showed students that a single source—the census—as useful as it was, was not enough to build a solid argument. Additional primary source evidence was required. In a subsequent lesson, he might devote more time to issues of reliability in census data collection.

In most cases, the students' role as text critic should not be ignored. As described earlier in this book, students tend to accept information at face value. This is particularly true with statistics, which appear to simply present objective facts. However, students must become aware that statistics are often manipulated to achieve a particular purpose. Students need to understand that private entities commission surveys with loaded questions, that organizations design websites containing statistics that support their purposes, that politicians spin data to promote their platforms, and that authors purposefully use statistical data as evidence to support their claims. The scale of graphs can be manipulated to exaggerate or downplay historical trends. As with all evidence, students must consider the origins, the author, the audience, the uses, and the context of numerical historical data and remain alert for ways that accurate numbers might be used to deceive.

Helping Students Use Numerical Data in Constructing Arguments

> Why do students, and most of the rest of society, fail to think critically about the statistics that are used to persuade?

The culmination of students' interaction with the census in Mr. Erikson's class was their use of numerical data to semi-independently develop a research question, search for historical evidence, make a claim, and substantiate that claim. Some students were asked to display the statistics in a bar graph they created using an online bar graph maker. His census work is meant as a mini-lesson on not only immigration but also on historical argumentation, with much of the class period spent with him modeling argumentative processes. As the school year continues, Mr. Erikson will require more argumentative writing and speaking from students, including more substantial research projects. And as students engage in independent research projects, Mr. Erikson will encourage them to find numerical data, when appropriate and available, to corroborate the other historical evidence that substantiates their claims. The census project has demonstrated for students both the advantages and disadvantages of numerical historical information. Numerical data are compelling evidence—often erroneously viewed by an audience as objective and unbiased. Numerical data, in contrast to primary sources like letters or journal entries, often provide a view of broad trends. Furthermore, historical statistics provide a springboard for authentic questions, as historians seek explanations for phenomena they observe in the numbers. Despite these strengths, numerical data present some disadvantages. Statistics do not stand alone as evidence but need documentation from other sources. Furthermore, statistics, like textbooks in students' eyes, may seem to be above criticism. Mistakenly, the student might pay little attention to the origin, author, context, and audience of statistical reports. Furthermore, the selective use of certain statistics and the omission of others can distort data. Like all other types of historical evidence, it takes great skill to use numerical data effectively to develop historical arguments.

Chapter Summary

Argumentation, including question formulation, claims, warrants, evidence, and rebuttals requires historical literacies. Strategies discussed throughout the chapters in this book, such as sourcing, corroboration, contextualization, historical empathy, and skepticism are vital argumentative reading skills to evaluate evidence in constructing solid arguments and planning to defend them in writing. Numerical historical data are evidence that can bolster a historian's argument. The internet increases the availability of numerical data such as census records, government statistics, and assorted charts and graphs. Students need support in decoding, comprehending, critiquing, and using numerical historical data to substantiate an argument.

Questions for Consideration

1. How is working with numerical evidence similar to and different from using other types of historical evidence? How has technology enhanced historians' ability to work with numerical data? How can numerical evidence be used to corroborate primary source evidence?
2. Why is argumentative reading and writing dependent on individuals approaching historical inquiry with a mature epistemic stance? How many different ways can you think of structuring activities that require argumentation?
3. How can teachers provide scaffolding to support students through the cognitively challenging task of historical inquiry that culminates in argumentative writing? How might teachers design activities that engage students in oral argumentation?

Additional Reading and Viewing

- Many social studies inquiries that follow the Inquiry Design Model are available at https://c3teachers.org
- A book on teaching argumentative writing with several writing-focused inquiries is Monte-Sano, C., De La Paz, S., & Felton, M. (2014). *Reading, thinking, and writing about history: Teaching argumentative writing to diverse learners in the Common Core classroom, Grades 6–12.* Teachers College Press.
- A thorough review of research on teaching argumentative historical writing can be found in Nokes, J. D. & De La Paz, S. (2018). Writing and argumentation in history education. In S. Metzger & L. Harris (Eds.), *International handbook of history teaching and learning* (pp. 551–578). Wiley Blackwell.
- Several websites present statistics and numerical data in interesting ways including the following:
  - A website that presents immigration trends, county by county https://dsl.richmond.edu/panorama/foreignborn/#decade=1890&county=G2901830

- A collection of maps that show immigration numbers https://www.vox.com/2015/1/12/7474897/immigration-america-maps
- A graphic display of immigration numbers http://metrocosm.com/us-immigration-history-map.html
- A site that graphically displays historical world poverty rates, life expectancy, and many other statistics https://www.gapminder.org
- A site that displays the racial makeup of the United States https://www.nytimes.com/projects/census/2010/explorer.html

References

Applebee, A. N., & Langer, J. A. (2006). *The state of writing instruction in America's schools: What existing data tell us*. Center on English Learning and Achievement. https://citeseerx.ist.psu.edu/viewdoc/download?doi=10.1.1.541.4136&rep=rep1&type=pdf

Common Core State Standards. (2010). *Common core state standards*. http://www.corestandards.org/

Crocco, M. S., Marri, A. R., & Wylie, S. (2011). Income inequality and U.S. tax policy. *Social Education, 75 (5)*, 256–262.

De Leur, T., Van Boxtel, C., & Wilschut, A. (2017). 'I saw angry people and broken statues': Historical empathy in secondary history education. *British Journal of Educational Studies, 65*(3), 331–352. doi:10.1080/00071005.2017.1291902

Durand, E. D., & Harris, W. J. (Directors). (1913). *Thirteenth census of the United States taken in the year 1910, volume 1, population 1910, general report and analysis*. Government Printing Office.

The Friends of Valley Forge (2011). *Valley Forge legacy, the muster roll project: The encampment*. http://valleyforgemusterroll.org/encampment.asp

Gaddis, J. L. (2002). *The landscape of history: How historians map the past*. Oxford University Press.

Grant, S. G., Swan, K., & Lee, J. (2017). *Inquiry-based practice in social studies education: Understanding the Inquiry Design Model*. Routledge.

Habermas, J. (1991). *The structural transformation of the public sphere: An inquiry into a category of bourgeois society*. MIT press.

Hayes, J. R. (2006). New directions in writing theory. In C. A. MacArthur, S. Graham, & J. Fitzgerald (Eds.), *Handbook of writing research (pp. 28–40)*. Guilford Press.

McGrew, S., Smith, M., Breakstone, J., Ortega, T., & Wineburg, S. (2019). Improving university students' web savvy: An intervention study. *British Journal of Educational Psychology, 89*(3), 485–500. doi:10.1111/bjep.12279

Monte-Sano, C., De La Paz, S., & Felton, M. (2014). *Reading, thinking, and writing about history: Teaching argumentative writing to diverse learners in the Common Core classroom, grades 6-12*. Teachers College Press.

National Council for the Social Studies (2013). *The college, career, and civic life (C3) framework for social studies state standards: Guidance for enhancing the rigor of K–12 civics, economics, geography, and history*. NCSS. https://www.socialstudies.org/sites/default/files/c3/c3-framework-for-social-studies-rev0617.pdf

Nokes, J. D., & De La Paz, S. (2018). Writing and argumentation in history education. In S. Metzger & L. Harris (Eds.), *International handbook of history teaching and learning* (pp. 551–578). Wiley Blackwell.

Nokes, J. D., & De La Paz, S. (2021, June 2). *It takes two (or more) to argue: The social nature of historical argumentation.* Paper presented at *the Argumentative Writing Conference. University of Maryland, [held remotely].*

Nokes, J. D., & Kesler-Lund, A. (2019). Historians' social literacies: How historians collaborate and write during a document-based activity. *The History Teacher, 52*(3), 369–410.

14

FINDING PATTERNS AND OVERCOMING BARRIERS IN TEACHING THROUGH INQUIRY

If you have read this book up to this chapter you hopefully have a vision of what inquiry might look like in your history classroom. The purpose of this chapter is to help you translate that vision into practice, overcoming the barriers that might prevent you from doing so. How can teachers teach and assess in a manner that makes historical inquiry a central part of their instruction?

In the following vignette, pay attention to the way Ms. Olson creates a practical assessment that gives her a sense of each student's ability to engage in sourcing. Also pay attention to the way that she uses information from the assessment to plan future instruction.

Ms. Olson wants to know whether the students in her eighth-grade history class can engage in sourcing when analyzing primary source documents. She finds the Stanford History Education Group's assessment instrument related to the 1621 harvest celebration that is sometimes considered the first Thanksgiving. She starts class one day with that activity, which she has modified slightly. Students are given four texts to rank: a painting created by Jennie Brownscombe in 1914; an excerpt of a letter written by Edward Winslow, who was present at the celebration and wrote about it a few days later; a passage from their textbook on the 1621 Thanksgiving; and an excerpt of a book written by William Bradford, who was also present at the celebration and wrote about it decades later. Along with the documents, students are given the source information of each. Ms. Olson asks students to evaluate each source, ranking them in order based upon their usefulness to a historian who is trying to figure out what happened at the 1621 Thanksgiving. She asks students to give a brief explanation for their ranking. Ms. Olson anticipates that students who are disposed to engage in sourcing

DOI: 10.4324/9781003183495-16

Score	Description
1 (Beginning)	no signs of sourcing, ranked documents randomly
2 (Approaching)	mention source information, provide faulty criteria for ranking
3 (Meeting)	critically evaluate the sources, rank all or almost all items correctly
4 (Exceeding)	list all documents correctly, list the positive and negative traits of each

FIGURE 14.1 A scoring guide used to score students' use of sourcing.

and who know criteria for evaluating sources will rank Winslow's letter first, because it was written by an eyewitness shortly after the event; Bradford's book second, because it was written by an eyewitness years later; the textbook and painting third and fourth, because historians do not use textbooks as evidence of the events textbooks describe, and the painting was produced centuries later by an artist whose perception of Thanksgiving had been shaped by Thanksgiving traditions at her time.

Ms. Olson develops a scoring guide that she uses to evaluate students' responses based on a 4-point scale (see Figure 14.1). Students who show no signs of sourcing and have ranked the documents randomly fit the *beginning* criteria. Students who mention source information but provide faulty criteria for ranking meet the *approaching* criteria. Students who critically evaluate the sources and rank all or most items correctly are marked as *meeting* criteria. Students who list all four documents in the correct order and address both the positive and negative traits of each source fit the *exceeding* criteria. Spending 10 seconds on each paper, Ms. Olson rapidly scores them using the scoring guide. She records the scores, creating a record of each student's ability to engage in sourcing in this context. After recording the scores, she looks over her class list. Noting that most of the students have met the *approaching* or *meeting* criteria but few have exceeded the objectives associated with sourcing, she decides to conduct another lesson on sourcing sometime during the next week. During that lesson, she will ask one of the three students who exceeded the expectations to model their thinking while analyzing a source. She also makes a mental note of the four students who fit the *beginning* criteria. During the next activity she will form them into a group and during the time dedicated to small-group work will work directly with them, providing additional explicit instruction.

How is Ms. Olson's assessment different from traditional multiple-choice assessments of students' knowledge of trivial information? How is her response to the assessment results also different than the traditional response to multiple-choice tests in history classes?

This chapter addresses many of the practical elements of engaging students in inquiry. Ms. Olson demonstrated several of these practical survival skills as she conducted this assessment. First, she borrowed and adapted from teaching materials that were available online. Next, she conducted an assessment that could be graded quickly and still yield useful and actionable information. Finally, she had developed routines for classroom activities that would allow her to differentiate instruction without major disruption to routines. In this chapter, I discuss strategies like these that make inquiry possible and practical in history classrooms.

Considering the Vignettes Together

Reread the vignette at the start of Chapter 2 on pages 16–18. How is your understanding of what was happening in each history class different now after having read this book? Why is preparing students for historical inquiry, and giving them many opportunities to practice, vital for their well-being in a democratic society and for the survival of that society?

I opened this book with the story of Ms. Cordova walking through the social studies department at McArthur Middle School observing a variety of teaching methods including lecture, textbook reading, memory drills, and the showing of documentary videos. She saw something different, however, in Mr. Rich's classroom, where students sifted through a variety of forms of evidence trying to determine whether child labor in factories was worse than child labor on family farms. A quick review of the vignettes across the chapters of this book shows other teachers, like Mr. Rich, helping students use evidence to engage in historical inquiry and to answer interpretive historical questions. For instance, the 10th-grade students in Mrs. Hansen's class used primary and secondary source accounts of the Crusades to decide whether the crusaders were motivated primarily by religious factors. The students in Miss Anderson's eighth-grade class used a historical novel and primary sources to gain a deeper appreciation for the historical context of the civil rights movement—to understand how White people and Black people interacted as the civil rights movement gained momentum. Mr. Erikson's 11th-grade students used census records to identify and explore patterns of immigration to the United States at the turn of the 20th century. And Mrs. Francis's students used tree rings, ruins of dwellings, and other artifacts to consider the changing culture of the Ancestral Pueblo people. In this chapter, I highlight a pattern followed by the innovative teachers described in the vignettes throughout this book in planning and executing lessons. The pattern involves four stages: (1) selecting objectives and planning assessments, (2) selecting texts, (3) identifying the support and instruction that students need to use the texts, and (4) executing the lesson. I then discuss potential barriers that might prevent teachers from using inquiry lessons in history classes, offering ideas for overcoming these barriers. I conclude the chapter with a few other practical suggestions for getting started in building students' historical literacies.

Stage 1: Selecting Objectives and Planning Assessments

What is the difference between a content objective and a literacy objective? What are dispositional objectives that might be associated with historical inquiry?

Content Objectives

The work of history teachers, like the work of historians, involves interpretive decisions about significance. Historians must decide which historical issues are worthy of investigation, which elements should be included in their narratives, and which can be left out. Similarly, history teachers make decisions about how to use their limited class time. Should they teach about specific battles of the Revolutionary War, spend greater time talking about the causes and outcomes of the war, or focus on the hypocrisy of a war for freedom that left slavery intact? Should they require students to memorize the Gettysburg Address, or should they skip it completely, as Lincoln suggested would be the case? Should they set a pace that allows students to learn about the Vietnam War and terrorism? Or will the end of the school year arrive while they are still studying World War II? From the vast domain of historical understanding, history teachers must make decisions about the content that would be significant, interesting, relevant, and important for students to understand. State curriculum guides often outline the content to be covered during the year. However, these guidelines typically leave much room for interpretation as history teachers determine the depth of coverage. For instance, the state curriculum guidelines might require teachers to teach about the causes, events, and effects of the Crusades, but the world history teacher decides whether the students spend 20 minutes or 3 days working toward that standard.

The teachers in this book integrate content and literacy objectives in their planning. Mr. Rich, for example, has high standards for students' mastery of content. He wants them to understand child labor in ways that extend beyond the iconic images of boys and girls standing in front of textile machinery staring emotionlessly at a photographer. He wants them to understand that children have always been involved in labor and that the Industrial Revolution simply changed the venue for their work and put into motion changes that would lead to public schooling and compulsory education. He is confident, and the research supports this notion (Nokes et al., 2007; Reisman, 2012), that the analysis of primary sources that students conduct will help them thoroughly understand and remember issues surrounding child labor, though they may come up with different interpretations about the impact of the Industrial Age on children.

Literacy and Skill Objectives

Some state curriculum guidelines say little about the skills that students should develop in their history classrooms, though many states have recently revised their standards to include historical reading, thinking, and writing skills (Stern et al., 2021). Pressured to "cover the historical content," many history teachers may fail to integrate skill and literacy objectives into their instruction. However, research on young people's historical thinking makes it possible to identify developmentally appropriate skills that history instruction might include. Furthermore, the Common Core State Standards (2010) and the National Council for the Social Studies (NCSS, 2013), through its C3 Framework, have established standards for reading, reasoning, and writing skills for history students. In addition, the National Council for History Education (NCHE, n.d.) outlines skills and habits of mind that guide historical inquiry. This book highlights these strategies and habits of mind associated with historical literacy that emerge from research on students' historical thinking and that are found in national standards documents.

Mr. Rich establishes literacy objectives in addition to the content objectives to be achieved during his lesson. In particular, he wants students to focus on the source of texts and to understand how considering the source influences the analysis of evidence. He wants students to think about the photographer behind the images and the creator's purpose, whether the text is a historical novel or a political cartoon. He wants them to consider the distance between the author and the event being described and to develop ways of thinking about text that allow them to view all sources as *accounts* and *evidence* rather than as conveyors of information. And students, with his support, are taught and practice these skills during the lesson and throughout the school year.

Chapters 5 through 13 of this book suggest eight historical literacy strategies that could become the focus of instruction over a school year: developing an appropriate epistemic stance, using historians' heuristics, making inferences, comprehending metaconcepts, showing historical empathy, remaining skeptical, avoiding reductionist thinking, and constructing evidence-supported arguments. Mr. Rich's lessons across the school-year cycle through these few historical literacy strategies. For example, he taught students about sourcing, one of the historians' strategies, on one of the first days of the school year, and reminds them about it repeatedly during subsequent lessons, adding to the complexity of their understanding. For instance, as students study events that occurred after the invention of the camera, Mr. Rich talks explicitly about sourcing again, raising awareness that photographs do not simply capture a moment of reality but that the person behind the camera, with their purposes in taking the picture, should be remembered as students analyze a photo. Mr. Rich provides explicit instruction on analyzing the source of photographs.

Mr. Rich will revisit sourcing as other new genres of evidence, such as audio and video recordings and internet sites are introduced as historical evidence. As strategies like sourcing are repeatedly reviewed, students transfer previously developed historical literacies to new genres of text. They learn the value of considering the source whether the text is a diary entry, a history textbook, a Depression-era photograph, an internet site, a social media post, or a current news report.

At the start of each new unit, as Mr. Rich considers his objectives, he reflects on the students' current skill levels and the literacies that can be fostered within the content to be taught. And, from unit to unit, when Mr. Rich considers his literacy objectives, his expectations steadily increase. He starts the year with a vision of what students will be able to do by the end of the year and provides repeated opportunities for students to learn and practice historical literacies with new genres of evidence, increasingly sophisticated questions, increasingly challenging texts, and decreasing teacher support. For example, posters that adorn the walls of his classroom early in the year, reminding students how to engage in sourcing, corroboration, and contextualization, are taken down as students start to use these strategies automatically, without conscious thought.

Dispositional Objectives

In addition to content objectives and skill or literacy objectives, teachers also promote dispositional objectives when they engage students in historical inquiry. Dispositions are character traits that are difficult to assess but vital for inquiry and for civic engagement. For example, *curiosity* is a disposition that motivates students during inquiry. Teachers want to nurture curiosity in students to motivate them during historical inquiry and to prepare them to be active participants in their communities. Academic humility, the tendency to change one's mind when exposed to better evidence, is another disposition that is vital in historical inquiry, a disposition observed in professional historians (Nokes & Kesler-Lund 2019). History students are more successful when they seek alternative perspectives, a tendency associated with academic humility. Other dispositions include the tendency to withhold judgment, to engage with ideas, to collaborate, to compromise, and to be resilient (which is especially useful when an original search for evidence does not pan out). Importantly, these dispositions that are helpful in historical inquiry are also essential for informed civic engagement. Unlike the content objectives and the literacy objectives described above, dispositional objectives are difficult to assess and especially hard to score. How can a teacher give a student a curiosity score or a resilience grade? Yet the failure to nurture these dispositions in students can interfere with their historical literacies in class and leave them unprepared for civic engagement in the adult world.

Assessing Students' Mastery of Objectives

With the exception of dispositional objectives, the development of assessments goes hand in hand with the selection of instructional objectives (Wiggins & McTighe, 1998). If a teacher's objectives include literacies, then their assessments should measure students' historical literacies. In other words, history assessments should evaluate students' ability to engage with diverse genres of historical evidence using target strategies. In Mr. Rich's case from Chapter 2, he should not only assess students' comprehension of the impact of the Industrial Revolution on children but should also evaluate students' ability to use source information to determine the trustworthiness and usefulness of historical evidence. Such assessments of literacies and skills differ substantially from the content-focused, multiple-choice history tests that merely measure students' ability to recall historical information. Teachers cannot use traditional, multiple-choice, content-focused assessments to measure students' learning of objectives associated with historical inquiry.

The vignette at the start of this chapter demonstrates one practical method for assessing the development of the skill of sourcing. Wineburg and his colleagues (2012) suggest that creating, administering, and scoring assessments of historical literacies is not as difficult as it might seem. They contend that quick tasks, like that given in the example at the start of this chapter, can help a teacher determine students' skill level in strategies such as sourcing, corroboration, and contextualization. They have created more than 100 field-tested *historical assessments of thinking* (HATS) that include a document-based assessment instrument, scoring guides and rubrics, and sample student responses (see the Beyond the Bubble history assessments at https://sheg.stanford.edu/history-assessments). Assessments such as these help history teachers measure students' proficiency. With such assessment data, teachers can set an appropriate pace and know whether to reduce or increase the level of scaffolding to provide, as Ms. Olson modeled at the start of this chapter.

According to the Inquiry Design Model (IDM), historical inquiries should include opportunities for students to communicate their understandings through a variety of media (Grant et al., 2017; Swan et al., 2018). Student products and presentations provide a more authentic opportunity for teachers to assess students' content knowledge and skill development. For example, a teacher might assess students' ability to engage in argumentative speaking during an oral presentation of an evidence-based interpretation constructed during a document-based inquiry. Students' argumentative writing provides an opportunity for teachers to assess students' ability to make claims, use warrants and evidence, and rebut alternative interpretations. Teachers may not be able to use these types of elaborate assessments as frequently as assessments like the HATS because of the time required to evaluate students' work and provide adequate feedback. However authentic argumentative speaking and writing can be used to assess students' ability to read, think, and write like a historian during historical inquiry.

Stage 2: Selecting Texts

How has the internet revolutionized the types of texts that students can access in history classrooms? What are the criteria a teacher can use for selecting appropriate texts for students?

The work of the historian and the history teacher are also comparable in their search for evidence. Historians scour archives searching for letters, diary entries, and newspaper clippings that will serve as evidence in answering a pressing historical question. History teachers too should search for evidence but for a different reason. The evidence they seek must be accessible to students, allowing them to engage in historical inquiry. Just as a historian feels euphoric after discovering an important piece of evidence, history teachers get excited when they find something suitable for students and their learning objectives.

There is no end to the number of possible texts that a history teacher might use to reach their content and literacy objectives. Collingwood (1993) suggests that anything perceptible to a historian might serve as evidence, given the right question. The chapters of this book describe history teachers using texts as varied as letters, paintings, speech transcripts, music, political cartoons, picture books, pottery shards, Hollywood-produced movies, maps, historical novels, census numbers, tree rings, line graphs, newspaper articles, monuments, and even textbooks. With such a rich array of potential resources, and with access to texts via the internet, teachers should be very selective about the texts they use. For instance, why would a teacher have students read a textbook passage about Dr. Martin Luther King's "I Have a Dream" speech when they could instead have students watch a video recording of King delivering the speech.

When choosing texts, a history teacher might ask questions such as "Will students learn the desired content by working with this text?" "Will students develop the target strategies by working with this text?" "Will this text be viewed as evidence by students or will they be seduced by objective sounding language into accepting it as informational?" "Will this text demand historical thinking on the part of the students?" "Do students have the literacies necessary to work with this text or can I help them build the needed literacies?" "Will this text expose students to a unique perspective of an event?" "Will this text be interesting and engaging for students?" "Is this a type of text that historians might use as evidence?" "Is this a genre of text that students will encounter in their adult world?" "Are the strategies that will be used to analyze this text transferable to online reading?" and "Is this the best text given the learning objectives or could I find something better?" History teachers should be purposeful in selecting the texts that students explore in their classrooms.

The most instructive historical literacy lessons include multiple texts. Corroboration is impossible without multiple pieces of evidence across which to make comparisons. And sourcing is facilitated when students read conflicting accounts from multiple perspectives—acknowledging the source often helps explain the disagreement. Furthermore, differences between genres can be highlighted when learning activities juxtapose different formats of text. For example, reading a detail-rich account in a historical novel followed by a relatively dry eyewitness account can improve students' understanding of the author's purposes in producing each. Furthermore, giving students reliable and unreliable accounts, side by side, can foster a healthy skepticism and can help them gain expertise in judging the credibility of the things they read. And introducing diverse perspectives can help students develop a more mature epistemic stance as well as a better understanding of the nature of history. Students of color feel like they belong in a history class when they read accounts produced by people who look like them and they feel marginalized when no accounts from people of color are included (Epstein, 2000; Thornhill, 2016; Woodson, 2015). All students see that textbooks present only one of many possible interpretations of an event. Historical empathy and perspective taking are improved when students read accounts showing multiple perspectives. Students learn to tolerate, respect, and eventually appreciate diverse perspectives on events (Goldberg, 2015)—both historical and current—a disposition often missing but sorely needed in the polarized societies of the 21st century.

Teachers in the vignettes in this book found texts in a variety of ways. Some received useful tips from colleagues. Some, like Mrs. Dahl who had recently visited the World War II memorial, found texts through their experiences. Journal articles, such as that on dendrochronology, inspired other teachers. Some teachers found texts while exploring the internet. Others remembered powerful texts that they experienced as students. What all teachers had in common, though, was that their planning included a search for engaging texts around which to build historical literacy lessons.

Stage 3: Determining the Support and Instruction Students Need

What can a teacher do to prepare materials for an inquiry lesson in a manner that will ensure that students can be successful?

After gathering texts for a lesson, a teacher should reflect on the support students will need to work effectively with the texts. Freebody and Luke's (1990) model of literacy, described in Chapter 4, provides a checklist for teachers. First, will students need help in their role as a code breaker? Reading old documents, written in cursive script, might present a challenge for students that a typed transcript would resolve. Unfamiliar genres of text, such as propaganda posters, political cartoons, or music, may use symbol systems that are foreign to students. Teachers should be sensitive to students' needs in breaking the code of each text they use. For instance, in Chapter 12, Ms. Chavez helped students identify the unique features of jazz music, by having them listen to examples of jazz followed by nonexamples. Over time, students began to recognize what made jazz jazz, identifying, in particular, improvisation and the unorthodox use of voice and instruments. Their breaking of the code of jazz music, in this manner, allowed them to understand its revolutionary nature and to consider attitudes about tradition and change during the Jazz Age.

Second, will students need help in their role as a meaning maker? A teacher can take several steps to help students comprehend texts. Texts might be modified to match students' reading levels. Vocabulary help, instruction on text structure, or peer support might aid students' comprehension of a text. In Chapter 13, Mr. Erikson dedicated a significant amount of class time to helping students comprehend the data presented in a relatively complex census table. Students could look at the table and see numbers, thus breaking the code, but many were not able to comprehend what those numbers meant without instruction and practice reading the table. He had students model for their peers how to use the rows and columns to comprehend what the numbers represented. Students must be able to comprehend a text in order to use it effectively as historical evidence. Figures 7.3, 7.4, and 7.5 (on pages 137, 138, and 139) show the same text, a letter from Confederate General Hood to Union General Grant during the Civil War in its original format, transcribed to facilitate code breaking, and revised to facilitate meaning making, respectively. (I encourage the reader to go back and try to read the letter in all three formats to anticipate why such modifications support students' deep thinking about the content of the text.)

Third, are students prepared for their role as a text critic? Do they have the disposition to approach a text with the appropriate epistemic stance and a healthy skepticism? Do they know how to use historians' strategies for working with the text? Teachers can foster students' ability to engage as text critics by providing conflicting accounts, creating cognitive dissonance. In order to achieve a resolution, students must make judgments about the trustworthiness and accuracy of conflicting sources. Teachers can create a classroom where all ideas and sources are subject to critical review. For example, in Chapter 11, Mr. Johnson had students use primary sources describing the Mongols to critique their textbook. By doing so, he modeled for students that all texts, including the textbook, should be considered *accounts* and that all accounts are open to critique. His conversations with students during the document analysis activity helped them think deeply about the source of the documents they analyzed. As a result, they became better evaluators of evidence.

Fourth, are students prepared for their role as a text user? In classrooms that build historical literacies, students use texts in ways that are authentic to the discipline of history, and not simply to answer factual questions or fill in boxes on a graphic organizer. History teachers design activities that require students to use texts in inquiry as historians do, to solve historical problems, answer historical questions, or settle historical controversies. Good historical thinking lessons begin with an authentic, engaging, and appropriately challenging question to answer or problem to solve. In the vignettes in each chapter, teachers established a purpose for working with texts that was more authentic to historians' inquiries than typical school work. In some instances, students considered a closed-ended question: Were the Crusades primarily motivated by religious factors? In other cases, teachers presented more open-ended questions: What does the evidence suggest about changes within the Ancestral Pueblo culture? Throughout this book, teachers produced graphic organizers, posters, and activities that facilitate sourcing and corroboration, and otherwise supported students as they worked as text critics and text users. T-charts and matrices were used to help students keep a record of their analysis of texts in order to help them solve the problems around which lessons were built. The graphic organizers served as a means to an end—part of a process rather than as the product of the inquiry. The product came as students communicated their interpretations to peers and defended their claims in argumentative speaking or writing. The graphic organizer facilitated this conversation.

Stage 4: Executing the Lesson

What do you think are the keys to executing a well-designed historical inquiry? Why is it important to focus on the process of inquiry and not just the products?

In most chapters of this book, I have given a rich description of a teacher who plans and executes an inquiry lesson. Several patterns can be seen across the vignettes illustrating successful teaching. In each vignette, the teacher gave students space to develop their own interpretations of the evidence. The 8th grade students in Miss Francis' class, for instance, used evidence to explore why many Ancestral Pueblo moved into homes built in the cliffs. They disagreed about the reasons for the move, some suggesting that it was because of a changing climate and others contending that it was because of enemies. Mr. Erikson gave 11th-grade students even more room to explore evidence, allowing them to identify a pattern in the census numbers and then search for an explanation for the pattern. The nature of history as a discipline allows historians to disagree over important historical questions. History classrooms that focus on inquiry and nurture historical literacies allow students the same room for independent thinking.

Another pattern across all of the vignettes was that the teachers fostered critical and creative thinking through their interactions with students. The modeling of historical thinking took place in whole-class discussions, during small-group work, and as teachers interacted with students one-on-one. During whole-class discussions and small-group work, teachers required students to make explicit their thought processes in working with texts by asking them to explain how they figured things out. Students who struggle benefit by this type of modeling and thinking aloud. Interactions with students focused on processes more than products. Thinking properly and strategically about the texts was more important than coming up with a predetermined correct answer. Teachers' standard was for students to work appropriately with texts and reach interpretations that they could defend using historical evidence. A correct answer, on the other hand, can represent a lucky guess, copying from a classmate, looking something up on Wikipedia, or countless other desirable or undesirable processes.

Additionally, the execution of lessons in this book shows teachers working flexibly in multiple roles with their students. At times they assume the position of the *sage on the stage*. They are the classroom authority on historical content and on historical literacies and they share their expertise with students when appropriate. They lecture at times, in order to build the background knowledge students need to approach historical questions. They provide explicit and implicit instruction on strategies and habits of mind, such as sourcing or showing historical empathy.

> *sage on the stage: the nickname, often used derogatorily, for a teacher who stands in front of the class and lectures to students during teacher-centered instruction*

At other times teachers assume the role of *guide on the side*, sometimes even withholding information that they know so that students can work through the process of discovering things for themselves. Rarely do classroom activities revolve around them. Instead, activities are centered on students' interaction with texts and ideas. The teachers are facilitators, gathering texts, imagining activities, designing support, and providing instruction that will allow students to work effectively with the texts and ideas. At times, teachers join the students as learners of history. They know that authentic inquiry is promoted not only by what they do but by who they are. They admit, without embarrassment, that they do not know everything about history—not even the most seasoned historians do. They show an interest in, and a critical respect for, the ideas presented by students. Like historians, these history teachers display academic humility by remaining open to new interpretations that are supported by evidence. Above all else, these teachers model a curiosity about the past—the driving force behind inquiry—with questions answered through the skillful use of evidence, a process that requires historical literacy.

> *guide on the side: a nickname for a teacher who serves a supporting role for students as they learn during student-centered instruction such as inquiry*

Barriers to Historical Inquiry

As you read this book you may feel a strong resolve to conduct historical inquiries and to nurture historical literacies. This commitment may wane when you enter or return to the classroom and face the realities of teaching. Several barriers might prevent you from engaging students in inquiry as frequently as you would like. I address each of these barriers and provide possible solutions. First, you may feel the constant pull of traditional instructional methods, particularly lecture. Lecture is the default instructional method in history classrooms. Lecture is a familiar teaching method, much more familiar than inquiry methods. Your mentors and colleagues will most likely lecture frequently. Your history professors undoubtedly lectured a great deal. When you imagine yourself teaching in your mind's eye, you are much more likely to see yourself standing in front of the class lecturing than kneeling beside a small group of students helping them analyze a document. You may find it easier to manage students' behavior during a lecture than during small-group work. For all of these reasons teachers experience a powerful pull towards traditional instructional methods. Teachers can resist the pull of traditional instruction in several ways. They might find mentors and colleagues who frequently engage students in inquiry. Having such a colleague, even if they teach in a different location, can provide much-needed support. You might collaboratively collect materials for document-based inquiry lessons and assessments. You might help each other resolve other issues related to inquiry, such as finding routines that you can use to help students remain on task during inquiry. Observing another teacher use inquiry methods, either live or through a video recording, can familiarize you with this instructional strategy. Remembering the dismal long-term impact of traditional instruction can serve as motivation to resist the constant pull of traditional methods.

Second, teachers may be discouraged from using inquiry methods or building historical literacies because of the pressure they feel to cover vast historical content. They recognize that information can be shared with students more quickly than students can discover it on their own. Historical inquiry takes time—time that could be spent covering more content. And teachers sometimes feel that students' historical education is blighted if they do not hear about this or that bit of historical trivia. Some teachers assume that everything in the textbook needs to be shared with students. They justify their drive for content coverage by suggesting that students need to know about Pickett's Charge, the XYZ affair, the Bull Moose Party, the TVA, and an avalanche of other content. The solution to this problem is relatively simple—it is to realize that students do not really need to know about all these things. In fact, research shows that when teachers try to cover too much content, students end up retaining very little (Bransford et al., 2000). Rather than trying to cover everything in the textbook, teachers should focus on the core standards that constitute the required curriculum. Teachers can free up time for inquiry by ignoring the pressure to try to cover everything that is worth teaching, a futile and unproductive endeavor (Wiggins, 1989).

Third, teachers may feel discouraged from engaging students in inquiry because of a lack of resources. Building inquiry lessons is a time-consuming process. Finding texts that meet all the criteria described earlier, poses a challenge. Teachers may not know where to turn for help. Teachers can overcome this barrier by using the lesson materials that have been prepared and are being shared by an increasing number of institutions. Here I provide an annotated list of organizations with websites that hold document sets, inquiry activities, or support for nurturing historical reading, thinking, and writing skills. This list may be the most useful resource in this book.

- **Stanford History Education Group** https://sheg.stanford.edu
This site includes hundreds of document-based lessons on U.S. and world history topics with simplified documents prepared by researchers at the Stanford History Education Group.
- **New York State Social Studies Resource Toolkit** https://www.engag-eny.org/resource/new-york-state-k-12-social-studies-resource-toolkit
This toolkit provides resources for inquiries following the Inquiry Design Model, divided into Grades K–4, 5–8, and 9–12 based upon the curriculum of New York state, and prepared by New York teachers and researchers.
- **Read. Inquiry. Write.** https://readinquirewrite.umich.edu
These resources, produced at the University of Michigan, hold materials for investigations in world geography, ancient world history, and U.S. history with study guides and tools to support students' reading, thinking, and writing.
- **Digital Public Library of America** https://dp.la
Primary source sets on hundreds of U.S. history topics, with about 15 documents in each set, are available at this site.
- **DOCSTeach** https://www.docsteach.org
Produced by the National Archives, this collection includes scores of document sets on U.S. history topics with ideas for lessons.
- **Library of Congress** https://loc.gov
A "teachers" tab links teachers to resources for teaching with primary sources, including study guides, blog posts, lesson plans, media presentations, and primary source sets. Chronicling America, https://chroniclingamerica.loc.gov, located within this site, provides a method of searching hundreds of newspapers for keywords.

- **C3 Teachers** https://c3teachers.org

An "inquiries" tab connects teachers to hundreds of Inquiry Design Model–based inquiries created by teachers using the template of compelling and supporting questions.

- **teachinghistory.org** https://teachinghistory.org/historical-thinking-intro

Created by the Roy Rosenzweig Center for History and New Media at George Mason University, this site includes introductory material on historical thinking and links to materials for teaching with documents, artifacts, photographs, and so on.

- **UC Berkeley History-Social-Science Project** https://ucbhssp.berkeley. edu

Produced by the University of California at Berkeley, a "teacher resource" tab links teachers to lessons developed by the California History Social-Science Project, organized by elementary, middle school, and high school grade levels, with many primary source lessons included.

- **Historical Thinking Matters** https://historicalthinkingmatters.org

Produced by the Roy Rosenzweig Center for History and New Media at George Mason University, this site includes materials for four inquiries on the Spanish American War, Scopes Trial, Social Security, and Rosa Parks.

- **America in Class** http://americainclass.org/primary-sources/

Produced by the National Humanities Center, this site includes collections with scores of texts related to U.S. history themes, with framing questions, resources, and reading guides.

- **Everyday Americans, Exceptional Americans** https://chnm.gmu.edu/ tah-loudoun/

Produced by the Roy Rosenzweig Center for History and New Media at George Mason University, this site holds primary source activities on Rosa Parks, the End of the Cold War, Sarah Green Probate Record (a plantation owner), and Westward Expansion, each with one or two carefully selected primary sources and guides for teaching with them.

- **Image Detective** http://cct2.edc.org/PMA/image_detective/index.html

This website is designed to support students as they analyze photographs associated with the turn of the 20th century.

- **The Historical Thinking Project** http://historicalthinking.ca

Created by Canadian researchers, this site includes primary source sets associated with Canadian history (including the French and Indian War, and the War of 1812), study guides, and other resources for promoting historical thinking.

- **TeachingAmericanHistory.org** https://teachingamericanhistory.org

Produced by the Ashbrook Center at Ashland University, this site includes collections of primary sources and important American documents related to general themes in U.S. history, such as the Revolutionary War, with introductory materials.

- **Uncovering   America**   https://www.nga.gov/learn/teachers/lessons-activities/uncovering-america.html

Produced by the National Gallery of Art, this resource includes collections of images with lesson ideas on 15 general topics in U.S. history.

- **World History Commons** https://worldhistorycommons.org

Produced by the Roy Rosenzweig Center for History and New Media at George Mason University, this site is an open educational resource with 1,700 annotated primary sources related to world history, organized into short or long teaching models.

- **World History Matters** https://worldhistorymatters.org

Produced by the Roy Rosenzweig Center for History and New Media at George Mason University, this site provides links to a number of other sites with resources on teaching about children, women, and other topics in world history including the following two topics:

- **Children and Youth in History** https://chnm.gmu.edu/cyh/

This resource includes primary sources and teaching modules related to children in world history.

- **Women in World History** https://chnm.gmu.edu/wwh/

This site has links to hundreds of documents with lesson ideas and materials for teaching about women in world history.

In addition to these educational and archival websites, teachers can find resources for historical inquiries from peers; from publications, such as the journal *Social Education*; from presidential libraries; and from special interest groups. The challenge of finding resources is fading as increasing numbers of institutions and teachers share inquiry materials that they have prepared.

Historians' monographs provide one additional source for developing historical inquiries. Historians often research interesting questions and always use primary source evidence. History teachers might find the resources for cutting-edge inquiries using historians' ongoing research. They might adapt the historian's research question for young learners. And they might tap into the evidence that the historian uses to substantiate their claims to create document sets for students to use. Reading the monograph would give the teacher confidence with the historical content and prepare them to provide students with background knowledge during a lecture and to answer questions during the inquiry. History teachers improve their practices when they remain abreast of ongoing historical research and using historians' work to frame a classroom inquiry can save them the time needed to develop an inquiry on their own.

Fourth, some teachers are discouraged from engaging students in inquiry because they are required to use schoolwide or districtwide lessons and assessments. Expectations of school administrators and colleagues may leave little room for inquiry. Curricular materials are often developed in collaboration with professional learning communities (PLCs). And some traditional teachers possess a strong voice within PLCs. However, PLCs are also a time to share data, including the results of research that shows the flaws of traditional instruction and the strengths of document-based historical inquiry (e.g., see De La Paz et al., 2014, 2016; Nokes, et al., 2007; Reisman, 2012). In addition, the core standards that should shape department objectives, lessons, and assessments sometimes require teachers to nurture historical reading skills, such as argumentative writing. Teachers may need to become curricular activists during PLC meetings, pushing for reform in the way departments teach and assess.

Fifth, some teachers are discouraged from using historical inquiry in their classrooms because of the challenge that document-based inquiries pose for students. They contend that students cannot read like historians and that attempting to make them do so is a wasted effort. The solution to this barrier lies in considering the students' four roles as a reader; diagnosing challenges they face with code-breaking, meaning-making, text-use, or text-criticism; and taking measures to support students in each of these roles. Of course, young people cannot read like trained historians with advanced degrees. But even the youngest students can engage in basic elements of historical thinking if given the needed support (Levstik & Barton, 2015). The fact that historical reading, thinking, and writing is challenging for students should not discourage teachers from taking on the challenge of teaching these vital skills—skills that transfer to online reading with the proper support.

Practical Suggestions for Getting Started

> How can a teacher who has used traditional methods throughout their career, or a new teacher start to use historical inquiries in their history classes?

I conclude this book with four practical suggestions for getting started in engaging students in historical inquiry and building students' historical literacies based on my experience and the experiences of others who have taught history or studied history teaching.

Start Small

First, start with small steps. In Chapter 1, I explain the long process I went through in integrating historical inquiry and historical literacy instruction into my curriculum. My experiences are similar to the process described by Bruce Lesh (2011), another high school history teacher with a drive to build historical literacies. During my first years of teaching, I used one or two historical thinking lessons each year. Eventually, I had developed at least one in-depth historical investigation for each unit. I eventually started to reduce the length of my lectures to make room for more regular mini-lessons involving students' work with texts. I was primarily driven by the success of the literacy lessons to try them with increasing frequency. A new teacher, or an experienced teacher attempting a new approach, should not feel pressured to have a literacy lesson each day but should be satisfied in making the transition to building historical literacies at a pace that will not cause undue stress. Furthermore, as with many aspects of teaching, it is difficult to have complete success in a first attempt. Unanticipated problems, such as using texts that are too difficult or unappealing to students, can cause literacy lessons to turn out disappointing. Teachers must be patient with themselves as they try, correct, and retry historical literacy lessons.

Use What's "Out There"

As a new teacher, studying history, planning lessons, grading students' papers, learning school policies, and fulfilling extracurricular responsibilities left me little time to explore innovative teaching methods. My first attempts at historical literacy lessons were based on materials collected by colleagues and shared with me. As mentioned, with the internet teachers today have unprecedented access to materials prepared by other teachers. The list provided in the previous section includes numerous websites with resources for historical inquiries. Furthermore, innovative colleagues, those who strive to build historical literacies, serve as valuable partners in developing and refining historical inquiry lessons. Teachers can save a significant amount of preparation time, perhaps preserving their sanity, by borrowing published resources and adapting them to meet the specific needs of the students they teach. In addition, I also recommend that teachers create at least one document-based lesson each year. Doing so requires them to develop a historical question, explore digital archives, gather resources, read secondary sources, and construct interpretations—the kinds of activities that likely nurtured their interest in history in the first place. Building new inquiry lessons sharpened my skills as a historian and helped me continue to learn the content that I love.

Build Structure and Accountability Into Literacy Lessons

With few exceptions, my historical literacy lessons have proceeded more smoothly when I build structure and student accountability into the lesson, often accomplished through graphic organizers. The graphic organizers that were used by the teachers in the vignettes in this book were designed for four purposes. First, as described in this book, they are a source of scaffolding, supporting students' strategic engagement with texts. For instance, the graphic organizers remind students of the need to use strategies. They prompt students to search for similarities and differences across texts. They help students weigh evidence from opposing perspectives. Well-designed graphic organizers serve an important role as scaffolding for students as they work with unfamiliar texts in historical inquiry

Second, the graphic organizers provide a record of the students' work that can be used to assess students' historical thinking. By looking at the students' notes in a "sourcing" column, for instance, the teacher can get a feel for the students' ability to appreciate the influence of perspective and audience on a source. Well-designed graphic organizers help make students' thought processes more evident to teachers so that they can adjust instruction according to the students' needs. Thus, graphic organizers serve as an ongoing formative assessment, helping teachers plan future learning activities.

Third, graphic organizers provide a record of the students' work that they can use to remember historical evidence during the inquiry and to monitor their own growth over a school year. Students can review historical evidence and historical content using the record of their argumentative reading as preserved on a graphic organizer. One particularly effective graphic organizer I designed was the "Evolving Concept Worksheet" (Nokes, 2010). Students would be exposed to a primary source related to a controversial issue (such as the guilt or innocence of Captain Thomas Preston in the deaths of American civilians during the Boston Massacre). After analyzing the first document, students would state their interpretation and rank their certainty on a scale of 1 to 5. After reading a second document they could switch their interpretation or keep it the same, ranking their certainty on a scale of 1 to 5. This process would be repeated through five or six documents. After completing the activity, students could trace their evolving interpretations. Typically, their level of certainty started high, as they accepted without question the evidence presented in the first document. After reading two or three different accounts, their certainty would usually decrease and their interpretation would sometimes shift. In the end, students would become more certain of their interpretation once again, but this time because of their familiarity with the evidence. The Evolving Concept Worksheet provided a record of their thinking throughout the activity and served as a resource in the metacognitive debriefing that followed the activity. It helped me assess their academic humility—the willingness to change their mind in the face of better evidence.

Fourth, graphic organizers build structure and accountability into a literacy lesson. Admittedly, managing a class can be more difficult during =small-group work than during a lecture, particularly when students are moving at their own pace, searching online, and engaging in lively debates with their peers. Graphic organizers provide a structure that helps students focus on the task at hand. Furthermore, knowing that a teacher will collect and evaluate their work can motivate students to stay on task throughout an activity. Other management-related problems may be avoided by establishing clear rules for small group work, appropriately pacing activities, and by purposefully forming groups. Giving students the freedom to develop independent interpretations of historical events does not need to result in a classroom full of students who are off-task or disruptive of other groups. But it can lead to chaos if teachers do not proactively address potential management issues.

Worry Less About Coverage

Most states have curriculum guidelines for history classes. Teachers should meet these standards. However, the guidelines typically leave considerable room for teachers to make curricular decisions. Unfortunately, many teachers choose to supplement the state standards with their own coverage standards. As mentioned, they feel like they are somehow short-changing students if they do not talk about every presidential election, battle of the Civil War, or New Deal agency. History teachers are notorious for putting pressure on themselves to cover everything (Tovani, 2004). Instead, history teachers must acknowledge that they cannot cover everything—they cannot even cover everything that is important (Wiggins, 1989). They must get over their concern for coverage, and use literacy lessons to meet their state or local curriculum guidelines. In the debate over depth or breadth, research on learning is firmly on the side of depth (Bransford, et al., 2000). And a focus on depth rather than breadth leaves room for historical inquiry and historical literacy instruction.

Chapter Summary

The teachers in the vignettes in this book went through four stages in the development and execution of historical literacy lessons. They chose content and literacy objectives and planned assessments, found appropriate texts for reaching the objectives, designed support for students' use with the texts, and flexibly carried out the lessons. They found ways to overcome the barriers that might prevent them from teaching through inquiry. I suggest that teachers who want to build historical literacies do not try to revolutionize their instruction overnight but start small, borrow from colleagues and from online sources, use graphic organizers to build structure and accountability into their literacy lessons, and worry less about content coverage.

Questions for Consideration

1. How would you argue in favor of using historical inquiries when meeting with traditional teachers in a professional learning community? What research could you show them to substantiate your claims about the benefits of historical inquiry?

2. Do the core social studies standards in your state include skills associated with historical inquiry such as document-analysis strategies or argumentative writing? If so, what skills are you required to teach? If not, how can you still provide skill instruction that enhances students' engagement with the content?

3. Which is more important, knowledge, skills, or dispositions in terms of both historical inquiry and civic engagement? How can you assess content in more meaningful ways than traditional multiple-choice tests? How can you assess skills in an efficient way? Is it possible to assess dispositions? If so, how?

Additional Reading and Viewing

- I recommend that you take some time to browse each of the sites on the list of online resources presented in this chapter.
- The Historical Assessments of Thinking (HATs) developed by the Stanford History Education Group can be accessed at https://sheg.stanford.edu/history-assessments.
- The rationale behind the HATs can be found in this article: Breakstone, J., & Smith, M (2013). *Using Library of Congress primary sources for assessment* at https://www.loc.gov/static/programs/teachers/about-this-program/teaching-with-primary-sources-partner-program/documents/assessing-historical-thinking.pdf.
- Bruce Lesh, a high school history teacher wrote a book with many practical ideas for implementing document-based inquiry found here Lesh, B.A. (2011). *Why won't you just tell us the answer?* Teaching historical thinking in grades 1–12. Stenhouse.

References

Bransford, J. D., Brown, A. L., & Cocking, R. R. (2000). *How people learn: Brain, mind, experience, and school.* National Academy Press.

Breakstone, J., & Smith, M (2013). *Using Library of Congress Primary Sources for Assessment* at https://www.loc.gov/static/programs/teachers/about-this-program/teaching-with-primary-sources-partner-program/documents/assessing-historical-thinking.pdf

Collingwood, R. G. (1993). *The idea of history.* Oxford University Press.

Common Core State Standards. (2010). *Common core state standards.* http://www.corestandards.org/

De La Paz, S., Felton, M., Monte-Sano, C., Croninger, R., Jackson, C., Deogracias, J. S., & Hoffman, B. P. (2014). Developing historical reading and writing with adolescent readers: effects on student learning. *Theory & Research in Social Education, 42*(2), 228–274. doi:10.1080/00933104.2014.908754

De La Paz, S., Monte-Sano, C., Felton, M., Croninger, R., Jackson, C., & Piantedosi, K. W. (2016). A historical writing apprenticeship for adolescents: Integrating disciplinary learning with cognitive strategies. [Online first]. *Reading Research Quarterly.* doi:10.1002/rrq.147

Epstein, T. (2000). Adolescents' perspectives on racial diversity in U.S. history: Case studies from an urban classroom. *American Educational Research Journal, 37,* 185–214. doi:10.2307/1163476

Freebody P., & Luke, A. (1990). Literacies programs. Debates and demands in cultural context. *Prospect: Australian Journal of TESOL, 5* (3), 7–16.

Goldberg, T. (2015). Looking at their side of the conflict? Effects of single versus multiple perspective history teaching on Jewish and Arab adolescents' attitude to out-group narratives and in-group responsibility. *Intercultural Education*, *25*, 453-467. doi:10.1080 /14675986.2014.990230

Grant, S. G., Swan, K., & Lee, J. (2017). *Inquiry-based practice in social studies education: Understanding the Inquiry Design Model*. Routledge.

Lesh, B.A. (2011). *Why won't you just tell us the answer? Teaching historical thinking in grades 1–12*. Stenhouse.

Levstik, L. S., & Barton, K. C. (2015). *Doing history: Investigating with children in elementary and middle schools* (5th Ed.). Routledge.

National Council for the Social Studies (2013). *The college, career, and civic life (C3) framework for social studies state standards: Guidance for enhancing the rigor of K–12 civics, economics, geography, and history*. NCSS. https://www.socialstudies.org/sites/default/files/c3/ c3-framework-for-social-studies-rev0617.pdf

NCHE. (n.d.). *History's habits of mind*. https://ncheteach.org/Historys-Habits-of-Mind

Nokes, J. D. (2010). The evolving concept instructional strategy: Students reflecting on their processing of multiple, conflicting, historical sources. *National Social Science Journal*, *35*(*1*), 104–117.

Nokes, J. D., Dole, J. A., & Hacker, D. J. (2007). Teaching high school students to use heuristics while reading historical texts. *Journal of Educational Psychology*, *99*(3), 492–504. doi:10.1037/0022-0663.99.3.492

Nokes, J. D., & Kesler-Lund, A. (2019). Historians' social literacies: How historians collaborate and write during a document-based activity. *The History Teacher*, *52*(3), 369–410.

Reisman, A. (2012). Reading like a historian: A document-based history curriculum intervention in urban high schools. *Cognition and Instruction*, *30*(1), 86–112. doi:10.10 80/07370008.2011.634081

Stern, J. A., Brody, A. E., Gregory, J. A., Griffith, S., & Pulvers, J. (2021). *The state of state standards for civics and U.S. history in 2021*. Fordham Institute. https://fordhaminstitute. org/sites/default/files/publication/pdfs/20210623-state-state-standards-civics-and- us-history-20210.pdf#page=15

Swan, K., Lee, J., & Grant S. G. (2018). *Inquiry Design Model: Building inquiries in social studies*. National Council for the Social Studies and C3 Teachers.

Thornhill, T. E. (2016). Resistance and assent: How racial socialization shapes black students' experience learning African American history in high school. *Urban Education*, *51*, 1126–1151. doi:10.1177/0042085914566094

Tovani, C. (2004). *Do I really have to teach reading? Content comprehension, Grades 6–12*. Stenhouse.

Wiggins, G. (1989). The futility of trying to teach everything of importance. *Educational Leadership*, *47*, 3, 44–59.

Wiggins, G., & McTighe, J. (1998). *Understanding by design*. Association for Supervision and Curriculum Development.

Wineburg, S., Smith, M., & Breakstone, J. (2012). New directions in assessment: Using Library of Congress sources to assess historical understanding. *Social Education*, *76*(6), 290–293.

Woodson, A. N. (2015). "What you supposed to know": Urban Black students' perspectives on history textbooks. *Journal of Urban Learning, Teaching, and Research*, *11*, 57–65.

INDEX